ISBN 978-1-332-24177-4
PIBN 10303094

1 MONTH OF
FREE
READING

at

www.ForgottenBooks.com

By purchasing this book you are eligible for one month membership to ForgottenBooks.com, giving you unlimited access to our entire collection of over 1,000,000 titles via our web site and mobile apps.

To claim your free month visit:

www.forgottenbooks.com/free303094

English
Français
Deutsche
Italiano
Español
Português

www.forgottenbooks.com

Mythology Photography **Fiction**
Fishing Christianity **Art** Cooking
Essays Buddhism Freemasonry
Medicine **Biology** Music **Ancient**
Egypt Evolution Carpentry Physics
Dance Geology **Mathematics** Fitness
Shakespeare **Folklore** Yoga Marketing
Confidence Immortality Biographies
Poetry **Psychology** Witchcraft
Electronics Chemistry History **Law**
Accounting **Philosophy** Anthropology
Alchemy Drama Quantum Mechanics
Atheism Sexual Health **Ancient History**
Entrepreneurship Languages Sport
Paleontology Needlework Islam
Metaphysics Investment Archaeology
Parenting Statistics Criminology
Motivational

HAND-BOOK

OF

STANDARD OR AMERICAN

PHONOGRAPHY.

IN FIVE PARTS.

BY ANDREW J. GRAHAM,

CONDUCTOR OF THE PHONETIC ACADEMY, NEW YORK; AND AUTHOR OF "BRIEF LONG-
HAND," "A SYSTEM FOR THE RAPID EXPRESSION OF NUMBERS," ETC.

New York:

ANDREW J. GRAHAM,

PHONETIC DEPOT.

DAVIES AND ROBERTS, Stereotypers,
113 Nassau Street, New York.

PREFACE.

A STANDARD system of shorthand for the English language must combine the following characteristics:

I. It must be capable of representing with accuracy the sounds of the English language, and of the principal languages quoted by English writers and speakers.

II. It must secure considerable speed of writing, with ample legibility, so as to answer all the purposes for which longhand is employed.

III. It must secure, for reporting purposes, ample speed of writing, without illegibility.

IV. Order and simplicity must be observed in every department.

Laying aside all exaggeration, and coming down to positive demonstration, the system of shorthand presented in this work can be shown to comply entirely with every one of these requirements, while it may be as demonstratively shown that every other system falls considerably short of them.

The English Phonography, the general features of which were invented by Mr. Isaac Pitman, and which is the basis of this system, though approaching these requirements more nearly than most other systems, is nevertheless found wanting in many important particulars when weighed in the balance of science. It can not express sounds, especially vowel-sounds, with such minute accuracy as this system; nor does it so closely follow general principles instead of arbitrary rules; nor can it secure, by from 30 to 50 per cent., so great a speed of writing.

Indeed, many who have perseveringly practiced the Old Phonography have been unable to secure by it sufficient speed for reporting purposes; and even of those whose natural facility of hand, whose temperament, and will, and talents would compensate for many a deficiency of a system, there are many who know that the English Phonography is inadequate for the *verbatim* reporting of the more rapid speakers; and if it has ever been made to fully answer this purpose, it has been by means which would not be recognized as a part of that system.

Mr. Pitman, up to 1852, had made eight Modifications or Changes of his original system, which was published in 1837, that is, a Change or Remodeling for every alternate year. Deeming his system yet incomplete, he has made still another modification within the past year (1857), in making which he has abandoned the Natural and Etymological order of the vowel-scale, and in some other respects detracted from the value which previously existed in his system.

These frequent changes, while they show that his

Phonography does not comply with what are felt to be the proper requirements of a Standard System, have subjected those who have employed his method, to frequent, inconvenient, and discouraging changes of habits of writing, and in several respects for the worse, especially of late years.

It is in view of the Fact that the system here presented complies with all the requirements of a standard system, and that *hence* its learners will not be subjected to the necessity of frequent and harassing changes of their writing in order to avoid the equally great inconvenience of having all their writing thrown out of fashion, that this system is denominated *Standard Phonography.* If the public generally should bestow upon it that approbation which it has won from accomplished writers of the Old Phonography, there will be added a third reason for this title, which, however (though it would come gratefully to the Author, who has labored under many difficulties, and been at great expense in the production of this work), would still be of less value in the scale of true merit than the approbation of the principles of Steno-Phonetic Science. In contradistinction from the Old, or English Phonography, and in honor of his Country, the author would also denominate this system AMERICAN Phonography.

That this art might go where the wants of the age demand it should go, into all our institutions of learning, there has been an endeavor to present it in a Scientific Form and Manner, with a Fullness yet Conciseness of Explanation, and a Completeness of Illus-

tration, which should place it, in these respects, upon
an equal footing with the other arts, and the sciences,
which are now made branches of education. While
the Hand-Book is thus best adapted to the requirements of School-instruction, it is eminently suited to
the wants of those who are unable to procure or afford
the assistance of a phonographic teacher.

All the Stenographic illustrations—which will be
found superior to the illustrations of all preceding
shorthand works—were executed by Mr. Chauncey B.
Thorne, the manifestation of whose genius and taste in
these little matters indicates in but an inferior degree
his fitness for the Profession of Art, to which he belongs.

As an introduction to the study of Phonography,
there has been presented a description of the principal
sounds of the language, accompanied by exercises designed to educate the vocal organs to the accurate and
facile, and therefore elegant, formation of the components of speech. While this department of the
work will prepare the reader for the successful study
of Phonography, it is hoped that it may increase the
number of those who would not detract from the glory
of our noble language by a slovenly pronunciation of
the elements of which it is composed.

As a means of familiarizing phonographic principles
and outlines, there is furnished in Part Third an extended series of progressive reading exercises, engraved
by Mr. Thorne. While these exercises possess fully the
merit of legibility, they afford an example of the ex-

quisitely beautiful phonography produced by an accomplished phonographic penman. By the imitation of this engraving the student may at least avoid the awkward stiffness of writing which would be induced by copying after inferior examples.

Part Fourth consists of an extended series of writing exercises. These, if written through in accordance with the directions, will make the student an accomplished phonographer, by requiring an exact and thorough knowledge of principles, by familiarizing phonographic outlines, by practically teaching the general principles for the determination of the best forms for words, and by requiring a desirable training of the hand. This department is so extensive as to constitute for one who has learned the plan of its arrangement a valuable Phonographic Thesaurus, by reference to which he may learn the best forms, as a general thing, for a large number of the more frequent words of the English language.

The legibility of the Old Phonography was seriously impaired in consequence of the diverse modes of writing adopted by different phonographers. This arose from the fact that it furnished no settled principles of orthography. The very authority that would have introduced harmony and uniformity failed, partially in consequence of its inconsistency with itself, but chiefly because of its inconsistency with the principles of stenographic orthography, which, indeed, had not been determined. In the Fifth Department of this work there has been presented a series of principles, con stituting an Orthographical Science for Phonography, which—while it will secure a uniformity of writing, that mere authority never could, enabling the writer to dispense with the guidance of either empirical practice or authoritative opinion, and determine accurately for himself the best phonographic outlines—affords a test of stenographic criticism, to which systems of shorthand, in respect of their speed, must be subjected in effect, however much it may be avoided in form.

Since it will be necessary for the student to refer quite frequently from one to another of the different parts of this work, it has seemed best that they should be comprised in one volume instead of several. This renders it possible to afford all the parts—every one of which will be needed by the student—at a cost considerably less than would otherwise be possible.

Finally, with the hope that his countrymen, in the cultivation of a just national spirit, will encourage American, rather than foreign, authors, especially when the works of the former are undeniably superior to those of the latter, this work and the system it explains are committed by the Author to the care of the American People.

ANDREW J. GRAHAM.

PHONETIC DEPOT, NEW YORK, *Aug.* 26, 1858.

AN

INTRODUCTION

TO

PHONOTYPY AND PHONOGRAPHY.

~~~~~~~~~~~~~~~~

PART FIRST

OF THE

Hand-Book of Standard Phonography.

PREFACE.

The objects of this treatise are three, namely—

1. To acquaint the general reader with the needs, objects, advantages, and general principles of a phonetic representation of language.

2. To serve as an accompaniment of a chart of the vocal elements of the English language. With this view, there have been given a general description and several examples of each sound. The exercises accompanying the descriptions are designed to assist the reader in familiarizing the elementary sounds and the mode of producing them.

3. To remove the various obstacles which, with the use of other manuals of Phonography, are usually encountered in the study of that art. To this end, there have been given—1. A general statement of the principles and characteristics of Phonography. 2. Specific directions for making the sounds denoted by the phonographic characters. 3. Exercises in phonetic analysis and synthesis.

Persons afflicted with stammering or other defects of articulation may make this work of decided service to them in overcoming their embarrassing difficulties, in the following manner:

1. Let them learn, by the careful study of §§ 10–64, 115–162, the nature and character of each of the sounds, and the method of producing them.

2. Utter these sounds many times, carefully, deliberately, distinctly, and with varying degrees of force, and with different inflections.

3. Repeatedly go through with the exercises in Phonetic Synthesis, in § 162, according to the directions there given.

4. Frequently repeat the sentences given as vocal exercises, in §§ 10–64.

By properly directed exercises in Phonetic Analysis and Synthesis, a complete cure of stammering may be effected in almost every case—where there are not serious organic defects (which is very rarely the case), and when the stammerer sufficiently desires a cure, to undertake the necessary practice.

Thousands who are subjected to the inconveniences and mortification of stammering, or some other defect in articulation, would *not* be, should they know that the actions of the vocal organs are as determinate, and as much under the control of the will as the actions of the arms, hands, fingers, legs, or feet. Speaking is an *art* as much as writing. The road to each is through certain elementary training. *First*, there has to be an idea of what is to be done; *secondl* , knowledge as to the mode of doing it; *thirdly*, practice in that mode.

He who would speak well needs but to have, *first*, a knowledge of the elements of the language; *secondly*, a knowledge of the vocal operations necessary for their production; *thirdly*, well-directed, thorough, energetic practice in producing the elements, and combining them into syllables, syllables into words, words into clauses, and clauses into sentences.

ANDREW J. GRAHAM.

Phonetic Depot, New York, *June 25th*, 1858

TABLE OF CONTENTS.

INTRODUCTION

TO

PHONOTYPY AND PHONOGRAPHY.

DEFINITIONS.

PHO-NET′ICS, PHON′ICS, or PHO-NOL′O-GY, *noun.* 1. A science which treats of the elements of language, their modifications, and their relations. 2. The science of representing the elements of language.

PHO-NET′I-CIZE, *verb.* To give instruction in phonology; to convert to the support of the Phonetic Reform.

PHO′NŎ-TYPE, *noun.* 1. A type to be used in printing the sign of a vocal element. 2. The sign produced by the type.

PHO′NŎ-TYPE, *verb.* To print with phonotypes; to print phonetically, that is, with a sign for each element of the voice,—no more, no less.

PHO-NOT′YP-Y, *noun.* 1. The printing produced with phonotypes—printing, in which each element of language is represented by a distinct letter or type. 2. The mode or system of printing phonetically.

PHO′NO-GRAPH, *noun.* The *graphic* or *written* sign of a vocal element.

PHO′NO-GRAPH, *verb.* To write with phonographs.

PHO-NOG′RAPH-ER, *noun.* A writer of phonography.

PHO-NOG′RAPH-Y, *noun.* 1. The system of representing language with phonographs. 2. The writing produced with phonographs. There are two kinds of phonography:

(1.) PHONETIC LONGHAND, or LONGHAND PHONOGRAPHY, writing produced with a phonetic alphabet consisting of most of the ordinary script letters and additional ones of the same general character for the additional sounds.

(2.) STEN′O-PHO-NOG′RAPH-Y, or PHONETIC SHORTHAND: writing produced with an alphabet composed of very simple signs. Of this there are two kinds:

(*a*) OLD, or ENGLISH, PHONOGRAPHY: a system of shorthand, the general features of which were invented by Mr. Isaac Pitman, of

England. Its tolerable perfection is due to the fact that its improvement has been contributed to by numerous persons who have practiced it. This system has not a sufficiency of signs for a perfectly phonetic representation, and is defective in other respects.

(*b*) STANDARD, or AMERICAN, PHONOGRAPHY: a system of shorthand writing, which, in its general features, resembles the English Phonography, but possesses many advantages over it.

ROMAN'IC PRINT, the printing produced by the Roman types or letters. This term applies to the printing of all the European nations who use the Roman alphabet.

ROMANIC, or COMMON, ORTHOGRAPHY. The ordinary mode of spelling, or representing language.—*Heterot'yp-y* is sometimes used as an equivalent term

---

SPOKEN AND WRITTEN LANGUAGE.

2. WHAT may have been the origin of language, it is not the object of this treatise to discuss. Whatever might be the speculative ideas of the author on that subject, they would not add to the positive knowledge of the reader, and would therefore be unprofitable. Whether human language originated from a few monosyllables, as *ha*, *he*, *hi*, *ho*, as Lord Monboddo contends in his work on "The Origin and Progress of Language;" whether it was developed, as Dr. Murray supposed, from nine monosyllables, *ag*, *bag*, *dwag*, *gwag*, *lag*, *mag*, *nag*, *rag*, *swag*, or whether, as Maupertuis thinks, "language was formed by a session of learned societies assembled for that purpose"—is a question of no practical moment. It is sufficient to know that spoken language exists, and is intended for a representative of ideas.

3. To the reflecting mind it must ever be pleasing to contemplate the wonderful process by which we reproduce, to a greater or less degree, in the minds of others, the mental sensations we ourselves experience. To make by no means an exhaustive enumeration of the links in the mysterious chain which connects soul to soul in feeling and thought,— we have a certain effect produced upon us by an oration, say, which oration is divisible into sentences, which can be divided into clauses, which are composed of words, which are constituted of syllables, which consist of indivisible parts of speech. These sounds we get by hearing, which is experiencing certain sensations indirectly produced by vibrations of the different parts of the ear; which vibrations were produced by certain vibrations of the air; which vibrations were caused by the ejection of the air from the lungs through the variously modified pas-

sages of the mouth and nose. We have not yet arrived at the fountain of power which, through various instrumentalities, has set in motion the organs of speech, and sustained them in numerous simultaneous, and rapid operations while producing the words which have impressed us. Not only have the words been delivered, but they have been modified by tone, accent, emphasis, modulation, etc., which concur with the words in effecting the desired result. Words are the viewless bearers of arbitrary meanings, and are variously grouped to suit the purposes of the speaker, and are clothed with the curious intertexture of tone, accent, emphasis, modulation, etc., furnished by each speaker as he sends them on their mission to his auditor.

Then, how wonderful is written or printed language! Here we have, or *should* have, certain signs as the representatives of the elementary sounds of speech; which signs being placed in the order of the sounds they represent, become the representatives of words, and sustain to the *light* and *sight* the same relations the words they indicate bear to the *air* and *ear*. Observe the circuit which a thought ordinarily travels in passing from the mind of an author to that of his reader. It passes from the brain of the author through his nerves, muscles, fingers, pen, and ink, to paper; then mounting through the eyes of the compositor to his mind, it comes back through his brain, nerves, muscles, and fingers, to types and ink, and then to paper again, whence the rays of light transmit it to the eye of the reader, whence it passes on its mysterious journey to his soul.

4. Languages vary in respect of their utility as instruments of communication. That language which, all things considered, is best, must eventually become the general medium of communication, or be the immediate predecessor of a universal language.

Excellence of the English Spoken Language.—The English language —which has drawn riches from various sources to answer the demands of the numerous and grand experiences of the race who use it—which is well adapted to poetry or prose, to science or art, to commerce or philosophy, to religion or law, to the delicate ornations of literature, or the sternest and most practical life-experiences—will become the universal medium of communication, both by reason of the indomitable energy of the Anglo-American race in every phase of life, and by reason of its superior merits as a spoken language, unless we shall prove blind to the anomalous orthography by which it is now represented, and fail to provide in its stead (which may be easily done) a scientific mode of writing and printing it.—Prof. Grimm, a noted German philologist, has paid no unmerited compliment to the English spoken language in the following paragraph :

" The English language possesses a power of expression such as never,

1*

perhaps, was attained by any other human tongue. Its altogether intellectual and singularly happy foundation and development has arisen from a surprising alliance between the two noblest languages of antiquity, the German and Romanesque—the relation of which to each other is well known to be such that the former supplies the material foundation, the latter the abstract notions.   Yes, truly, the English language may call itself a universal language, and seems chosen to rule in all future times in a still greater degree in the corners of the earth. In richness, sound reason, and flexibility, no modern tongue can be compared with it, not even the German, which must shake off many a weakness before it can enter the lists with the English."

K. M. Rapp, another noted German philologist, in his "Physiologie der Sprache," has given the following testimony in favor of the English language :

"Although the French has become the common language in a diplomatic and social sense, it has never acquired a firm footing in extensive regions out of Europe.   The English, on the contrary, may pass for the universal language out of Europe; and by its bold fusion and consequent decomposition of the forms of its Gothic and Roman elements, this idiom has acquired incomparable fluency, and powers especially destined by nature more than any one of the other living languages to undertake that part.   Were not the impediment of a bizarre, antiquated orthography in the way, the universality of this language would be still more apparent; and it may perhaps be fortunate for us other Europeans that the Englishman has not made the discovery."

5. *Defects of our Written Language.*—But we are beginning to make the discovery.   Read what Sheridan says of it :

"Such is the state of our written language, that the darkest hieroglyphics, or the most difficult ciphers ever invented by the art of man, were not better calculated to conceal the sentiments of those who use them, from all who do not have the key, than the state of our spelling is to conceal the true pronunciation of our words from all except a few well-educated individuals."

It is said, in "Chambers' Papers for the People," that "we violate every principle of a sound alphabetical system more outrageously than any other nation whatever.   Our characters do not correspond to our articulations, and our spelling of words can not be matched for irregularity and whimsical caprice."

DEFECTS OF THE COMMON ORTHOGRAPHY.

TOO MANY SIGNS FOR A SOUND.

6. LET it be understood to be a principle of a correct alphabet that no elementary sound of the voice should have more than one sign provided for its representation, and, in that respect, the common orthography will appear defective. It does not, however, furnish a sufficient number of *single* signs for the elements of the language; and of those provided, so far as the representation of single elements is concerned, *c*, *q*, and *x* are redundant; for *c* = *k* or *s*; *q* = *k*, and not *kw*, as Dr. Latham says; and *x* = *ks*, *kz*, or *z*. But let the *combinations* of letters (which are used as the signs of single sounds) be regarded as so many separate signs, and the proposition that the common orthography employs too many signs for a sound can be easily sustained. It is a fact, that the number of signs employed to represent about thirty-four elements is not less than three hundred; and instead of every sound having its uniform representative, as should be the case in a correct orthography, *not a single element of the language has a uniform representation in the common spelling!* The elementary sound produced in naming ‘a’ is represented by sixteen different signs; thus, by *a* in *mating*, *a-e* in *mate*, *ai* in *pain*, *aigh* in *straight*, *ao* in *gaol*, *au* in *gauging*, *au-e* in *gauge*, *ay* in *pray*, *aye* in *prayed*, *ea* in *great*, *ei* in *veil*, *eig* in *reign*, *eigh* in *weigh*, *eighe* in *weighed*, *ey* in *they*, *eye* in *conveyed*.

The elementary sound produced in naming the letter ‘e’ is represented by seventeen different signs; thus, by *e* in *be*, *ee* in *bee*, *e-e* in *complete*, *ea* in *each*, *ea-e* in *leave*, *eg* in *impregn*, *ei* in *conceit*, *ei-e* in *conceive*, *eo* in *people*, *ey* in *key*, *eye* in *keyed*, *i* in *albino*, *i-e* in *magazine*, *ie* in *grief*, *ie-e* in *grieve*, *uay*, in *quay*, *ui* in *mosquito*.

The sound heard in naming the letter ‘i’ has sixteen different signs. The sound indicated by *ew* has nine different representatives.

The sound of *k* is indicated by *c* in *can*, *ch* in *chasm*, *ck* in *back*, *gh* in *lough*, *k* in *kill*, *lk* in *walk*, *q* in *quack*.

The sound of *t* is indicated by *bt* in *debt*, *ct* in *indict*, *ed* in *lacked*, *phth* in *phthisic*, *pt* in *ptarmigan*, *t* in *to*, *th* in *Thomas*, *tt* in *letter*.

The sound of *f* as in *for* is indicated by *ff* in *off*, *gh* in *laugh*, *ph* in *physic*, *pph* in *Sappho*.

The sound of *s* in *sin* is represented by *c* in *cede*, by *ps* in *psalm*, *sc* in *scene*, *ss* in *loss*, *sch* in *schism*, *sw* in *sword*.

The sound of *l* in *low* is represented by *ll* in *ball*, by *ln* in *kiln*, by *tle* in *castle*, *llesl* in *belles-lettres*

TOO MANY SOUNDS TO A SIGN.

7. Let it be understood that in a perfect alphabet but one sound should be given to a letter, and the common orthography, in that respect, will appear defective; because very few of the single letters or combinations of letters are employed with unvarying powers.

The insufficiency of the alphabet to represent the elements of the language has led to the use of the combinations of letters as single signs, and giving several different powers to the single letters and combinations of letters. To represent thirty-four distinct sounds the common alphabet provides but twenty-six signs. To indicate sixteen vowels it furnishes but five letters (a, e, i, o, u). A few instances of this defect may be given.

The letter 'a' has eight different sounds, as in the following words : *mate, many, pare, at, farm, pass, all, what.*

The letter 'e' has six different sounds, as in *mete, pretty, they, met her, there.*

The letter 'i' has five different sounds, as in *machine, if, bird, bind, union.*

The letter 'o' has nine different sounds, as in *woman, form, hop, ope, whole, son, move, women, one.*

The letter 'u' has seven different sounds, as in the following words *busy, bury, cut, rule, usage, persuade, pull, unite.*

8. Not only are single letters employed with varying powers, but, contrary to the principles of a correct orthography, combinations of letters have many different significations. If the combination IE, as in *grief*, is used to indicate the sound of *ee*, the principles of a correct mode of language-representation would require it to be used with that power invariably; but this combination is employed in the common spelling to represent eight different sounds; as in " grief, pitied, friend, soldier, lie, medieval, conscientious, science."

The combination EA represents four different sounds; as in " pea, great, heart, head."

The combination EO represents seven different sounds; as in " people, leopard, yeoman, galleon, theology, aureola, MacLeod."

The couplet

" *Though* the *tough cough* and *hiccough plough* me *through*,
O'er life's dark *lough* my course I will pursue,"

presents the combination *ough* with seven different sounds. It has another sound in the word 'bought.' If a uniform pronunciation were given to the termination 'ough' in each word, the first line of the above couplet would read in some one of the following ways:

(Though)	Tho the to co and hicco plo me thro
(Tough)	Thuf the tuf cuf and hiccuf pluf me thruf
(Cough)	Thof the tof cof and hiccof plof me throf
(Hiccough)	Thup the tup cup and hiccup plup me thrup
(Plough)	Thow the tow cow and hiccow plow me throw
(Through)	Thoo the too coo and hiccoo ploo me throo.

In analogy with one or another of the uses of ' ough,' the name "Brougham" may be pronounced "Bro-am, Bruffam, Broffam, Bruppam, Brow-am, Broo-am, Brock-am, or Braw-am." It is not surprising that the Frenchman should complain of a "cow [cough] in his box" [chest]; or that Voltaire, upon learning that *ague* is pronounced as two syllables and *plague* as one syllable, should wish one half the English had the *ague* and the other half the *plague!*

EVILS OF THE COMMON ORTHOGRAPHY.

9. The evils of the common orthography may be summed up in the following manner :

(1.) Much time is required to learn to read and write by the common orthography which would be saved by a correct mode of representing language. A vast amount of drilling in reading and spelling is now required before the pupil can read or write with tolerable accuracy, to say nothing of facility. In consequence of this, children are sent to school at an early age and confined to the school-house many hours a day, in violation of very obvious physiological laws. The common orthography is chargeable with the weakening and ruining of the constitutions of many children who have been set at the work of mastering our anomalous spelling, at a very early age, under the impression that children from five to eight years of age will acquire it more readily than those who are older. Not only does it result in the waste of much time, but in the useless expenditure of large sums of money which might be devoted to higher uses, if we had a phonetic orthography. The money now required for the education of one million children in the arts of reading and writing, would educate three millions of children in those arts, if we had a phonetic orthography

(2.) The common orthography requires that the child at the most impressible age should be trained to read and write in a manner violating the dictates of his common sense. The natural effect of learning a deceptive, inconsistent, absurd system of representing language is, to a degree, to blunt the child's sense of truth, consistency, and rationality.

(3.) It engenders in the minds of thousands a distaste for study. To this may be traced very much of the ignorance of reading and writing known to exist in Great Britain and America.

(4.) So great are the irregularities of the common mode of spelling, that no person is able to pronounce a word which he may see printed but which he has never heard pronounced.

(5.) No person can tell the common spelling of any word which he has heard pronounced but has never seen written .or printed. The result of the two last-mentioned defects is, that reading and writing are felt to be difficult; whereas, by a correct orthography, they would almost " come by nature,"—and differences in pronunciation constantly increase; whereas, a phonetic orthography would bring about the most accurate and uniform pronunciation.

(6.) Our spoken language is hindered in, if it shall not be absolutely prevented from, becoming the universal medium of communication.

(7.) The common orthography occasions great difficulties to those who endeavor to represent unwritten languages.

(8.) It occasions much difficulty to elocutionists, etc., in writing concerning the elements of our language.

(9.) It results in a general profound ignorance of the elements of that language which is in hourly use by millions.

(10.) It enhances the cost of books, etc., above what they would cost with a phonetic orthography, millions of dollars annually.

All these evils may be replaced with as many important blessings by the adoption of a phonetic mode of representing language

---

THE ELEMENTS OF THE ENGLISH LANGUAGE.

10. An investigation as to the elements of the English language will not only serve to lay the foundation for the presentation of a phonetic mode of representing language, but will assist the student of Phonography to overcome the difficulties which are sometimes presented in this study in consequence of false ideas suggested by the common orthography.

11. By an element of speech is meant an indivisible portion of language. Reference is here had to spoken language; hence it is not to be understood that the letters (a, b, c, d, etc.) or their names (a, be, ce, de, etc.) are elements. To illustrate, the lips being rounded in a manner indicated by ◯, and vocalized breath being emitted through them, there will be produced an indivisible portion of English language. This *sound* occurs in the word represented by *oath*. Its SIGN in the common spelling, in this instance, is a combination of letters (oa). The NAME of this sign is *owe-a*. This sound also occurs in the word *though*. Its sign, in this instance, is a combination of four letters (ough) ! The name of this sign is *owe-you-gee-aitch ! !* The sound represented by x is not an element, for it is capable of being resolved

into the sounds usually denoted by *k* and *s*. Nor is the sound usually indicated by *j* in *join* an element, but a double sound. Further illustrations will be seen in the following paragraphs. A general division of the elements may be made into consonants and

VOWELS.

12. A vowel is a smooth emission of sounding breath, modified but not obstructed by the organs of speech. Such are the sounds represented by *ea* in *eat*, *a* in *ale*, *a* in *arm*.

ꞁ ᵢ (Phonotype); ℋ ᵢ̇ (Phonograph).

13. The sound indicated in Graham's Phonetic Alphabet by the letters given above, and by the *italic* letters in the words "*eat, each, eel*," is a long vowel. It has, in the common spelling, fourteen different signs, *æ* as in *ægis*, *e* as in *me*, *ea* as in *eat*, *ee* as in *bee*, *eg* as in *impregn*, *ei* as in *conceit*, *eip* as in *receipt*, *eo* as in *people*, *ey* as in *key*, *i* as in *Albino*, *i-e* as in *magazine*, *ie* as in *grief*, *uay* as in *quay*, *ui* as in *mosquito*.

14. This sound is erroneously regarded as the long sound of the vowel of *ebb*. That it is more nearly related to the vowel of *it* than to the vowel of *ebb* is proved thus: In passing from the vowel of *eat* to the vowel of *ebb*, the change in the position of the vocal organs is considerable ; while in passing from the vowel of *eat* to the vowel of *it*, the change is scarcely appreciable. For this reason *ee* and *ĭ* are regarded as mates, and have like signs appropriated to them in the phonetic alphabet.

I i ; 𝒥 ᵢ̇.

15. The sound represented by *i* in *it* is a short vowel. It is erroneously called the short sound of *i* in *ire*. It has twelve different signs : *i* as in *if*, *ie* as in *duties*, *ia* as in *carriage*, *ea* as in *guinea*, *ee* as in *been*, *ei* as in *forfeit*, *ey* as in *barley*, *eigh* as in *Burleigh*, *o* as in *women*, *u* as in *busy*, *ui* as in *build*, *y* as in *hymn*.

Exercise.—"Isabella Ingleton inherited an immense incomprehensible, inimitable, idiosyncratical imagination. To ignorant ignoramuses and impertinent individuals, Isabella Ingleton indifferently indicated ineffable indignation. And on the Illuminati, Isabella Ingleton invariably inflicted her irresistible and inestimable idiosyncratical imaginations."

Ɛ ɛ ; 𝒮 ɛ .

16. The sound indicated by *a* in *ale* is a long vowel. It is errone-

ously regarded as the long sound of the vowel of *at*. It more nearly resembles the vowel of *ebb*, with which it is paired in the phonetic alphabet. It has fourteen different signs: *a* as in *fading*, *a-e* as in *fade*, *at* as in *pain*, *aig* as in *campaign*, *aigh* as in *Laight*, *ao* as in *gaol*, *au* as in *gauging*, *au-e* as in *gauge*, *ay* as in *pray*, *e* as in *tête*, *ei* as in *their*, *eig* as in *reign*, *eigh* as in *weigh*, *ey* as in *they*.

Exercise.—"Amy Amiable owned an ape with eighty-eight aches, ailings, and ailments. Amy Amiable essayed to aid her ape with eighty-eight aches, ailings, and ailments. But ere Amy Amiable's amiable intentions could aid the ape, he ailed and ached, and ached and ailed, and ailed and ached, and died."

E e; *Ĕ e*.

17. The sound indicated by *e* in *end* and *ebb* is a short vowel. It has ten different signs: *a* as in *any*, *ai* as in *said*, *ay* as in *says*, *e* as in *ebb*, *ea* as in *head*, *ei* as in *heifer*, *eo* as in *leopard*, *ie* as in *friend*, *u* as in *busy*, *ue* as in *guess*.

Exercise.—"Ethelbert Englehart, an emigrant from Essex, encountered and engaged an enthusiastic enemy. But this enterprising emigrant embarrassed his exasperated enemy."

E e; *ĕ̆ æ*.

18. The sound of *ea* in *earth* and of *e* in *mercy* is a short vowel This vowel and the vowel of *up* are supposed to be the same by many in whose pronunciation they are distinct. A difference may be discovered by repeating the first syllable of *mercy* and comparing it with the word *murmur;* thus, *mermer, murmur*. This vowel uttered alone will be perceived to be the vowel of *ebb* modified by the tongue in assuming the position to pronounce the following *r*. When the *r* is united to a following vowel, a preceding vowel remains unmodified, as in *merry*. In this word two *r*'s are printed to indicate that the preceding *e* is "short," but the only one pronounced is joined to the following vowel. For ordinary printing, an *e* followed by *r* in the same syllable is, perhaps, a sufficient sign for the vowel of *her*. For critical purposes the distinct sign for it given above will be necessary. This vowel has four different signs: *e* as in *herd*, *ea* as in *earth*, *i* as in *bird*, *y* as in *satyr*.

Exercise.—The mirthful girl Gertrude, the daughter of Herbert Werner, is ever observing the birds that perch on the fir-trees.

E o; *Ĕ́ a*.

19. The sound of *ai* in *air* is a long vowel. Words of the class of *air*, *fair*, *dare* are variously pronounced: by some, with the vowel of *ale;*

and by others, with a lengthened quantity of the vowel of *ebb ;* but they are generally pronounced with a lengthened quantity of the vowel of *at.* In ordinary phonetic printing, this vowel is, perhaps, sufficiently indicated by the sign for the vowel of *ale* followed by *r* in the same syllable. This vowel has six different signs: *a* as in *daring, a-e* as in *dare, ai* as in *pair, aye* as in *prayer, e-e* as in *there, hei* as in *heir.*

Exercise.—Blair Hair married the fair heir of a millionaire, and care scarce dared to his house repair or ascend his stair till poor Blair Hair offended the fair heir of the millionaire by daring to compare her to the candle-flare, when the fair heir rushed up stairs, and pulled out his hair, and threw it in air, and made him stare and care to be somewhere, anywhere but there.

Ꞛ a ; 𝒜 𝒶.

20. The sound of *a* in *at* is a short vowel. It is the short quantity of the vowel of *air.* It has three different signs: *a* as in *at, aa* as in *Isaac, ai* as in *plaid.*

Exercise.—" Adam Adams attacked an antiquated African alligator in Abyssinia. This African alligator angrily and acrimoniously attempted to avenge himself on Adam Adams. But Adam Adams actively accumulated additional assistance and accomplished the assassination of the angry animal."

21. Many do not distinguish the vowel of *at* from the vowel of *ask,* and in ordinary phonetic printing no confusion can arise from representing it by ' a,' the sign for the vowel of *ask.*

Ꞛ ɞ ; 𝒜 𝒶.

22. The sound of *a* in *arm* is a long vowel. It has six different signs: *a* as in *arm, aa* as in *baa, ae* as in *Haerlem, ah* as in *ah, ea* as in *heart, ua* as in *guard.*

Exercise.—The Bard of Farven alarmed at the darts of his barbarous enemies departed one dark, dark night from Farven and embarked for Parma.—There, guarded by the arms of the Czar, the large-hearted Bard of Farven by his art charms the farmers of Parma who stroll in the parks by starlight.

A a ; 𝒜 𝒶.

23. The sound of *a* in *ask* approximates the short quantity of the vowel of *arm.* It ends such words as *America, data, Cuba,* and is heard in the unaccented syllables of *about, around, ago, dollar,* etc. It is the usual sound of the article " a." It is the first element of the diphthong indicated by *i* in *find.* It has two different signs: *a* as in *ask, au* as in *aunt.*

Exercise.—Pulaski Trask passes away a vast amount of time in counting the vast masses of gold he has by chance and task amassed, but alas! he must pass, at last, from the vast amount of wealth he has by chance and task amassed; and then, I ask, to whom shall pass the vast amount of wealth Pulaski Trask by chance and task amassed.

O o ; *W̄ a.*

24. The sound of *a* in *all* is a long vowel. It has nine different representatives in the common print: *a* as in *all*, *au* as in *laud*, *aw* as in *awl*, *awe* as in *awe*, *augh* as in *aught*, *eo* as in *George*, *o* as in *form*, *oa* as in *broad*, *ough* as in *bought*.

Exercise.—"All were appalled at the thralldom of Lord Walter Raleigh, who was almost scalded in a caldron of water."

'Augustus Hauley, the auctioneer, audibly awed an audience all one long day in August with his awful voice. The audience all appalled with Augustus Hauley's awful voice audaciously hauled Augustus Hauley out of the long auction hall with a halter.'

O o ; *O̱ a̱.*

25. The vowel of *on* is regarded by phoneticians generally as the short quantity of the vowel of *all*. It is the first element of the diphthong represented by *oi* in *oil*. It has four different representatives: *a* as in *what*, *o* as in *on*, *ow* as in *knowledge*, *ho* as in *honor*.

Exercise.—"Oliver Operose occasionally offered to operate on the obstreperous Opheclyde. But an obstinate orchestral oligarch opposingly obstructed Oliver Operose's occasional offer. The obnoxious objection of this obstinate orchestral oligarch offended Oliver Operose's officious and obsequious observers."

O̅ o̅ ; *O̅ a̅.*

26. The sound of *o* in *old* is a long vowel. It has sixteen different signs: *aut* as in *hautboy*, *eau* as in *beau*, *eo* as in *yeoman*, *ew* as in *sew*, *o* as in *old*, *oa* as in *oar*, *oe* as in *foe*, *o-e* as in *ore*, *oh* as in *oh*, *oo* as in *floor*, *ot* as in *depot*, *ou* as in *four*, *ough* as in *though*, *ow* as in *snow*, *owe* as in *owe*, *gh* as in *Edinburgh !*

Exercise.—Homer Overly, groaning, openly owned that his old coat shone no more as in the days of yore; and more, a hole in the shoulder torn showed his linen below. So Homer Overly slowly strolled over his floor, out of his door, and the road o'er, to the tailor More, who sold a coat to Homer Overly for his golden ore. Then Homer Overly o'er the road strode to his own door and threw his old coat with a hole in the shoulder torn, behind the door, and reposed on his sofa to take a snore.

O o ; *O̶ o*.

27. The vowel of *whole*, *none*, is the short quantity of the vowel of *old*. These words are better pronounced with the long vowel; and for ordinary phonetic printing, a sign for the short vowel of *whole* is not required.

IJ ɒ ; *𝒲 ʌ*.

28. The sound of *u* in *up* is a short vowel. It is slightly lengthened in *cur*, as most vowels are preceding *r* in the same syllable. In the short phonetic alphabet it is paired with the vowel of *old*. It has nine different signs : *o* as in *son*, *oe* as in *does*, *o-e* as in *love*, *oo* as in *flood*, *ou* as in *tough*, *u* as in *up*, *ub* as in *subtle*, *uo* as in *liquor*, *up* as in *cupboard*.

Exercise.—" Ulric Ulithorn had an ugly, uncouth, unintelligible utterance, utterly unfit to unlock unlearned understandings. Unbending umpires took umbrage at Ulric Ulithorn's ungainly, uncommon, unconscious, undistinguishable, unfathomable utterance. Until Ulric Ulithorn, with unusual urbanity, undertook to unriddle his untoward unintelligibility."

Ɯ ɯ ; *𝒲 ʌ*.

29. The sound of *oo* in *food* is a long vowel. It has nine different signs : *o* as in *do*, *oe* as in *shoe*, *o-e* as in *move*, *oo* as in *food*, *ou* as in *soup*, *ous* as in *sous*, *oux* as in *billet-doux*, *ough* as in *through*, *wo* as in *two*.

Exercise.—As the moon at noon of night moodily moved on its tour to its gloomy tomb, the troops removed the poor drooping youth from his gloomy room that he might be soothed by the silver beams of the moon before he met his doom.

Ʊ u ; *𝒰 u*.

30. The vowel of *foot* is the short quantity of the vowel of *food*. It is the second element of the diphthongs indicated by the *italic* letters in " n*o*w, o*u*t; ne*w*, m*u*te, d*u*e." It has five different signs : *o* as in *wolf*, *oo* as in *foot*, *ou* as in *could*, *u* as in *pull*, *w* as in *now*.

Exercise.—A cook, with a hook pulled a rook by its foot from a nook in the rookery and stood on it till dead, and then put it in sooty wool and buried it in the woods.

VOCAL DIPHTHONGS.

31. Two vowels *pronounced together by a single effort* constitute a vocal diphthong. In a strictly phonetic alphabet, diphthongs should be represented by the signs of their elements; but as some desire single signs, they have been provided in Graham's Phonetic Alphabet.

Double signs — ai , *ai;* Ŧ ɟ , *Ŧ ɟ* — Single signs.

32. The diphthong represented by the letters given above is composed of the vowels of *ask* and *it*. It has fourteen different signs: *ai* as in *aisle*, *ei* as in *eider*, *eigh* as in *height*, *ey* as in *eying*, *eye* as in *eye*, *i* as in *bind*, *ic* as in *indict*, *ie* as in *pie*, *i-e* as in *fine*, *igh* as in *high*, *is* as in *island*, *uy* as in *buy*, *y* as in *by*, *ye* as in *rye*.

Exercise.—"Iamblicus Ideality, the identical itinerant Irish idealist, idolized his isolated ideas into an iambic hypothesis, idly identifying his idle-headed, high-flown, hyperbolical idealities with wisdom. Finally Iamblicus Ideality ended his idling life on an island of ice."

There are different pronunciations of *i* in *bind* besides the general one indicated above. Some say "beind;" some, "baind;" some, "bɒind;" and others, "boind."

oi, *oi* — Θ ɵ, *Θ ɵ*.

33. The diphthong represented by the letters presented above is composed of the vowel of *on* and *it*. It has two different signs: *oi* as in *oil*, *oy* as in *boy*.

Exercise.—Lloyd Floyd was annoyed by noisy boys who enjoyed sport devoid of sense; but Lloyd Floyd, by some toys, decoyed the noisy boys into his garden, and counterpoised their senseless joys by the "oil of beech," till the noisy boys with dolorous voice assured Lloyd Floyd that he should be no more annoyed by their boisterous voices.

ou, *ou* — Ȣ ȣ, *Ȣ ȣ*.

34. The diphthong indicated by these letters is composed of the vowels of *on* and *pull*. Instead of this, the following combinations are heard: eu, au, au, ɒu. This diphthong has six different signs: *o* as in *compt*, *ou* as in *out*, *oub* as in *doubt*, *ough* as in *bough*, *ow* as in *now*, *hou* as in *hour*.

Exercise.—Downe, the clown, prowling round about town found a brown fowl, which he pronounced an eagle, but which without doubt was an owl. When the brown fowl powerfully plowed his brown talons into the hands of the clown Downe, he scowled and threw the owl to the ground; but to this hour the clown Downe prowls round about town, pronouncing all who announce that he found an owl, foul-mouthed owls themselves, and denouncing them as outrageous out-and-out doubters of astounding facts—robbers of his renown.

iu, *iu* — Ш ɥ, *Ш ɥ*.

35. The diphthong indicated by these letters is composed of the vowel of *it* and *pull*. It has twelve different signs: *eau* as in *beauty*, *eo* as in *feod*, *eu* as in *feud*, *ew* as in *new*, *ieu* as in *lieu*, *iew* as in *view*, *u* as

in *duty*, *ue* as in *due*, *u-e* as in *tune*, *ugh* as in *Hugh*, *ui* as in *juice*, *ui* as in *puisne*.

Exercise.—Hugh Newton, the beautiful, dutiful son of the rude Jew, Newton, blew on his flute a few new beautiful tunes that drew—be assured it is true—a crew of blue-birds to hear; but they flew when they knew Hugh Newton's flute was mute. But Hugh Newton's flute and eyes so blue near him drew a beautiful Jewess, who flew not when she knew Hugh Newton's flute was mute; and now the beautiful Jewess sings with her Hugh the beautiful tunes the young Hugh Newton blew on his flute.

CONSONANTS.

36. A consonant is a sound made either by a complete or partial contact of the vocal organs obstructing the whispered or sonant breath, in some degree, varying, from an entire break or stoppage of it (as in producing the sound of *p* or *b*), to a simple aspiration (as the sound of *h* in *hate*).

H h; *H h*.

37. The sound of *h* in *he* is a consonant. It has two signs: *h* as in *hut*, *wh* as in *who*.

Exercise.—His heavy-headed highness held up his shrunk shank, and hopping, hied himself home, happy to have his hands, his head, and his heart whole.

W w; *W w*.

38. The sound of *w* in *way* is a consonant. In producing the sound of *oo*, a clear vocal sound is heard. Now, if the lips be compressed slightly, the clear vocality ceases, and a hum or buzz (the sound of *w*) is heard. It has three different signs:—as in *one*, *u* as in *quire*, *w* as in *we*.

Exercise.—" Weave well the warp of life. The waves wandered with the wild and wanton winds that wail and weep."

Q q; *Q q*.

39. The sound of *wh* in *when* is a whispered consonant related to that of *w*. Strictly phonetic principles demand a character for it, and, in Graham's Phonetic Alphabet, *q* is used as its sign: but for ordinary phonetic printing it is best represented by *hw*—the *h* preceding *w* indicating the aspirated sound of *w*, or, what is the same thing, the sound indicated by *q* in the phonetic alphabet, and by *wh* in the common spelling.

Exercise.—A wheezing, whimsical, whimpering, whining whiffler, while attempting to wheedle a wharfinger out of some white wheat, whalebone, whetstones, whipcords, wheelbarrows, whistles, whisky, whey-tubs, and what not, was whipped by the wharfinger with whale-bone, whereupon the wheezing, whimsical, whimpering, whining whiffler whistly left the wharf.

Y y ; *Y y .*

40. The sound of *y* in *yet* is a sonant or spoken consonant. When the organs are in the proper position to produce the vowel of *eat*, let the tongue be raised toward the palate till the clear vocality of the vowel ceases—till a murmur or buzz is heard—and the sound of *y* will be produced. This sound has four different signs : *i* as in *union*, *j* as in *hallelujah*, — as in *use*, *y* as in *yet*.

Exercise.—Yes, you yet use your useless yellow uniforms. Yesterday the yawning youngster yelling yielded to the yoke

41. The whisper corresponding to the sonant *y* occurs in the English pronunciation of *human* (which is *hyooman*), and, perhaps, also in the American pronunciation of *inhumanity*, which is occasionally pronounced " inhyŏŏmanity." It may be represented by *hy*.

L l ; *L l .*

42. The sound of *l* in *let* is a sonant consonant, produced by trilling the sides of the tongue while its tip is pressed against the superior incisory teeth. It has six different signs : *l* as in *let*, *ll* as in *ill*, *ln* as in *kiln*, *lle* as in *bagatelle*, *tle* as in *whistle*, *llesl* as in *belles-lettres*.

Exercise.—The long, lean, lank, lolling lubber little likes the " limbs of the law," who leave him little leisure.

Respecting the whispered *l* see the Phonetic Quarterly, vol. i., p. 14, par. 7.

R r ; *R r .*

43. The letter *r* is used to indicate two sounds—one, the trilled *r* produced by vibrating the tongue against the gums of the upper incisory teeth as in pronouncing *ray*—the other, the smooth *r*, produced by placing the sides of the tongue against the sides of the hard palate and emitting sonant breath over the tip of the tongue (which is curled upward and backward), as in pronouncing *air*, *hear*. They have seven different signs : *r* as in *run*, *rh* as in *rhetoric*, *rr* as in *burr*, *rrh* as in *myrrh*, *rt* as in *mortgage*, *rps* as in *corps*, *wr* as in *write*.

Exercise.—The rolling, raging, raving, roaring river rushed wrathfully round and round the rough, rugged rocks which rose high in air. " A rat in a rat-trap, ran through the rain on a rail, with a raw lump of red liver in his mouth."

The smooth *r* occurs frequently in the exercises on the vowels of *air* and *far*, which see.

Respecting the whisper corresponding to the smooth *r*, see the Phonetic Quarterly, vol. i., p. 14, par. 8.

M m ; *M m* .

44. The sound of *m* in *met* is a sonant consonant. It has four different signs: *m* as in *me*, *mb* as in *dumb*, *mm* as in *crammed*, *mn* as in *condemn*.

Exercise.—The mad musician, Maestro, made magical, massive, majestic music with his mammoth melodeon, but Maestro's marked mannerisms mortified his musical master, whose mild mournful melodies many musicians mournfully remember.

N n ; *N n* .

45. The sound of *n* in *no* is a sonant consonant. It has seven different signs: *gn* as in *gnaw*, *kn* as in *know*, *mn* as in *mnemonic*, *mp* as in *compt*, *n* as in *no*, *nn* as in *sinned*, *pn* as in *pneumatic*.

Exercise.—Nineteen nervous nonsensical nobles nodded assent to the nominations, but their newly-fangled notions will, for the nonce, be knocked into nonentity.

ŋ ŋ ; *y y* .

46. The sound of *ng* in *sing* is a sonant consonant. It has three different signs: *n* as in *think*, *ng* as in *sing*, *ngue* as in *tongue*.

Exercise.—The young man languidly sung a long song and jingled a long string of shining rings which hung from his long strong fingers.

47. The letters *m*, *n*, *ŋ* represent sounds which are called *nasals,* because the breath is emitted through the nasal passages. With the exception that the breath is emitted through the nose instead of the mouth, these sounds are nearly the same as the sounds of *b*, *d*, *g*. Persons who have a severe "cold in the head" use the latter sounds instead of the nasals.

Respecting the whispered *m*, *n*, *ng*, see the Phonetic Quarterly, vol. i., p. 14.

B b ; *B b* .

48. The sound of *b* in *be* is a sonant consonant. The mode of producing it will be seen in pronouncing *bay, rob*. It has two different signs: *b* as in *be*, *bb* as in *ebb*.

Exercise.—The babbling of the blabbing, black-browed, bombastic bibber was as bad as the babbling of a Babylonian black-bird.

P p ; *P p* .

49. The sound of *p* in *pay* is a whispered consonant. It is cognate with *b*. It has three different signs: *p* as in *pay*, *gh* as in *hiccough*, *pp* as in *stopped*.

Exercise.—Peter Piper put pen to paper to produce a peerless production, proudly presuming to please princes, princesses, parliament, pastors, and people. " Pigmies are pigmies still though perched on pyramids "

D d; *D d.*

50. The sound of *d* in *do* is a sonant consonant. It has four different signs ; *bd* as in *bdellium*, *d* as in *do*, *dd* as in *add*, *ed* as in *signed.*

Exercise.—Dionysius Didymus delivered dogmatical declamations against dangerous dabblers in philosophy whose distempered minds disturbed dominant doctrinal distinctions.

T t; *T t*

51. The sound of *t* in *too* is a whispered consonant, and closely related to the sound of *d.* It has eight different signs : *ct* as in *Ctesiphon*, *d* as in *hoped*, *ed* as in *lacked*, *phth* as in *phthisic*, *pt* as in *ptyalism*, *th* as in *Thomas*, *tt* as in *Pitt*, *tte* as in *Gazette.*

Exercise.—The temper of the taciturn Titus Ptolemy was terribly tried by table-talk of the traveling tradesmen.

G g; *G g.*

52. The sound of *g* in *go* is a sonant consonant. It has four different signs : *g* as in *go*, *gg* as in *Hogg*, *gh* as in *ghost*, *gue* as in *rogue.*

Exercise.—Gabriel Goldfinch giggled at the great green gilded goggles his great-grandfather gave to Godfrey Gardner's gardener.

K k; *K k.*

53. The sound of *c* in *Coe* is a whispered consonant, and closely related to the sound of *g* in *go.* It has seven different signs : *c* as in *can*, *ch* as in *chord*, *ck* as in *lack*, *gh* as in *lough*, *k* as in *kill*, *qu* as in *piquant*, *que* as in *pique.*

Exercise.—Catherine Kickshaw kept a cat and kitten to catch and kill the crickets that came in her cousin's kitchen.

V v; *V v.*

54. The sound of *v* in *vine* is a sonant consonant. It has four different signs : *f* as in *of*, *ph* as in *Stephen*, *v* as in *vie*, *ve* as in *have.*

Exercise.—The ventriloquist was vain, vexatious, vicious, venal, and venturesome.

F f; *F f.*

55. The sound of *f* in *fine* is a whispered consonant, and closely related to the sound of *v* in *vine.* It has seven different signs : *f* as in

for, *ff* as in *off*, *ft* as in *often*, *gh* as in *cough*, *lf* as in *calf*, *ph* as in *phonic*, *pph* as in *Sappho*.

Exercise.—The fashionable, fastidious fellow found fiction and far-fetched fables of fairies far more favorable to his finical fashions than familiar facts.

ꭰ �; ⑀ ⑂.

56. The sound of *th* in *then* is a sonant consonant. It has two different signs: *th* as in *then*, *the* as in *wreathe*.

Exercise.—Gather together the roses that have withered in this rather cool though fine weather. "Thát is the man that said that you saw him. I say that thát that thát man said is not thát that thát man told him. Thát that I say is this: that thát that thát gentleman then advanced, is not thát that he should have spoken; for he said that thát *that* that thát man pointed out is not thát *that* that thát lady said that it was, but is *another that*."

Ꮋ ꞛ; ℏ ɀ.

57. The sound of *th* in *thin* is a whispered consonant, and closely related to the sound of *th* in *then*. It has five different signs: *h* as in *eight-h*, *th* as in *thin*, *the* as in *withe*, *tth* as in *Matthew*, *phth* as in *apophthegm*.

Exercise.—Thingumbob Thimblerig thievishly thought to thrive through thick and thin by throwing his thimbles about.

Z z; 𝒵 z.

58. The sound of *z* in *zeal* is a sonant or spoken consonant. It has nine different signs: *c* as in *suffice*, *cz* as in *czar*, *s* as in *is*, *sc* as in *discern*, *se* as in *raise*, *ss* as in *scissors*, *x* as in *Xenia*, *z* as in *zeal*, *zz* as in *buzz*.

Exercise.—Xenophon Zealous the zoologist zealously sought for zinc and zoophytes in the Zuyder Zee. The zany on his zebra resumed his zigzag journey through the desert.

S s; 𝒮 𝒎.

59. The sound of *s* in *seal* is a whispered consonant, and is closely related to the sound of *z* in *zeal*. It has eleven different signs: *c* as in *cider*, *ce* as in *fleece*, *ps* as in *psalm*, *s* as in *see*, *sc* as in *scene*, *sce* as in *coalesce*, *sch* as in *schism*, *se* as in *mouse*, *ss* as in *kiss*, *st* as in *listen*, *sw* as in *sword*.

Exercise.—Sally Simper stuttered, stammered, and lisped unceasingly from sunrise to sunset. "He boasts he twists the texts and suits the several sects. Sam Slick sawed six slim slippery saplings. Amidst the mists he thrusts his fists and insists he sees the ghosts."

2

J j; *J j*.

60. The sound of *si* in *vision* is a spoken consonant. It has five different signs: *ge* as in *ledge*, *j* as in *jet-d'eau*, *si* as in *vision*, *ssi* as in *scission*, *z* as in *azure*. English orthoëpists frequently use *zh* as the sign of this sound.

Exercise.—Free from seizure, intrusion, obtrusion, invasion, or derision, the miser in his inclosure leisurely measures his profusion of treasures obtained by usury, and experiences as much pleasure at the vision as a vizier.

C c; *C c*.

61. The sound of *ce* in *ocean* and *sh* in *shall* is a sonant consonant, and is closely related to the sound of *si* in *vision*. It has nine different signs: *c* as in *appreciate*, *ce* as in *ocean*, *ch* as in *etch* and *chaise*, *ci* as in *musician*, *s* as in *sure*, *sch* as in *Schiller*, *sh* as in *shall*, *ss* as in *assure*, *ssi* as in *mission*.

Exercise.—" Shun sheepish shame nor wish to shine in transient passion." He is an efficient, proficient, judicious, social, conscientious, cautious, veracious, patient, dispassionate practitioner, whose judicial acquisitions put to shame the pretensions of his unsocial, inefficient, officious, superficial, capricious, injudicious, ingratiate, irrational, shallow-headed, charlatan opponents.

CONSONANTAL DIPHTHONGS.

62. The two consonantal diphthongs requiring notice are those represented by *ch* and *j* in the common spelling. Double and single signs have been provided for them.

dj, *dj* — D d, *D d*.

63. The sound represented by these letters, is composed of *d* and the sound represented by *si* in *vision*—which last sound is represented by *j* in the phonetic alphabet. Germans usually substitute for this diphthong *dc* = *dsh*, saying *dcob* = *dshob* for *djob* (*job* in the common print). The analysis given above is intimated in the common spelling of such words as *ledge*, in which *ge* has the sound of the phonetic *j*, or, what is the same thing, the sound of *si* in *vision*. This diphthong has six different signs in the common orthography: *dg* as in *ledger*, *dge* as in *ledge*, *dj* as in *adjective*, *g* as in *gem*, *ge* as in *age*, *j* as in *join*.

Exercise.—The jovial German judge adjudged the jocose genius guiltless, when General John Johnson justified the generous jovial German judge's just judgment.

tc, *tc* — C g, *C j*.

64. The consonantal diphthong represented by these letters is com-

posed of the sound of *t* and the sound of *ce* in *ocean* = *sh* in *shall*. It is represented in German by *tsch*, the letters *sch* representing the sound of *sh* in *shall* = *ch* in the French representation, which is *tch*, as in *Tchernaia*. This analysis is intimated by the common spelling of such words as *etch*, in which *ch* = *ce* in *ocean* = *sh* in *shall* = *c* in the phonetic alphabet. This diphthong has two different signs in the common spelling: *ch* as in *chin*, *tch* as in *etch*.

Exercise.—"Three chubby children in Richfield were each choked with choice chunks of cheese, much of which was purchased of Charles Chickering on Chimborazo."

NUMBER OF THE VOCAL ELEMENTS.

65. The number of simple and proximate elements of the English language (exclusive of whispered *l*, *m*, *n*, and *ng*) is forty-six. They may be classed as follows:

a. Simple Vowel Elements.—There are sixteen vowels, which may be represented by twelve signs, provided no distinction is made, by means of signs, between the vowels of *ale* and *air*, *ebb* and *her*, *at* and *ask*, *old* and *whole*.

b. Proximate Vowel Elements.—There are four vowel diphthongs. These may be represented by the signs of their elements or by single signs. For *stenographic* reasons, single signs are used in phonetic shorthand; but, for phonotypy, double signs are best.

c. Simple Consonant Elements.—There are twenty-four consonants, inclusive of whispered *w* and *y*, and exclusive of whispered *l*, *r*, *m*, *n*, and *ng*. If whispered *w* be represented by *hw*, and whispered *y*, by *hy*, the number of distinct consonant signs may be reduced to twenty-two. The "Short Phonetic Alphabet" is composed of thirty-four signs, namely, twenty-two consonant signs, and twelve vowel signs.

d. Proximate Consonant Elements.—There are two consonantal diphthongs. In phonotypy they are best represented by the signs of their constituents. In phonetic shorthand, for stenographic reasons, they are represented by single signs, and classed among the vocal elements.

ANDREW J. GRAHAM'S

PHONETIC ALPHABET.

Note.—The sound of each letter is shown by the *italic* letter or letters in the word opposite or beneath it. The "superiors" refer to the scripts of the new letters.

Long Vowels.			Short Vowels.		
Ɩ	ɩ [1]	*ea*t, f*ea*r	I	i	*i*t
Ɛ	ɛ [2]	*a*le (*ai*r)	E	e	*e*ll (h*e*r)
Ᵽ	ᴃ [3]	*a*rm	A	a	*a*sk (*a*t)
Ꞷ	ꞷ [4]	*a*ll, f*o*rm	O	o	n*o*t, *o*n
Ꝋ	ꝋ [5]	*o*pe (wh*o*le)	Ʊ	ʊ [7]	*u*p, c*u*r
Ɯ	ɯ [6]	f*oo*d	U	u	f*oo*t, f*u*ll.

Consonants.

Ꟈ	ꟈ [8]	*th*en.	b, d, f, g, h, k,
Ƕ	ƀ [9]	*th*in.	*b*e, *d*o, *f*oe, *g*o, *h*e, *k*ey,
Ŋ	ŋ [10]	si*ng*.	l, m, n, p, r, s,
C	c	o*c*ean, *sh*all.	*l*et, *m*e, *n*o, u*p*, *r*oa*r*, *s*o,
J	j	vi*s*ion, *zh*.	t, v, w, y, z. —
and in their usual sense,			*t*o, *v*ie, *w*e, *y*e, *z*eal. —

Diphthongs.				Optional Letters.		
Double letters.	Single letters.					
ai	Ɨ ɨ [11]	*ai*sle, f*i*nd	Ɛ	ɛ [17]	*ai*r, where
oi	Θ ɵ [12]	*oi*l, b*oy*	Ꭿ	a [18]	*a*t, *a*n
ou	Ȣ ȣ [13]	*ou*t, n*ow*	Ɐ	ɐ [19]	h*e*r, b*i*rd
iu	Ɥ ɥ [14]	n*ew*, m*u*te	Ꝋ	ɵ [20]	wh*o*le
dj	Ɗ ɗ [15]	e*d*-*ge*, *j*oin	Q	q	*or* hw = wh in *wh*en;
tc	Ꞓ ꞓ [16]	e*t*-*ch*, *ch*in.			thus, "qen" or "hwen."

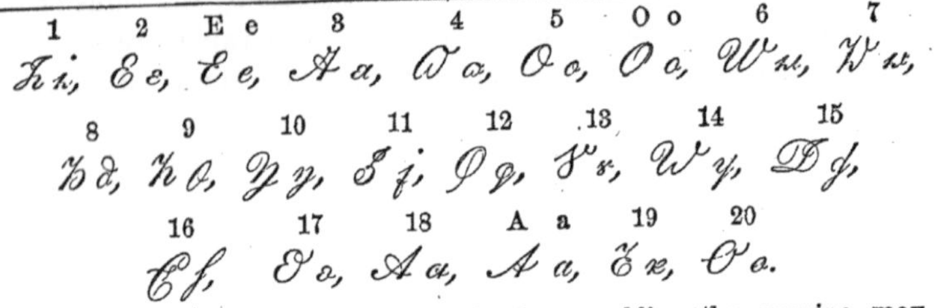

Transition Phonotypy.—Phonotypy closely resembling the genuine, may be produced, with the common types, by substituting

ɹ	ɐ	ᴀ *or* ʌ	ɔ	ƍ	ɯ	ʊ	th *or* dh,	th,	ng	for
ɩ	ɛ	ᴃ	ꞷ	ꝋ	ɯ	ʊ	ꟈ	ƀ	ŋ	

PRINCIPLES OF THE PHONETIC ALPHABET.

68. The phonetic alphabet presented in this treatise has been constructed in view of certain well-defined and obviously correct prin. ciples.

(1.) All the common Roman, italic, and script letters are used as far as they can be without violating entirely the analogies of Romanic print; and the phonetic print, therefore, closely resembles the common print.

(2.) The new letters are constructed in accordance with the principles of the old letters, and are such as admit of good italic and script forms.

(3.) The old vowel-letters being settled, by their most usual signifi-cation, as the signs of the short vowels of *pass, pet, pit, pot, put,* signs resembling the old vowel-letters are appropriated to the long vowels, in accordance with the principle that—*sounds of a given degree of like-ness should be represented by signs of a corresponding degree of like-ness.*

(4.) Reference has been had to the wishes of different classes of pho-neticians, and the alphabet has been so constructed that while they may differ as to the use of signs for the vowels of *air, at, her, whole* as distinct from the vowels of *age, ask, met, ope;* or as to the use of double or single types for the diphthongs,—they will all agree as to the signs for the generally recognized sounds.

69. In respect of the four particulars above mentioned, no phonetic alphabet has been constructed which can compare with the one explained in this work. For a chart of all the principal phonetic alphabets, and for various matters pertaining to the phonetic reform which do not come within the province of this treatise, see Vol. I. of the Phonetic Quarterly

---

SPECIMENS OF PHONETIC PRINT.

TRUTH.

(*With distinct signs for the sounds of the italic letters in " air, at, her, whole, when;" and with monotypes for the diphthongs.*)

70. Fœrs ov ðat me bi put fœrð tu amás welb for selfic grati-fikecon, tu giv ðe individyual pꭓer œver ꭒðerz, tu blꭓnd ꭒðerz, tu wꭓv a web ov sofistri, tu kast a desɪtful lꭒster on vꭓs, tu mɛk ðe wꭒrs apɪr ðe beter kœz. But enerᖤi ov ðat sœ emplœd iz sꭒisꭓdal. Ꭸe intelekt, in bikꭒmꭓꭨ a pander tu vꭓs, a tul ov ðe paconz, an advœket ov lꭓz, bikꭒmz not œnli degrɛded, but disꭓzd. It lꭒzez ðe kapasiti ov distꭓꭨgwiciꭨ trꭒb from fœlshud, gud from

ivil, rįt from roŋ; it bikumz az wʋrƀles æz an į hwiᵹ kanot dis-
tiŋgwic bitwin kʋlorz or fɔrmz.   Wɔ tu ƌat mįnd qiᵹ wɔnts ƌe
lʋv ov trʏƀ!   For wɔnt ov ƌis, ᶁinyʋs haz bikʋm a skʋrᶁ tu ƌe
wʋrld; its breƀ a pezonʋs ekshalɛcon; its brįtnes a sedʏser intu
paᵭz ov pestilens and deƀ.   Trʏƀ iz ƌe ljt ȯv ƌe Infinit mįnd,
and ƌe imeᶁ ov God in hiz krįtyurz.   Nʋƀiŋ endʏrz bʋt trʏƀ.
Ƌe drįmz, fikconz, ƀioriz qiᵹ mon wud sʋbstitʏt for it, sʋn dį.
Widʊt its gįdans, efort iz ven, and hɵp besles.   Akɔrdiŋli, ƌe
lʋv ov trʏƀ, a dip ƀɛrst for it, a deliberet pʋrpʋs tu sįk it and
hɵld it fast, me bį konsiderd az ƌe veri fɵndɛcon ov hʋman
kʋltyur and digniti.   Precʋs az ƀot iz, ƌe lʋv ov trʏƀ iz stil
mɵr precʋs; for widʊt it, ƀot wonderz and wɛsts itself, and pre-
sipitɛts men intu gįlt and mizeri.   Dr. Ꞓaniŋ.

TRUE COURAGE.

*(Printed with distinct signs for the sounds of the italic letters in
" air, at, her, whole, when," and with double letters for the diph
thongs.)*

71. Ƌer iz a vertyuʋs, glɵriʋs kʋredj; but it hapenz tu bį
found list in ƌoz hu ɛr most admaird for breveri.   It iz ƌe
kʋredj ov prinsipel, qitc dɔrz tu du rait in ƌe fes ov skɔrn, qitc
puts tu hazard repyutɛcon, raŋk, ƌe prospekts ov advansment,
ƌe simpaƀi ov frendz, ƌe admirɛcon ov ƌe wʋrld, raƌer ƌan
vaiolɛt a konvikcon ov diuti.   It iz ƌe kʋredj ov benevolens and
paieti, qitc kounts not laif dįr in widstandiŋ eror, siupersticon,
vais, oprecon, indjʋstis, and ƌe maitiest fɵz ov hiuman imprʋʋv-
ment and hapines.   It iz moral enerdji, ƌat fɵrs ov wil in adoptiŋ
diuti, ɵver qitc mēnɛs and sʋferiŋ hav nɵ pouer.   It iz ƌe
kʋredj ov a sɵl qitc reverensez itself tu mʋtc tu bį gretli mʋʋvd
about qot bifɵlz ƌe bodi; qitc ƀɛrsts sɵ intensli for a piur inward
laif, ƌat it kan yild ʋp ƌe animal laif widout fįr; in qitc ƌe
aidįa ov moral, spirityual, selestyal gud haz bin ʋnfɵlded sɵ
braitli az tu obskiur ɵl wʋrldli interests; qitc aspairz after
imɵrtaliti, and, ƌerfɵr, hįdz litel ƌe penz or plejurz ov a de;
qitc haz sɵ konsenterd its hɵl pouer and laif in ƌe lʋv ov God-
laik vertyu, ƌat it įven faindz a djoi in ƌe perilz and sʋferiŋz
bai qitc its loialti tu God and vertyu me bį aprʋʋvd.   Ƌis kʋredj
me bį kɵld ƌe perfekcon ov hiumaniti, for it iz ƌe eksersaiz,
rezʋlt, and eksprecon ov ƌe haiest atribiuts ov our netyur.
                                                Dr. Tcaniŋ.

MINIATURE WRITING.

(Printed with single types for the diphthongs, but without distinguishing by signs between the vowels of age *and* air, ask *and* at, met *and* her, ope *and* whole, *and with* hw *for* wh *in* when.)

72. Sisero rekordz ðat ðe hol ov ðe Iliad ov Homer woz riten on a pis ov pɛrçment in so smol a karakter, ðat it mįt bi enklozd in ðe kumpas ov a koko-nut-cel! Ꝺer woz olso wun in Kw.in Elizabeð's tįm huu rot ðe Ten Komandments, ðe Krid, ðe Pater Noster, ðe Kwin'z nɛm, and ðe Yir ov ɤr Lord, wiðin ðe kumpas ov a peni; and gev Her Maǵesti a pɛr ov spektakelz ov suç an ɛrtifical mek, ðat bį ðer ɛd ci plɛnli dizernd everi leter. Anuðer penman in ðe miniatywir stįl, wun Fransis Almonus, rot ðe Krid and ðe ferst fortin versez ov St. Don'z Gospel in ðe kumpas ov a peni. In ðe ljbrari ov St. Don'z Koleǵ, Oksfurd, iz a piktyur ov Ꞓɛrlz ðe Ferst dun wið a pen, ðe ljnz ov hwiç konten ol ðe Sɛmz in a leǵibel hand. At Halston, in Cropcir, ðe sit ov ðe Mitunz ⟨Myttons⟩, iz preservd a kɛrviŋ ov ðe portret ov Ꞓɛrlz ðe Ferst, ful-fɛst, on a piç-ston; abuv iz a krɤn; hiz fɛs, and klodz, hwiç ɛr Vandįk dres, ɛr pented; on ðe revérs iz an įgel transfikst wįð an aro, and rɤnd it ðis moto, "Ꝼ feðerd ðis aro." Ꝺe hol iz admirabli eksekųted, and iz set in gold, wið a distaf on iç sįd; it probabli woz ðe wurk ov Nikolas Bįot, a grɛt grever ov ðe Mint in ðe tįm ov Ꞓɛrlz ðe Ferst. In ðe Roal Mųziụm at Kopenhegen, iz a komon çeri-ston, on ðe surfɛs ov hwiç ɛr engrevd 220 heds; but ðer smolnes mɛks ðem apir raðer imperfekt.　　　　　　　　　Iŋglic "Foṅetik Durnal."

OSSIAN'S ADDRESS TO THE SUN.

(Printed with double types for the diphthongs, with hw *for* wh *in* when, *and without distinguishing by signs between the vowels of* age *and* air, ask *and* at, met *and* her, ope *and* whole.)

73. Ơ ðou ðat rolest abuv, round az ðe cild ov mai fɛðerz! Hwens ɛr ðai bimz, o Sun, ðai everlastiŋ lait? Ꝺou kumest forb in ðai oful biuti; ðe stɛrz haid ðemselvz in ðe skai; ðe Muun, kold and pɛl, siŋks in ðe western wɛv. But ðou ðaiself muuvest alon: huu kan bi a kompanyon ov ðai kors.

Ꝺe oks ov ðe mountenz fol: ðe mountenz ðemselz deké wið yirz; ðe ocan criŋks and groz agen; ðe Muun herself iz lost in Heven; but ðou ɛrt for ever ðe sɛm, redjoisiŋ in ðe braitnes ov ðai kors.

Hwen ðe wɔrld iz dɑrk wid tempests, hwen ðunder rɵlz and laitniŋ flaiz, ðou lukest in ðai biuti from ðe kloudz, and lafest at ðe stɔrm.   But tu Ocan ðou lukest in vɛn ; fɔr hi biholdz ðai bimz nɵ mɵr, hweðer ðai yelɵ herz flɵ on ðe istern kloudz, or ðou tremblest at ðe getṣ ov ðe west.

(In Phonetic Longhand.)

74. But ðou art perhaps laik mi—for a sizon : ðai yirz wil hav an end. Ðou calt slip in ðe kloudz, herles ov ðe vois ov ðe morniŋ. Ehzult, ðen, o Sun in ðe strenþ ov ðai yuþ! Edj iz dark and unluvli : it iz laik ðe glimeriŋ lait ov ðe Mun, hwen it sights þru broken kloudz; and ðe mist iz on ðe hilz, ðe blast ov ðe norþ iz on ðe plen, ðe travler crinks in ðe midst ov hiz djurni.

WHAT PHONOTYPY WILL DO.
(Printed with the Transition Phonetic Alphabet.)

75. Fɵnotipi siks sɵ tu reform our prezent alfabet, bai a fiu olterɛ-conz, az tu mɛk our Ingglic *speling an izi and ekzakt saiens*.   Striktli spiking, let that bi dun, and speling wud not hav tu bi gon ɵver at ol. Lern the alfabet, and ðe *prinsipel* ov speling-kombinɛcon,—and ɔl *speling kumz ov itself*.   Hens, ai understand the Tcerokı Indian, Ges (Guess) bai nɛm, invented for hiz traib an alfabet sɵ komplit that eni ordinari tcaild, after a fiu morningz, kud spel eni wurd in the langwɵdj the ferst taim hı herd it.   Nou, wı nıd tu hwip up and ɵver-tɛk thız Tcerokız.   But our bɑrbarizm iz mɵr inveterɛt than thɛrz, inazmutc az wı hav a vail, laiing, dementing ɵld orthografi tu get rid ov, bɑfɵr eni uther kan bı introdiust.   Sɵ our pɛrents must gɵ on driling thɛr dɑrlingz tu deth, or stiupiditi, bai fɵrsing intu thɛr tender brɛnz, in thɛr tcaildic yirz, a labɵrius, ɑrbitrari, memoraizd mas ov mis-spelingz ov an entair langgwɵdj in dıtel, ov hwitc hɵl langgwɵdj not siksti wurdz ɑr speld unekwivɵkali, and nesesarili rait!   Adopt fɵnotipi, and ther iz nɵ nıd ov a memoriter dril.   The brɛn task iz spɛrd; the inkyubus disipɛts.   A niu yır or tm ov brait, piur laif iz aded tu boihud.   Niu rum iz mɛd for tcıri akwizicon.   Edyukɛcon, tm, in rıding and raiting, iz tcıpend and yuniversalaizd.   Milyonz ov anyual edyukɛconal ekspens iz spɛrd, and milyonz ov ignɵrant tcildren ov poverti ɑr brot intu the pɛl ov noledj.   The grɛt obstakel tu the ızi akwairment ov our langgwɵdj bai forenerz iz remuvd, and our spɵken Ingglic, if simpli and triuli riten, promisez, when bɵrn bai komers,

konkwest, travel and kolinizecon ȯver distant landz, tu bɪkʊm the predominant langgwedj ov the wʊrld.   Rev. Dr. Hwɪdon.

IMMEDIATE ADVANTAGES OF PHONOTYPY.

76. PHONOTYPY not only offers benefits to future generations who may adopt it, but, as an educational instrument, it is now capable of saving at least one half of the time, money, and labor now devoted to the acquisition of the art of reading by the common orthography. Let a child first acquire the ability to read phonotypy (which may be done with thirty or forty hours' instruction); let him continue phonetic reading, say three months—until he becomes familiar with the general appearance of words ; and then, by reason of the general resemblance of phonotypy to the common orthography, he will be able to make a transition to the latter almost at once, in the same manner that the reader of the common print makes a transition to phonetic print.

77. Dr. Látham, author of the "Hand-Book of the English Language," says:

"The present writer is prepared with facts by which he could verify the following position :—that if a child were taught at first on the phonetic principle, and, by graduated lessons, brought up to a comprehension of the present orthography, his reading would be taught at half the time, half the trouble,—and consequently half the risk of having a distaste for learning engendered by the difficulties of his first studies—involved in the present system."

78. Another recommendation of the phonetic method of teaching reading is that it induces accuracy of pronunciation, and gives the pupil a thorough knowledge of the elements of the language, either of which (without special instruction) is rarely attained by those who are taught the common orthography alone.

79. The several above-mentioned advantages of phonotypy point to, and demand, two things: 1. The use in all our primary schools of the phonetic plan of teaching reading. 2. The use of phonotypy by Home-Missionary Societies, and by private individuals, in teaching ignorant adults the art of reading, at least by a phonetic orthography.

80. The phonetic system of teaching reading is already in use in a considerable number of schools in the United States; and the results justify the expectations of the most ardent phoneticians; and a large number of parents unwilling to subject their children to twelve or eighteen months' useless toil in learning to read, with the risk of rendering study distasteful to them, teach them at home by means of the

Phonetic Readers; by following the directions in which, the phonetic plan of teaching may be used by the most inexperienced.

81. Phonotypy, by furnishing a sign for each element of the language, is a very efficient instrument in the cure of stammering, lisping, and other defects of articulation, and in giving instruction to avoid foreign accents or other peculiarities of pronunciation.

ADVANTAGES OF A PHONETIC ORTHOGRAPHY.

82. LET a phonetic orthography be generally adopted, and the follow ing-mentioned advantages may be expected to result from it :-

(1.) Reading and writing will be rendered absolutely certain. In the phonetic alphabet, a letter being assigned to each sound, and the sound being the name of the letter, the mere rapid naming of the letters in a printed word, in their order, will not only tell us *how* to pronounce it, but pronounce it. In writing, the only thing required will be the writing, in the order of the sounds to be represented, those letters which are named by the sounds. The labor of learning to read will consist in merely becoming familiar with the forms and names of the letters, which may be done with thirty or forty hours' instruction. Conse-quently, phonetic writing and printing will save much of the time, money, and labor now lost in learning to read by an anomalous orthog-raphy. The school-days of the child will be virtually lengthened, and the sphere of his studies enlarged ; and the teacher will be saved from a vast amount of drudgery. The art of reading the common orthogra-phy is rarely attained without eighteen or twenty months' instruction, when the old plan of teaching is followed. And even then, what is prop-erly called the art of reading has not been attained. To be able to read and write the entire language with facility and accuracy requires years of study, practice, and observation. And who, even after years of study of the language, is not under the necessity of referring to a dictionary to ascertain the pronunciation of an unusual word? And what good speller even, thinks of writing an article for the press with-out consulting a dictionary to verify his orthography.

(2.) Phonetic writing and printing will eventually settle the orthography and pronunciation of every word in the language. Pro-vincialisms will disappear ; and the pronunciation of the English language, the world over, will be uniform, exact, elegant.

(3.) The doors of learning will be opened to millions who would never learn to read by the common orthography. A large number of adults now are unable to read and write ; and many who are said to possess the ability rarely read because they can not do so with facility. Adopt a phonetic orthography, and the reading public will be increased by millions. As there will be no excuse for being ignorant of the art of reading, but few, if any, will be.

(4.) Every one who learns to read by a phonetic orthography will possess an accurate knowledge of the elements of the language; and elocutionists and lexicographers will be able to write concerning the elements of the language, with the full assurance that they will be understood.

(5.) The business of representing unwritten languages will be rendered sure and easy.

(6.) A phonetic representation of language will most effectually tend to a wide diffusion of our language among foreigners, if it should not lead to its adoption as a universal medium of communication.

(7.) It will save millions of dollars in the expense of books, etc., annually

OBJECTIONS ANSWERED.

83. The principal objections which are made to the adoption of a phonetic orthography are: 1. That it will change the venerated English language. 2. That it will obscure the origin or etymology of words. Both of these objections are founded in ignorance of the nature and objects of the phonetic reform; instead of a change being effected in the English language by the adoption of a phonetic orthography, the language will be made more permanent than it could be in any other way; for it is not proposed by a phonetic orthography to change the pronunciation of a single word, but simply to give a definite, absolutely certain representation of whatever pronunciation may be settled as best. The principal difference between the phonetic and the common orthography is this:—By the common orthography, no one can tell with certainty the pronunciation of a single printed word except as he has learned it by tradition; while, by a phonetic orthography, the pronunciation of every word is indicated with greater certainty than it usually is by the ordinary pronouncing dictionaries. By the common orthography, the man who sits at your elbow can not tell, except he hears you utter them, what pronunciation you would give to the words you have written; while by a phonetic orthography, a Chinese, ignorant of every word of the English language, but knowing the signification of the phonetic letters, could tell, with absolute certainty, your pronunciation of words expressed by the phonetic letters. Such is the basis of the principal objection brought against the phonetic reform, and considered as countervailing all the advantages mentioned in the preceding chapter.

84. The second objection is like unto the first. It supposes either that the present orthography will be inaccessible after the adoption of a phonetic mode of representation, or that, to save etymologists from the

slight trouble of an additional step in their researches respecting the
origin of words, children to the end of time should be subjected to the
waste of millions of years and money in learning our present bar
barous orthography—an orthography unequaled for its anomaly—instead of giving them a mode of representing language, with which the
labor of learning to read and pronounce words with infallible accuracy,
and to write them with as much accuracy as they might pronounce
them, would consist in merely becoming familiar with the names and the
forms of the typic and graphic phonetic letters. If the objection is
founded upon the latter consideration, it can never avail with the
masses who have derived so little benefit from the rather uncertain
speculations and researches of etymologists thus far. Even supposing
that, after the adoption of a phonetic orthography, the books in the common print were to be mostly destroyed, nothing is more certain than that
all the etymological advantages of the present spelling could be retained
by simply placing in dictionaries the common spelling after the phonetic spelling. Etymologists would not fail to have this done before all
the works in the common orthography would disappear. But it is idle
to suppose that the books in the common print would cease to be printed.
They would continue to be produced for reasons similar to those which
give us the works of the principal Greek authors. With the alphabet
offered by the author, all the types required to produce a book in the
ordinary spelling would be found in the "case" of the phonetic printer.
Since, on account of the general resemblance of phonotypy to the common print, the phonetic reader would be able, at once—or, at most,
with a few minutes' study,—to make the transition to the common
print, all the advantages of the old orthography would be nearly as
accessible as now—in fact, more so ;—because had we but the common
orthography, eighteen or twenty months would have to be spent by
each pupil in learning to read it. On the contrary, a phonetic orthography being first familiarized by two or three months' study, the
transition to the common spelling is at once made, with a saving of
from twelve to fifteen months' study. Thus is the phonetic reform im-
pregnable to all the assaults that can be made upon it, turning out a
blessing wherever an evil is predicted of it, in accordance with the
general law of the universe, that blessings always attend the footsteps
of Truth, while Evil is evil continually

PHONOGRAPHY;

OR,

PHONETIC SHORTHAND.

85. THE Phonetic Alphabet previously explained is admirably adapted to the wants of the reader, being both beautiful and legible ; but the script forms of these letters, each consisting of two or more strokes, do not answer all the wants of the writer. There is required a system of shorthand, which to be worthy of general adoption should combine the following characteristics :

1. It should be capable of expressing all the vocal elements which in any way enter into the language to be represented.

2. It should secure a tolerable degree of speed of writing with ample legibility, so that it may answer all the purposes for which longhand is employed.

3. It should secure sufficient speed for reporting purposes without illegibility.

4. It must observe, in every department, order and simplicity.

86. A system of shorthand which shall fully comply with all of these requirements, may justly be regarded as the standard system ; and when it shall have appeared, the conditions for the general adoption of shorthand for all the purposes for which longhand is now employed will have been secured. These requirements were more fully met by the Old or English Phonography than by any of its predecessors. It may, however, be shown to fall short, in many important particulars, of the requirements of a standard system of shorthand. Upon the basis furnished by the English Phonography has been constructed a system which is denominated Standard or American Phonography. It can be demonstratively shown that this fully complies with the requirements of a standard stenography, and that therefore the long-sought desideratum has been attained. Standard Phonography, with its different styles or degrees of contraction, is explained in detail in the "Compendium." It is the object of this chapter to furnish a general statement of the principles and uses of the system.

87. Phonography, or Phonetic Shorthand, is based upon the pho-

netic principles heretofore explained, harmonized with certain stenographic principles, or laws of speed in writing, which it is the purpose
of a phonographic text-book to explain. No phonographic sign of a
single sound requires more than one movement of the hand to form
it; and it is not unfrequently the case that several sounds are expressed by a single stroke of the pen. The characters for the elements
are formed of the simplest geometrical signs—simple lines for the consonants, and dots and dashes for the vowels.

88. As the phonographic characters are explained, it will be observed that the straight lines are written in four different directions,
and that the curves are written in eight different positions, in accordance with the following diagrams:

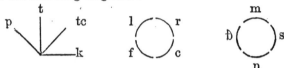

89. A class of consonants known as *Mutes* or *Abrupts* are represented
in Phonography by straight lines, thus:

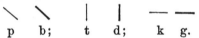

p   b;   t   d;   k   g.

90. The likeness between several of the signs given above—one
being light and another distinguished from it, simply by its being
heavy,—intimates a corresponding likeness between the consonants
they represent—some sounds being what are frequently designated as
whispers, and others being what are called *sonants* or *spoken sounds*. This
relation exists between the sounds indicated by

p, b—t, d—k, g—f, v—Ð, đ—s, z,

as is intimated by their phonographic signs. The similarity will be
observed by comparing the initial sounds of the following words:

Pay, bay—tie, die—Coe, go—fie, vie—thigh, thy—seal, zeal—sure,
jour (a French word, pronounced *zhoor*).

91. By making the simple lines light and heavy, a sufficient number of simple signs for all the elements is obtained. After a little
practice, the writer will find that the heavy signs for the spoken
sounds will be made without any particular thought or effort—it
seeming very natural to write a heavy sign for such sounds, while it
will be felt to be equally natural to write a light sign for a whisper.
Such is the similarity between the sounds represented by light and
heavy lines, that if the signs of cognate sounds were to be inter-
changed by accident, but little difficulty would be experienced in
arriving at the word intended to be written. The word "Pŭvălō,"
for instance, in connection with other words of a sentence, would

readily be understood as meant for "Bŭfălō;" so "Vranklin" would be seen to be a mistake for "Franklin."

92. As ╱ ╱ are not required as signs of any simple consonants, they are employed to represent the consonantal diphthongs,

g (t-sh) and ɉ (d-zh).

93. A class of consonants usually known as *Continuants* are indicated in Phonography by curved lines, thus:

ᴖ ᴖ (( )) ᴗ ᴗ
f, v; þ, đ; s, z; c, j.

94. Two sounds, usually called *Liquids* (because of their ready coalescence with other consonants), are indicated in Phonography thus:

( ) or ╱
l, r.

95. The consonants indicated by the signs *l* and *r* in the words *low*, *row*, are spoken sounds; and, in accordance with the principles thus far observed in the Phonographic Alphabet, they should be represented by heavy lines; but, on the supposition that the corresponding whispers do not occur in English, the light lines are employed to represent them; and the corresponding

96. Heavy lines are employed to represent the two sounds frequently called *Semivowels*, thus:

╲ ╭
w, y.

These sounds are sometimes represented by briefer signs, thus:

c or ɔ = w; ᴗ or ᴖ = y.

97. Three sounds, called *Nasals* (because, in forming them, the breath is expelled through the nose), are represented in Phonography thus:

⌒ ᴗ ᴗ
m n ŋ.

98. What is known as the *aspirate* is indicated in Phonography thus:

╱ h,

when a dot placed before the vowel is not more convenient.

99. Six of the twelve generally recognized vowels are represented by a dot, and six by a dash. The value of either of these signs depends upon its position respecting a consonant.

100. A heavy dot, according as it is placed opposite the *beginning, middle*, or *end* of a consonant sign, signifies

i, ε, ʙ.

101. A heavy dash, according as it is placed opposite the *beginning middle*, or *end* of a consonant sign, signifies

ω, ℧, ɯ.

102. The corresponding short vowels indicated by

i, e, a,
o, ℧, u,

are represented by light dots (for the first three) and dashes (for the remainder) opposite the *beginning, middle*, or *end* of a consonant. The dashes are to be made about the length of a hyphen (-) and are written at right angles with the consonant-signs.

103. Thus two characters are made to represent twelve sounds. These signs are placed before or after the consonants, as may be desired. As the consonants of a word are first written, and the vowels written beside them, the reporter (who reads mainly by consonants) can omit the vowels to any desirable extent. It is frequently the case that a phonographer in writing a letter, writes merely the consonants of the words employed, and inserts the vowels as he revises what he has written.

104. The four vowel-diphthongs are represented by small angles, for the mode of writing which the reader is referred to the *Compendium of Standard Phonography.*

105. *Speed of Phonography.*—As soon as the writer becomes sufficiently familar with the system to be able to omit most of the vowels, he will find, by calculation, that to write a given number of words phonographically will require but one seventh of the number of strokes necessary to write them in the common longhand. Hence a person who is able to write by the common longhand twenty-five words per minute, can write by phonography 175 words per minute, as soon as he has thoroughly familiarized the phonographic letters. The average rate of speaking is 120 words per minute.

106. *Arrangement of the Consonant Signs.*—When describing the consonantal elements in the previous pages, the sonant consonants were made to precede the whispered consonants, because this is the natural order,—the importance of the elements of speech being in the ratio of their vocality. In the Phonographic Alphabet, however, the whispers are made to precede the sonant consonants, because they are more easily pronounced than the spoken consonants. On the contrary, the long vowels which correspond to the spoken consonants precede the short vowels, because their pronunciation is easier than that of the short ones.

CONSONANTS

p	b	t	d	ç=tc	ɟ=dj	k	g
\	\	|	|	/	/	—	—
pay	bay	to	do	ctch	edge	cain	gain

f	v	þ	đ	s	z	c	j
(	(	(	(	) ○	) ○	)	)
fie	vie	thin	then	sec	zee	she	zhe

l		r		m		n		ŋ
(		\/		⌢		⌣		⌣
lie		roar		me		no		sing

w				y				h
\	c ɔ			(	∪ ∩			/
we				ye				he

LONG VOWELS.

i	ε–o	ɹ	ɔ	o–o	ɯ
•|	•|	.|	⌐|	-|	_|
eat	age (air)	arm	all	ope (whole)	food

SHORT VOWELS.

ɪ	e–ɐ	a–ɑ	o	ʊ	u
'|	·|	.|	⌐|	-|	_|
it	edge (her)	ask (at)	on	up, cur	foot

NOTE—The sound of each sign is shown by the phonotype above it, and by the *italic* letter or letters in the word or words beneath it. The vowels of parenthetic words are provided with distinct signs, whose use is optional.

STANDARD PHONOGRAPHIC ALPHABET.

OPTIONAL VOWEL-SIGNS.

o	a	ɐ	ϴ
air	*at*	her	*whole*

CLOSE DIPHTHONGS.

ai = i̯	oi = ϴ	ou = ⴄ	iu = ɥ
*a*isle=*isle*	*oil,* boy	*out,* now	*dew=due*

OPEN DIPHTHONGS.

ɐi	ɑi	ii	ɛi	ɔi	ϭe	ϭa	ɯi
aye	*sawing*	Deity	*clayey*	*snowy*	*Owen*	Noah	Louis

W WITH VOWELS.

ɹ	i	ɛ	e	ɐ	ɔ	a	ʁ	a	ɔ	o	ϭ	o	ɹɹ	ɯ	u	i̯	o	ⴄ

Y WITH VOWELS.

ɹ	i	ɛ	e	ɐ	ɔ	a	ʁ	a	ɔ	o	ϭ	o	ɹɹ	ɯ	u	i̯	o	ⴄ

Entered, according to Act of Congress, in the year 1857, by ANDREW J. GRAHAM, in the Clerk's Office of the District Court of the United States for the Southern District of New York.

ADVANTAGES OF PHONOGRAPHY.

GENERAL STATEMENT.

107. UPON each individual who learns it, Phonography confers, doubtless, some advantage peculiarly adapted to his individual circumstances. Upon the reporter it confers the power of taking the exact words of a speaker, even at the rate of 180 or 200 words per minute. It enables the student of a foreign language to visualize its *pronunciation*—to put down on paper, as it were, the voice of his teacher. To him who aims to be a public speaker it is of inestimable value, on account of its turning his attention to pronunciation. Phonographers are said to pronounce the English language better than any other class of persons. To the clergyman it is of peculiar value, as it enables his pen to keep pace with his powers of composition, and saves him five sixths of the manual labor required in the use of the common longhand. It is exceedingly serviceable to the lawyer in taking notes of testimony, decisions, and rulings of a court, and in rough-sketching business papers of every description. The principal of a commercial establishment may conduct the largest correspondence in a fraction of the time ordinarily required (thus saving much time and energy for other important duties) by dictating his letters, even with the rapidity of speech, to a competent phonographer, who would afterward write them out and prepare them for the mail. Ministers who use Phonography claim that they can read it better than longhand, and with more of the freedom of extemporaneous delivery. Authors whose "living flocks of thoughts trudge it slowly and wearily down the pen and along the paper, hindering each other as they struggle through the strait gate of the old handwriting"—whose "kind and loving thoughts, warm and transparent, liquid as melted from the hot heart," now "grow opaque, and freeze with a tedious dribbling from the pen," can not fail to duly appreciate Phonography, which enables them to write at "breathing ease." The Rev. Dr. Raffles, of Liverpool, says: "Phonography is a railroad method of communicating thought; a railroad by reason of its expedition—a railroad by reason of its ease."

It is hardly necessary to speak further upon the *peculiar* advantages of shorthand, since the bare mention of the art is sufficient to suggest many benefits, even in addition to those *general* ones which it bestows upon all, in correspondence, writing literary compositions, in keeping a diary, in book-keeping, in copying letters, in making memoranda, in sketching lectures and sermons, in making abstracts of, and quotations from, books read. For these and all other purposes for which writing is available, it requires but a tithe of the time, labor, and space needed in the use of longhand.

108. The following testimonial as to the benefits of shorthand is from the pen of Mr. Gawtress, the publisher of an improved edition of Byrom's system. Of course, whatever advantages could be predicated of the old systems of stenography, undoubtedly belong to Phonography, the best system of stenography yet given to the world.

109. "Shorthand is capable of imparting so many advantages to persons in almost every situation of life, and is of such extensive utility to society, that it is justly a matter of surprise that it has not attracted a greater share of attention, and been more generally practiced.

"In England, at least, this art may be considered a national blessing, and thousands who look with the utmost indifference upon it, are daily reaping the fruits of its cultivation. It is scarcely necessary to mention how indispensable it is in taking minutes of public proceedings. If all the feelings of a patriot glow in our bosoms on a perusal of those eloquent speeches which are delivered in the senate, or in those public assemblies where the people are frequently convened to exercise the birthright of Britons—we owe it to shorthand. If new fervor be added to our devotion, and an additional stimulus be imparted to our exertions as Christians, by the eloquent appeals and encouraging statements made at the anniversaries of our various Religious Societies—we owe it to shorthand. If we have an opportunity, in interesting judicial cases, of examining the evidence, and learning the proceedings with as much certainty, and nearly as much minuteness, as if we had been present on the occasion—we owe it to shorthand. In short, all those brilliant and spirit-stirring effusions which the circumstances of the present times combine to draw forth, and which the press transmits to us with such astonishing celerity, warm from the lips and instinct with the soul of the speaker, would have been entirely lost to posterity, and comparatively little known to ourselves, had it not been for the facilities afforded to their preservation by shorthand. Were the operations of those who are professionally engaged in exercising this art, to be suspended but for a single week, a blank would be left in the political and judicial history of our country, an impulse would be wanting to the public mind, and the nation would be taught to feel and acknowledge the important purposes it answers in the great business of life.

"A practical acquaintance with this art is highly favorable to the improvement of the mind, invigorating all its faculties, and drawing forth all its resources. The close attention requisite in following the voice of the speaker, induces habits of patience, perseverance, and watchfulness, which will gradually extend themselves to other pursuits and avocations, and at length inure the writer to exercise them on every occasion in life. When writing in public, it will also be absolutely necessary to distinguish and adhere to the train of thought which runs through the discourse, and to observe the modes of its connection. This will naturally have a tendency to endue the mind with quickness of apprehension, and will impart an habitual readiness and distinctness of perception, as well as a methodical simplicity of arrangement, which can not fail to conduce greatly to mental superiority. The judgment will be strengthened, and the taste refined ; and the practitioner will, by degrees, become habituated to seize the original and leading parts of a discourse or harangue, and to reject whatever is commonplace, trivial, or uninteresting.

"The *memory* is also improved by the practice of stenography. The obligation the writer is under to retain in his mind the last sentence of the speaker, at the same time that he is carefully attending to the following one, must be highly beneficial to that faculty, which, more than any other, owes its improvement to exercise. And so much are the powers of retention strengthened and expanded by this exertion, that a practical stenographer will frequently recollect more without writing, than a person unacquainted with the art could copy in the time by the use of common-hand.

"It has been justly observed, 'this science draws out all the powers of the mind ;—it excites invention, improves the ingenuity, matures the judgment, and endows the retentive faculty with those superior advantages of precision, vigilance, and perseverance.'

The *facility it affords to the acquisition of learning* ought to render it an indispensable branch in the education of youth. To be enabled to treasure up for future study the substance of lectures, sermons, etc., is an accomplishment attended with so many evident advantages that it stands in no need of recommendation. Nor is it a matter of small importance, that by this art the youthful student is furnished with an easy means of making a number of valuable extracts in the moments of leisure, and of thus laying up a stock of knowledge for his future occasions. The pursuit of this art materially contributes to improve the student in the principles of grammar and composition. While tracing the various forms of expression by which the same sentiment can be conveyed ; and while endeavoring to represent, by modes of contraction, the dependence of one word upon another, he is insensibly initiated in the science of universal language, and particularly in the knowledge of his native tongue.

"The rapidity with which it enables a person to commit his own thoughts to the safety of manuscript, also renders it an object peculiarly worthy of regard. By this means many ideas which daily strike us, and which are lost before we can record them in the usual way, may be snatched from destruction, and preserved till mature deliberation can ripen and perfect them.

"In addition to these great advantages, Science and Religion are indebted to this inestimable art for the preservation of many valuable lectures and sermons, which would otherwise have been irrecoverably lost. Among the latter may be instanced those of Whitfield, whose astonishing powers could move even infidelity itself, and extort admiration from a Chesterfield and a Hume, but whose name would have floated down-the stream of time, had not shorthand rescued a portion of his labors from oblivion. With so many vouchers for the truth of the remark, we can have no hesitation in stating it as our opinion, that since the invention of printing, no cause has contributed more to the diffusion of knowledge and the progress of refinement, we might also add, to the triumphs of liberty and the interests of religion, than the revival and improvement of this long-neglected art.

"Such are the blessings which shorthand, like a generous benefactor, bestows indiscriminately on the world at large. But it has additional and peculiar favors in store for those who are so far convinced of its utility as personally to engage in its pursuit. The advantages resulting from the exercise of this art are not, as is the case with many others, confined to a particular class of society; for though it may seem more immediately calculated for those whose business it is to record the eloquence of public men, and the proceedings of popular assemblies, yet it offers its assistance to persons of every rank and station in life—to the man of business as well as the man of science—for the purpose of private convenience as well as of general information.''

TWO MODES OF REPRESENTING LANGUAGE NECESSARY.

110. A CONSIDERATION of the different wants of the reader and writer makes it apparent that two different systems of representing language are required:—1. A system combining a tolerable degree of facility of execution with very great legibility. 2. A system combining tolerable legibility with the greatest facility of execution.—Phonetic print is an example of the former. Phonography is an example of the latter. The use of a phonetic alphabet based upon the common alphabet is seconded by various considerations besides those of legibility. At the same time that we are furnished by it, with phonetic printing which can be equaled by no other system in respect of beauty

and legibility, there is required the least possible expenditure of money and time in procuring new types; and all that has been invested in the ordinary types will be saved. Furthermore, the transition from the new to the old spelling is rendered so easy that all who learn to read phonetic print can read works in the old orthography without any instruction in it. This will be possible on account of the general resemblance of the new to the old print. In consequence of this, all the advantages of the old orthography in respect of etymology, etc., will be nearly as accessible as they are now. Moreover, the reader of the common print can, with a very few minutes' instruction, make the transition to the new spelling; and phonetic print will encounter far less opposition than it would if an entirely new alphabet were to be employed, to read by which would require considerable study. Then the use as an educational instrument of a phonetic orthography closely resembling the common print will be a powerful aid in securing the prevalence of phonetic spelling—an aid, without which the phonetic reform might struggle in vain for centuries to come—but with which it is destined to have a speedy triumph.

111. The unbounded admiration for phonetic shorthand, entertained by those who have recently learned it, frequently leads them to desire that Phonography should supplant all other modes of representing language; and makes them opponents, rather than promoters, of phonetic printing. It is presumed that, in forming their opinions, they have overlooked the above-mentioned considerations, which demand a system of printing differing from their favorite system of shorthand; and they are, perhaps, not aware of the apparently insuperable obstacles in the way of printing phonography from letter-press. Thus far phonographic works have had to be produced by processes three or four times as costly as the ordinary letter-press printing. Even if there were some process as cheap as letter-press printing for producing phonography just as it should be written, yet, not being as legible as phonotypy, phonography could not take its place in respect of legibility;— nothing being said of the fact that Phonography could not secure several important advantages which would be obtained by phonotypy. Let Phonography supplant other modes of representing the language, and the ability to read the old orthography could be attained only by the present tedious processes.

It is earnestly to be hoped that all phonographers will lend the printing department of the phonetic reform that aid which it merits at their hands

SPECIFIC DIRECTIONS FOR MAKING THE ELEMENTARY SOUNDS.

112. THE reader will scarcely have reached this point in this treatise, without having acquired a definite knowledge of the method of forming each of the elements of the English language.

113. The purpose of the exercises which have been given on each element, has been to render it distinct, by placing it in a great variety of situations, and by rendering it very prominent by the frequency of its occurrence. However, lest the student should fail to acquire from the preceding account an accurate knowledge of the vocal elements, it is deemed advisable to furnish specific directions for their formation.

114. By way of introduction to these directions, it is well that the reader's attention should be called to the principal distinguishing characteristics of vocal utterance. Then, first, let it be observed that the term *Voice* is here used to denote all the different sounds heard in speech. When the breath is so emitted as to call into action the vocal ligaments, a species of musical sound is produced, which if unimpeded constitutes a *Vowel;* if impeded, as in the production of the spoken consonants, a sort of murmur is produced, which may be termed an *Undertone,* or *subvocal* sound.

115. When the breath is emitted without a distinct vibration of the vocal ligaments, and is simply impeded by entire or partial contacts of the organs of speech, an effect is produced, which may be termed a *Whisper.* Instances of such whispers occur in the formation of those consonants which have heretofore been described as *whispered consonants.* The sonant or spoken consonants differ from the whispered consonants, principally by their having a subvocal sound in connection with a whisper. The sound of *b*, for instance, requires that there should be made a contact in almost the same manner as for the production of the sound of *p;* but in sounding *b*, it will be observed that the undertone, or subvocal sound, is heard previous to the sudden separation of the lips, which is required for the completion of the sound.

1. DIRECTIONS FOR PRODUCING THE CONSONANTS.

116. To produce the sound indicated by ⟍ close the lips, and suddenly force them apart with the breath. Or, gradually separate the sounds of the syllable *āp*, and finally drop the sound denoted by *ā;* thus, ā-p, ā-p, ā—p, —p, *P*.

117. To produce the sound indicated by $\searrow$ close the lips, produce the undertone—a sort of murmur in the throat,—and suddenly force apart the lips by the breath at the moment of the cessation of the undertone. Or, having distinctly pronounced the syllable ōb several times, gradually separate the two sounds, and finally drop the sound denoted by ō, when the desired sound, denoted by b, will remain; thus, ōb, ō-b, ō–b, ō—b, —b, B. Or, having deliberately pronounced the word bay several times, gradually separate the two sounds, and finally omit the sound denoted by ay; thus, bay, b-ay, b-ay, b—ay, b—, B.

118. To produce the sound indicated by | separate the sound of t from eat or tea; thus, eat, ea-t, ea–t, —t, T: tea, t-ea, t–ea, t—ea, t—, T.

119. To produce the sound indicated by | gradually separate the sound of d from that of o in do, and finally drop the sound of o; thus, do, d-o, d–o, d—, D. Or, separate the sound of d from the word aid; thus, aid, ai-d, ai–d, ai—d, —d, D.

120. To produce the sound indicated by ╱ separate the sound of ch from chin, or the sound of tch from etch; thus, chin, ch-in, ch–in, ch—in, ch—, Ch: etch, ĕ-tch, ĕ–tch, ĕ—tch, —tch, Tch = Ch. Or, rapidly unite the sounds of t and ch. This process may be represented by phonotypes thus:

$$t \quad c \qquad t\ c \qquad t\ c \qquad tc \qquad ç.$$

121. To produce the sound indicated by ╱ separate the sound of j from the word joy, or the sound of dge from edge; thus, joy, j-oy, j–oy, j—oy, j—, J: edge, ĕ-dge, ĕ–dge, ĕ—dge, —dge, Dge = J. Or, rapidly unite the sounds of d and si (as in vision). This process may be represented by phonotypes thus:

$$d \quad j \qquad d\ j \qquad d\ j \qquad dj \qquad ḏ.$$

This sound, as previously explained, is not a simple, but a proximate, element.

122. To produce the sound indicated by——, separate the sound of k from ken or oak; thus, ken, k-en, k–en, k—en, k—, K: oak, oa-k, oa-k, oa—k, —k, K.

123. To produce the sound indicated by ——, separate the sound of g from go or egg; thus, go, g-o, g–o, g—o, g—, G: egg, ĕ-gg, ĕ–gg, ĕ—gg, —gg, Gg = G.

124. To produce the sound indicated by $\diagdown$ separate f from foe or

if; thus, foe, f-oe, f—oe, f—oe, f—, *F:* if, ĭ-f, ĭ–f, ĭ—f, —f, *F.* To produce this sound, the upper teeth are required to be placed upon the lower lip.

125. To produce the sound indicated by ⌞ separate the sound of *v* from *vie* or *eve;* thus, vie, v-ie, v-ie, v—ie, v—, *V:* eve, e-ve, e-ve, e—ve,—v, *V.*

126. To produce the sound indicated by (separate the sound of *th* from *thin* or *earth;* thus, thin, th-in, th-in, th—in, th—, *Th:* earth, ear-th, ear-th, ear—th, —th, *Th.*

127. To produce the sound indicated by (place the tongue against the crowns of the upper front teeth, so that breath may be slightly emitted at the time of the production of the undertone, and then suddenly withdraw the tongue from the teeth. Or, separate the sound of *th* from *then* or *with;* thus, then, th-en, th-en, th—en, th—, *TH:* with, wĭ-th, wĭ-th, wĭ—th, —th, *TH.*

128. To produce the sound indicated by) separate the sound of *s* from *see,* or that of *ss* from *hiss;* see, s-ee, s-ee, s—ee, s—, *S:* hiss, hĭ-ss, hĭ–ss, hĭ—ss, —ss, *SS = S.*

129. To produce the sound indicated by) separate the sound of *s* from *zeal,* or that of *zz* from *buzz;* thus, zeal, z-eal, z-eal, z—eal, z—, *Z:* buzz, bŭ-zz, bŭ-zz, bŭ—zz, —zz, *ZZ = Z.*

130. To produce the sound indicated by ⌡ separate the sound of *sh* from *show* or *hush;* thus, show, sh-ow, sh-ow, sh—, *SH:* hush, hŭ-sh, hŭ-sh, —sh, *SH.*

131. To produce the sound indicated by ⌡ separate the sound of *j* from the French *jour* (pronounced *zhoor*), or the sound of *ge* from *rouge* (pronounced *roozh*); thus, jour, j-our, j-our, j—, *J = ZH:* rouge, rou-ge, rou-ge, —ge, *GE = ZH.* This sound is represented by *ge* in *edge = edzh =* phonetic *edj.*

132. To produce the sound indicated by ⌒ , separate the sound of *l* from *low* or *ail;* thus, low, l-ow, l-ow, l—, *L:* ail, ai-l, ai-l, —l, *L.*

133. To produce the sound indicated by ⟍ or ⟋ , separate the sound of *r* from *ray* or *air;* thus, ray, r-ay, r-ay, r—, *R:* air, ai-r, ai-r, —r, *R.*

134. To produce the sound indicated by ⌒, close the lips, emit the undertone through the nose, and suddenly separate the lips, at the moment of the cessation of the subvocal sound. Or, separate the

sound of *m* from *may* or *aim;* thus, may, m-ay, m-ay, m—, *M;* aim, ai-m, ai-m, —m, *M.*

135. To produce the sound indicated by ‿ , separate the sound of *n* from *no* or *own;* thus, no, n-o, n-o, n—, *N:* own, ow-n, ow-n, —n, *N.* The production of this sound requires the emission of the undertone through the nose.

136. To produce the sound indicated by ‿ , separate the sound of *ng* from *sing;* thus, sing, sĭ-ng, sĭ-ng, —ng, *NG.* This sound commences no syllable in the English language. Its production requires that the undertone should be emitted through the nose.

137. To produce the sound indicated by ╲ , separate the sound of *w* from *wall;* thus, wall, w-all, w-all, w—, *W.* Or, while prolonging *oo,* gradually compress the lips till the clear vowel sound is destroyed, and the sound of *w* will be the result. Some phonologists consider this sound and that of *oo* identical; but to be convinced of their error, they have but to pronounce *woo-woo-woo;* and observe the varying position of the lips, and the changes in the character of the sound. Students of phonography should avoid naming the sign of this sound *Double-U.* When mentioned in conversation, it should be called *Wā.*

138. To produce the sound indicated by ⌠ separate the sound of *y* from *yawl;* thus, yawl, y-awl, y-awl, y—, *Y.* Or, while prolonging the sound of *ee,* elevate the tongue, till the clear vowel sound is destroyed, and until a murmur is heard, and the sound of *y* will be the result. The pronunciation of *ye-ye-ye* will serve to illustrate the mode of arriving at the sound of *y* from the sound of *ee,* and also demonstrate that these sounds are not identical, as some phonologists have thought. The sign for the sound of *y* should not be called *Wĭ.* When mentioned in conversation it may be named *Yā.*

139. To produce the sound indicated by ╱ , separate the sound of *h* from *hall;* thus, hall, h-all, h-all, h—, *H.* Or, emit the breath suddenly with all the organs open. The sign of this sound should not be called *Aitch.* When mentioned in conversation, it may be named *Hā* or *Haitch.*

2. DIRECTIONS FOR PRODUCING THE VOWELS.

140. To produce the sound indicated by ˙| pronounce the common name of the letter *e.* Or, pronounce the word *eat* distinctly several times; and finally leave off the sound indicated by *t.*

141. To produce the sound indicated by ˙| , deliberately pronounce the word *it* several times, and finally omit the sound indicated

by *t*. Or, speak the word *if*, as nearly as possible, without bringing the under lip in contact with the upper teeth.

142. To produce the sound indicated by •| pronounce the common name of the letter *a*. Or, pronounce the word *aid* several times, and finally omit the sound denoted by *d*. Or, pronounce the word *ape*. as nearly as possible, without the contact of the lips. Or, having distinctly pronounced *pay* several times, dwelling upon the sound denoted by *ay*, finally omit the sound denoted by *p*.

143. To denote the sound indicated by ·| , speak the interjection *eh !* Or, having distinctly pronounced the word *ell* several times, finally omit the sound indicated by *ll*. Or, pronounce the word *ebb*, as nearly as possible, without a contact of the lips.

144. To produce the sound indicated by ι| , distinctly pronounce the word *earth* a number of times ; and finally omit the sound indicated by *rth*.

145. To produce the sound indicated by ι| , deliberately pronounce the word *air* several times, dwelling upon the sound of *ai*, and finally omit the sound denoted by *r*.

146. To produce the sound indicated by ι| , deliberately pronounce the word *at* several times, and finally omit the sound denoted by *t*. Or, pronounce the syllable *ap*— as nearly as possible without bringing the lips into contact.

147. To produce the sound indicated by ι| , distinctly pronounce the word *arm* a number of times, and finally omit the sounds represented by *rm*. Or, pronounce the word *ah !* Or, distinctly pronounce the word *are* several times, and finally omit the sound denoted by *re*.

148. To produce the sound indicated by | having distinctly pronounced the word *ask* several times, omit the sounds denoted by the letters *sk*. This vowel is not that of *at*. Observe, by the aid of a looking-glass, that the vowels of *air* and *at* require that the tongue should be elevated in the middle,—to assume a position which is very well indicated by ⌒. On the contrary, in producing the vowel of *ask*, the tongue is nearly straight. An exercise on this vowel will be found at paragraph 23.

149. To produce the sound indicated by ⁻| , pronounce the word *awe*.

150. To produce the sound indicated by ⁻| , forcibly pronounce the word *on* several times, and finally omit the sound denoted by *n*. Or,

pronounce the syllable *op*, as nearly as possible, without bringing the lips together.   Observe that the vowel of *arm* requires that the corners of the mouth should be slightly drawn back.   On the contrary in producing the vowel of *on*, the mouth is more open than in pronouncing *ah*, and the corners of the mouth are not retracted.

151. To produce the sound indicated by -| , pronounce the common name of the letter *o*, or the word *oh!* Or, pronounce the word *owe*. Or, pronounce the word *ope*, as nearly as possible, without closing the lips.

152. To produce the sound indicated by ∖| , pronounce the word *only* several times ; and finally omit the sound indicated by *nly*. This vowel occurs in the common pronunciation of *whole*, *most*, and *none*.

153. To produce the sound indicated by -| , pronounce *up*, as nearly as possible without a contact of the lips. The vowel of the word *cur* is precisely the same in quality as that of *up*. This sound must not be confounded with the vowel of *her*, *earth*, or *bird*.

154. To produce the sound indicated by _| , distinctly pronounce the word *ooze* several times, dwelling upon the sound indicated by *oo*, and finally omit the sound denoted by *ze*. Or, pronounce the word *do* several times, and finally omit the sound indicated by *d*.

155. To produce the sound indicated by _| , having pronounced the word *foot* several times, omit the sound of *f ;* and finally omit the sound denoted by *t*, when the desired sound will be heard.

156. To produce the sound indicated by ᵛ| , pronounce the name of the letter *i*. Or, pronounce the word *eye*. Or, unite the vowel of *ask* and *it*.

157. To produce the sound indicated by ^| , pronounce the word *oil* several times, and finally omit the sound denoted by *l*.   Or, blend the vowels of *on* and *it*, accenting the first.

158. To produce the sound indicated by ₐ| , pronounce the word *out* several times, and finally omit the sound denoted by *t*.   Or, unite the vowels of *on* and *full*, accenting the first.

159. To produce the sound indicated by ₍| , pronounce the word *dew*, and finally omit the sound denoted by *d*. Or, unite the vowels of *it* and *full*, accenting the first. This sound is a pure vowel-diphthong, and must not be confounded with the sound denoted by *you* in the word *youth*, or by *u* in the word *unit*.

PHONETIC SYNTHESIS.

160. PHONETIC SYNTHESIS, or spelling by sound, consists in uniting vocal elements so as to form words. To name separately the sounds of *p* and *ay*, and then pronounce them in rapid succession, in other words, to say *pay*, is to spell this word by its sounds, or to perform an act of Phonetic Synthesis.

161. Practice in Phonetic Synthesis will serve three useful purposes. 1. It will render the student thoroughly familiar with the different elements of the English language. 2. It will tend to produce a distinct and elegant pronunciation. 3. It will be of material service as a preparation for reading phonetic shorthand.

162. In making use of the following exercises, the reader should be careful to remember that he is to deal with sounds and not with letters, except as they are representatives of sounds; and that the only names that should be given to the letters are the sounds they denote.

EXERCISE IN PHONETIC SYNTHESIS, No. 1.

b-ɛ	n-ω	i-ŋ-k	o-n
bay	gnaw	ink	on
b-ʒ	đ-ơ	e-l-m	f-u-t
bough	though	elm	foot
b-ө	w-ɛ	ɐ-r-đ	n̄-ө-n
boy	weigh	earth	none
đ-ө	c-ʙ	b-ɐ-r-d	h-ө-l
joy	shah	bird	whole
đ-ω	v-ʉ	a-s-k	k-ʋ-p
jaw	view	ask	cup
k-ᴊ	f-ө-r	a-n-t	t-ʋ-f
key	fair	aunt	tough
çʉ	k-ө-r	a-n-t	ω-d
chew	care	ant	awed
g-ɛ	đ-ө-r	p-a-đ	ᴊ-d
gay	there	path	eyed
m-ᴊ	k-ɯ	p-a-t	ʒ-l
my	coo	pat	owl

EXERCISE IN PHONETIC SYNTHESIS, No. 2.—GROUPED CONSONANTS.

NOTE.—The first time through this exercise, pronounce each element separately. The second time through, pronounce the consonants in groups, as is indicated by the grouping of their signs.

r-ɛ-z	l-ʙ-rd	st-ɵ-r	ʂw-ɐ-rv
raise	lard	stair	swerve
pr-ɛ-zd	bl-a-nks	st-ʙ-rts	ꝧw-a-kt
praised	blanks	starts	thwacked
kr-ᴅ-sts	fl-ɐ-rt	sk-ɛ-n	ꝧw-ɔ-rt
crusts	flirt	skein	thwart
tr-a-nst	kl-a-sps	sf-i-r	bw-ɵ
tranced	clasps	sphere	buoy
fr-e-nd	gl-ɵ	sl-ɪ̯-t	kw-ɔ-rt
friend	glow	slight	quart
ꝧr-ᴅ-sts	gl-i-nd	sm-ɷ-l	d-e-lvd
thrusts	gleaned	small	delved
cr-ɪ̯-nz	spl-i-n	sn-i-r	tw-e-lfꝧ
shrines	spleen	sneer	twelfth
dr-i-mz	kl-i-vd	sw-i-ŋz	m-ᴅ-nꝧs
dreams	cleaved	swings	months
ʂpr-ɛ	kl-ɵ-ꝧd	sw-ɵ-rn	br-ed-ꝧs
spray	clothed	sworn	breadths
str-ɛ-nd	kl-a-mp	tw-ɐ-rl	si-ks-ꝧs
strained	clamp	twirl	sixths
skr-i-mz	sp-ɯ-lz	dw-ɔ-rf	ɛt-ꝧs
screams	spools	dwarf	eighths

h-ʙ-rps	ᴅ-rꝧd	f-ɵ-rth	b-ʙ-rnz
harps	urged	forth	barns
ɷ-rbz	w-ᴅ-rkt	f-ɐ-rst	b-ᴅ-rnd
orbs	worked	first	burned
c-ɵ-rd	t-ᴅ-rf	h-ʙ-rɕ	st-ɷ-rmd
shared	turf	harsh	stormed
ʙ-rɕt	k-ʙ-rvd	ɐ-rlz	f-ɷ-rmz
arched	carved	earls	forms

h-e-lps	m-i-lɕ	tw-e-lvz	ɛ-lz
helps	milch	twelves	ails
kw-i-lts	b-ᴅ-lɟ	h-e-lꝧ	W-e-lc
quilts	bulge		Welsh
h-ɵ-ldz	b-ᴅ-lk	e-ls	e-lm
holds	bulk	else	elm

EXERCISE IN PHONETIC SYNTHESIS, No. 3.—SYLLABICATION.

NOTE.—The first time through this exercise, sound each element separately, and unite them into syllables, and finally into words. The second time through, speak the elements in syllables, and then unite them into words. This exercise should be repeated till both processes become easy.

bi-kʊm	nᴏ-tᴏ-ri-ʊs	fᴏ-no-graf-ik
men-i	sprʒt-ed	yʊ-ni-vers-al
ᴏl-redi	fab-yu-list	in-trᴏ-dʊk-coṅ
dᴏ-ter	kin-dred	ad-i-con-al
ᴏ-bʊrn	pɛv-ment	mʊ-zi-ʊm
en-dʊr	sʊb-di-vj̇d	kar-ak-ter
eks-pél	eks-plan-ɛ-con	im-pʉr-fekt
mod-est	kom-pend-i-ʊm	fᴏ-net-ik
smuᵭ-li	kon-trak-con	il-ʊs-trɛt-ed
kron-ik	sʊk-ses-ful	kor-ekt-nes
kri-ɛ-con	am-big-yu-ʊs	pros-trɛ-con
sit-yu-ɛ-ted	meᵭ-od-i-kal	kon-di-con

PHONETIC ANALYSIS.

163. PHONETIC ANALYSIS, the precise opposite of phonetic synthesis, consists in dividing words into their vocal elements. Phonetic analysis is useful because of its directing the attention to pronunciation and leading to an appreciation of the finest shades of sound. It is especially serviceable to the student, as a preparation for the study of phonography; since the phonetic analysis is invariably required before any word can be phonographically represented.

164. To combine the elements into words, when they are represented by phonetic types, is comparatively easy. Phonetic analysis is rather more difficult, especially when words are represented by the common spelling; for if the student allows himself to be guided to any extent by the common bewildering and chaotic orthography, he will be very likely to be led astray. He should, therefore, entirely disregard the suggestions of the common spelling, and seek to analyze the *spoken* word. Most persons unaccustomed to phonetic analysis are led to infer the presence of the sound of *l* in such words as *walk, talk*, etc., because they observe the letter *l* in the common spelling of these words. But analysis of the spoken words indicated by this orthography, will show them their error. Further illustration of these points is unnecessary, since by the preceding portions of this treatise the

reader must have discovered that the common orthography is very far from being a certain index of the sounds of words. If the combination *ough* occurs in the common spelling, care must be taken, before attempting to write its phonetic equivalents, to ascertain whether it represents the sound of *ō* as in *though*, of *uf* as in *tough*, of *of* as in *cough*, of *up* as in *hiccough*, of *ou* as in *bough*, of *oo* as in *through*. It must be remembered, that each common vowel letter has several different values, which must be distinguished by reference to their pronunciation. *A*, for instance, has eight different sounds, it representing "ε" as in *mate*, 'e' as in *many*, 'ɔ' as in *pare*, 'a' as in *it*, 'ʙ' as in *farm*, 'a' as in *pass*, 'ɷ' as in *all*, 'o' as in *what*. Which one of these sounds *a* represents in any particular word, the student must determine by carefully analyzing the spoken word. An analysis of the word represented by *farm*, for instance, discovers that the letter *a* has a sound entirely different from the sound given it in naming the letter.

165. The correct pronunciation of the words in the following exercises having been ascertained either by knowledge of the pronunciation of good speakers, or by reference to a pronouncing dictionary, they should be deliberately and distinctly pronounced several times, and then divided into their elements. Assistance will be derived from representing the analysis by means of phonetic longhand or shorthand signs.

Exercise in Phonetic Analysis.

166. Resolve into their elements the following words:

Aid, ail, air, ought, aught, eyed, owed, talk, food, height, shawl, edge, phthisic, Ptolemy, Thomas, George, John, sew, so, sow, Wright, rite, right, write, ail, ale, know, no, faint, feint, air, heir, bard, barred, all, awl, claws, clause, key, quay, meed, Mede, mead, caught, enough, sight, cite, site, limb, pique, bdellium, condemn, tongue, schism, I'll, aisle, isle, Xenia, czar, who, rode, rowed, road, hue, hew, Hugh, honor, ghost, chaise, side, sighed, wait, weight, chord, guard, quart, cent, scent, sent, sleigh, lack, brow, three, eighth, ease, aunt, weighed, straight, essay, buy, though.

167. Key to the Preceding Exercise.

ε-d, ε-l, ɔ-r, ɷ-t, ɷ-t, ɪ-d, ɵ-d, t-ɷ-k, f-ɯ-d, h-ɪ-t, c-ɷ-l, e-ʤ, tizik, Tolemi, Tomas, Dɔrʤ, Don, sɵ, sɵ, sɵ, Rɪt, rɪt, rɪt, rɪt, εl, εl, nɵ́, nɵ, fεnt, fεnt, ɔr, ɔr, bʙrd, bʙrd, ɷl, ɷl, klɷz, klɷz, kɪ, kɪ, mɪd, Mɪd, mɪd, kɷt enɷf, sɪt, sɪt, sɪt, lim, pɪk, delyɷm, kondem, tɷŋ, sizm, ɪ'l, ɪl, ɪl, Zinia, zʙr, hɯ, rɵd, rɵd, rɵd, hɷ, Hɷ, onor, gɵst, cεz, sɪd, sɪd, wεt, wεt, kɔrd, gʙrd, kwɷrt, sent, sent, sen sle, lak, brɵ, ƀri, εtƀ, iz, ant, wεd, strεt, ésε, bɪ, ɗɵ.

3*

COMPENDIUM

OF

STANDARD PHONOGRAPHY.

~~~~~~ ~~~~~~~

PART SECOND

OF THE

Hand-Book of Standard Phonography.

PREFACE.

It is believed that this Work presents the principles of Standard Phonography in such a form and manner as to place the art within the reach of every person who may desire to be possessed of the valuable advantages and benefits it is capable of conferring.

The principal features of this Work are the following:

1. It presents in coarse print only those matters which must necessarily be learned in order to write phonography at all. Thus is furnished the shortest possible course of phonographic study, while the entire work in connection with the other portions of the Hand-Book furnishes a course of study as thorough as can be desired, and one which is calculated to make of the student an accomplished phonographer.

2. It is amply illustrated with phonographic letters and words, which have been cut with great accuracy and finish, and the imitation of which will tend to beauty of writing.

3. It presents a system of phonographic Nomenclature, which furnishes the means of indicating, with the utmost precision, phonographic outlines, and their vocalization and position, and enables the pupil to avail himself of his experience in deriving the powers of letters from their names, as in the common spelling, and obviates the discouraging inconvenience and delay of learning to spell by making the separate sounds of the elements.

4. It so classifies the principles, and presents them in such a manner, as both to facilitate their comprehension and materially assist the memory in their retention.

5. It is nearly if not quite free from the ambiguities and the absolute errors of expression which abounded in the works on the Old Phonography to such an extent as to discourage many a person from the study of the art they were intended to teach.

6. It furnishes a series of carefully-considered questions on the text, which, while they adapt the work to the requirements of schools, make it a complete self-instructor.

The Appendix furnishes a new and natural analysis of vocal elements; which analysis lays the foundation for an orderly and convenient phonetic representation (shorthand, typic, and longhand), not only of foreign consonants and the minutest distinguishable divisions of vowels, but of many sounds of the voice, which, while they enter in some form into language, have not previously been provided with signs, nor furnished a place in a scientific inventory of vocal elements. Not only does this department of the work, in connection with the explanation of Phonogra- phy as applied to the representation of English, furnish the linguistic student with a very valuable means of familiarizing more thoroughly than would otherwise be possible the pronunciation of a foreign language, by enabling him to give that pro nunciation a complete representation, as it were an embodiment, thus distinguish- ing it from the misleading orthography or dress,—but the very classification of the sounds is such that by means of it, and by a knowledge of the elements of his own language, he is enabled to attain (though it may be with considerable practice) the accurate pronunciation of foreign elements, whose correct pronunciation is rarely acquired, without the guidance of phonetic science, even under the instructions of a native teacher.

The Appendix also exhibits a plan for producing by means of the common types a very fair phonetic representation of English and the foreign languages, so that every author or printer who chooses may become a phonetic printer without the expense of phonotypes.

ANDREW J. GRAHAM.

Phonetic Depot, New York, *August 25th* 1858.

ANALYSIS OF CONTENTS.

INTRODUCTION.

INTRODUCTION TO PHONOGRAPHY AND PHONOTYPY.

IN order to remove the usual difficulties which arise in the study of phonography in consequence of incorrect ideas induced by the common imperfect orthography, the Author of this treatise has prepared a work entitled Introduction to Phonotypy and Phonography, which the student is advised to peruse carefully before commencing the study of this volume. Those who may not be possessed of that work should the more carefully read what may be said in these pages about the elementary sounds and the mode of arriving at their separate pronunciation.

STENOGRAPHIC AND PHONOGRAPHIC ALPHABETS.

Most of the old systems of stenography provided signs corresponding to the letters of the present imperfect alphabet. On the other hand, the system of phonetic shorthand, explained in the subsequent pages, entirely dispenses with both the common alphabet and the imperfect mode of spelling resulting from its employment, and furnishes a series of the simplest possible signs, exactly corresponding to, and coextensive with, the simple and proximate elements which a careful analysis discovers in the English language.

SIMPLE AND PROXIMATE ELEMENTS.

A searching analysis reveals the fact that the large number of words constituting the English language are made up of about thirty-eight simple, indivisible sounds, or elements. Six double sounds or diphthongs increase the number of simple and proximate elements to forty-four ; for the representation of which the common alphabet provides but twenty-six letters. The phonographic and phonotypic alphabets, on the other hand, contain a distinct letter for each element.

FAMILIARITY WITH THE ELEMENTS AND THEIR PHONOGRAPHIC SIGNS.

The first business of the student of phonography is to become acquainted with the phonographic signs and the sounds they represent.

However easy it may be to pronounce the elements of speech when connected in words, to most persons who have not been accustomed to vocal analysis, the separate pronunciation of the elements is quite difficult.

A knowledge of the distinct sounds of the language, and the mode of producing them, is best acquired by the aid of oral instruction. However, when this aid can not be procured, no serious difficulty will be experienced in attaining the necessary knowledge, if the student will carefully observe the distinction between signs and the sounds they represent—bear in mind that the phonographic signs in the following phonographic alphabet do not stand for the italic *letters* in the words beneath them, but for the SOUNDS indicated by the italic *letters* in those words ; and that these signs or their equivalents occur invariably for these sounds, however they may be represented in the common orthography. To arrive at these sounds, the student, having carefully pronounced the illustrative words and observed the mode of producing the particular sound required, should drop all the sounds but the one indicated by the *italic* letter or letters. To illustrate more particularly : To arrive at the sound indicated by ⎮ , the word ' *to* ' having been distinctly and slowly pronounced, and the mode of producing the sound indicated by *t* observed, the other element should be gradually separated from the *t ;* and, finally, being entirely dropped, the separate *sound* of *t* will be heard. Now be it especially observed that the phonograph ⎮ , or its equivalent, represents this sound, however it may be denoted in the common orthography ; whether by *tt* as in *Pitt, ct* as in *indict, ed* as in *looked, th* as in *Thomas, phth* as in *phthisic ; pt* as in *ptyalism,* or *cht* as in *yacht.* It is better to name this sign by its sound rather than by the syllable Tee. So also the sign (——) is best named by the *sound* of *g* in *gain ;* but if a syllable-name is applied at all, it should be Gay, and not Jee, which would lead to error.

MATERIALS FOR WRITING.

Ruled paper should always be employed for phonographic writing. In his early practice, the double-line paper will afford the pupil assistance in determining the proper length and proportion of the letters. A good steel pen is usually preferred to gold pens for fine phonographic writing. The Author has made use of the finest steel pens, for a number of years, even for reporting purposes. The student is recommended to make use of a pen from the very commencement of his writing, as it leads to an accuracy and beauty of writing that would very rarely be acquired with the use of the pencil. Contrary to what is generally supposed, a pen is to be preferred to a pencil, for rapid writing, especially by those who accustom themselves to the use of a pen on all convenient occasions. Occasional practice with a pencil, however, is recommended, for the purpose of accustoming the hand to its use, as the writer may sometimes be so situated that the employment of pen and ink would be exceedingly inconvenient. When pencils are employed, they should be of a fine quality of drawing-pencils. Faber's No. 3, it is believed, is best adapted to phonographic writing. Soft and rather rough paper should be employed for pencil practice. Very much of the beauty of phonographic manuscript depends upon the quality of the ink employed. Pale and corrosive inks are to be avoided.

METHOD OF HOLDING THE PEN.

The best and most rapid phonographic writers, for the most part, hold the pen the same as for ordinary writing. Some, however, have supposed that ease of phonographic writing is best secured by holding the pen or pencil between the first and second fingers, the thumb being employed in controlling the pen, as in the ordinary mode. Whether this is the best method or not, the occasional use of it will serve to relieve the muscles when they become fatigued in holding the pen in the ordinary position. The position given to the pen and hand in backhand writing, seems best adapted for the easy and graceful formation of phonographic characters. The pen should be held very loosely, so that the nib may be readily turned and suited to the execution of characters made in various directions.

METHOD OF STUDY.

The student, having familiarized the phonographic consonant signs by repeatedly copying them from the following alphabet, and by availing himself of the mnemonic assistance contained in a following chapter, entitled "Aid in Learning the Consonant Signs," is advised to adopt the following method of study : Having learned, by reference to the first exercise in the Phonographic Reading Exercises, what sections of the Compendium are referred to as preparatory to the use of that exercise, turn to those sections and make yourself thoroughly conversant with all the statements contained in the coarse print, testing your knowledge by means of the questions at the bottom of each page. As soon as all the questions referring to the coarse print can be readily and certainly answered, read, several times through, the whole portion (including the fine print) to which reference is made. Then answer all the questions referring to the sections read. Next turn to the first phonographic reading exercise, and read it several times through, seeking to have a perfect understanding of every thing therein contained. If any difficulty is experienced here, the student should attribute it to his failure to comply strictly with the preceding instruction; and, if he will accept advice of vital importance to his success in the study of phonography, he will carefully review the sections referred to, and assure himself, once for all, that their principles are thoroughly fixed in his memory. The exercise having been read several times, should be repeatedly copied, care being taken to make the signs as nearly as possible like those of the exercise, rather than to write rapidly. Next turn to the first writing exercise, and repeatedly write in phonography the letters and words there given. The same course should be pursued with all the subsequent exercises. Previous, however, to commencing another exercise, benefit will be derived from a careful review of the sections to which the first exercise refers.

Phonographic teachers should assign such a number of these exercises for each lesson as will be necessary to bring all the principles they propose to teach, within the course of lessons. The most rapid progress will be made by assigning brief lessons at the commencement of the course, and until the pupil has become thoroughly grounded in the fundamental principles of the system, when his lessons may be made to embrace a greater number of exercises. There should never be an attempt to embrace more principles in a series of lessons than the pupil can perfectly master. Rather, lay the foundation for his further successful study of phonography in private, by teaching only as many principles as can be thoroughly familiarized in the proposed course of instruction. Otherwise the pupil will become confused, and hindered in his progress, if not discouraged from the further study of the art.

The course of study here recommended is such as will result in the attainment, in the shortest possible time, of a thorough knowledge of phonography, and the ability to use it with freedom and accuracy. The chief benefits of phonography can be secured only by becoming entirely conversant with its principles and the established phonographic outlines for words. This requires considerable study and practice; yet, if the pupil will follow the directions of this work, he will find himself possessed of an art which he will deem almost invaluable, and that, too, with considerably less study than is required for the attainment of any one of the usual branches of education, which would be of inferior service.

The present work has been written with the view of placing a thorough knowledge of this very valuable art within the possession of every person who is willing to make an effort any way proportionate to the good he desires. While the Author has endeavored to remove every needless difficulty in the attainment of phonography, and labored to provide the student with every assistance which the extensive practice and teaching of phonography have suggested to him, he has had no hope of making it so simple and easy as to bring it within the comprehension of that pitiable class of minds, who are so averse to intellectual exertion that nothing is acquired by them which, so to speak, may not be comprehended at a glance; and who, even though they may be so fortunate as to possess considerable natural brilliancy of talent, prove entirely deficient when compared, by a just standard, with those who have not perhaps been fortunately endowed by nature with any remarkable intellectual ability, but who have had the spirit to *work* perseveringly with the moderate talent which has fallen to their lot, for the accomplishment of whatever object may have seemed to them desirable; and whose mental acquisitions will eventually give them a power and intellectual position which genius, however brilliant, unaccompanied by mental application, can not hope to equal.

DEFINITIONS.

PHO-NET'ICS, PHON'ICS, or PHO-NOL'O-GY, *noun*. 1. A science which treats of the elements of language, their modifications, and their relations. 2. The science of representing the elements of language.

PHO-NET'IC, *adj.* Denoting sounds, as *phonetic* writing or printing. Pertaining to phonetics, as *phonetic* journals or books.

PHO-NET'IC-AL-LY, *adv.* In a manner expressive of sounds or letters, as to write or print *phonetically*.

PHO'NŎ-TYPE, *noun.* 1. A type to be used in printing the sign of a vocal element. 2. The sign produced by the type.

PHO'NŎ-TYPE, *verb.* To print with phonotypes; to print phonetically, that is, with a sign for each element of the voice,—no more, no less.

PHO-NOT'YP-Y, *noun.* 1. The printing produced with phonotypes—printing, in which each element of language is represented by a distinct letter or type. 2. The mode or system of printing phonetically.

PHO'NO-GRAPH, *noun.* The *graphic*, or *written* sign, of a vocal element.

PHO'NO-GRAPH, *verb.* To write with phonographs.

PHO-NOG'RAPH-ER, *noun.* A writer of phonography.

PHO-NO-GRAPH'IC, *adj.* 1. Belonging, or pertaining, to phonography, as a *phonographic* sign, exercise, book, or journal.

PHO-NOG'RAPH-Y, *noun.* 1. The system of representing language with phonographs. 2. The writing produced with phonographs. There are two kinds of phonography:

(1.) PHONETIC LONGHAND, or LONGHAND PHONOGRAPHY, writing produced with a phonetic alphabet consisting of most of the ordinary script letters and additional ones of the same general character for the additional sounds.

(2.) Sten'o-pho-nog'raph-y, or Phonetic Shorthand : writing produced with an alphabet composed of very simple signs. Of this there are two kinds :

(a) Old, or English, Phonography : a system of shorthand, the general features of which were invented by Mr. Isaac Pitman, of England. Its tolerable perfection is due to the fact that its improvement has been contributed to by numerous persons who have practiced it. This system has not a sufficiency of signs for a perfectly phonetic representation.

(b) Standard, or American, Phonography : a system of shorthand writing, which, in its general features, resembles the English Phonography, but possesses many advantages over it.

Roman'ic Print, the printing produced by the Roman types or letters. This term applies to the printing of all the European nations who use the Roman alphabet.

Romanic, or Common, Orthography. The ordinary mode of spelling, or representing language. *Heterot'yp-y* is sometimes used as an equivalent term.

ANDREW J. GRAHAM'S PHONETIC ALPHABET.

NOTE.—The sound of each letter is shown by the *italic* letter or letters in the word opposite or beneath it. The "superiors" refer to the scripts of the new letters.

LONG VOWELS.				SHORT VOWELS.		
ι	ɪ [1]	*ea*t, f*ea*r		I	i	*i*t
ε	ε [2]	*a*le (*ai*r)		E	e	*e*ll (h*e*r)
ͷ	ʙ [3]	*a*rm		A	a	*a*sk (*a*t)
ɷ	ω [4]	*a*ll, f*o*rm		O	o	n*o*t, *o*n
ʊ	ʊ [5]	*o*pe (wh*o*le)		Ս	ɒ [7]	*u*p, c*u*r
ɯ	ɯ [6]	f*oo*d		U	u	f*oo*t, f*u*ll

CONSONANTS.

ɗ	ɗ [8]	*th*en.	b,	d,	f,	g,	h,	k,	
Ƀ	Ƀ [9]	*th*in.	*b*e,	*d*o,	*f*oe,	*g*o,	*h*e,	*k*ey,	
ʍ	ŋ [10]	si*ng*.	l,	m,	n,	p,	r,	s,	
C	c	*o*cean, *sh*all.	*l*et,	*m*e,	*n*o,	u*p*, *r*oar,	*s*o,		
J	j	vi*s*ion, *zh*.	t,	v,	w,	y,	z. —		
and in their usual sense,			*t*o,	*v*ie,	*w*e,	*y*e,	*z*eal. —		

DIPHTHONGS.

Double letters.	Single letters.			
ai	Ŧ	ʝ [11]	*ai*sle, f*i*nd	
oi	Θ	ɵ [12]	*oi*l, b*oy*	
ou	४	૪ [13]	*ou*t, n*ow*	
iu	ɰ	ч [14]	n*ew*, m*u*te	
dj	Ꟈ	ɟ [15]	e*d-ge*, *j*oin	
tc	Ͼ	ɕ [16]	e*t-ch*, *ch*in.	

OPTIONAL LETTERS.

Ꞓ	ɘ [17]	*ai*r, wh*e*re
Ⱥ	a [18]	*a*t, *a*n
Ƚ	ʙ [19]	h*e*r, b*i*rd
Ø	ø [20]	wh*o*le
Q	q	or hw = wh in *wh*en; thus, "qen" or "hwen."

[Script forms:]

1. 2. E e. 3. 4. 5. O o. 6. 7.

8. 9. 10. 11. 12. 13. 14. 15.

16. 17. 18. A a. 19. 20.

TRANSITION PHONOTYPY.—Phonotypy closely resembling the genuine, may be produced, with the common types, by substituting

ɪ.	ʙ	A or ʌ	ɔ	ʊ	ɯ	ʊ	th *or* dh,	th,	ng	for
ɪ	ε	ʙ	ɷ	ʊ	ɯ	ɒ	ɗ	Ƀ	ŋ	

CONSONANTS							
p	b	t	d	ç=tc	ɉ=dj	k	g
\	\	|	|	/	/	⌐	—
pay	*bay*	*to*	*do*	e*tch*	e*dge*	*c*ain	*g*ain
f	v	ƀ	đ	s	z	c	j
⌐	⌐	(	(	) ∘	) ∘	⌐	⌐
*f*ie	*v*ie	*th*in	*th*en	*s*ee	*z*ee	*sh*e	*zh*e
l		r		m		n	ŋ
⌐		\/		⌐		⌐	⌐
*l*ie		*r*oar		*m*e		*n*o	si*ng*
w			y				h
⌐ c ɔ			⌐				⌐
*w*e			*y*e				*h*e

LONG VOWELS.

i	ɛ-ᴏ	ß	ᴏ	ᴏ-ᴏ	ɯ
·|	·|	.|	⁻|	⁻|	₋|
*ea*t	*a*ge (*air*)	*a*rm	*a*ll	*o*e (*whole*)	*foo*d

SHORT VOWELS.

i	e-ɐ	a-ɑ	o	ʊ	u
·|	·|	.|	⁻|	₋|	₋|
*i*t	e*dge* (*her*)	a*sk* (*at*)	*o*n	*u*p, c*u*r	*foo*t

NOTE—The sound of each sign is shown by the phonotype above it, and by the *italic* letter or letters in the word or words beneath it. The vowels of parenthetic words are provided with distinct signs, whose use is optional.

STANDARD PHONOGRAPHIC ALPHABET.

OPTIONAL VOWEL-SIGNS.

ɔ	ɐ	ʚ	o
air	at	her	whole

CLOSE DIPHTHONGS.

ai = į	oi = ө	ou = ᚷ	iu = ų
aisle=isle	oil, boy	out, now	dew=due

OPEN DIPHTHONGS.

ɛi	ɵi	.ii	ɛi	ɵi	ɵe	ɵa	ɰi
aye	sawing	Deity	clayey	snowy	Owen	Noah	Louis

W WITH VOWELS.

ị	i	ɛ	e	ʚ	ɔ	ɐ	ʙ	a	ɔ	o	ơ	ө	ɯ	ɯ	u	ị	ө	ᚷ

Y WITH VOWELS.

ị	i	ɛ	e	ʙ	ɔ	ɐ	ʙ	a	ɵ	o	ơ	ө	ʊ	ɯ	u	ị	ө	ᚷ

Entered, according to Act of Congress, in the year 1857, by ANDREW J. GRAHAM, in the Clerk's Office of the District Court of the United States for the Southern District of New York.

THE COMPENDIUM.

SIMPLE-CONSONANT SIGNS.

§ 1. A CONSONANT may be defined as a sound made either by a complete or partial contact of the vocal organs, obstructing the whispered or sonant breath, in some degree, varying from an entire break or stoppage of it (as in producing the sound of *p* or *b*) to a simple aspiration (as the sound of *h* in *hate*).

REM. 1. It is convenient as well as usual to employ the term Consonant to denote both a certain kind of sound and its sign, though, in strictness, the sign of a consonant should be called a Consonant-sign.

REM. 2. The proximate elements ch (=t-sh), j (=d-zh) are, for stenographic reasons. treated as simple elements, and provided with simple signs.

CLASSIFICATION OF THE CONSONANTS.

§ 2. The characteristics and relationships of the consonants are exhibited in the following table.

Group.	Utterance.	Labial.			Dental.		Palatal.	Guttural.
Explodents	Whispered	p			t			k
	Sonant	b			d			g
Continuants	Whispered	..	f	th		s	sh	
	Sonant	..	v	TH		z	zh	
Liquids	Sonant				l		r	
Nasals	Sonant	m			n			ng
Semi-vowels	Whispered	wh					(hy)	
	Sonant	w					y	
Aspirate	Whispered							h

REM. 1. The Explodents are so named because of their explosive character They are sometimes termed Abrupts.

---

§ 1. What is a consonant? What is the sound of *p*? *t*? *k*? *s*? *l*? If these sounds are consonants, how are they determined to be such? [Remarks.] How is the term Consonant usually employed? What, in strictness, should the sign of a consonant be called? What proximate elements are provided with simple signs? What are the elements of the sounds of *ch* and *j*?

§ 2. How many Explodents are there in the English language? How many Continuants? Liquids? Nasals? Semi-vowels? How many Sonants? How many Continuants are whispered? Are the liquids whispered or spoken? Are the sounds of *n*, *m*, *ng*, whispered or spoken? Are the sounds of *w* and *y* whispered or sonant? Produce the whisper corresponding to the sonant *w*? How many Labials are

Rem. 2. The Continuants are so called because they are capable of being prolonged; as, for instance, the sound of *ss*, as in *hiss*. These sounds are sometimes denominated Semi-vowels, but very improperly.

Rem. 3. The third group of consonants are called Liquids, because of the readiness with which they unite with other consonants, as in *play, pray, flee, free*, etc.

Rem. 4. The Nasals derive their name from the fact that, in their production, the breath is required to be emitted through the nose (Latin *nasus*).

Rem. 5. Semi-vowels are so named because they possess nearly perfect vocality.

Rem. 6. The Aspirate derives its name from the fact that its production requires the full emission of the breath, the word Aspirate being a derivative from the Latin *aspiro*, to blow

Rem. 7. The term Sonant is employed to denote those consonants which are spoken, or which require an undertone, or murmur, in their production.

Rem. 8. Whispers are those consonants which require the breath simply, to be emitted in their production.

Rem. 9. The terms Labial, Dental, Palatal, Guttural, in the preceding table, denote that the consonants arranged under them are produced by contacts at the lips, teeth, palate, and throat.

MNEMONIC ASSISTANCE IN LEARNING THE CONSONANT-SIGNS.

§ 3. The student will be assisted in committing the consonant-signs to memory by supposing, with reference to the following diagram:

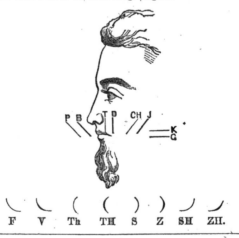

there? What are they? How many Dentals? Pronounce them. How many Palatals? Pronounce them. How many Gutturals? Pronounce them. [Rem.] What kind of consonant is denoted by the term Explodents? What kind, by the term Continuants? by the term Liquids? by the term Nasals? by the term Semi-vowels? Why is the sound of *h* called an Aspirate? What kind of consonants is denoted by the term Sonants? What kind, by the term Whispers?

§ 3. Why do the signs of *p* and *b* proceed, in the Diagram, from the lips? Why

1. P AND B.—That the signs of P and B proceed from the lips, because their sounds are produced by a contact of the lips.

2. T AND D.—That the signs of T and D are placed upright at the teeth, because these sounds are produced with a contact of the Tongue and Teeth.

3. CH AND J.—That the signs of CH and J are inclined midway between T and K, because in part formed with a contact midway between the T and K contacts.

4. K AND G.—That the signs for K and G are placed at the throat, because these sounds are produced with a contact at that point.

5. F AND V.—That the signs of F and V are written in the same direction as the sign for P, because their sounds are produced in part with the lips.

6. Th AND S.—That the signs for Th and S are written in the direction of the sign for T, because the sounds of Th and S are produced by a partial contact at the teeth.

7. SH AND ZH.—That the signs of SH and ZH are written in the direction of the signs for CH and J, because these sounds are the final elements of these compound sounds. See § 1, Rem. 2.

§ 4. L AND R.—The curve signs for L and R may be regarded respectively as the Left and Right portions of an arch:

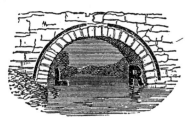

§ 5. W.—The stroke and brief signs of W may be regarded as portions of a script W, as in the following figures:

§ 6. Y.—The stroke and brief signs of Y may be regarded as portions of a script Y in its natural and inverted positions, as in the following figures:

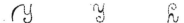

§ 7. T AND D.—The signs of T and D may be regarded as the upright straight lines of

T, D.

are the signs of *t* and *d* placed upright at the teeth? Why are the signs of *ch* and *j* inclined midway between the signs of *t* and *k*? Why are the signs for *k*, *g* placed at the throat? Why are the signs of *f* and *v* written in the same direction as the sign for *p*? Why are the signs for *th* and *s* written in the direction of the sign for *t*? Why are the signs for *sh* and *zh* written in the direction of the signs of *ch* and *j*?

§ 4. How may the curve-signs for *l* and *r* be remembered?

§ 5. How may the signs for *w* be remembered?

§ 6. How may the signs for *y* be recalled?

§ 7. Of what common letters may the signs for *t* and *d* be considered a portion?

§ 8. CH AND J.—The sign of J may be regarded as an abbreviated *J.* The sign of CH, the kindred sound, should, of course, be written by a light sign in the same direction.

MANNER OF WRITING THE CONSONANTS.

§ 9. Each stroke consonant-sign is to be written in the direction of one of the lines of the following diagram :

the lines in the first and third directions being inclined midway between a vertical and a horizontal line.

§ 10. Perpendicular letters, and those inclined to the left, are al· ways written downward.

§ 11. Horizontal letters are written from left to right.

§ 12. Of signs inclined to the right, some are written downward, and some upward.

1. ╱ ch, ╱ j, ⌐ y, and ⌐ zh are always written down-ward.

2. (*a*) When standing alone, ⌐ sh is always written downward. (*b*) When joined with other stroke-signs it may be writen upward or downward, as may be most convenient ; thus ⟋ shd, ⟍ shk.

3. (*a*) When standing alone, ⌐ l is always written upward. (*b*)

---

§ 8. What letter abbreviated gives the phonograph for *J?*

§ 9. In how many, and in what, directions are the consonant-signs written ? How much are those in the first and third directions inclined ?

§ 10. How are perpendicular letters, and those inclined to the left, to be written ? How should you write the stroke for *p? f? w?* How should the curve for *r* be written ? the sign for *v? d?*

§ 11. How are the horizontals written ?

§ 12. How are the signs inclined to the right to be written ? How is *ch* to be written ? *zh? j?* the stroke for *y?* How is the sign for *sh* to be written ? Is it ever written upward ? In what cases may it be written upward ? How is it to be written when standing alone ? Write some outline with the upward *sh.* Write *sh* downward, and join it with *p*—with *k.* How is the sign for *l* to be written ? Is it ever written downward ? When must it be invariably written upward ? How is it to be written when standing alone ? When joined with other strokes, may it be written downward ? How is the straight sign for *r* to be written ? At what incli-nation is it to be written, when standing alone ? How is it distinguished from *ch,* when joined with other signs ? How, when standing alone ? Show how *r-p* is

When joined with other stroke-signs, it may be written upward or downward, according to convenience; thus. ⌐ ld, ⌐ lm, ⊂ lng.

4. (a) The straight sign for r is invariably written upward,—and, when standing alone, at an inclination of thirty degrees. (b) It is thus distinguished from / ch, which, when standing alone, is written at an inclination of sixty degrees. (c) When ch and the straight line for r are joined to other stroke-signs, they are distinguished by their directions; ch being always written downward, while r is invariably written upward; thus, ⟋ rch, ⟋ chr, ⟋ rt, ⟨ cht.

5. The h-stroke is invariably written upward.

REM. 1. A sign is always to be regarded as standing alone, unless it is joined with some other sign by which its direction may be determined.

REM. 2. There is but one exception in Phonography to the rule that all heavy perpendicular and sloping strokes must be written downward.

REM. 3. No difficulty is experienced in giving different inclinations to ch and upward r; because the common writing has accustomed the hand to making the upward strokes more inclined than the downward ones.

PHONOGRAPHIC GEOGRAPHY.

§ 13. Benefit will be derived from describing geographically the *direction* of the straight lines and the *direction of the convexity* of the curves. To illustrate, the Teacher may say *P*, and the Student answer, South-east, light. Teacher—*B*. Student—South-east, heavy.—Teacher—*F*. Student (describing the *direction of the convexity*)—South-west, light. The h-stroke may be described as 'North east, hooked.'

NAMES OF THE CONSONANT-SIGNS.

§ 14. From first to last, the learner who wishes to make the surest and most rapid progress, should name the *signs* by their *sounds*, or by the following syllables: Pee,

---

distinguished from *ch-p*. Show how *p* with the straight *r* joined, is distinguished from *p-ch*. How is the h-stroke written? [Rem.] When is a sign to be regarded as standing alone? In what direction, as a general rule, are the heavy sloping strokes to be made? Why is it easy to make an upward *r* more sloping than the sign for *ch*?

§ 13. Describe, geographically, the direction of the straight-line signs, and the direction of the convexity of the curves. What is the direction of *p*? *ch*? of upward *r*? of *t*? of *k*? What is the direction of the convexity of *f*? *m*? *ng*? *sh*? *l*? downward *r*?

§ 14. What are the best names for the phonographic signs? What syllable-names are recommended to be used when the signs are not named by their sounds? What is the name for the sign of *l* when written upward? What sign is denoted by the syllable Ray? by Lay? Write Pee, Ef, Zee, Chay, Ish, Lay, Gay, Ing, Ith, Zee, Way, Hay, Yay. [Rem.] How is the brief sign for *w* to be distinguished, by name, from the stroke-sign? Write Wĕh. Write Wŭh. What is the name for the brief sign of *y*? Write Yĕh—Yŭh. What is the name of the s-circle? How is it named when joined at the beginning of Pee? How should it be named when written at the end of Kay? How must it be named when joined at the beginning of Bee?

Bee, Tee, Dee, Chay, Jay, Kay, Gay, Ef, Vee, Ith, Thee, Es, Zee, Ish, Shay (for up-ward *sh*), Zhay, El (for the downward *l*), Lay (for the upward *l*), Ar (for the downward *r*), Ray (for the upward *r*), Em, En, Ing, Way, Yay, Hay.

REM. 1. The brief sign for *w* may be named Wĕh. If it is deemed advisable to distinguish by name between c and ɔ , the first may be named Wĕh, and the second, Wŭh.

REM. 2. The brief sign for *y* may be named Yĕh. If it should seem desirable to distinguish ᴜ from ᴖ by name, the first may be called Yĕh, and the second Yŭh.

REM. 3. The circle for *s* and *z* may be named Iss, when its sound can not be con-veniently spoken in one syllable with the name of the stroke to which it is joined. For example, Pee with Iss joined at the beginning may be called Spee; Chay with Iss joined at the end, may be named Chays; but Bee with Iss at the beginning, must be named Iss-Bee, because it would be difficult to say Sbee.

SIZE OF THE CONSONANT-STROKES.

§ 15. The learner should make the consonant-strokes about one sixth of an inch in length, as in these pages. The practiced phonographer may advantageously reduce them to one eighth of an inch, as in the Phonographic Reading Exercises. (*b*) Beauty of phonographic writing requires that the light lines should be very light; that the heavy lines should be barely distinguishable from the light signs; that the heavy curves should gradually taper to a fine line.—(*c*) To lay the foundation of good phonographic penmanship, it is necessary that the phonographs should, for a considerable time, be written with the utmost care. Do not attempt, at first, to write rapidly, but *well*. Speed in phonographic writing is the result principally of familiarity with phonographic letters and principles.

JOINING THE CONSONANT-STROKES.

§ 16. All the consonants in a word should be written without tak-ing off the pen, the second sign commencing where the first ends, the third being continued from the end of the second, and so on; thus,

    pk,   nv,   rg,   nj,   kml.

CONSONANT-SIGNS REPEATED.

§ 17. Two consonant-strokes of the same kind occurring together are written thus:

    gg,   mm,   nn.

---

§ 15. What length should the learner make the consonant-strokes? To what length may they be reduced by the practiced writer? For beauty of writing, how should the light lines be made? the heavy lines? the heavy curves?

§ 16. Repeat the directions for writing the consonants of a word. Should the pen be taken off in making the consonants of a word? Where should the second con-sonant of a word begin?

§ 17. Write m-m, n-n, k-k, j-j, p-p, t-t, f-f, b-b.

POSITION OF WORDS.

1. *With Perpendicular or Sloping Strokes.*

§ 18. The first perpendicular or inclined stroke of a consonant out-line should rest upon the line of writing ; thus,

rp, kj, nvt, rg.

2. *Composed entirely of Horizontal Strokes.*

§ 19. Until otherwise instructed, the learner should write upon the line all words composed entirely of horizontal consonants.

CAUTION.—ORDER OF READING THE STROKES.

§ 20. It will sometimes happen that a stroke which is further along than another in the line of writing must be read first ; thus, ⌡ is

t-ch and not *r-t.*

(*b*) Tee is known to be the first letter, because, according to § 18, the first perpen-dicular or sloping stroke should rest upon the line; and the second sign is known to be Chay and not *Ray*, because as Tee must be made downward, and Ray up-ward, they could not be joined as above without violating the rule of § 16.

MODE OF JOINING CERTAIN STROKES.

§ 21. There should always be an angle between Ef and En, Vee and En; and in similar combinations ; thus, ⌣ vn.

§ 22. The novitiate phonographer will generally make an angle between Pee and En, Ith and En, and in similar cases ; but the advanced writer will unite these letters without an angle. In his writing Ef will flow, as it were, into Kay ; Tee into Ef, Lay into Ar ; and Lay into the downstrokes Es and Ish. The correct mode of making these combinations is exhibited in the following examples :

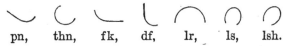

pn, thn, fk, df, lr, ls, lsh.

---

§ 18. Where should the first perpendicular or inclined stroke of an outline rest? Which stroke of Ray-Gay should rest upon the line? of Em-Zee? of Em-Chay? Of Lay-Kay, where must Kay be written?—on or above the line? Where must Em be written, in writing Em-Ray, in order to have the sloping stroke rest upon the line?

§ 19. Where, till further instructions are given, should words composed entirely of horizontal strokes be written? Should Em-Kay be written on or above the line? If on the line, why? Where should En-Kay be written? En-Em?

§ 20. Which stroke of a word should be read first? Write Chay-Tee? Which should be read first, Chay or the Tee? How do you know that the Tee is not made first, and therefore to be read first? How do you know the upper stroke is not Ray, instead of Chay?

§ 21. What is said in respect of the junction of Ef and En, of Pee and En, of Ith and En? How should the practiced writer unite Pee and En and Ith or En?—with or without an angle?

§ 22. Write, according to directions, Ef-Kay ; Tee-Ef ; Lay-Ar ; Lay-Es ; Lay-Ish.

§ 23. Heavy and Light Lines Joined.—A heavy line when joined, without a distinct angle, to a light line, should taper toward the point of union, and be so joined that no precise point of junction shall be discernible; thus,

| dt,   \ pb,   ⌞ fg.

§ 24. *Heavy Curves Joined to Heavy Straight Lines.*—A heavy curve joined, without a distinct angle, to a heavy straight line, should *not* taper toward the point of junction, but should be written as in the following examples:

\ bng,   ⌞ vg, | dv.

§ 25. *Variation of Inclination and Curvature.*—(a) The inclination of the sloping consonants may be considerably varied in order to secure an easy junction with a preceding or following stroke. (b) The ease of junction between signs joined at an angle is in proportion to the acuteness of the angle. Hence, the junction becomes easier between Pee and Tee, or Tee and Pee, by giving more than ordinary inclination to Pee; between Kay and Pee, or Pee and Kay, by inclining Pee less than usual. (c) The acuteness of the angles and consequent ease of junction in words containing curves, is considerably affected by variations in the curvature of the curve-signs; thus, the junction between Em and Tee is rendered easier by making Em nearly straight; while Em requires to be considerably curved for ease of junction with a preceding or following Kay.

BRIEF SIGNS FOR S AND Z.—LOOPS AND LARGE CIRCLE.

§ 26. On account of the frequent occurrence of the sounds of *s*, *z*, they are furnished with brief signs, o , o , which are particularly convenient for joining.

---

§ 23. How is a heavy line to be made, when joined, without a distinct angle, to a light line? Write, according to directions, Dee-Tee; Tee-Dee; Kay-Gay; Bee-Pee; Gay-Ar; Ar-Dee; Ith-Gay; Em-Bee; Dee-Ef; Chay-Jay; Bee-En.

§ 24. How is a heavy curve-sign to be written, when joined, without a distinct angle, to a heavy straight line? Write, according to directions, Bee-Ing; Vee-Gay; Dee-Vee.

§ 25. Is it allowable to vary the inclination of a sloping stroke? For what purpose is the inclination ever varied? How else is the ease of junction increased? How is the ease of junction between two consonants joined at an angle measured? Is the curvature of the curve-signs ever varied? If so, for what purpose? In joining Em and Tee, should the Em be made straighter or more curved than usual, for convenience of junction? In joining En and Kay, would you make the En straighter or more curved than usual, for convenience of junction? Why would you make it more curved?

§ 26. Make the brief signs for *s* and *z*. Why are brief signs provided for the sounds of *s* and *z*? For what are these signs particularly convenient? [Rem.] Does any confusion result from employing a light circle for *s* and *z*? When a distinction is desired between *s* and *z*, how may it be made, with the use of the circle?

Rem. No inconvenience or confusion, except in rare cases, is found to result from the common practice among phonographers of employing the light circle for *z* as well as *s;* because we are already accustomed to this confusion of signs in the common print. When necessary, as in distinguishing 'the *loss* of a kingdom' from 'the *laws* of a kingdom,' the circle may be made heavy on one side for *z*.

ON JOINING THE CIRCLE.

§ 27. The circle is joined

1. *To the Straight Lines*—by a motion contrary to that of the hands of a clock; thus,

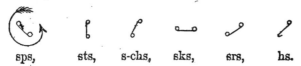

sps, sts, s-chs, sks, srs, hs.

2. *To the Hook of H*—by making the hook into a circle; thus, ⟋ sh.

3. *To Curves*—by following the direction of the curve; thus,

ᗕ sfs, ᗞ sls, ◝ srs, ᗢ sñs.

4. *Between two Strokes*—by turning the circle in the most convenient manner; thus, ⌐ tsk, ⅄ pst, ⌐ rsg, ⌒ msk, ⌒ nsm, ⋋ fsl, ⌥ fslt, ⌣ nsld.

Rem. 1. To distinguish Iss-Ray from Iss-Hay, observe that in the former case the circle is on the left side of the stroke, and on the contrary side in the latter case. See § 14, and Rem. 3.

Rem. 2. Iss-Hay is distinguishable from Chays by the latter being less inclined than the former.

Rem. 3. Iss-Hay should never be employed instead of Ish for the sound of *sh* in *shade*.

Rem. 4. *The Circle between Curves.*—In cases like *nsm, fslt, nsld*, the circle should be written on the back of the first curve; in cases like *msn, msth*, on the concave side of the first curve.

---

§ 27. How is the circle joined to straight lines? to the hook of *h?* to curves? How is the circle written between two strokes? Join a circle at the beginning of Pee, Gay, Ray, Jay, Dee. Join a circle to the end of Hay. Write a circle at the beginning of Hay. Write a circle at the beginning and end of Vee, Ish, Lay, Way, Yay, Ing. Write a circle between Kay and Tee; Em and Chay; En and Tee; Ray and Kay; Em and Lay; En and El; En and Lay; Way and Kay; Tee and Pee. [Rem.] How is Iss-Ray distinguished from Iss-Hay? On which side of the stroke is the circle in Iss-Ray? on which side, in Iss-Hay? How is Iss-Hay distinguished from Chay-Iss? Which is the more inclined, Iss-Hay or Chay-Iss? Is Iss-Hay ever employed to represent the sound of *sh* in *shade?* On which side of En is the circle to be made in the combination En-Iss-Em? on which side of Ef in Ef-Iss-Lay? on which side of En in En-Iss-Lay? on which side of Em in Em-Iss-En? in Em-Iss-Ith?

§ 28. The circle may be enlarged for *s-s* (*ses, sez, zes,* or *zez*)*;* thus,

    ⌐○ ks,   ⌐○ ks-s,   ↳○ fs,   ↳○ fs-s.

Rem. 1. When great precision is required, one side of this circle may be made heavy when one or both of the sounds denoted by it is *z,* as in *races, causes.*

Rem 2. *Syllable-Name of the Large Circle.*—The large circle may be named Sez or Ses.

§ 29. To express *t* following *s* (as in *lost, most*) or *d* following *z* (as in *amazed, raised*), make the circle into a small loop; thus, ⌒○ ls,

⌒ lst, ╱ rz, ╱ rzd, ⌠ st, ⌠ stt.

Rem. 1. When great accuracy of representation is required, the loop may be made heavy for *zd;* thus, ╱ rzd.

Rem. 2. *Name of the Small Loop.*—The small loop may be named Stĕh when its sound can not be conveniently spoken in one syllable with the name of the stroke to which it is attached. Ef with the small loop at the beginning may be called Stef; but Chay with Steh at the beginning must be named Stĕh-Chay′. Kay or Bee with Steh at the end may be named respectively Kayst, Beest; but Ef with Steh added must be called Ef-Steh; or Ef may be changed to Fee, when the sound of Stĕh can be added, forming Feest.

§ 30. *Large Loop.*—To express *tr* following *s* (as in *pastor, Chester, Lester*), make the circle into a large loop; thus, ↘○ ps, ↘ pst,

↘ pstr, ⌒ ls, ⌒ lst, ⌒ lstr.

§ 28. Is the circle ever enlarged? for what purpose? [Rem.] How can it be denoted that one of the sounds represented by a large circle is *z?* What is the syllable-name of the large circle?

§ 29. Is the circle ever made into a loop? for what purpose? How may *t* following *s* be expressed? *d* following *z?* Give some word in which *t* follows the sound of *s;*—some words in which *d* follows the sound of *z.* [Rem.] How may *zd* be distinguished from *st,* with the use of the loop? What is the syllable-name of the small loop? Is this syllable-name always to be employed? How is Ef with the small loop at the end to be called? How is Ef with the small loop at the beginning to be named? How is Chay with the small loop at the beginning to be named? Write Stĕh-Pee. Write Stĕh-Dee, Stĕh-Chay, Stĕh-Kay, Stĕh-Ray. Write Stĕh at the beginning of all the curves. Write Stĕh at the end of all the straight lines.

§ 30. Is the circle ever made into a large loop? if so, for what purpose? How may *tr* following *s* be expressed? Give some words in which *tr* follows *s.* Write a large loop at the end of the curves; at the end of the straight lines. [Rem.] Is the large loop ever employed for *str* at the commencement of a word? What is the syllable-name of the large loop? How is its name to be pronounced in connection with the preceding syllable-name? What is the name of Bee with the large loop joined at the end? What is the name of Kay with the large loop joined at the end? What is the name of Lay with the large loop joined at the end?

REM. 1. CAUTION.—The large loop is never employed for *str* at the commencement of a word.

Rem. 2. *Name of the Large Loop.*—The large loop may be named Ster. To distinguish it from the name of another letter, it should form, with the name of the preceding letter, a single word, which should be accented on the first syllable. For example, En, Bee, Kay form with Ster the words En'ster, Bee'ster, Kay'ster.

LOOPS AND LARGE CIRCLE IN THE MIDDLE OF WORDS.

§ 31. The loops and large circle may be used occasionally in the middle of a word, as in 'testify, distinguish, Chesterfield, necessary, necessity.'

S ADDED TO LOOPS AND THE LARGE CIRCLE.

§ 32. *S* or *Z* may be added to a loop or large circle; thus, ⟍ psts, ⟍'pstrs, ⟋ ksrszz.

WORD-SIGNS.

§ 33. Certain words of frequent occurrence (called Sign-Words or Grammalogues) are indicated in Phonography by one or more of their important letters. These contractions are denominated Word-Signs or Logograms.

REM. It is found, by careful calculation, that certain words of frequent occurrence (most of which are provided with word-signs requiring each but one movement of the pen) constitute nearly two thirds of spoken and written English; that is, in every ten thousand words of a book, sermon, or lecture, about six thousand words will be found to consist of the words which in Phonography are represented by word-signs. By one estimate it appeared that, in ten thousand words, taken from twenty books (five hundred from each), *it* occurred 119 times; *for*, 121; *is*, 136; *that*, 138; *a*, 150; *in*, 214; *to*, 228; *of*, 396; *and*, 413; and *the*, 675 times. A slight contraction then in words of such frequent recurrence results in a great saving of the time and labor of writing; and when familiarized, they are more easily read than the uncontracted outlines.

§ 34. *Double Letters, etc.*—In the lists of word-signs, a word is occa-

---

§ 31. Are the loops ever employed in the middle of a word? Recite the words given as instances of such use. Is the large circle ever employed in the middle of a word?

§ 32. How can *s* and *z* be added to the loop or large circle? Write Pee-Steh-Iss—Ray-Sez-Iss—Kay'-Ster-Iss—Ef'-Ster-Iss.

§ 33. What are those words called, which are denoted by one or more of their important letters? What is an equivalent name for *sign-word?* What name is given to the imperfect representation of the *sign-words?* What word is synonymous with *word-sign?*

§ 34. What, in the list of *word-signs*, does a double letter indicate? What does the printing of a word with a hyphen denote? When a *word-sign* represents more than one word, how is it determined which word is intended in any case?

sionally printed with a hyphen, thus, *give-n;* or with a double letter; thus, th^{ee}_{y}; to intimate that the corresponding word-signs represent *give* and *given; thee* and *thy.* The context will readily show which word is intended.

§ 35. *Dot-Lines.*—The dot-lines which appear in this work in connection with certain words, serve to indicate the position of those words with respect to the line of writing. (*b*) All word-signs whose position is not thus indicated, should rest upon the line of writing.

§ 36. *Method of Learning the Word-Signs.*—A knowledge of the word-signs and sign-words may be readily acquired according to the following plan. 1. Cover a line of the word-signs with a slip of paper or card, and write the proper signs for sign-words. After becoming familiar with one line, pursue the same course with all the succeeding ones. 2. Cover the sign-words and speak the words for which the word-signs stand.

§ 37. LIST OF SIMPLE-CONSONANT WORD-SIGNS.

up, hope, by, be, to be, subject, [subjected], it, at *or* out,

its, itself, do, had, each, which, much, advantage,

common, kingdom, [commonly] come, because, give-n, together,

if, for, few ever, have, however, several, think, thank-ed,

th^{ee}_{y}, the^{m}_{y}, though *or* thou, these, this, those *or* thus,

$this^{is}_{has}$ *or* themselves, see, so, us, use (noun), was, use (verb), is,

as, [his, has,] is $^{as}_{his}$, his $^{s}_{h\text{-}as}$, as $^{h\text{-}is}_{has}$, has $^{his}_{as}$, first, wish, she

shal$^{l}_{t}$, usual-ly, wil$^{l}_{t}$, whole, he$^{re}_{ar}$ *or* her, are, our, her$^{s}_{self}$

---

§ 35. What is denoted by the dot-lines in connection with the word-signs? Where should all word-signs rest, whose position is not indicated by the dot-lines?

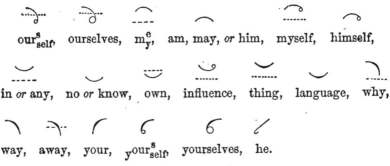

our^sself, ourselves, m^ey, am, may, *or* him, myself, himself,

in *or* any, no *or* know, own, influence, thing, language, why,

way, away, your, your^sself, yourselves, he.

REM. 1. *His and Has.*—*His* and *Has* may be expressed by placing the h-dot before the signs for *is* and *as*. No confusion, however, results from the common practice of omitting the aspirate, the context enabling the reader to distinguish very readily between *is* and *his, as* and *has*.

REM. 2. (*a*) *Are* when written separately, is usually represented by Ar. (*b*) A slight advantage results from employing Ray as the sign for *are* in case the preceding word ends on, or below, the line of writing, and the following word commences above the line. (*c*) Ray is frequently the most convenient sign for *are* when joined, without lifting the pen, to other words.

REM. 3. When a word-sign represents two or more words, they are of different parts of speech, or have some other difference by which in connection with the context they may be readily distinguished.

PLURALS, POSSESSIVES, ETC.

§ 38. The small circle may be added to word-signs to indicate

1. The plural number, or possessive case, of a noun ; thus, ⌣

thing, ⌣ things ; ⎯ kingdom, ⎯ kingdoms *or* kingdom's. •

---

§ 37. Cover the word-signs and write the signs for the sign-words. Next cover the sign-words and speak the words denoted by the signs. [Rem.] How are *his* and *has* expressed ? Does any confusion result from using the signs for *is* and *as*, for *his* and *has* ? How is *are* usually represented when written separately ? When may Ray be employed as a sign for *are* ? When is Ray frequently used as a sign for the word *are* ? When a sign represents more than one word, how are the words distinguished ?

§ 38. For what purpose may the small circle be added to word-signs ? How may *is* or *has* be added, to pronoun word-signs ? How may *is* or *his, as* or *has*, be added to conjunctions, adverbs, etc. ? How may *his* be added to the signs for prepositions ? How may the addition of *self* to the sign of a pronoun, be indicated ? Write *kingdom's, things, hopes, advantages, uses, influences, languages, ways, why's*. Write *gives, subjects, comes, wishes, thinks, thanks, uses* (*yuzez*). Write, in accordance with § 38, 3, *it is* or *has ; each is* or *has ; which is* or *has ; he is* or *has ; she is* or *has ; if his ; so as ; much as*. Write in accordance with § 38, 4, *by his, at his, if his, for his, in his*. Write in accordance with § 38, 5, *myself, himself, thyself, yourself, ourself, herself*. [Rem.] How may *thyself* be written ? What change should be made in a verb word-sign ending in a circle, in order to denote the third person, singular, of the present tense, or the perfect participle ? Write *influence*,

2. The third person, singular, of a verb in the present tense; thus, ___ come, ___○ comes.

3. The addition of *is* or *his*, *as* or *has*, principally to pronouns, conjunctions, and adverbs; thus, | it, | it is *or* it has, ⌐ if his,) so as.

4. The addition of *his* to prepositions; thus, \ for, \ for his.

5. The addition of *self* to pronouns; thus, ⌢ him, ⌢ himself.

REM. 1. THYSELF may be indicated by adding a circle to the sign for *thy*.

REM. 2. THIRD PERSON SINGULAR AND PERFECT PARTICIPLE.—When a word-sign representing a verb ends in a circle, the third person, singular, of the present tense, is indicated by enlarging the circle; the perfect participle, by making the circle into a small loop; thus, ⌐ influence, ⌐ influences, ⌐ influenced.

REM. 3. SELVES.—The large circle is attached to signs of pronouns to indicate the addition of *selves*, as to the sign for *them*, for *themselves;* to the sign for *our*, for *ourselves*.

REM. 4. IS, HIS, AS, HAS ADDED.--The circle for *is* or *his* and *as* or *has* may be enlarged to indicate the addition of *is* or *his*, *as* or *has*. (*b*) *Is* or *has* may be added to the sign for *this* or *thus* by enlarging the circle.

POSITION OF WORD-SIGNS.

§ 39. By the preceding list of word-signs it will appear that the word-signs are written in three different positions.

1. THE FIRST POSITION, for horizontals, and vowel-signs, is the height of a Tee stroke above the line of writing; (*b*) and, for all other consonant-signs, half the height of a Tee stroke above the line.

2. THE SECOND POSITION, for any kind of sign, is on the line of writing.

·3· THE THIRD POSITION, for horizontals, is below the line; (*b*) for half-length sloping and perpendicular signs, commencing on the line or slightly below it; (*c*) for all other signs, through the line.

REM. 1. With double-line paper, for the first position, horizontals are made to touch the lower edge of the upper line; perpendicular and sloping full-length letters are written half above and half below it; and half-length sloping and perpendicular letters commence upon it and descend half the distance to the lower line. The second and third positions are the same as with single-line paper. Full-length perpendicular signs in the second position extend from line to line.

---

influences, and *influenced*. How may the addition of *selves* to the sign of a pronoun be indicated? For what purpose is the circle for *is* or *his*, *as* or *has*, enlarged? In accordance with this principle, write *is his, is as, as is, as has, as his, has his*. Write *this is, it is as, it has his, which is as, which has his, much as is, this has as, thus is, he has his, he is as*.

§ 89. In how many different positions are the word-signs written? What is the first position for horizontals? for all other consonant signs? what is the second position? What is the third position for horizontals? for half-length sloping and

§ 40. LIST OF WORDS REPRESENTED BY THE SIMPLE-CONSONANT SIGNS.

A.
advantage
am
any
are
as
as has § 38, R. 4.
as h-is § 38 R. 4.
at
away

B.
be
because
by

C.
come
common
[commonly]

D.
do

E.
each
ever

F.
few
first
for

G.
give
given

H.
had

has
has as § 38, R. 4.
has his § 38, R. 4.
have
he
hear
her
here
hers
herself
him
himself
his
his has § 38. R. 4.
his is § 38, R. 4.
hope
however

I.
if
in
influence
influences, § 38, R. 2.
influenced, § 38, R. 2.
is
is as, § 38, R. 4.
is his, § 38, R. 4.
it
its
itself

K.
kingdom
know

L.
language

M.
may
me
much
my
myself

N.
no

O.
our
ours
ourself
ourselves
out
own

S.
see
several
she
shall
shalt
so
subject
[subjected]

T.
thank
thanked
thee
them
themselves
these
they
thing

think
this
this has, § 38, R. 4.
this is, § 38, R. 4.
those
thou
though
thus
thy
thyself, § 38, R. 1.
to be
together

U.
up
us
use (noun)
use (verb)
usual
usually

W.
was
way
which
whole
why
will
wish

Y.
your
yours
yourself
yourselves.

REM. 1. In the preceding list the sign-words are presented in alphabetical order, so that, by reference to it, the writer may at once determine whether or not a given word is to be represented by a contracted outline. If it should be found in this list, and the sign should not be remembered, reference must be made to § 37, where the sign will be found. This list may also be made of service in learning the word-

---

perpendicular signs? for all other signs? [Rem.] With double-line paper, where are the first-place horizontals written? How are first-place perpendicular and sloping letters written with respect to the upper line? How are half-length sloping and perpendicular letters written with respect to the upper line? What are the second and third positions, with the use of double-line paper?

§ 40. Write the word-signs for the words given in the list of § 40.

signs, by writing from memory the sign for each word as tne list is read through. This practice should be continued till each word of the list instantly suggests the correct sign.

REM. 2. *Derivatives from Sign-words.*—To represent a derivative from a sign-word, add to the sign of the primitive the additional consonant or consonants of the derivative, usually joining them if the last consonant of the primitive is represented in its sign; but generally *disjoining* the additional consonant, if the last consonant of the primitive is *not* represented in its sign. Hence, since the last consonant of *advantage* is represented in its sign, write *advantageous* by joining Ess, the additional consonant, to Jay, the sign of the primitive. In like manner, write *advantageously*, by joining Lay, the additional consonant, to the last letter of *advantageous* But, since the last consonant of *subject* is *not* represented in its sign, write *subjected*,

by disjoining Dee, the additional consonant of the derivative; thus, ⟍| sub-jected.

REM. 8. *Important Advice.*—It is very desirable that the word-signs should be so thoroughly fixed in the memory that they shall be suggested the instant the sign-words are seen or heard; and the pupil who would take those steps which most surely lead to rapid writing, will apply himself *diligently and patiently* till he has acquired a complete mastery of this department of the phonographic art. A valuable means of acquiring the desired thorough knowledge of the word-signs, is, while reading any work, to note the sign-words, calling to mind their signs. Until the word-signs are familiarized, do not hesitate to copy dozens of pages, writing the proper phonographic signs for the sign-words, and, for the present, writing the others in longhand. This plan should at once be adopted in all writing for the student's own use; and if he will thus continue to apply phonographic principles as he acquires them, his longhand will soon be entirely displaced by the brief and beauti-ful characters of Phonography.

VOCALIZATION—SIMPLE VOWELS.

§ 41. *Vocalization.*—In Phonography, the term Vocalization is employed to denote the act of indicating, in accordance with established principles, the vowels of a word.

REM. The consonant expression of a word is called a Skeleton, Word-form, Consonant-Outline, or simply Outline. Outlines may be vocalized, that is, have the vowels placed beside the consonants, as explained in subsequent sections. The advantage of this mode of vocalization is that the outlines used by the reporter need rarely differ from those used by the correspondent; the vocalization of a phonographic report being nearly sufficient to reduce it to the simplest style of phonography.

§ 42. *Vowel Defined.*—A vowel may be defined as a smooth emission of sounding breath, modified but not obstructed by the organs of speech. Such are the sounds represented by *ea* in *eat*, *a* in *ale*, *a* in *arm*.

REM. Convenience sanctions the common use of the term Vowel to denote both a certain kind of sound and its sign, though in strictness the sign of a vowel should be called a *Vowel-Sign.*

NUMBER OF THE VOWELS.

§ 43. By a careful analysis, the English language is found to contain sixteen vowels, seven long and nine short. They are denoted by the *italic* letters in the following words:

LONG VOWELS— *ea*T, *a*LE, *ai*R, *a*RM, *aw*E, *ow*E, F*OO*D.
SHORT VOWELS—*i*T, *e*LL, H*e*R, *a*T, *a*SK, *o*N, WH*O*LE, *u*P, F*OO*T.

SHORT VOWEL-ALPHABET.

§ 44. For all of the vowels, Standard Phonography provides appropriate signs, more or less of which may be used according to the writer's purposes, ability to distinguish sounds, taste, etc. But for ordinary purposes the vowel-alphabet may be reduced to twelve signs, in the following manner:

1. The sign of the vowel of *ell* may (without confusion) be employed to represent

---

§ 41. What is the term vocalization employed to denote? What is the consonant expression of a word denominated? What is a consonant-outline? What advantages result from the phonographic mode of vocalization?

§ 42. What is a vowel? What kind of sound is denoted by *ea?* Is or is not the sound denoted by *owe* a vowel? What kind of sound is that heard in the pronunciation of the word *ah?* If these several sounds are vowels, how are they determined to be such? [Rem.] What is the term Vowel commonly used to denote? What in strictness should the sign of a vowel be called?

§ 43. How many vowels are there in the English language? how many long? how many short? what are they?

§ 44. For ordinary purposes, how many vowels is it necessary to recognize? How may the vowel of *her* be represented? If represented by the sign of the vowel also the vowel of *her*, it being observed that the former never occurs before *r* not followed by a vowel, nor even before *r followed* by a vowel in certain derivatives—as *preferring* from *prefer*—in which the vowel of *her* is retained from the primitive.

2. The sign of the vowel of *ale* may (without confusion) be employed to represent also the vowel of *air*, it being observed that the former rarely occurs before *r* not followed by a vowel, nor even before *r followed* by a vowel in certain derivatives—as *caring* from *care*—in which the vowel of *air* is retained from the primitive.

3. The vowel of *at* (which to many ears is not different from the vowel of *ask*) may be represented by the sign for the vowel of *ask*. Little difficulty can result from this practice, because the same practice of confusing these sounds under one sign (namely, ' a') obtains in the common orthography. It may be observed that the vowel of *ask* occurs principally before the sounds of *f*, *th*, *s*, and in the unaccented syllables of *about*, *ago*, *Cuba*, *America*, and similar words.

4. The vowel of *whole* may be represented by the sign for the vowel of *owe*, it being observed that the latter occurs rarely, if ever, in unaccented syllables, and that the former occurs under the accent, in but few words, as *whole*, *none*, etc.

§ 45. The vowels being divided with considerable accuracy into two groups—Lingual Vowels and Labial, or Lip, Vowels—the reduced vowel-scale may be presented thus:

First Group—Linguals.			*Second Group—Labials.*		
LONG— ē	ā	ah	au	ō	ōō
eat	*ale* (*air*)	*arm*	*awe*	*owe* (*whole*)	*food*
SHORT— ĭ	ĕ	ă	ŏ	ŭ	ŏŏ
it	*ell* (*her*)	(*at*) *ask.*	*on*	*up*	*foot.*

REM. 1. The Lingual Vowels are so named because the tongue (Latin, *lingua*) is principally concerned in the formation of the apertures requisite for their production.

REM. 2. The second-group vowels are named Labial, or Lip, Vowels, because in the formation of the peculiar apertures required for their production, the lips are chiefly concerned.

VOWEL-SIGNS.

§ 46. (*a*) Of the generally-recognized vowels of the English language, six (Linguals) are represented by a dot, and six (Labials) are denoted by a dash, each made heavy and light to correspond to long and short

---

of *met*, how is it to be distinguished from the latter sound? In what manner may the use of a distinct sign for the vowel of *air* be avoided? How is this vowel distinguished from that of *mate*, when no distinct sign is used for it? How may the use of a distinct sign for the vowel of *ask* be avoided? Why does no confusion result from employing the same sign for the vowels of *ask* and *at?* What are the principal cases in which the vowel of *ask* occurs? How may the use of a distinct sign for the vowel of *whole* be avoided?

§ 45. How many vowels are there in the First Group? how many in the Second Group? How many Linguals are there? how many Labials? [Rem.] Why are the first-group vowels denominated Linguals? Why are the second-group vowels denominated Labials?

§ 46. How are the Linguals represented? How are the Labials denoted?

vowels, and, in order to distinguish between the vowels, placed at three different points beside the consonant, namely, at the BEGINNING (or the point at which the pen commences to make the consonant), the MIDDLE, and the END (or the point at which the pen ceases in the formation of the consonant).

(b) To particularize :

1. OF THE LINGUALS.

Write, beside the consonant, for the vowels

ē —ĭ ⎫   ⎧ in the FIRST PLACE, or at the Beginning
ā —ĕ ⎬ a DOT ⎨ in the SECOND PLACE, or at the Middle
ah—ă ⎭   ⎩ in the THIRD PLACE, or at the End.

2. OF THE LABIALS.

Write, beside the consonant, for the vowels

au—ŏ ⎫   ⎧ in the FIRST PLACE, or at the Beginning
ō —ŭ ⎬ a DASH ⎨ in the SECOND PLACE, or at the Middle
ōō—ŏŏ ⎭   ⎩ in the THIRD PLACE, or at the End.

(c) This plan of representing the vowels is illustrated in the following scheme, in which the vowels are placed by an upright stroke, or letter Tee, to show their respective positions, namely, opposite the beginning, middle, or end of the consonant.

§ 47. STANDARD VOWEL-SCHEME.

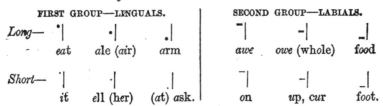

FIRST GROUP—LINGUALS.			SECOND GROUP—LABIALS.		
Long— eat	ale (air)	arm	awe	owe (whole)	food
Short— it	ell (her)	(at) ask.	on	up, cur	foot.

REM. 1. The scheme given above is called the Standard Vowel-Scheme, because it is the one usually employed by phonographers. Another vowel scheme (whose use is optional) will be given in a subsequent section, in which distinct signs will be provided for the vowels of the words inclosed in curves in the preceding table.

REM. 2. *The Dot and Dash Vowels.*—The first-group vowels being denoted by a

How are the long-vowel signs distinguished from the short-vowel signs? How are the long vowels represented? the short vowels? How are the different vowels distinguished, by means of the signs? In how many places beside the consonants are the vowels written? What is the beginning of a consonant? what is the end? How are the vowels ē and ĭ represented? ā and ĕ? ah and ă? au and ŏ? ō and ŭ? ōō and ŏŏ? What is the First Place for a vowel? what is the Second Place? what is the Third Place?

§ 47. For what purpose is the upright stroke, or letter Tee, employed in the vowel-scheme? How is the vowel of *air* denoted? of *her?* of *at?* of *whole?* [Rem.] Why is the Standard Vowel-Scheme so named? Why are the first-group dot, are called Dot-Vowels; while, for a corresponding reason, the second-group vowels are denominated Dash-Vowels.

REM. 3. The vowel-signs should be written at a little distance from the consonants by which they are placed. If allowed to touch, they would occasion mistakes.

REM. 4. The dashes should generally stand at right angles with the consonants. Slight variations, however, from such a position are occasionally convenient and allowable. They frequently add to the beauty of phonographic writing. But when the "Optional Vowel-Signs," to be subsequently explained, are employed, the dash for ' ŭ' at least must be written at a right angle with the consonant, lest it should be mistaken for the vowel of *whole*, which is written at an oblique angle with the consonant.

REM. 5. *Mnemonic Assistance.*—The following mnemonic lines may be of service to the student in fixing in the mind the order and representation of the vowels:

FIRST GROUP—DOT-VOWELS.			SECOND GROUP—DASH-VOWELS.		
Long— Near	*eight*	palms	Saw	so	blooming
Short— Wh*i*ch	s*ai*d	l*a*d	Hobb's	h*u*t	stood
Beginning.	Middle.	End.	Beginning.	Middle.	End.

In these lines, *palms* should be pronounced as if written *pahms*.

REM. 6. The pupil will derive additional assistance in remembering the order of the vowels, from observing the order of the positions assumed by the organs in producing the long vowels—ē, ă, ah, au, ō, ōō. Commencing with a close position for *ē*, the lower jaw and the tongue are gradually depressed till *ah* is arrived at; then commencing with an open position for *au*, the lower jaw is gradually elevated, and the lips brought gradually nearer each other, until *ōō* is produced. These changes may be indicated by the following diagram:

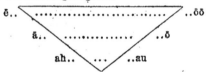

To produce this series of vowels, the mouth is required to be gradually opened and closed, the vowel-apertures being produced chiefly by the tongue, when opening the mouth; and by the lips, when closing the mouth.

CAUTIONS.

REM. 7. Observe that the first-place vowels—ē, ĭ, au, ō—are always written opposite the beginning of the consonant; and that the third-place vowels—ah, ă, ōō, ŏŏ— are always placed at the end. Hence, before writing a first-place, or third-place

vowels denominated Dot-Vowels? Why are the second-group vowels called Dash-Vowels? Why must the vowels be written at a little distance from the consonants? How should the dashes stand with reference to the consonant? Is it allowable to vary the direction of the dash-vowels in reference to the c nsonants? When the optional vowel-signs are employed, how must the dash *ŭ* be written? Repeat the lines given as an assistance in remembering the order and representation of the vowels. What lines correspond to the dot-vowels? What lines correspond to the dash-vowels? What lines contain the long vowels? What lines contain the short vowels? How should the word *palms* be pronounced in these mnemonic lines? What is said with reference to the movements of the mouth when pronouncing the long vowels in the order of the vowel-scheme? Which vowel requires the closest position? which the most open position? At what point beside the consonants are vowel, the direction of the consonant must be determined; and the student should, therefore, make himself familiar with §§ 10, 11, and 12. As Ray is always written upward (see §12, 4 a), its beginning is, of course, at the bottom, and the end, at the top; but not so in respect to the phonograph for l, for that is not always written upward: it may be, and sometimes is, written downward when joined with other signs by which its direction may be determined. It should be observed that sh is usually, *but not always*, written downward. As Ray is always written upward, a first-place vowel in connection with it must always be placed at the bottom, and a third-place vowel, at the top. Horizontal consonants being written from left to right, first-place vowels must be placed opposite their left extremity; a third-place vowel, opposite their right extremity. Carefully peruse §§ 10, 11, and 12; and then observe the method of placing the vowels in the following phonographic words:

Downstrokes.

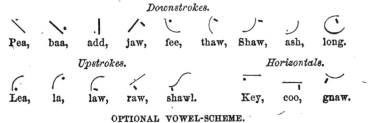

Pea, baa, add, jaw, fee, thaw, Shaw, ash, long.

Upstrokes. *Horizontals.*

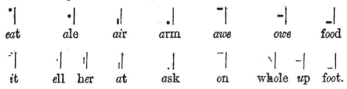

Lea, la, law, raw, shawl. Key, coo, gnaw.

OPTIONAL VOWEL-SCHEME.

§ 48. In the Standard Vowel-Scheme (§ 47), the signs of the vowels of 'ale, ell, ask, owe,' are used to represent also the vowels of 'air, her, at, whole.' For a perfectly phonetic representation, however, the latter vowels require distinct signs, as in the following scheme:

eat	ale	air	arm	awe	owe	food

it	ell	her	at	ask	on	whole	up	foot

REM. 1. The sign of the vowel of *whole* should be written at an oblique angle

---

the first-place vowels always written? Before writing a first-place or third-place vowel beside a consonant, what is first to be considered? For vowels written beside *Ray*, what is the first place? what is the third place? For vowels written beside any upstroke consonant, what is the first place? what is the third place? What is the first place for vowels in connection with Ray? What is the first place and third place for vowels in connection with horizontal consonants? Why, in the phonographic words given at the close of Rem. 7, is the vowel *au* written opposite the top of El in the word *long*, and opposite the bottom of Lay in the word *law*? Why is the vowel *au* placed at the top of Jay in the word *jaw*, and at the bottom of Ray in the word *raw*? Why is *au* placed at the top of Ish in the word *shaw*, and at the bottom of Shay in the world *shawl*? Why is *ah* at the bottom of Bee in the word *baa*, and at the top of Lay in the word *la*? Why is the vowel *ē* placed at the top of Pee in the word *pea*, and at the bottom of Lay in the word *lea*?

§ 48. In the optional vowel-scheme, what is the sign provided for the vowel of *air*? for the vowel of *her*? for the vowel of *at*? for the vowel of *whole*? How, with this scheme, is the vowel of *ask* represented? [Rem.] How should the vowel with the consonant. The signs of the vowels of *air*, *at*, *her*, should be written parallel with the consonant.

REM. 2. The distinct signs for the vowels of *her*, *air*, *at*, *whole*, are denominated Optional Vowel-Signs, because their use is optional.

NAMES OF THE VOWEL-SIGNS.

§ 49. The vowel-signs should be named by the *single sounds which they represent*, and not " *double-ē, long-ā, a-eye, a-aitch, a-you, long-ō, double-ō, short-ĭ*," etc. (*b*) For convenience of conversation, the vowels of *her, ask, whole,* may be named *èr, àf, òl ;* these syllables being pronounced as *er* in *hèr, aff* in *stàff, ole* in *whòle.*

METHOD OF PLACING THE VOWELS IN RESPECT TO THE ORDER OF READING.

§ 50. (*a*) When a vowel is placed
above a horizontal consonant, or
to the left of any other, it is read
BEFORE the consonant; thus, ⸱ ache, ⸱| aid.

(*b*) When a vowel is placed
below a horizontal consonant, or
to the right of any other, it is read
AFTER the consonant; thus, ⸱ gay, |⸱ day.

MODE OF WRITING SINGLE VOWELS.—NOMINAL CONSONANT.

§ 51. A consonant-sign which is not to be pronounced, but which is used merely to show the place of a vowel—as in writing initials of names, indicating single vowels, and in writing words composed entirely of vowels—should be canceled—

(*a*) Either by striking an oblique line through it at any convenient point; thus, ⸱⌋ ĕ, ⌉ ă, ⸱⸱ Eah.

---

of *whole* be written with respect to the consonant? the vowels of *air?* *at?* *her?* What are the Optional Vowel-Signs? Why are they thus named?

§ 49. How are the vowel-signs named? For convenience of conversation, what name is provided for the vowel of *her?* of *ask?* of *whole?*

§ 50. On which side of a consonant-sign should a vowel be written, when it is to be read *after* the consonant? On which side of horizontal consonant-signs is a vowel to be placed, when it is to be read *before* a consonant? on which side, when it is to be read *after* the consonant? On which side of all other consonants should a vowel be placed, when it is to be read *after* the consonants? on which side is it to be placed when it is to be read *before* the consonant?

§ 51. How may it be indicated that a consonant-sign is not to be pronounced? For what purpose may a consonant-sign be canceled? How may a consonant-sign be canceled? How, when a dot-vowel is to be written beside it? How, when (*b*) Or by writing the vowel-sign, if a dash, through it at a right angle; thus, ⊤ awe, ⊤ ŏ, + ŭ, ⊥ ōō.

REM. 1. As a canceled consonant has no value as the sign of a sound—that is, has the form, but not the power, of a consonant,—it is denominated a Nominal Consonant.

REM. 2. Single vowels are usually written to a letter Tee; but any other consonant may be employed which may be more convenient, provided, of course, that it should be canceled.

REM. 3. The letter Tee may be employed as a nominal consonant, even without cancellation, in all cases, as in the preceding vowel-schemes, when no confusion would be likely to result from such use.

REM. 4. The words *ah!* and *eh!* may be written thus: ⟋ ah, ⟋ eh. When these words are forcibly spoken, the aspirate is actually heard, and is therefore properly indicated. However, the sign may be regarded as simply serving to show the place of the vowel, and not requiring cancellation.

REM. 5. The optional vowel-signs, when written singly, should be placed beside a canceled Tee.

POSITION OF WORDS.

1. WORDS COMPOSED ENTIRELY OF HORIZONTAL CONSONANTS.

§ 52. Words composed entirely of horizontal consonants should be written above the line, when their accented vowel is first place; otherwise, on the line. Hence, 'gnaw, key, in, me, my' are written above the line, while 'know, go, gay, am, coo' are written on the line.

2. WORDS HAVING PERPENDICULAR OR INCLINED STROKES.

§ 53. Words having perpendicular or inclined strokes should be written in the second position; that is, so that the first perpendicular or inclined stroke shall rest upon the line of writing.

---

it serves to denote the place of a dash-vowel? [Rem.] What is a canceled consonant called? What is a Nominal Consonant? How are single vowels usually written? What consonant-sign is sometimes used for a nominal consonant, even without cancellation? How may the words *ah* and *eh* be written? When is the sound of *h* heard in these words? If not heard, how is the stroke-sign for *h* to be regarded?

§ 52. Where, that is, in what position, should words composed entirely of horizontal consonants be written? When should such words be written above the line? when on the line? Where should you write *gnaw! key! scheme! sick! sake! sum! sane! awn!* Why should *me, awn, key, gnaw, sing, song, scene* be written above the line? Why should *neigh, snow, son, some, same, coo, sang* be written *on* the line?

§ 53. Where, that is, in what position, should words containing perpendicular or sloping strokes be written? What is the second position for such words?

§ 54. With few exceptions, the reporter subjects all words of few consonants (horizontals or not) to the reporter's rule of position, placing them, not in two positions only, as in the corresponding style of phonography, but in three different positions, according as their accented vowel is first-place, second-place, or third-place. Words with first-place accented vowels are written in the first position (see § 39, 1); those with second-place accented vowels are written in the second position (§ 39, 2); and those with third-place accented vowels are written in the third position (§ 39, 3). By observing this rule of position, the reporter is enabled, for the most part, to dispense with vocalization, the mere position of words pointing out very nearly the accented vowel—which is one of the most important prerequisites in deciphering reporting outlines. These three positions are partially recognized in the word-signs of the corresponding style of phonography (the style explained in this work). They are specified in § 39. The student will now be able to understand why the sign for *at* is written through the line (that is, in the third position); why the signs for *if, give, me, common,* are written above the line (that is, in the first position); while the signs for *come, together, so,* and *they* are written on the line (that is, in the second position).

§ 55. EXCEPTIONS TO THE RULE OF POSITION FOR WORD-SIGNS.

(*a*) *Position Changed to Avoid Confusion.*—It is necessary to write a few word-signs out of the position denoted by their accented vowel, to prevent their being confounded with other words (of the same consonants) which, according to the rule, would occupy the same position. The sign for *any,* for example, is written above the line, to prevent its being mistaken for *no;* while the sign for *him* is written on the line, so that it may not be mistaken for *me.* For the same reason, the sign for *own* is written in the third position, though it strictly belongs to the second.

(*b*) *Position Changed for the Convenience of the Writer.*—Some word-signs which properly belong to the first or third position, are put in the second position, because that is the most convenient for the writer. *Do* and *be,* for this reason, occupy the second position, though *do* properly belongs to the third position, and *be* to the first.

---

§ 54. What is the reporter's rule of position? How many different positions does the reporter recognize for words of few consonants? In what position does he write such words when their accented vowel is first-place? when it is second-place? when it is third-place? How does this rule benefit the reporter? In the Reporting Style, what does the position of a word serve to point out? Are the three positions of the Reporting Style recognized to any extent in the Corresponding Style? Why is the sign for *at* written through the line, that is, in the third position?

§ 55. Are word-signs ever written out of the position denoted by their accented vowel? and if so, why? Why is the sign for *any* written in the first position? Why is the sign for *him* written on the line? Why is the sign for *own* written below the line? What is the most convenient position for writing words? Are word-signs which strictly belong to the first or third position ever put in the second position? Give some examples.

VOCALIZATION OF CONSONANT-STROKES WITH CIRCLES OR LOOPS ATTACHED.

CIRCLE OR LOOP AT THE BEGINNING OF A STROKE.

§ 56. A circle or loop at the beginning of a consonant-stroke is read before the consonant-stroke or any vowels placed beside it; thus,

$\diagdown$ ope, $\diagdown$ s-oap, $\diagdown$ st-eep; $\diagup$ eel, $\diagup$ s-eal, $\diagup$ st-eal; $\vert$- toe, $\vert$- s-tōw; $\diagup$ lōw, $\diagup$ s-lōw; $\curlyvee$ no, $\curlyvee$ s-nōw.

§ 57. In other words—In reading a consonant-stroke with a circle or loop at the beginning, read the circle first; and then read the consonant-stroke and the vowels beside it (if any) precisely as though no circle or loop were attached; thus, "s-oap, st-eep, s-eal, st-eal, s-tōw, s-lōw, s-nōw."

RULES FOR REPRESENTING S AND Z AT THE BEGINNING OF A WORD.

§ 58. (a) The small circle should usually be employed to represent s at the beginning of a word; as in the examples in § 56;

(b) Except—

1. When two vowels follow, as in $\diagup$ science.

2. When another s follows, as in $\diagup$ cease, $\diagup$ system.

REM. The object of the first exception is to provide two strokes, between which the vowel-signs may be conveniently divided, instead of being written in a confused manner beside one stroke, as would be necessary if the s in such cases were represented by a circle.

§ 59. The sound of z at the commencement of a word is always represented by a z-stroke, as in $\diagup$ zeal.

REM. This rule results in a clear distinction between words commencing with s and those commencing with z, as seal, zeal.

CAUTION.

§ 60. The sound of s or z following an initial vowel should be denoted by a stroke, as in $\diagup$ ask, $\diagup$ Ezra, $\cdot$) ace, -) owes.

REM. This is necessary, because, according to § 56, a vowel can not be written so as to read before a circle, at the commencement of a word. Hence, $\circ$— is not ask, but sack; $\diagup$ is not Ezra, but Sēra.

---

§ 56. How is a circle or loop at the beginning of a consonant-stroke read?

§ 57. How should a consonant-stroke with a vowel or vowels beside it be read, when a circle is joined at the beginning of the stroke?

§ 58. Repeat the rule for representing initial s. How is initial s represented when two vowels follow it? when another s follows it, as in cease, system? [Rem.] What is the object of using Ess for initial s followed by two vowels?

§ 59. How is initial z represented? [Rem.] What is the object of this rule?

§ 60. How should you represent s or z following an initial vowel, as in ask, easy, Ezra? [Rem.] Why is it necessary in such cases to write the stroke-sign for s or s? Why may not the s in ask be represented by Iss?

CIRCLE OR LOOP AT THE END OF A STROKE.

§ 61. A circle or loop at the end of a consonant-stroke is read after the consonant or any vowels placed beside it; thus, ⟍ pă-ss, ⟍ pă-sses, ⟍ pă-st, ⟍ pă-stor, ⟍ ope-s, ⟍ arrŭ-st, ⟍ ămă-ssed.

§ 62. In other words—In reading a consonant-stroke with a circle or loop at the end, read the consonant-stroke with the vowel or vowels beside it, as though no circle or loop were attached, and then add the circle or loop; thus, pă-s, pă-sez, pă-st, pă-str, ŏp-s, ărĕ-st, ămă-st.

RULES FOR REPRESENTING S AND Z AT THE END OF A WORD.

§ 63. (a) The small circle should usually be employed to represent the sound of s or z at the end of a word; as in the examples in § 61;

(b) Except—

1. When two vowels precede it, as in ⟍ chaos.

2. When another s precedes it, as in ⟍ access, ⟍ amaurosis.

CAUTION.

§ 64. The sound of s or z preceding a final vowel should be denoted by a stroke; thus, ⟍ see, ⟍ also, ⟍ rosy.

REM. This is necessary, because, according to § 61, a vowel can not be written so as to be read after a circle at the end of a word. Hence ⟍ is not also, but aulōs.

VOCALIZATION OF THE LARGE CIRCLE.

§ 65. The large circle is used to represent a syllable containing the vowel ĕ. (b) It may be vocalized for other vowels by writing their signs within the circle; as in ⟍ exist.

USES OF THE LARGE CIRCLE.

§ 66. The large circle is used in the following cases:

1. To express two s-sounds at the end of a word—principally in the

---

§ 61. When is a circle or loop at the end of a consonant to be read? Should it be read *before* or *after* a vowel following the consonant-stroke?

§ 62. How should a stroke with a vowel or vowels beside it be read, when a circle or loop is joined at the end of the stroke?

§ 63. Repeat the rule for representing final *s*. How should final *s* be represented when two vowels precede it? when another *s* precedes it, as in *access, amaurosis?*

§ 64. How should you write *s* followed by a final vowel? Why may not *s* in such cases be represented by Iss? Write *see, essay, rosy, massy, lessee, Vesey, Asă, racy, also.*

§ 65. What kind of a syllable is the large circle employed to represent? How may it be vocalized for other syllables, as in *exist, exhaust, insist, Crassus?*

§ 66. Repeat the rule for the use of the large circle. Is it ever used in the middle representation of such words as *passes, causes, faces;* rarely in writing such words as *Crassus, amaurosis, exercise.*

2. Occasionally in the middle of a word; as in ⌒ necessary, ⊤ exhaust.

3. Occasionally at the beginning of words, for such syllables as *sus, sis,* in such words as *sustain, sister, system, suspect.*

REM. *Caution.*—A third-place vowel preceding the syllable denoted by the large circle, should not be placed within the circle, because a vowel thus written should be read *between* the two *s*-sounds denoted by the circle, and not *before* them.

RULE FOR VOCALIZING A STROKE WITH A CIRCLE OR LOOP ATTACHED.

§ 67. In vocalizing a consonant-stroke which has a circle or loop attached, place the vowel-sign before or after the stroke, according as the vowel precedes or follows the consonant, precisely as though no circle or loop were attached.

(*b*) For example, in vocalizing Iss-Jay for *siege*, determine, in the first place, whether the vowel ē precedes or follows the sound of *j* heard in the word. If it precedes, write it before the Jay; if it follows that consonant, write it after the sign Jay; and do not give yourself *any* trouble as to whether or not the circle will be read before or after the vowel. Place the vowel correctly with reference to the strokes, and the correct reading of the circle will be found to be governed by rules given in §§ 56, 57, 61, 62.

VOWEL WORD-SIGNS.

§ 68. The vowel dots and dashes are employed in different positions as signs for certain words of which they constitute a portion.

REM. 1. Some of the vowel-dashes are written in different directions to distinguish between their different uses. For example, *au* as the sign of *all* takes a south-eastern direction; as the sign of *already,* a southern direction; and as the sign of *ought,* a south-western direction. The dash for ŏ is written south-east, south, or south-west, as a sign, according to the direction, for *of, or, on.*

---

of a word? ever at the beginning of a word? Give some examples of its use at the end, beginning, or middle of words. Write *passes, causes, noses, insist, necessity, accessory, necessary, exist.* [Rem.] Should third-place vowels preceding a large circle be written within it? If not, why not?

§ 67. Repeat the rule for vocalizing a consonant-stroke to which a circle or loop has been attached. Write *siege, sage, mass, ax, sick, sake, sack.* In writing the last three words, should the vowels be written above or below the Kay? If above, why? In *sick,* how is it known that the vowel should not be read before the circle? See §§ 56, 57.

§ 68. Are the vowel-signs employed as word-signs? [Rem.] How can you distinguish the different uses of the vowel-dashes when they are employed as word-signs? In how many different directions is *au* written when employed as a word-sign? What is the direction of *au* when it represents *all?* when it represents *already?*

REM. 2. *Position of the Dashes and Dots.*—As but two positions (above and on the line) can be conveniently recognized for the dots and dashes when not written beside a consonant-stroke, the second-place dots and dashes, when used as word-signs, have to be carried up to the first place or brought down to the third place. For example, the dashes for ō and ŭ are brought down to the third place, and used as signs for *oh !* and *but;* while the dot for ĕ is carried up to the first place, and employed as a sign for *the*. *The* is usually pronounced *thĕ*, especially before consonants ; thus, *thĕ man, thĕ book.* Some, however, regard the word-sign for *the* as ĭ.

§ 69. LIST OF VOWEL WORD-SIGNS.

.....˙_ ĕ   . ā   . ă

the,   a,   an-d,

↘ au | au   ╱ au   ↘ ŏ | ŏ   ╱ ŏ

all,   already, awe,   ought,   of,   or,   on.

↘ ōō | ō   ╱ ōō   ↘ ōō | ŭ   ╱ ōō

two, too,   oh, owe,   who-m,   to,   but,   should.

REM. 1. THE, when emphasized, may be denoted by the dot for ĕ written above the line.

REM. 2. In rapid writing, *a* is rarely distinguished from *an-d;* and yet no difficulty is experienced on this account in reading phonographic notes, the correct word being very readily determined by means of the context.

REM. 3. WHOSE may be written by adding a circle to the sign for *who;* thus, ₅ whose. No confusion results from writing *who is* or *has* in the same manner.

REM. 4. Zee may be vocalized for *owes;* Dee, for *owed;* and *owing* may be represented by the word-sign for *owe*, with a small dot below it.

'THE' JOINED BY A TICK.

§ 70. *The* may be joined to a preceding or following word, by a tick written upward or downward in the direction of Pee ↘ or Chay ╱ ;

thus, ↳ for the, ⌣..... in the, ⌐ is the, ╱ which the, ⌐..... of

---

when it represents *ought?* How many positions can be conveniently recognized for the vowel dots and dashes when written alone? Where must the second-place vowel-signs be written? Where is ĕ written when used as a sign for *the?* How do some regard the light dot when used in the first position as a word-sign for *the ?*

§ 69. Cover the word-signs and write the proper signs for the words in the List of Vowel Word-Signs. What is the direction of ŏ when used as a sign for *of?* or? on? What is the direction of ŏŏ when used as a sign for *to?-should?* What is the direction of ōō when used as a sign for *too? two? who? whom?* What is the direction and position of ŭ when used as a sign for *but?* of ō when used as a sign for *oh, owe?* [Rem.] How may emphasized *the* be denoted? How may *a* be distinguished from *an* or *and*, when, in rapid writing, the dot for *a* happens to be made light? How may *whose* be written? How may *owes, owed,* and *owing* be written?

§ 70. What is the direction of the tick for *the?* May it be written either upward

the, ⟩ to the, ⟋ on the, ⩗ or the, ⌐ but the, ⟋ should
the, ⟿ the first, ⟍ the way.

REM. 1. The ease of writing *or the* and *but the* is slightly increased by inclining
the dashes for *or* and *but;* thus, ⩗ or the, ⌐ but the.

REM. 2. The joining of *the* to a following word is of comparatively rare occurrence in the writing of the best phonographers.

'A-N-D' JOINED BY A TICK.

§ 71. *A, an,* or *and* may be joined to a preceding or following word,
by a horizontal or perpendicular tick; thus, ⌣ in a, ⌐ is a,
⌐ or a-n, ⌐ but a-n, ⌐ and the, ⌐ and a-n, ⟍ to a-n, ⌐ of
a-n, ⌐ and for a-n, ⌣ and in a-n.

REM. 1. A-n-d is joined nearly as often to a following as to a preceding word.
REM. 2. (*a*) Observe that in *and but* the last stroke rests upon the line; while in
and a-n the first stroke rests on the line, and the second (perpendicular) stroke extends below the line. (*b*) *And should* is distinguished from *and the* in a corresponding manner.

DIRECTION OF 'ON' AND 'SHOULD.'

§ 72. *On* and *should* are generally written downward, when standing
alone; (*b*) when joined with other words, the upward direction is
usually the most convenient.

POSITION OF THE DASH WORD-SIGNS OF THE FIRST PLACE.

§ 73. The first-place dashes, when used as word-signs, should be commenced the
height of a Tee above the line of writing. With double-line paper, they commence
on the upper line.

§ 74. LIST OF WORDS REPRESENTED BY SIMPLE-VOWEL SIGNS.

a—§ 68, R. 2; § 71	and—§ 71
all	awe
already	but—§ 68, R. 2; § 71, R. 2, *a.*
an—§ 71	of

---

or downward? [Rem.] What is the advantage of varying slightly the direction of
or and *but* in writing *or the* and *but the?* What is said of joining *the* by a tick to a
following word? Write 'for the, if the, by the, on the, of the, all the, in the, is the,
as the, it is the, this is the.'

§ 71. What are the directions of the tick for *a-n-d?* [Rem.] What is said of joining *a-n-d* by a tick to a following word? How is *and but* distinguished from *and
a-n?* Write 'and a, is an, as a, it is a, it has a, or a, but an, of a, on a, and in a,
and for a, should a, by a, if a, give a, and may a, and may the, and the, and it, and
should, and the, and because a, and give, a common.'

§ 72. How are *on* and *should* generally written when standing alone? when
joined with other words?

§ 73. Where should the first-place dash-wordsigns be commenced? where, with
double-line paper?

§ 74. Write the proper signs for the words in this list.

oh!—§ 68, R. 2   to
on—§ 72   too
or   two
ought   who
owe—§ 69, R. 4   whom
should—§ 72   whose—§ 69, R. 3.
the—§ 69, R. 1; § 70; § 71, R. 2, *b*.

QUALITY AND QUANTITY OF UNACCENTED VOWELS.

§ 75. Without guidance of rules, it is frequently difficult for the phonographic writer to determine satisfactorily the quality and quantity of vowels without a primary or secondary accent; as the vowels denoted by *italic* letters in the following words :—'am*o*ng, def*i*ne, r*e*tain, pr*e*fer, met*a*l, tail*o*r.' Good phonographers are now quite generally agreed, as shown by their practice, that a correct, distinct pronunciation supports the following rules:

1. TO DETERMINE THE QUALITY OF AN UNACCENTED VOWEL.

§ 76. Generally, when the precise quality of a vowel without a primary or secondary accent can not be readily determined, regard it as the short sound of the letter used to represent it in the common spelling, unless another sound is indicated by the analogy of some related word. Hence, write 'dĕfĭne, rĕfer, prĕfer, mĕtăl, saĭlŏr,' but ' dĭspōsĭtion' instead of ' dĭspŏsĭtion,' because of ' dĭspōse.'

Rem. 1. The ordinary pronunciation of a word is occasionally changed, in order to distinguish it from some other word of similar sound; as, "I did not say *prĕcede* but *prŏceed ;* not *dĕclaim* but *rĕclaim ;* not *dĕfer* but *rĕfer.*" In such cases, write the distinguishing, instead of the ordinary, pronunciation—writing ' prĕcede, dĕclaim, rĕclaim, dĕfer, rĕfer,' instead of the common pronunciation, ' prĕcéde, dĕclaim', rĕclaim', dĕfer', rĕfer'.'

Rem. 2. Some writers regard ē as the vowel of the unaccented prefixes, *de, re, pre*, and usually write them with this vowel in primitive words, though a change to ĕ in the derivatives is almost invariably necessary ; thus, ' dēfine, dĕfinition ; rēfer, rĕference ; prēfer, prĕference. The correct rule is to write these prefixes with ē, whenever the sound is clearly heard in a proper, deliberate pronunciation, as in *rē-seat, rē-bound, rē-form ;* and when a vowel immediately follows the prefix, as in *re-enter, pre-emption ;* but write ĕ whenever the vowel is obscurely pronounced, as in *reform, defer, prefer.* The observance of this rule secures a distinction in writing, *corresponding to the difference in speech*, between such words as re-seat, receipt ; re-dress (to dress again), redress (to amend) ; re-form (to form anew), reform (to correct) ; re-bound (to bound again), rebound (to spring back) ; and also secures in the primitive the vowel which generally appears distinctly in the derivative ; thus, dēfine, dĕfinition ; rēfer', rĕf'erence ; rēlate', rĕl'ative ; prēfer, prĕf'erence.

2. TO DETERMINE THE QUANTITY OF AN UNACCENTED VOWEL.

§ 77. Generally, when the quality of a vowel is clear, but the writer doubts whether to employ the long or short vowel of any particular pair, the short vowel should be employed in preference to the long one ; thus, ŏ instead of *au* in 'reformation ;' ă instead of *ah* in 'peculiar ;' ĕ instead of ā in 'certain, captain ;' ŏ instead of ō in ' obey ;' ŏŏ instead of ōō in ' to-day.'

PUNCTUATION, ACCENT, NUMBERS, ETC.

PUNCTUATION.

§ 78. THE marks of punctuation employed in Phonography are the following :

PERIOD	× or /	DOUBT	(?)
COLON	:	PLEASANTRY	
SEMICOLON	,	HYPHEN	
COMMA	,	PARENTHESIS	( )
EXCLAMATION	!		
WONDER or IRONY	(!)	BRACKETS	[ ]
GRIEF		OBSOLESCENT	
INTERROGATION	§ or §	DASH	

PERIOD.

REM. 1. (a) The first mark of a period should be made quite small. It is employed, in preference to any other sign, in the Corresponding Style. It has a neat appearance when properly made, and is readily distinguished from phonographic words. (b) The second sign of a period is employed chiefly by reporters. It may be occasionally used instead of a colon or semicolon. (c) Instead of the long sign for a period, some reporters employ this sign ⟋ It is, however, inferior to the long stroke in two important respects: it is not so readily made, and is not so distinct and conspicuous.

REM. 2. *Period after Common Letters.*—When a period is required immediately after common letters, as in writing titles, etc., write very near to them the common sign (.); thus, *A. B., M. D., LL. D.*

INTERROGATION.

REM. 3. The first mark of interrogation given above should be employed only when the writer prefers to place the sign of a question at the beginning, instead of the end, of the interrogation. There is not sufficient advantage, however, to justify

§ 78. What marks of punctuation are employed in Phonography? How many are the same as in common print? [Rem.] What sign is most generally employed, in Phonography, as the sign of a period? How should it be made? For what is the long sign employed? How do reporters occasionally indicate a colon or semicolon? What sign do some reporters employ instead of the long sign for the period? Which is the best?——How is a period immediately after common letters to be written?——When should the first mark of interrogation be employed? What is said as to the advantage of a change from the usual mode of indicating a ques the change from the usual practice of placing the Interrogation at the end of a question. In most cases, the form of an interrogative sentence or clause is of itself sufficient to indicate its character.

DOUBT.

Rem. 4. Doubt is indicated, as in common writing and printing, by an Interrogation inclosed in curves; thus, (?). Doubt of the accuracy or propriety of remarks quoted from the writings of another, is denoted by introducing, at the required place, an Interrogation inclosed in brackets; thus, [?].

IRONY—WONDER.

Rem. 5. An Exclamation within parenthetical curves is employed in Phonography, as in common writing, to denote wonder, irony, contempt; as, "This accurate scholar (!), who went to Eton and graduated at Cambridge, has actually made a dozen grammatical mistakes within the compass of one short paragraph." Wonder at, or contempt of, the remarks quoted from the writings of another, is indicated by introducing, at the proper place, an Exclamation inclosed in brackets; thus, [!]

PLEASANTRY.

Rem. 6. In writing, pleasantry may be denoted by the sign given above. In printing, an appropriate sign is secured by inverting the common mark of interrogation; thus, ¿.

OBSOLESCENT.

Rem. 7. The Obsolescent is used to inclose words in the common spelling. Some phonographers very improperly employ the Obsolescent instead of the Parenthesis.

DASH.

Rem. 8. In Phonography, the dash must be made wave-like, to prevent its being mistaken for a phonographic Kay.

ACCENT—EMPHASIS—CAPITALS.

§ 79. The Accent of a word may be shown by writing a small cross near the accented vowel; thus, ⤳ árrows, ⤳ aróse. (b) It is best, however, in marking accents, to use phonetic longhand.

§ 80. Emphasis is indicated, as in longhand, by one, two, or more lines drawn beneath the word or words to be emphasized. (b) A single line under a single word should be made wave-like, to prevent its being mistaken for Kay.

---

tion ?——How is doubt indicated ? How is it indicated in a quotation ?——How is pleasantry denoted ? How may it be indicated in common printing ?——What is the Obsolescent ? and for what purpose is it employed ? For what is it improperly used ?——How is the dash distinguished from Kay ?

§ 79. How is accent indicated ? Write éssay, essay'; áffix, affíx; Au'gust, augúst; árrows, aróse.

§ 80. How is emphasis indicated ? When must a single subscript, or underwrit-

Rem. In longhand "copy" for the printer, a single subscript line denotes *italics;* two lines, SMALL CAPITALS; three lines, CAPITALS. Minute directions for preparing copy for the printer, and for correcting "proofs," are given in the Author's work entitled "Brief Longhand."

§ 81. A capital letter is denoted in Phonography by two short lines under the letter; thus, ⟍⟍ Rome. (*b*) This is generally unnecessary.

NUMBERS.

§ 82. Numbers may be expressed phonographically, or by the common figures.

Rem. 1. *One, Two, and Six.*—The numbers *one* and *two* are most easily written in Phonography; thus, ⌣ *one*, ⟍ *two*. (The sign for *one*, as will be subsequently learned, is *wn*.) The figures 1 and 6, when written singly, will not be liable to be mistaken for phonographic characters, if formed thus, *1 6.*

Rem. 2. *Phonographic Numerals.*—A mode of expressing numbers more rapidly than by the common figures, has been devised by the Author, and is explained in a phonographic work entitled "Phonographic Numerals: A System for the Rapid Expression of Numbers."

INITIALS—TITLES—PROPER NAMES.

§ 83. The initials of names should be written in the common hand, or such phonographs employed as will surely indicate the correct longhand initials.

Rem. 1. If Philip —— should employ a phonographic Ef for the initial of his name, his correspondent will infer therefrom that the initial of his name is F. rather than P.; and, if Philip should fail to get a response to his communication, it will, in all probability, be due to his not having written the initial of his name in the common hand, *or with such a phonograph* (namely, Pee) *as would surely indicate the initial letter of his name in the common spelling.* George should not employ **Jay** for the initial of his name, for this would indicate 'J' instead of 'G.' Gay,

---

ten, line be made wave-like? and for what purpose? [Rem.] In longhand, what is denoted respectively by one, two, and three subscript lines?

§ 81. How is a capital letter denoted in Phonography? Is it generally necessary in Phonography, to indicate capitals?

§ 82. How, in Phonography, may numbers be expressed? [Rem.] How is it best to write *one, two,* and *six?* What is the form, in Phonography, for the common figures 1 and 6 when written separately? Why is it necessary to give them this particular form?

§ 83. How should the initials of names be written? [Rem.] Carefully read Remarks 1 and 2.

however, would surely indicate 'G.' The Chaunceys and Charleses may employ Chay for their initials, for this unmistakably indicates 'C.,' the common-hand initial of their names. The Theodores may employ Ith for the initial of their name, because Ith surely indicates a name commencing with T. The Cyruses must be careful not to write Es for their initial, for that indicates 'S.,' and the Calebs must be equally cautious not to employ Kay for the initial of their name, for that would suggest 'K.' as the longhand initial.

REM. 2. The vowel-letter initials are best written in the common hand; they may, however, be indicated phonographically according to the method explained at § 51. When the phonographs are employed, it is better to denote by them the *names* rather than the various *sounds* of the common vowel-letters used as initials; that is, phonographically write ă for 'A.,' whether this letter should be the initial of Alfred, Augustus, Arthur, or Aaron. In like manner, phonographically, write ĕ for 'E.,' whether this letter should be the initial of Edith, Ebenezer, Ernest, or Eurydice. 'U.' must be written in longhand, or have its name (*Yoo*) phonographically expressed.

§ 84. The initials of titles should usually be written in the common longhand; thus, *M.D., LL.D., A.B.*

PROPER NAMES.

§ 85. When the pronunciation of a proper name is doubtful, it should be written in the common hand. (*b*) When a word is written in the common longhand, it should be inclosed in an Obsolescent, if there could otherwise be doubt as to whether the letters were used with their phonetic or with their common value.

OTHER MARKS USED IN PHONOGRAPHY.

§ 86. The following signs may be used in Phonography as in the common hand:

QUOTATION POINTS........	" "	The ASTERISK	※
The CARET..............	∧	The OBELISK, or DAGGER	†
The INDEX, or HAND	☞	The DOUBLE DAGGER	‡
The PARAGRAPH	¶	The PARALLELS	‖
The SECTION.............	§		

REM. 1. For phonographic writing, the Caret should be made quite acute, and with strokes sufficiently long to distinguish it from the sign for the diphthong *ow* (See the Phonographic Alphabet, under 'Close Diphthongs.')

REM. 2. Five of the above illustrations have been cut especially for this work, in order to furnish the student with graceful writing forms for the printing signs for the Caret (∧), Index (☞), Paragraph (¶), Section (§), and Asterisk (*).

REM. 3. No Apostrophe (') is required for phonographic writing.

---

§ 84. How should the initials of titles usually be written?

§ 85. How should a proper name be written when its pronunciation is doubtful? [Rem.] When should longhand words be inclosed in an Obsolescent?

§ 86. Make the Quotation Points, the Caret, the Index, the Section, the Asterisk, the Paragraph, the Parallel, the Double Dagger, the Obelisk. [Rem.] How, in Phonography, must the Caret be made to distinguish it from the angular sign for *ou?* Is any sign required, in Phonography, for the Apostrophe?

C · C C C

VOCALIZATION—DIPHTHONGS.

DEFINITION, ENUMERATION, AND CLASSIFICATION.

§ 87. A Diphthong may be defined- as a coalition or union of two simple vowel-sounds, pronounced in one syllable ; as in *oil, out, feud.*

Rem. 1. The vowels composing a diphthong are called its *elements*.

Rem. 2. The word Diphthong does not necessarily denote a peculiar union of vowels only. It may be appropriately applied to corresponding combinations of two consonants, as of *d* and *zh*, as in *edge=edzh*. The term, however, is usually and conveniently employed, without a restrictive word, to denote vowel-diphthongs only. When reference is made to similar combinations of consonants, the words consonantal diphthongs' should be employed.

Rem. 3. *Diphthong* is derived from the Greek δίφθογγος (díphthonggos), a word composed of δὶς (double) and φθόγγος (fthonggos) a sound. The etymology of the word, therefore, indicates *dif'thong* as its correct pronunciation.

Rem. 4. Dr. K. M. Rapp, a profound phonologist, in defining the conditions necessary in order that two vowels should constitute a diphthong, says : " First, the diphthong must constitute a single syllable ;" and secondly, " the accent must fall upon the first of the two component vowels."

§ 88. The diphthongs may be divided, with reference to the intimacy of the connection of their elements, into *Close,* and *Open,* diphthongs.

1. Of the Close Diphthongs.

§ 89. The close diphthongs are those denoted by *italics* in *i*sle, *oi*l, *ou*t, *n*ew.

Rem. 1. It will be seen, by reference to the Phonographic Alphabet, that the elements of the close diphthongs are short vowels; while only one of the elements of the open diphthongs is short.

---

§ 87. What is a diphthong? Give some examples of diphthongs. [Rem.] What are the sounds composing a diphthong called? May the word Diphthong be appropriately applied to close combinations of two consonants? Give some examples of consonantal diphthongs. What is the general use of the term Diphthong? From what Greek words is the word Diphthong derived? What is its correct pronunciation? What conditions are defined by Dr. Rapp as necessary for the formation of a diphthong?

§ 88. How may the diphthongs be divided with reference to the intimacy of the connection of their elements?

§ 89. What are the close diphthongs? [Rem.] What is said in respect to the quantity of the elements of the close diphthongs? How, in respect of the quantity of their elements, do they differ from the open diphthongs?

§ 90. I.—The diphthong denoted by *i* in *isle* and *ice*, and by *ai* in *aisle*, is composed of the vowel of *ask* (not *at*) and *it*, the voice accenting the first and *gliding* to the second.

REM. Various peculiar pronunciations of ī are heard, namely, ŏĭ, ăĭ, ŭĭ, very rarely ŏi, and ŏi (ŏ denoting the vowel of *whole*).—*See Introduction to Phonotypy and Phonography*, § 32.

§ 91. OI.—The diphthong represented by *oi* in *oil*, and by *oy* in *boy*, is composed of the vowel of *on* (o) and *it* (i), the voice accenting the first and *gliding* to the second.

§ 92. OU.—The diphthong represented by *ou* in *out* consists of the vowels of *on* (o) and *foot* (u), the voice accenting the first and *gliding* to the second.

§ 93. EW.—The diphthong represented by *ew* in *few*, and *u* in *duty*, is composed of the vowels of *it* (i) and *foot* (u), the voice accenting the first and *gliding* to the second.

REM. In English Phonography, this pure diphthong is represented by a sign equivalent to *yoo*. Hence *duty, tube*, are spelled *dyooty, tyoob*, insteady of *dūty, tūbe*. This is pronouncing *u* by its name (Yoo) instead of its proper sound.

§ 94. From the preceding remarks we arrive at the following

Table of Close Diphthongs.

Common Symbols—	I,	OI,	OU,	EW.
Phonetic Symbols—	ai,	oi,	ou,	iu.
Examples—	isle, aisle, eye	oil, toy	owl, out	feud, dew, due, pure.

2. OF THE OPEN DIPHTHONGS.

§ 95. The principal open diphthongs are those represented by *italics* in the following words : *aye*, dr*awing*, d*ei*ty, cl*ayey*, sn*owy*, *Owen*, N*oah*, L*oui*s.

REM. 1. The open diphthongs differ from the close diphthongs in having a long, instead of a short, initial element, and, as a consequence, greater quantity, and a less intimate connection of their components.

REM. 2. The open diphthongs are intermediate between perfect, close diphthongs, and a dissyllabic connection of two vowels. They are imperfect diphthongs. Compared with the close diphthongs, they appear dissyllabic; but when contrasted with undoubted vowel dissyllables, they appear diphthongal. On the one hand, compare *ahi* with *i; aye* with *eye; aui* with the close diphthong *oi*. On the other hand, contrast *e'i* as in *deist* with *ē-i'* in *deistic;* *ŏ'ĕ* in *poet* with *ŏ-ĕ'* in *poetic*.

---

§ 90. What are the elements of *i?* Which element is accented? Contrast the correct pronunciation of *i* with the diphthong formed by a union of the vowels of *it* and *it*. [Rem.] Give the various incorrect pronunciations of *i*.

§ 91. What are the elements of *oi?* Which element is accented ?

§ 92. What are the elements of *ou?*

§ 93. What are the elements of *ew?* Which is accented ? [Rem.] In English Phonography, what sounds are written instead of this pure diphthong?

§ 94. Separately pronounce the close diphthongs.

§ 95. What are the principal open diphthongs ? Give some words in which they occur. [Rem.] How do the open diphthongs differ from the close ones ? How do they appear when compared with dissyllabic unions of vowels ? when compared with perfect diphthongs ?

§ 96. The elements of the open diphthongs are indicated by the phonetic symbols in the following

Table of Open Diphthongs.

Common Symbols—	ahĭ,	auĭ,	ĕĭ,	āĭ,
Phonetic Symbols—	ʙi,	ᴏi,	ᴊii,	ɛi,
Examples—	a*ye*,	dra*wi*ng,	de*i*ty,	cla*yey*.

Common Symbols—	ŏĭ,	ŏĕ,	ŏă,	ŏŏĭ,
Phonetic Symbols—	ᴇ'i,	ᴇe,	ᴇa,	ɯi.
Examples—	sn*owy*,	O*w*en	No*ah*,	Lo*uis*.

I. CLOSE-DIPHTHONG SIGNS.

§ 97. The four close diphthongs are represented by small angular marks, whose direction and place are indicated by the following illustrations:

ſ   OI   OU   EW

*i*sle, *ai*sle   o*i*l   out   dew, d*u*pe.

Rᴇᴍ. 1. The diphthong-signs should be written in an invariable direction, whatever may be the direction of the consonant to which they are placed; that is, the sign for *ī* should always open upward; that for *oi* and *ou*, downward; and that of *ew*, to the right.

Rᴇᴍ. 2. Both of the strokes of the close-diphthong signs are made *light*, to correspond to the *short* elements composing the diphthongs which they denote.

Rᴇᴍ. 3. Each of the close diphthongs is written in the place of its last element; hence, *ai* (*ī*) and *oi* are written in the first place, because this is the place of *i*; while *ou* and *iu* (*ew*) are written in the third place, because this is the place of *u* (ŏŏ).

Rᴇᴍ. 4. The sound of *ew* in *new* never begins a syllable.

§ 96. Pronounce separately the open diphthongs. Give their elements separately.

§ 97. How are the four close diphthongs represented? What, as shown by the illustration, is the direction of *ī?* of *oi?* of *ou?* of *ew?* What, as shown by the illustration, is the place of *ī?* of *oi?* of *ou?* of *ew?* Write *ī, oi, ou, ew, ī, ou, oi, ew.* [Rem.] What is said with reference to the direction of the diphthong-signs when written beside consonants of different directions? How should the sign for *ī* invariably open—upward or downward? the sign for *oi?* for *ou?* How should the sign for *ew* invariably open? Why are both of the strokes of the close-diphthong signs made light? How is the fact that both of the elements of the close diphthongs are short indicated by their signs? How is the place of each of the close diphthongs determined? Why are *ī* and *oi* written in the first place? Why are *ou* and *ew* written in the third place? Does *ew* ever begin a syllable?

II. OPEN-DIPHTHONG SIGNS.

§ 98. The open diphthongs are represented by angular marks, whose form, place, and direction are shown by the following illustrations:

ahĭ	auĭ	ēĭ	āĭ	ōĭ	ōĕ	ōà	ōōĭ
ᴠ⟨	ᴧ⟨	<⟨	>⟨	>⟨	>⟨	<⟨	⟨
ꜱi	ꙍi	.ii	ɛi	ꝍi	ꝍe	ꝍa	ꙍi
aye	*drawing*	*deity*	*clayey*	*snowy*	*Owen*	*Noah*	*Louis.*

Examples.— ⌒⌒ sōlfaing (present participle of *sōlfa*, to sing), ⌒ laity, ⌒ being, ⌒ Caughey, ⌒ snowy, ⌒ Owen, ⌒ Noah, ⌒ Louis.

REM. 1. The preceding list of open diphthongs does not include all the open diphthongs of even the English language; but the additional ones—such as ē′à, au′à, ōō′à, ōō′ĕ—are so easily represented by the signs of their elements, that distinct signs for them are not required in the representation of English.

REM. 2. The open-diphthong signs are made heavy on one side or the other, according to the convenience of the writer, to indicate that one of the elements (the first) of the diphthong represented, is long. As the chief difference between *ahĭ* and *ài* (*ī*), or *auĭ* and *oi*, is in respect to the quantity of their elements, this fact is indicated by a corresponding difference between their signs in respect of the heaviness of their strokes. Turn to the Phonographic Alphabet, and compare the signs for *ahĭ* and *ai*; *auĭ* and *oi*.

CONCURRENT VOWELS WRITTEN WITH SEPARATE SIGNS.

§ 99. When two vowels occurring together are represented by separate signs, that which is heard next before or after the consonant should be written nearest to the consonant-sign; thus, ᴠ⟨ iota, ᴠ⟨ idea.

REM. 1. The open diphthongs presented in the preceding section *may* be repre-

---

§ 98. How are the open diphthongs represented? What, as shown by the illustration, is the place and direction of ahĭ? auĭ? ēĭ? āĭ? ōĭ? oĕ? ōà? ōōĭ? What is the place of ahĭ? auĭ? ēĭ? āĭ? ōĭ? ōĕ? ōà? ōōĭ? Write 'solfaing, being, deity, Caughey, Ow′en, No′ah, Go′a, Geno′a, Louis, la′ity, snowy.' [Rem.] Does this list of open diphthongs include all the open diphthongs in the English language? If not, give some words containing other open diphthongs. How may the additional open diphthongs be represented? Why is one stroke of the signs for the open diphthongs made heavy? Which stroke should be made heavy? How does the sign for *ahĭ* differ from that for *ī*? How does the sign for *auĭ* differ from that for *oi*?

§ 99. When two vowels occurring together are to be represented by separate signs, how are they written so as to determine which is to be read first? Which vowel is written nearest the consonant-stroke? [Rem.] May the open diphthongs be represented, in accordance with this principle, by the signs of their elements; thus, ⌣. Noah.

REM. 2. When two vowels occur together between two consonants, one should be written to each consonant-sign, if that can be done conveniently; thus, ⤳ vowel, ⤳ poem; otherwise, both should be written to the same consonant-sign; thus, ⎰ duel, ⎰ towel.

§ 100. *Names of the Diphthong-Signs.*—The diphthong-signs should be named by the *sounds* they represent, and not "long ī, owe-eye, owe-you, ē-double-you, ā-aitch-eye, ā-you-eye," etc. .

CERTAIN DIPHTHONG-SIGNS JOINED.

§ 101. When the junction would be easy, initial *ī* or *oi* may be joined to a following stroke, (b) and *ou* or *iu* (*ew*), to a preceding one; thus, ⎰ eyed, ⌒ oil, ⟍ bŏw, ⎯ cue.

WORD-SIGNS AND CONTRACTIONS.

1. DIPHTHONG WORD-SIGNS.

§ 102. The signs for *ahĭ*, *ī*, and *ou* are employed as signs for the following words:

v	v	·v	ʌ
-----	-----	......	
ay, aye	I, eye	[high]	how.

REM. 1. The sign for *eye* may be joined to Zee for *eyes;* to Dee for *eyed;* and to Ing for *eying.*

REM. 2. No confusion results from writing *high* the same as *eye*, that is, without the h-dot. (b) The *ī* may be joined to En-Iss for *highness;* to Tee for *height;* to Ar for *higher.* (c) The first stroke of the *ī* may be joined to Lay for *highly.*

---

sented by the signs of their elements, in accordance with this principle? Write, in accordance with this principle, the words 'No'ah, Go'a, Owen.' When two vowels occur together between two consonants, how should they be written? When they can not be conveniently divided between the two consonants how should they be written? Write 'vowel, poem, duel, towel.'

§ 100. How should the diphthong-signs be named?

§ 101. When may *ī* or *oi* be joined to a following stroke? When may *ou* or *iu* (*ew*) be joined to a preceding stroke? Join the diphthongs in writing 'eyed, eyes, eying, height, highness (§ 102, Rem. 2), oily, ire, ivy, vow, Dow, bough, cue.'

§ 102. For what word is *ahĭ* employed as a sign? What words are represented by *ī?* How is *high* represented? What word is represented by the sign for *ou?* [Rem.] Write *eyes, eyed, eying.* How may *high* be written? Write *highness*—

Rᴇᴍ. 3. The word *ay*, or *aye*, when signifying *yes, yea, certainly*, is pronounced *ah'ĭ*. (*b*) The word *aye*, signifying *always, ever*, is pronounced *ā*. This may be written thus, •⌴ (*c*) Ahĭ may be joined to Zee for *ayes*.

Rᴇᴍ. 4. *Position of Aye and I.*—The signs for these words, as indicated above, should be written in the first position (§ 39, 1 *a*); that is, with double-line paper, so that they will barely touch the lower side of the upper line; with single-line paper, so that their tops will just touch an imaginary line running, at the height of Tee, above the line of writing.

ABBREVIATED ĭ JOINED.

§ 103. The pronoun *I* is sometimes joined to a following word, by one stroke of the sign, written, according to convenience, in the direction of Pee, Tee, or Chay ; thus, ⌒······ I am, | I do, (I think.

Rᴇᴍ. The reporter does, and the practiced writer of the Corresponding Style may, join *I* to a *preceding* word, or between two words, by one stroke of the sign, written, according to convenience, in the direction of Tee or Kay ; thus, ⌐······ if I, ⌐ may I.

2. ᴄᴏɴᴛʀᴀᴄᴛɪᴏɴs ᴡɪᴛʜ ᴅɪᴘʜᴛʜᴏɴɢs.

§ 104. A single stroke of the signs for *ĭ*, *ou*, and *ew* may be joined to the phonographs Lay and En for the following words :

✓······

highly, I will   now   new, knew.

Rᴇᴍ. 1. *Highly* should be written in the first position (see § 39, 1, *a*) ; *now* and *new*, in the second (see § 39, 2).

Rᴇᴍ. 2. *Contraction and Word-Sign.*—For the sake of distinction, the term Contraction is employed to denote an imperfect representation consisting of two or more strokes (whether consonant or vowel strokes) ; while the term Word-Sign is applied to an imperfect representation containing but a single stroke, with or without a hook, loop, or circle. Hence, the imperfect representations for *highly, now*, and *new* are contractions ; while those of *I, how, subject, this is*, etc., are word-signs.

---

higher—height—highly. How should you write *ay*, or *aye*, signifying *yes, certainly ?* How should you write *aye* when it signifies *always, ever ?* Write *ayes* (the plural of *aye*). What is the position of the signs for *ay* and *eye ?*

§ 103. How is the pronoun *I* sometimes expressed in connection with a following word ? In such cases, in what direction is the single stroke written ? [Rem.] In what direction is the abbreviated ĭ written, when *I* is joined to a preceding word ? Write, in accordance with the principles of this section, ' I do, I shall, I wish, I am, if I, had I, shall I, may I.'

§ 104. What is the contraction for *highly ?* for *now ?* for *new* or *knew ?* [Rem.] In what position should *highly* be written ? In what position should *now* and *new* be written ? What is denoted by the term Contraction ? What is denoted by the term Word-Sign ? Is the sign for *now* a contraction or a word-sign ? If it is a contraction, how is it determined to be such ? Are the signs for *I* and *how* word-signs or contractions ? If word-signs, how are they known to be such ?

METHOD OF PLACING VOWELS BETWEEN CONSONANT STROKES.

§ 105. Vowels, whether simple or compound, occurring between two consonant-strokes, are written thus:

      1. ALL *first-place*, and
         LONG *second-place*, vowels are written
         AFTER the first consonant.

Examples.— beam, king, tick, ball, doll, mire, boil, make, roam.

      2. ALL *third-place*, and
         SHORT *second-place*, vowels are written
         BEFORE the second consonant.

Examples.— car, bat, rouge, rook, rude, pull, neck, love.

§ 106. In other words—

1. *First-place Vowels* are written after the first consonant.

2. *Second-place Vowels* when *long* are written after the first consonant; when *short*, before the second consonant. The length of a second-place vowel is thus determined by *position*, if it should not be indicated by *size*.

3. *Third-place Vowels* are written before the second consonant.

REM. The object of this rule is to insure uniformity of writing and to avoid the ambiguity which has been found to result frequently from its non-observance. The effect of the rule is to take the vowel from the angles, where it would be doubtful with what stroke it should be read. If in writing *rack*, for example, the vowel were to be placed after the Ray; thus, *rack;* instead of before Kay, as the rule would require, it would be doubtful whether the vowel, unless written with great care, should be read as ă after Ray, or as ĭ after Kay. But, on the other hand, the strict observance of the rule would, in some cases, bring the vowel into an angle, and thus result in the very ambiguity which the rule generally avoids. Hence, the following rule.

---

§§ 105, 106. Repeat the rule for placing vowels between two consonant-strokes. Where, in such case, should you write the first-place vowels? the long second-place vowels? the short second-place vowels? all third-place vowels? When occurring between two consonant-strokes, to which stroke should ĕ be written? If written after the first stroke, why? To which should *au* or ŏ be written? Why? Should *ah* be written after the first or before the second? and why? Should ĕ or ŭ be written after the first stroke or before the second? If before the second, why? Should ā or ō be written after the first stroke or before the second? If after the first, why? [Rem.] What is the object of this rule? What is the effect of the rule? If, in writing *rack*, the vowel were placed after Ray instead of before **Kay**, how would the vowel be liable to be read, unless written with great care? Would not the observance of the rule in some cases result in ambiguity?

§ 107. Occasionally, in writing words of more than one syllable, greater clearness will result from a non-observance of the rules relating to the first-place and third-place vowels; as in ⟋⟍— arsenic, ⟍⟍ calmly.

REM. The parts of compound words should be vocalized the same, if possible, as when separate, even though this should require the violation of the rule of § 105. For instance, in vocalizing En-Zee for *uneasy*, it seems better to place ē before Zee rather than after En, because, by so doing, we secure the natural syllabication of the word; thus, *un-easy*.

CAUTION.

§ 108. In such words as ⌐ task, ⌐ desk, ⌐ dusk, it should be observed that the vowels do not occur between two long consonants; but between two consonants, the second of which is represented by a circle; hence the rule of § 105 does not apply, and the vowels of whatever place must be written by the stroke next which they are heard. If, in these cases, the vowels were placed before the Kay, the words would have to be read *tsăk, dsek, dsuk.* See §§ 56, 61.

DIVIDING CONCURRENT VOWELS BETWEEN TWO STROKES.

§ 109. When two vowels occur between two consonant-strokes, one vowel is written to each consonant, if that can be conveniently done; otherwise, both vowels are written by one; thus, ⟍⟋ poem, ⟋ vowel, but ⟋ duel, ⟋ towel, ⟍⟍ power.

METHOD OF READING WORDS OF SEVERAL CONSONANTS.

§ 110. In reading words composed of more than one consonant-stroke, read the first stroke (with the vowel or vowels beside it, if any) as though it were a single word; then read the next in the same manner; and so on till the word is completed. Thus, ⟋ = ⟋ ăm, ⟋ ĕrĭ, ⟍ kă = America. ⟍ = ⟍ bĭz, ⟍ nĕss = business. ⟍⟍ = ⟍ pŏ, ⟍ lĭ, ⟍ sĭ = pŏ-lĭ-sĭ = policy.

---

§ 107. Does any advantage ever result from the non-observance of the rules for placing the first-place and third-place vowels? [Rem.] How should the parts of compound words be vocalized? Why, in vocalizing En-Zee for *uneasy*, does it seem best to place the ē before the Zee?

§ 108. When only one of the consonants between which a vowel occurs is represented by a stroke, how must the vowels be written? Where must the vowel of *dusk* be written? of *task?* of *desk?*

§ 109. How are two vowels occurring between two consonant-strokes to be written? In case they can not be conveniently divided between the two strokes, how should they be written?

§ 110. What method of reading is recommended in reading words composed of

REM. 1. It will be of very great advantage to the student to adhere strictly to this method of reading, for by it the longest words may be read as easily as words having but a single consonant.

REM. 2. CAUTION.—Do not acquire the pernicious habit of reading a portion of a word and 'guessing' the remainder. Do nothing by guess-work. Shirk no labor requisite for advancement in knowledge; determine to enjoy the pleasure of overcoming the obstacles to your progress.

PREFIXES AND AFFIXES.

PREFIXES 'CON' OR 'COM' AND 'ACCOM.'

§ 111. A light dot placed at the commencement of a word signifies *con* or *com; (b)* a heavy dot, *accom;* thus, ⟨ conscience, ⟨ commit, ⟨ accommodate, ⟨ accompany.

REM. 1. The writer should accustom himself to writing the signs for these prefixes before commencing the remainder of the word.

REM. 2. The practiced reporter usually omits the signs for *con, com,* or *accom;* and experiences no difficulty therefrom in reading his notes.

AFFIXES ING, INGS.

§ 112. The affix *ing* may be expressed by a light dot at the end of a word; *(b)* the affix *ings*, by a heavy dot; thus, ⟨ dying, ⟨ doings. *(c)* Instead of the heavy dot, Ing-Iss, ⟨, is generally employed, when it can be conveniently joined; thus, ⟨ sayings.

REM. The dot should not be employed for *ing* or *ings* when it is not an affix; that is, when a complete word does not remain when *ing* or *ings* is omitted. Hence the dot must not be employed for *ing-s* in *ring, sing, kings, wings.* *(b)* As a general rule, the affix *ing, when it forms part of a noun,* is best written with the stroke Ing, when it can be conveniently joined; as in *a casing, the rising, an etching,* etc.

---

more than one consonant-stroke? [Rem.] What is the advantage of the method recommended?

§ 111. How is the prefix *com* and *con* denoted? What is indicated by a heavy dot at the commencement of a word? by a light dot? In writing a word with a prefix *con, com,* or *accom,* which should be written first—the prefix? or the remainder of the word? What is said as to the omission of these prefixes by the reporter?

§ 112. How may the affix *ing* be expressed? What is denoted by a heavy dot at the end of a word? by a light dot? When is *ings* represented by Ing-Iss? Write *sayings.* [Rem.] When should not the dot be employed for *ing* or *ings?* Should the dot be employed for *ing* in *sing, ring, king?* How can *ing* be determined to be an affix? What is said with regard to writing *ing* when it forms a portion of a noun? Give some nouns ending in the affix *ing.*

-ING THE.

§ 113. The affix *ing* and a following *the* may be expressed by writing the tick for *the*—namely, ⟍ or ⟋ according to convenience, in the place of the dot for *ing*; thus, ⟍ showing the, ⟍ passing the.

REM. Of the two directions of the tick for *the*, that one should be chosen which is most variant from the direction of the preceding stroke.

-ING A-N-D.

§ 114. The affix *ing* and a following *a, an,* or *and*, may be expressed by writing the tick for *a-n-d*—namely, ⟍ or ⟋ according to convenience—in the place of the dot for *ing*; thus, ⟍ eating a-n-d, ⟍ giving a-n-d.

REM. Of the two directions of the tick for *a-n-d*, that one should be chosen which is most variant from the direction of the preceding stroke.

---

§ 113. How may the tick *the* be written to express a preceding *ing*? How, for this purpose, should the tick for *the* be written? Write *showing the, passing the, doing the, giving the.* [Rem.] What direction of the tick is best for *ing the*?

§ 114. How may the tick for *a-n-d* be written to express a preceding *ing*? Write *eating a-n-d, giving a-n-d.* [Rem.] What direction of the tick is best for *ing a-n-d*?

DIFFERENT SIGNS AND DIRECTIONS.

§ 115. BY providing two or more signs for several sounds, and by allowing certain signs to be written in different directions, Phonography not only avoids many difficult forms and junctions which would otherwise be required, but affords opportunity, in many cases, for distinguishing, by difference of outline merely between words of the same consonants, which must otherwise be written alike.

I. DIFFERENT MODES OF EXPRESSING W AND Y.

1. W AND Y EXPRESSED BY STROKES.

§ 116. The strokes for *w* and *y* are ⟍, ⌒; which the student will be assisted in remembering by observing that they are respectively portions of the capital scripts for

W   and   Y.

REM. These strokes, if named by syllables, should be called Way, Yay. See § 14.

USES OF THE WAY-STROKE.

§ 117. The Way-stroke is usually employed in the following cases:

1. In all words except *we*, in which *w* is the only consonant; as in ⟍ weigh, ⟍ woe.

2. When initial *w* is followed by *s;* as in ⟍ weighs, ⟍ waste, ⟍ wasp.

3. When initial *sw* are the only consonants, or when they are followed by any other consonant (except *r*) which can be conveniently joined to the Way-stroke; as in ⟍ sway, ⟍ sways, ⟍ sweep, ⟍ swallow, ⟍ swim, ⟍ swing.

4. When *w* follows an initial vowel; as in ⟍ awoke.

---

§ 115. What advantages does Phonography secure by providing several signs for certain sounds, and by writing several signs in different directions?

§ 116. What are the stroke-signs for *w* and *y?* How may they be fixed in the memory? [Rem.] What is the syllable-name of the stroke for *w?* for *y?*

§ 117. In what cases is Way employed? Write 'weigh, woe, weighs, waist, wasp; sway, sways, sweep, swallow, swim, swing; awoke, awake.'

USES OF THE YAY-STROKE.

§ 118. The Yay-stroke is employed principally in the follcwing cases :

1. In all words, except *ye* and *you*, in which *y* is the only consonant; as in ⌐⋅ yea, ⌐ yew.

2. In the words *yes, yeas, yeast, yews*, and a few others in which initial *y* is followed by *s*.

3. When *y* follows an initial vowel; as in ⟨ oyer.

---

2. W AND Y EXPRESSED BY BRIEF SIGNS JOINED.

§ 119 For convenience and speed of writing, brief signs have been provided for the sounds of *w* and *y*, namely, c or ɔ for *w*, and ᴜ or ᴧ for *y*.

REM. For convenience of conversation, and to avoid the injurious practice of calling these signs Double-Yoo and Wy, the names Wĕh and Wŭh have been provided for the brief signs of *w*; and Yĕh and Yŭh for the brief sign of *y*. They may be called Brief Way and Brief Yay, though these names do not indicate the direction of the curvature of the signs. See § 14, Rems. 1, 2.

JOINING THE BRIEF WAY.

§ 120. The brief Way may be joined at the beginning of consonant-strokes—

1. *As a Hook*—to Lay, El, Ray, Em, or En ; thus, ⌐ wail, ⟨ wore, ⌐ we may, ⌣ wine ; in which case it is called the Way-Hook.

2. *At an Angle*—to all other letters ; thus, ⋅| wet, ⋅| weighed, ⌐ wedge, — week, ⌐ woke, ⌐ wave.

REM. When brief Way is joined at an angle with a stroke, either Wĕh or Wŭh

---

§ 118. Repeat the rule for the use of Yay. Are *ye* and *you* written with Yay ? Write 'yea, yew, yes, yeast, yews, yeas, ōyer.'

§ 119. Make the brief sign for *w* and *y*. For what purpose are these signs provided ? [Rem.] What are the syllable-names of the brief signs for *w* and *y* ? What may they be called besides Wĕh and Yĕh ?

§ 120. How may brief Way be joined at the beginning of Lay ? El ? Ray ? Em ? En ? How may it be joined to all other letters ? Join it to Tee, Jay, Ef, Kay, Thee, Ing. Write 'wail, wine, wore, wear, wire.' Write 'weave, wedge, weighed, wake, watch, web.' [Rem.] When brief Way is joined at an angle, with reference to what is the choice of Wĕh or Wŭh made ? When brief Way is joined as a hook, may be used, according to convenience of joining. (*b*) Brief Way joined as a hook takes the direction of the stroke.

REM. 2. Em, En, Lay, and Ray in connection with the Way-hook may be named Wem, Wen, Wel, Wer.

JOINING THE BRIEF YAY.

§ 121. The brief Yay must always be joined at an angle; thus, ‿ yawn, ⸢ Yale, ·⸥ Yates, ⸗ yore, ⌐ yoke, ⸜ yellow, ⸜ yarrow.

REM. When brief Yay is joined, either Yĕh or Yŭh may be chosen, according to convenience of joining.

METHOD OF READING BRIEF WAY OR YAY JOINED TO A CONSONANT-STROKE.

§ 122. In reading a consonant-stroke with a brief Way or Yay joined at the beginning, read the Way or Yay first, and next, the consonant-stroke with the vowel or vowels beside it, precisely as though no Way or Yay were joined; thus, ·⸥ = w-āt = weight; ⸝⸍ = y-aul = yawl; ⸝⸍ = w-ērĭ = weary.

USES OF THE WAY-HOOK.

§ 123. The Way-hook should usually be employed in the following cases:

1. For *w* at the commencement of a word, when *l*, *r*, *m*, or *n* is the second consonant; as in § 120, 1.

2. When initial *sw* is followed by *r*; thus, ⸝⸍ swore.

3. Whenever the hook can be conveniently used for *w* between two consonant-strokes, the second of which is Lay, Ray, Em, or En; thus, ⸡ twain, ⸠ Edwin, ⸝⸍ acquire.

USES OF THE BRIEF WAY JOINED AT AN ANGLE.

§ 124. The brief Way joined at an angle is employed—

1. Usually for an initial *w* followed by any consonant except *l*, *r*, *m*, *n*, or final *s* or *z*; as in § 120, 2.

2. Occasionally in the middle of a word; as in ⸝⸥ unweighed.

---

what direction is given to it? Which is most convenient for joining with Bee—Wĕh or Wŭh? Which is most convenient for joining with Kay? with Ish? with Chay? § 121. How must the brief Yay be joined? Join it to En, Ar, Lay, Ray, Tee, Kay, Em. Write 'yawn, yellow, Yates, yore, yoke, yarrow, yam.' [Rem.] With reference to what is the choice made between Yeh and Yuh, when brief Yay is joined? § 122. Repeat the directions for reading brief Way or Yay joined at the beginning of a consonant-stroke. After the brief Way or Yay has been read, how should the following consonant-stroke and the vowels beside it be read? Write *weight, yawl, weary*. §§ 123, 124. Specify the cases for the use of the Way-hook. Specify the cases for the use of brief Way joined. [Rem.] How may the reporter, without lifting the pen, express the consonants of *sweet, switch*, etc.?

REM. In order to secure the complete consonant-expression of such words as *sweet*, *switch*, without lifting the pen, the reporter may prefix a circle to the brief Way; using, for instance, Iss-Weh-Tee ⸨ as an outline for *sweet*, *sweat*, etc.

USES OF THE BRIEF YAY JOINED.

§ 125. The brief Yay joined to a consonant-stroke is employed to a limited extent for an initial *y* followed by any consonant except final *s* or *z;* as in § 121.

---

3. W AND Y EXPRESSED BY BRIEF SIGNS IN THE VOWEL PLACES.

§ 126. It is occasionally desirable to write the brief Way and Yay, the same as the vowel-signs, beside the consonant-strokes, the following vowel being indicated *without writing it*, according to the method explained in the following sections:

BRIEF WAY WRITTEN IN THE VOWEL-PLACES.

§ 127. *W Followed by Dot, or First-Group, Vowels.*—The particular FIRST-group vowel following *w* may be indicated by writing ⸦ Wĕh (the FIRST part of ⸦\/⸣) in that vowel's place, making this sign *heavy*, if the vowel is long ; *light*, if the vowel is short; thus, ⸠ sweet, ⸝ switch, ⸦ swayed, ⸦ sweat.

§ 128. *W Followed by Dash, or Second-Group, Vowels.*—The particular SECOND-group vowel following *w* may be indicated by writing ⸥ Wŭh (the SECOND part of \/⸠) in that vowel's place, making this sign *heavy*, if the vowel is long ; *light*, if the vowel is short; thus, ⸗— walk, ⸝ watch, ⸥ wooed, ⸥ wood.

---

§ 125. What is said of the use of brief Yay joined?

§ 126. Is brief Way or Yay ever written in the vowel-places? If so written, how is the following vowel indicated?

§ 127. When brief Way is written in the vowel-places, how is it indicated that a first-group, or dot, vowel follows the *w?* What kind of vowel is denoted by Weh written in the vowel-places? If a Weh so written indicates a dot-vowel, how is the particular vowel, as *ē*, *ā*, or *ah*, indicated? How is it indicated that a long or short vowel follows? In what place must Weh be written to indicate that the following vowel is *ē* or *ĭ?* if *ē*, should it be made heavy or light? How should it be made if the following vowel is *ĭ?* Write 'sweet, switch, swayed, sweat.'

§ 128. When brief Way is written in a vowel-place, how is the particular second-group, or dash, vowel following the *w* denoted? Which of Weh or Wuh written in the vowel-places denotes that a dash-vowel follows? In what vowel-place must Wuh be written to indicate a following *au* or *ŏ?* How should it be made when a long dash-vowel follows? when a short dash-vowel follows? Write 'walk, watch, wooed, wood.'

BRIEF YAY WRITTEN IN THE VOWEL-PLACES.

§ 129. *Y Followed by Dot, or First-Group, Vowels.*—The particular FIRST-group vowel following *y* may be indicated by writing ◡ Yĕh (a part of ⌐⌐ in its FIRST, or natural, position) in the place of that vowel, making this sign *heavy*, if the vowel is long; *light*, if the vowel is short; thus, ⌐ year, ⌐ Yale, ⌐ yell, ⌐ yam.

§ 130. *Y Followed by Dash, or Second-Group, Vowels.*—The particular SECOND-group vowel following *y* may be indicated by writing ⌒ Yŭh (a part of *y* in its SECOND, or inverted, position ⌒) in the place of that vowel, making this sign *heavy*, if the vowel is long; *light*, if the vowel is short; thus, ⌒ yore, ⌒ yon, ⌒ young, ⌒ youth, ⌒ unite= yŏŏníte.

§ 131. TABLE SHOWING BRIEF WAY AND YAY WRITTEN IN THE PLACES OF THE DIFFERENT DOT-VOWELS.

Long—								
i	ɛ	ʙ	wi	wɛ	wʙ	yi	yɛ	yʙ
Short—								
i	e	a	wi	we	wa	yi	ye	ya

§ 132. TABLE SHOWING BRIEF WAY AND YAY WRITTEN IN THE PLACES OF THE DIFFERENT DASH-VOWELS.

Long—								
ꞷ	ꬰ	ɯ	wꞷ	wꬰ	wɯ	yꞷ	yꬰ	yɯ
Short—								
o	ꭒ	u	wo	wꭒ	wu	yo	yꭒ	yu

§ 129. How must brief Yay be written to indicate, without writing it, the particular vowel of the first group following the *y?* How must it be written to indicate the particular dash-vowel following the *y?* Which of Yeh or Yuh is used in the vowel-places to indicate dot-vowels? Write 'year, yell, Yale, yam.'

§ 130. Which of Yeh or Yuh written in the vowel-places is employed to indicate a following dash-vowel? How is the particular dash-vowel following Yuh indicated? In what place must Yuh be written to indicate a following *au* or *ŏ?* *ō* or *ŭ?* *ŏŏ* or *ŏŏ?* How should it be made when a long vowel follows? when a short vowel follows? Write 'yore, yon, young, youth, unite.'

§§ 131, 132. Observe how wĕ, wă, wah—yĕ yă, yah, correspond, in respect of their

§ 133. The brief Way and Yay are joined to the optional vowel-signs at an angle ; thus,

<table>
<tr><td>wə</td><td>waː</td><td>wɐ</td><td>wɵ</td></tr>
<tr><td>yə</td><td>yaː</td><td>yɐ</td><td>yɵ</td></tr>
</table>

Rem. When brief Way or Yay is joined to a vowel-sign, either Weh or Wuh, Yeh or Yuh, may be employed, according to convenience of joining.

§ 134. The brief Yay may be joined to the signs for *ī*, *oi*, *ou*, thus :

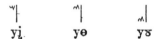

yi̩.   yɵ   yʊ

USE OF THE BRIEF WAY AND YAY DETACHED.

§ 135. (*a*) The brief Way or Yay is usually employed where previous rules (§§ 117, 118, 123–125) would not authorize the use of a stroke, or a brief sign joined. (*b*) Brief Way detached, is usually employed in the following cases:

1. For the sound of *w* between an initial *s* and a following *t, d, ch, j, f,* or *v ;* as in ˹ sweet, ⟋ switch, ◂˹ swayed.

2. For the sound of *w* between two stroke-consonants, if in such case it would not be allowable or convenient to represent it by the Way-hook; thus, ⎰⌐ dwell, ⌐‿ twig, ⎯‿ quake, ⌇‿ quill; but ‿ⱴ acquire, ⌐ Edwin.

YA USED FOR ĬA.

§ 136. The sound of *y* in connection with a vowel so nearly resembles ē or ĭ in a

---

position, with ē, ā, ah. In this respect, compare wĭ, wĕ, wă—yĭ, yĕ, yă, with ĭ, ĕ, ă. Observe also that Weh and Yeh, which are written in the vowel-places to denote a following first-group vowel, have in their names the vowel ĕ, which is *one* of the *first-group* vowels ; while ŭ, one of the second-group vowels, is contained in the names of Wuh and Yuh, which are written in the vowel-places to denote following second-group vowels. Compare, in respect of their position, wau, wŏ, wōō—yau, yō, yōō, with au, ō, ōō ; also, wŏ, wŭ, wŏŏ—yŏ, yŭ, yŏŏ, with ŏ, ŭ, ŏŏ.

§ 133. How are brief Way and Yay joined to the optional vowel-signs? Join brief Way to the signs of the vowels of *air, at, earth,* none. Join brief Yay to the same. [Rem.] Which of Weh or Wuh, Yeh or Yuh, is chosen when brief Way or Yay requires to be joined to a vowel-sign?

§ 134. Join brief Yay with the signs for *ī, oi, ou.*

§ 135. Specify the cases for the employment of brief Way and Yay detached. Write 'sweet, switch, swayed, dwell, twig, quake, quill, acquire, Edwin.'

similar situation, that no confusion, but considerable convenience, is found to result from employing

yă, yŏ, yō, yŭ,' etc.,
for ēă, ĕŏ, ēō, ĕŭ,
or ĭă, ĭŏ, ĭō, ĭŭ, etc.

Hence we may write

Arminyăn	for	Armĭnĭăn
inferyŏr	"	inferĭŏr
thyŏlogy	"	thĕŏlogy
Arabya	"	Arabĭạ
ŏdyŭs	"	odĭous
ōpyate	"	opĭate.

'YOO' DISTINGUISHED FROM 'EW.'

§ 137. The student should carefully distinguish between the different uses, in the common spelling, of *u, eu, ew, ue,* etc. They sometimes represent *iu* (*ew*), a pure diphthong (§ 93), and sometimes represent a combination of a consonant, *y*, with a vowel, ōō or ŏŏ—usually ōō in accented syllables, and ŏŏ in unaccented syllables. To avoid error in these cases, the writer has only to observe a correct pronunciation carefully, and then accurately represent it. Observe and compare the following words:

Ew.	*Yōō.*	*Yŏŏ.*
mute = mewt	union = yōōn'ion	unite = yŏŏnīte'
dew = dew	Ewing = Yōō'ing	nephew = nĕɹ h'yŏŏ
feud = fewd	euphony = yōō'phony	euphonic = yŏŏphon'ic.

REM. 1. The diphthong *ew* never begins a syllable.

REM. 2. *Euphonic Changes from Ew to Yoo, or from Yoo to Ew.*—The pure diphthong *ew* (*iu*) seems to require the primary accent to sustain it; and having lost that in the course of derivation, and having been brought at the beginning of a syllable, it falls into *yoo;* that is, its first element is changed into the closely related consonant *y*. Hence the *ew* (*iu*) of *refuse', repute'* = phonetic *refiuz', repiut',* becomes yoo (yu) when it loses the accent in *ref'use, rep'utable* = phonetic *ref'yus, rep'yutabel.* (*b*) On the other hand, *yoo* seemingly will not admit, except at the beginning of a word, of a primary accent, though it sometimes takes a secondary accent; hence, when, in the course of derivation, it falls under the primary accent, *yoo* becomes *ew* (*iu*), that is, the consonant *y* is changed to the closely related vowel ĭ. Hence the *yoo* (*yu*) of *fu'ture, distrib'ute* = phonetic *fiut'yur, distrib'yut,* becomes *ew* (*iu*) when it comes under the accent in *futu'rity, distribu'tion* = phonetic *fiutiu'riti, distribiu'con.*

---

§ 136. For what may yă, yŏ, etc., be employed? What may be written for *Arminian? inferior? theology? Arabia? odious? opiate?*

§ 137. What is the difference between *ew* and *yoo?* In what kind of syllables does *yōō* occur? *yŏŏ?* What sound is denoted by *u* in *mute?* in *union?* in *unite?* What sound is represented by *ew* in *dew?* in *Ewing?* in *nephew?* What sound is denoted by *eu* in *feud?* in *euphony?* in *euphonic?* [Rem.] Does the diphthong *ew* ever begin a syllable? What change does *ew* undergo when it loses the primary accent and comes at the beginning of a syllable? Give some examples of such change. What change does *yoo* suffer when it takes a primary accent? Give some examples of such change. Does *yoo* ever take the secondary accent?

4. W SOMETIMES EXPRESSED BY A RIGHT ANGLE.

§ 138. It is sometimes convenient to indicate that *w* is prefixed to

$$^{\text{v}}|\ i, \qquad ^{\wedge}|\ \Theta, \qquad _{\wedge}|\ \mathbf{8},$$

by opening their signs to right angles; thus:

$$^{\llcorner}|\ w\underline{i}, \qquad ^{\urcorner}|\ w\Theta, \qquad _{\urcorner}|\ w\mathbf{8},$$

as in $\llcorner$ twice, $^{\urcorner}\ \diagdown$ quoif.

REM. Instead of employing the angular sign for initial *wi*, as in *wife, wide*, etc., the reporter will find it more convenient to omit the expression of ī, and to represent the *w* by a brief Way joined to the following consonant.

Wī, Yă, AND Yoo JOINED.

§ 139. Whenever the junction would be convenient, it is allowable to join

1. *Initial Wī*—to a following stroke; thus, $]$ wide.

2. *Final Yă or Yoo*—to a preceding stroke; thus, $\frown$ ammonia, $\diagdown$ nephew.

WORD-SIGNS AND CONTRACTIONS.

§ 140. LIST OF WAY AND YAY WORD-SIGNS.

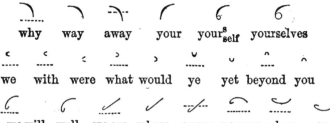

why	way	away	your	your$_{\text{self}}^{\text{s}}$	yourselves

we	with	were	what	would	ye	yet	beyond	you

while, we will	well	we are	where	aware	we may	when	one

REM. 1. No difficulty will be experienced in distinguishing between *while* and *we will*, notwithstanding both are represented by the same sign.

---

§ 138. How is it convenient at times to indicate that *w* is prefixed to *i, oi, ou?* Write 'twī, twoi, twou.' Write 'twice, quoif.' [Rem.] What, for the reporter, is the best mode of representing initial *w* followed by ī?

§ 139. Specify the cases for joining wī, yă, and yoo.

§ 140. Cover the word-signs with a card, and write the signs for the words below. Cover the sign-words, and speak the words denoted by the signs above. [Rem.] Are *while* and *we will* confusible if written by the same sign? How does the reporter write *with me* or *with my?* How does he write *with him? we know?*

REM. 2. The reporter employs Wem above the line for *with me* or *with my* as well as for *we may ;* on the line for *with him.* (*b*) He also writes Wen above the line for *we know* as well as for *when.*

REM. 3. *You* is generally pronounced yŏŏ, and is therefore properly represented by the sign of that sound. (*b*) This sign made heavy—in other words, the sign for yŏŏ ⌒ may be employed as a correct representation of this word when emphasized.

§ 141. LIST OF WORDS REPRESENTED BY WAY AND YAY.

aware	where
away	while
beyond	why
one	with
way	with me—§ 140, R. 2.
we	with my—§ 140, R. 2.
we may	would
we will	ye
we are	yet
well	you—§ 140, R. 3.
we know—§ 140, R. 2, *b.*	your
were	yours
what	yourself
when	yourselves

§ 142. LIST OF CONTRACTIONS.

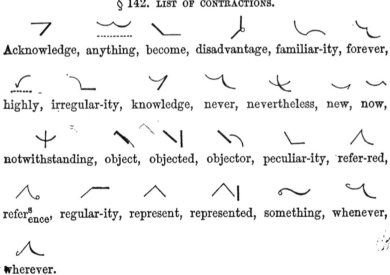

Acknowledge, anything, become, disadvantage, familiar-ity, forever,

highly, irregular-ity, knowledge, never, nevertheless, new, now,

notwithstanding, object, objected, objector, peculiar-ity, refer-red,

refer$_{ence}^{s}$, regular-ity, represent, represented, something, whenever,

wherever.

§ 141. Write the signs for the words in this section, till the words instantly sug-gest the correct word-signs.

§ 142. Cover the phonographic characters, and write the contractions for the words below. Next cover the words, and read the phonographic contractions. [Rem.] What is the contraction for *object ?* What is said of the omission of the

REM. 1. *Object.*—The sign given above for *object* is 'ŏb.' The reporter always omits the vowel; and it may be safely omitted even in the Corresponding Style.

REM. 2. No confusion arises from having a contracted outline stand for two words, as *regular* and *regularity;* for the context at once indicates whether the outline should be read as an adjective or as a noun.

REM. 3. *Derivatives.*—Signs for *regularly, irregularly, peculiarly,* and *familiarly* may be formed by writing Lay near the end of the last stroke of the signs for *regular,* etc. Derivatives from other contracted words may be written in accordance with § 40, Rem. 2. (*b*) *References* is written by enlarging the circle of *reference.*

§ 143. LIST OF WORDS REPRESENTED BY CONTRACTED OUTLINES.

Acknowledge	object—§ 142, Rem. 1.
anything	objected
become	objector
disadvantage	peculiar
familiar	peculiarity
familiarity	refer
forever	reference
highly—§ 104.	referred
irregular	refers
irregularity	regular
knowledge	regularity
never	represent
nevertheless	represented
new—§ 104.	something
now—§ 104.	whenever
notwithstanding	wherever

II. DIFFERENT MODES OF EXPRESSING H—ASPIRATION.

§ 144. The word Aspiration (derived from the Latin *Aspiro, to blow*) signifies the forcible expulsion of the breath denoted by the letter *h* in *heat, hope. Secondarily,* it denotes the marking of such action by means of determined signs. To *aspirate a vowel* is to sound *h* before it, or to write the sign of aspiration before a vowel-sign. In Phonography, four different methods of denoting aspiration are employed: 1. By a stroke. 2. By a light dot. 3. By a tick. 4. By widening a Way-hook. The different modes of aspiration may be treated under three heads: 1. Aspiration of the Simple and Double Vowels. 2. Aspiration of the Way-Stroke. 3. Aspiration of the Brief Way.

vowel of this sign? Does any confusion result from using Ray-Gay for *regular* and *regularity?* Why not?

§ 143. Repeatedly write the contracted outlines for the words in the list of § 143.

§ 144. What is signified by the word *Aspiration?* From what is it derived? What does it signify secondarily? What is meant by the *aspiration of a vowel?* How many different methods of aspiration are employed in Phonography?

1. ASPIRATION OF SIMPLE VOWELS AND DIPHTHONGS.

§ 145. The simple vowels and the diphthongs may be aspirated by writing a light dot before them; thus, ⁀\ hear, ＿: hack, ·— hawk, ·| hide. See § 101.

MANNER OF PLACING THE HAY-DOT.

§ 146. The Hay-dot should be written beside the dash-vowels; thus, ⁀\ hope, ‿⌒ hall. (b) It should be so written by the dot-vowels that a line drawn through the two dots shall be at right angles with the consonant; thus, ·| not :| for *head;* ·\ heap.

Rem. 1. The Hay-dot may be distinguished by name from the stroke, by calling it Hēh or Hetch; (b) but when reading phonography, it should always be read in connection with the following vowel; thus, hē, hā, hah, etc.

Rem. 2. The Hay-dot is never mistaken for a short dot-vowel sign, for a short vowel never occurs in English before another vowel in the same place.

Rem. 3. The reporter almost invariably omits the Hay-dot, even when he deems it necessary to write the vowel following it. The writer of the Corresponding Style may, without endangering legibility, omit the dot in writing the words *his, has, high, highly, height,* and a few other similar words.

Rem. 4. *H-Tick.*—It is sometimes convenient, especially in the Reporting Style, to represent *h* by a joined tick, written, according to convenience, in the direction of Pee or Chay; thus, / hedge, ⁀\ horse, ‿ hem. (b) This mode of writing *h,* as will appear from a subsequent section, is sometimes employed for the aspiration of the Way-stroke; thus, ⁀\ hwā = whey.

Rem. 5. *The H-Tick used for He in the Reporting Style.*—(a) In the Reporting Style, *he* is represented by a tick, on the line, written downward in the direction of Pee, but usually upward or downward in the direction of Chay; thus, / he, ‿ he may, ⌒ he will. (b) When joined to a preceding word, it assumes the position required for the junction; thus, ⌣ for he, ⌐ and he, ⌐ but he, ‿ is he, ⌐ or he. (c) Practice shows that the different uses of this tick for *he* and *the* can be readily distinguished.

---

§ 145. How are the simple vowels and the diphthongs aspirated? Write 'hide, hack, hawk, Hague.'

§ 146. How should the Hay-dot be written by the dot-vowels? by the dash-vowels? Write 'hall, hop, head, heap, heat, hitch, hack.' [Rem.] How is the Hay-dot distinguished by name from the Hay-stroke? How should it be read? How is Heh distinguished from a short dot-vowel? What is said of the omission of Heh by the reporter? From what words may it be omitted by the writer of the Corresponding Style? Is *h* ever conveniently written by a tick? How is the h-tick joined to the following stroke? Write 'hedge, hem, horse, whey.' How is *he* represented in the Reporting Style?

2. ASPIRATION OF THE WAY-STROKE.

§ 147. There are two modes of aspirating the Way-stroke:

1. By a small tick joined at the beginning; thus, ⌐ whey, ⤳ awhile.

2. By a Hay-dot placed before the following vowel; thus, ⌐˙ whey.

REM. 1. This last method of indicating whispered *w* corresponds precisely with the method of the common orthography, in which the aspiration of *w* is denoted by placing *h* after it; as in *when, where.*

REM. 2. The second mode of aspirating *w* is to be preferred by those intending to acquire the Reporting Style.

---

3. ASPIRATION OF THE BRIEF WAY.

§ 148. The brief Way is aspirated—

1. *When Written in the Vowel's Place,*—by placing a dot before it; thus, ˙\ whip, ˙| wheat, (˙| white).

2. *When Joined at an Angle,*—(*a*) either by prefixing the h-tick, (*b*) or by placing a dot before the following vowel; thus, ˙| *or* ˙| wheat.

3. *When Joined as a Hook,*—(*a*) either by placing the Hay-dot before the following vowel, (*b*) or by making the hook heavy; thus ˙ʃ or ˙ʃ for *wheel,* (*c*) or by prefixing the h-tick; thus, ⌣ whine, ⌐ whim.

REM. 1. When initial brief Way is to be aspirated, and it can not be joined as a hook, it is best, in the Corresponding style, to write it in the vowel's place. (*b*) But since in the Reporting Style the aspiration of the *w* may be omitted, the reporter may conveniently, in almost all cases, join an initial brief Way to the following stroke. He will, for instance, write Weh-Tee for *wheat* or *white;* Weh-Tee-Lay for *Whateley* or *whitlow;* Wuh-Gay for *Whig.*

---

§ 147. How is the Way-stroke aspirated? Write *whey,* aspirating Way with the tick. Write *whey,* aspirating Way with the Hay-dot. Where is the Hay-dot written when employed to aspirate Way? [Rem.] Which mode of aspirating *w* is to be preferred by those intending to acquire the Reporting Style? To what in the common orthography does the second mode of aspiration correspond?

§ 148. How is the brief Way aspirated when written in the vowel-places? Write, with brief Way detached, the following words: 'whip, wheat, white, Whig, whitlow.'——How is the brief Way aspirated when joined at an angle? Write 'whip, wheat, Whig,' with the brief Way joined, and aspirated by the h-tick. Write the same words again, aspirating the brief Way by the Hay-dot before the vowel.——How is the brief Way aspirated when joined as a hook? Apply these different modes in writing 'whine, whim, wheel, whale, wherry, whence.' [Rem.] How is it best, in the Corresponding Style, to write an aspirated brief Way when it is initial and can not be joined as a hook? How is it written, in such cases, in the Reporting Style? How

REM. 2. The Way-hook on Lay and Ray is aspirated conveniently by making the hook heavy. (*b*) But the Way-hook on Em and En is aspirated most conveniently by writing a dot before the following vowel, or by prefixing the h-tick. (*c*) In either case, however, the reporter makes no attempt to indicate aspiration ; (*d*) and reporting habits and forms in this respect, will be most easily attained by those writers of the Corresponding Style who either adopt the plan of aspirating the Way-hook by writing a dot before the following vowel, or who accustom themselves to dispensing with every mode of expressing aspiration in these cases.

REM. 3. *Wī, Woi, Wou.*—The angular signs for *wī, woi, wou* may be aspirated by writing the Hay-dot before them, as in § 148, 1.

USES OF THE HAY-STROKE.

149. The Hay-stroke is used principally in the following cases :

1. In all words except *who, high, how,* in which *h* is the only consonant, or the only one that can be conveniently represented by a stroke; as in ⟋ Ohio, ⟋ hay, ⟋ ah ! ⟋ eh ! ⟋ Yahoo.

2. Next following an initial vowel; as in ⟋ ahead.

3. For initial *h* preceding a consonant which is followed by a vowel; as in ⟨ haughty.

4. When *s* follows an initial *h ;* thus, ⟋ house, ⟋ hasten.

5. When *p, t, ch,* or *k* follows *h* in the past tense of monosyllabic verbs; as in *hoped, heated, heeded, hedged, hooked.*

REM. 1. *Ah ! Eh !*—As previously remarked, when *ah ! eh !* are forcibly uttered, the aspirate is heard following the vowels, and is therefore properly indicated; otherwise, the Hay-stroke serves merely as a nominal consonant.

REM. 2. *H* followed by *p, t, ch,* or *k* in the *present* tense of such monosyllabic verbs as *hope, heap, heat, heed,* is represented by a Hay-dot. The stroke is employed in the cases mentioned in subsection 5 for the purpose of availing, without vocalization, of the advantage of the halving principle (to be subsequently explained).

does the reporter write *wheat, Whig, Whateley?* What is the best mode of aspirating the Way-hook on Ray and Lay? on Em and En? Is it the practice of the reporter to indicate the aspiration of the brief Way? How may the angular sign for *wī, woi, wou* be aspirated?

§ 149. How is the aspirate expressed in words containing no other consonant? Specify the other cases for the use of the Hay-stroke. Write 'Ohio, ah ! hay, eh ! Yahoo, ahead, haughty, house, hasten.' [Rem.] When the aspirate is not pronounced in *ah !* and *eh !* what purpose does the Hay-stroke serve? How is *h* represented in the present tense of such verbs as *heap, heat?* Why is it represented by the Hay-stroke in the past tense of such verbs?

III. DIFFERENT MODES OF EXPRESSING S AND Z.

§ 150. Directions for the use of several different modes of representing S and Z have been given in preceding sections of the Compendium.

See §§ 58–60 for Rules for representing S and Z at the beginning of
a word.

See §§ 63 and 64 for Rules for representing S and Z at the end of a
word.

See §§ 65 and 66 for the uses of the large circle.

IV. DIFFERENT MODES OF REPRESENTING R.

§ 151. The sound of *r*, as previously explained, is represented by
two different signs, namely, ⟍ Ar, ╱ Ray. The means of distinguishing Ray from Chay were pointed out in § 12, 4. It now only
remains to specify the cases for the use of each of these signs.

USES OF AR—THE DOWNWARD SIGN FOR R.

§ 152. Ar is usually employed in the following cases:

1. For *r* following an initial vowel; as in ⟍ ark; except when the junction
of Ar with a following consonant would be comparatively difficult, in such words,
for instance, as *arsenic, arch, arrayed, earth, erroneous.*

2. At the end of words—
Except—

(*a*) After Em or Ith; as in ╱ mar, ╱ Thayer.

(*b*) Sometimes when the derivative would require Ray; as in ⟍ *future,*
from which ⟍ *futurity* is derived.

(*c*) When Ar would run too far below the line; as in ╱ Shakspeare.

USES OF RAY—THE UPWARD SIGN FOR R.

§ 153. Ray is usually employed in the following cases:

1. For *r* next preceding a final vowel; as in ╱ ray, ╲ fury.

2. For *r* at the beginning of a word; as in ╱ race, ╱╲ reap; unless the

------

§ 150. Answer the questions on §§ 58–60; 63–64; 65–66.

§ 151. What are the two strokes for *r*? How is Ray distinguished from Chay?

§ 152. Specify the cases for the use of Ar. What are the exceptions to the use of
Ar at the end of words? Write 'ark, arsenic, arch, urge, arrayed, earth, erroneous,
mar, Thayer, future, futurity, Shakspeare, bear, fear, dare, jeer, gore, shore, lore,
ôyer.'

§ 153. Specify the cases for the use of Ray. Write 'rays, fury, race, reap, roam, second consonant is *m*, or some other consonant or consonants which can not be easily joined to Ray; as in 〰 roam, 〰 resume.

3. For *r* next following an initial vowel when Ar could not be so conveniently employed; as in ⟋ arch, ⟋ urge, ⟋ arrayed, ⟋ earth.

4. For final *r* in the cases specified at paragraphs *a*, *b*, and *c* under § 152, 2.

5. (*a*) For both of two *r's* at the end of a word; as in ⟋ rare, ⟋ rarer, ⟋ terror; (*b*) unless Ar is required for the first *r* ; when the second is represented by Ray or Ar, according to preceding rules; thus, 〰 aurora—see § 153, 1; 〰 error—see § 152, 2.

V. DIFFERENT DIRECTIONS OF THE STROKE FOR L.

§ 154. As previously explained, the stroke for *l* may be written upward or downward. The sign written upward is called Lay ; El, when written downward. The best direction in any particular instance may usually be determined by the following specifications.

USES OF LAY.

§ 155. Lay should be employed in the following cases:

1. Always for *l* when it is the only stroke-consonant in the word; thus, ⟋ ale, ⟋ less.

2. For *l* at the commencement of a word; as in 〰 like, 〰 lime; unless El would secure an easier junction with a following consonant; as in the words *lion, long, lessen.*

3. Usually for *l* next preceding a final vowel; as in 〰 folly, 〰 rely ; unless it is preceded by some letter after which El is more conveniently written than Lay; as in *only.*

4. Usually for final *l;* as in 〰 pull, 〰 ball, 〰 doll, 〰 quill; unless preceded by some letter or letters, as Ef, Iss-Kay, or En, after which El is written more conveniently than Lay.

REM. En requires El after it in order to prevent the change of the circular movement of the pen ; En and El being arcs of circles struck in the same direction. For a similar reason, Iss-Kay requires El after it. On the other hand, Em requires Lay

---

resume, urge, arrayed, earth, arch, mar, Thayer, future, Shakspeare, rare, rarer, terror, aurora, error.'

§ 154. In how many different directions may the sign for El be written ? What is it named when written upward ? when written downward ?

§ 155. Specify the cases for the use of Lay. Write 'ale, less, lime, like, lion; long, lessen, folly, rely, only, pull, ball, doll, quill, feel, skull, nail.' [Rem.] Why does after it; for El after Em would demand a change of the circular movement of the pen; Em and El being arcs of circles written in *different* directions.

USES OF EL.

§ 156. El is usually employed in the following cases:

1. For *l* next following an initial vowel, and followed by *k* or *m;* thus, .⌒ alike, .⌒ alum.

2. For *l* initial, when followed by some letter before which El is more conveniently written than Lay; thus, ⌒ lion, ⌒ long, ⌒ lessen.

3. For final *l;* as in ⌒ vowel, ⌒ scale, ⌒ nail; unless preceded by some letter, as Pee, Tee, Chay, Kay, Ar, to which Lay is joined more conveniently than El.

REM. The preceding rules for the use of El and Lay, when preceded by another consonant-stroke, may, for purposes of reference, be presented thus:

(*a*) After Ef, Vee, Ray, Yay, write Lay or El, according as *l* is, or is not, followed by a vowel.

(*b*) After En, Ing, Ish, Zhay, and Iss-Kay, write El, whether a vowel follows or not.

(*c*) In all other cases write Lay, whether a vowel follows or not.

VI. DIFFERENT DIRECTIONS OF THE STROKE FOR SH.

§ 157. As previously explained, the stroke for *sh* may be written downward or upward. In the former case it is called Ish; and Shay in the latter case. Whether this sign is best written upward or downward in any particular instance, may usually be determined by the rules of the following section:

§ 158. USES OF ISH AND SHAY.

1. Use Ish for the sound of *sh* when it is the only stroke-consonant in the word.

2. Usually write Shay for *sh* preceding *l;* thus, ⌒ shawl, ⌒ shallow.

3. Usually write Shay for *sh* when final and preceded by *l;* thus, ⌒ polish.

4. Usually write Shay for *sh* after Tee and Dee; thus, ⌒ dash.

5. Ish is almost invariably used in all other cases.

En require El rather than Lay after it? Why does Iss-Kay take El instead of Lay after it? Why does Em demand a following Lay rather than El?

§ 156. Specify the cases for the use of El. Write 'alike, alum, lion, long, lessen, vowel, scale, nail.' [Rem.] After what strokes is the sign for *l* to be written upward or downward according as a vowel does, or does not, follow? After what strokes is it to be written downward whether a vowel does, or does not, follow? In what other cases should it be written upward whether a vowel does, or does not, follow?

§ 157. In what direction may the stroke for *sh* be written? What is it named when written upward? when written downward?

§ 158. Specify the cases for the use of Ish and Shay. Write 'show, ash, Shah, shawl, shallow, polish, relish, dash, tissue, push, cash, gnash, mush.'

GROUP-CONSONANT SIGNS.

§ 159. PHONOGRAPHY obtains over most other systems of shorthand a decided and very important advantage, in respect of brevity, facility, and legibility, by providing signs for the expression of certain groups of consonants, such as 'pl, fr, pn, fshn, ktv, pt, pnt, pln, prf,' etc. With the use of these signs it is possible and easy, in very many instances, to express with a single stroke of the pen what would require from two to five strokes in the old systems of stenography.

§ 160. If, to express groups of consonants, letters were to be devised which would bear no obvious relation to the consonant-signs previously explained, the labor of learning such new signs would be much more than that required to become acquainted with the simple-consonant alphabet. But let the new signs be formed by regular modifications of the simple-consonant letters, and the student can readily familiarize a large number of virtually distinct signs, merely by learning the principle of the modification. There are five modes of modifying the primary letters to form group-consonant signs:

1. By an initial hook.
2. By a final hook.
3. By widening.
4. By lengthening.
5. By halving.

I. INITIAL HOOKS.

---

1. THE EL-HOOKS.

§ 161. (a) A small hook on the circle-side (§ 27, 1, 3), and at the beginning of any consonant-stroke (except *l, r, m, n, ng, s, z, w, h*), indicates that an *l* follows it; thus,

    pl   tl   chl   kl

    fl   thl   shl   yl

(b) Shel and Zhel never stand alone, have their hooks at the bottom, and are always written upward.

---

§ 159. What is the advantage of signs for groups of consonants?

§ 160. What modes of modifying the simple signs, to form group-consonant signs, are employed in Phonography?

§ 161. What consonant-strokes take the small El-hook? With hook-signs, write 'pl, tl, chl, kl, fl, vl, thl, shl, yl.' Do Shel and Zhel ever stand alone? In what direc-

REM. 1. The sentence "No MeRRy SoNGS[Z] We'LL HeaR," contains all the consonants whose signs do not take the small El-hook.

REM. 2. *El-hook on Em, En, Ray.*—The reporter uses a large initial hook on Em, En, Ray for *l;* thus, ⌒ ml, ⌣ nl, ⟋ rl. (*b*) The El-hook must be made large in these cases, to distinguish it from the Way-hook.

REM. 3. The object of the rule to write Shel and Zhel upward, and not to use them alone, is to secure a distinction between these letters and the group-signs for *shn, zhn; shr, zhr,* to be subsequently explained.

REM. 4. The student will be assisted in remembering the side for the El-hook on the straight lines, by observing that if the *L*eft hand, with the first finger bent, be held up in the directions of Kay, Pee, Tee, Chay, the outlines for *kl, pl, tl, chl* will appear; thus,

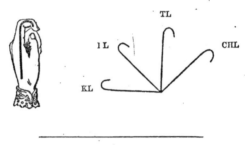

2. THE AR-HOOKS.

§ 162. Signs to indicate the combination of *r* with a preceding consonant (except *s, z, l, r, m, n, ng, w, y, h*), are obtained by turning over sidewise the corresponding El-hook signs, except Shel, Zhel, which are turned over endwise; thus,

╲ pl   ⌐ tl   ⟋ chl   ⌐ kl   ⌞ fl   ⌠ thl   ⌣ shl

╲ pr   ⌐ tr   ⟋ chr   ⌐ kr   ⟍ fr   ⌐ thr   ⟋ shr

(*b*) Sher and Zher have their hook at the top, and are always written downward. See § 161 *b*, and Rem. 3.

---

tion are they always written? [Rem.] What sentence contains the consonants whose signs do not take the small El-hook? On what consonant-strokes does the reporter write a large hook for *l?* Why must the hook for Mel, Nel, Rel be made large? How is the El-hook on Em, En, Ray distinguished from the Way-hook? Why must Shel and Zhel be written upward and joined to some other stroke? How may the side for the El-hook on straight lines be remembered?

§ 162. How are signs obtained to express *r* in connection with certain preceding consonants? What consonant-signs do not take an Ar-hook? How are Sher and Zher formed, and in what direction are they written?

R ADDED TO EM AND EN.

§ 163. R may be added to Em and En by a small initial hook, provided they are widened; thus, ⌒ mr, ⌣ nr.

REM. 1. The widening of Em and En when they take the Ar-hook serves to distinguish *mr* and *nr* from *wm* and *wn*. See § 120, 1.

REM. 2. As Ar, Es, Ing, Way do not take the Ar-hook, *fr*, *thr*, *nr*, *vr* can not be
mistaken for *rr*, *sr*, *ngr*, *wr*.

REM. 3. Sher and Zher, having their hook at the top, and being always written
downward, are readily distinguished from Shel and Zhel, which have their hook at
bottom, and are always written upward.

REM. 4. The sentence "HiS eRRiNG WiLL You See" contains all the consonants whose signs do not take the Ar-hook.

REM. 5. The student will be assisted in remembering the side for the Ar-hook on
the straight lines, by observing that if the *R*ight hand, with the first finger bent, be
held up in the directions of Kay, Pee, Tee, Chay, the outlines for *kr*, *pr*, *tr*, *chr*,
will appear; thus,

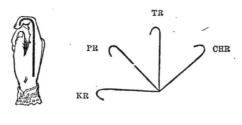

IMPERFECT EL OR AR HOOKS.

§ 164. In some cases when an El or Ar hook sign is joined to a preceding letter, the hook can not be perfectly formed; as in ⋀ reply, ⌐ explore, ⌐ dimmer, ⌐ farmer, ⌐ tiger.

REM. 1. In such cases, a slight offset of the pen serves instead of the hook. (*b*) In
slow writing, the hook may be added, in some cases, after lifting the pen.

REM. 2. *Ter or Der following Ray.*—Tee or Dee following Ray may be made
into Ter or Der by rounding the junction; thus, ∕| write, ∕| writer.

---

§ 163. What signs are widened when they take the Ar-hook? With hook-signs,
write *mr*, *nr*. [Rem.] Why must Em and En be widened when they take the Ar-
hook? Why can not the sign for *fr* be mistaken for *rr*? *thr* for *sr*? *nr* for *ngr*?
vr for *wr*? How are Sher and Zher distinguished from Shel and Zhel? What
sentence contains all the consonants whose signs do not take the Ar-hook?

§ 164. Is an El or Ar hook ever imperfectly formed? Write 'reply, explore,
dimmer, farmer, tiger.' [Rem.] In these cases, what serves instead of the hook?
How may Tee or Dee following Ray be made into Ter or Der? Write 'write,
writer.'

§ 165. The El and Ar hook signs should not be called ' Pee-El, Pee-Ar,' etc., but should be named by the final syllables of such words as ' sam-ple, ta-per, set-tle,' etc., or by syllables containing the vowel ĕ; thus, Pel, Per; Tel, Ter; Chel, Cher, etc.; (b) and are to be regarded as indivisible signs. (c) The series of El and Ar hook signs may be spoken of as the " Pel and Per Series of Signs," or as the " Pel and Per Signs."

USE AND VOCALIZATION OF THE PEL AND PER SIGNS.

§ 166. *General Use.*—The El-hook and Ar-hook signs are used principally for such close combinations of *l* and *r* with a preceding consonant as occur at the commencement of *clay, fly, pray, fry,* etc. ; (b) and in cases where *l* is separated, by a slight, unaccented vowel, from the consonant preceding in the same syllable ; as in ' Bible, sober, able, Abel, novel, river, awful, labor, evil.' (c) In these cases the expression of the obscure vowel is unnecessary.

Rem. In the cases specified above, it is occasionally better, when an El or Ar hook sign can not be conveniently joined to a preceding sign, to write in its stead its equivalent simple signs; as Bee-Lay instead of Bel for the last syllable of *sensible, forcible,* or *admissible;* Tee-Ray instead of Ter for the last syllable of *ministry.*

§ 167. *General Rule of Vocalization.*—A vowel written beside an El-hook or Ar-hook sign should not be read between the two consonants, but before or after both, according as it is written before or after such sign ; thus, ╲ apple, ╲ plea, ⌐ offer, ⌐ free, ⌐ eater, ⌐ tree.

§ 168. *Special Use.*—Long and inconvenient outlines are occasionally avoided by the employment of El-hook and Ar-hook signs, even when there occurs between the consonants indicated by them a clear, accented vowel, as in ' term, charm, corner:' (The principal words in whose representation this use is convenient will be given in the Phonographic Writing Exercises.) In these cases, if the word is not sufficiently legible *without* vocalization, the vowel may be written so as to read between the two consonants, by the following rule.

---

§ 165. How are the El and Ar hook signs named ?

§ 166. What is the principal use of the El and Ar hook signs ? [Rem.] When, in the cases specified, should the equivalent simple signs be written instead of the group-sign ? How is it best to write the last syllable of *sensible, forcible, admissible, ministry ?*

§ 167. In what order is a vowel read when written beside an El or Ar hook sign ? On which side of a Pel or Per sign should a vowel be written when it is to be read before both of the consonants ? on which side, when it is to be read *after* both the consonants ?

§ 168. Is it ever allowable to employ an El or Ar hook sign to represent two consonants with a clear accented vowel between them ?

§ 169. *Special Rule of Vocalization.*—Vowels to be read between the consonants denoted by an El-hook or Ar-hook sign are written thus :

1. *Dots* are made into circles, and written

(a) *Before* the group-sign, if the vowel is long ; thus, ⌐ dark.

(b) *After* the group-sign, if the vowel is short ; thus, ⌐ term.

(c) *Either side* of the group-sign, when the preceding rules (a and b) can not be conveniently applied ; thus, ⌐ engineer, ⌐ paralyze.

2. *Dashes Written Parallel with the Consonant* are made into small ellipses and written beside the group-sign in the same manner as the small circles ; thus, ⌐ germ, ⌐ calcine.

3. *Dashes Written at an Oblique or Right Angle* with the consonants are written through the group-sign ; thus, ⌐ course, ⌐ portray, ⌐ burst, ⌐ school, ⌐ correct.

4. *Angles or Semicircles* are written through the group-sign ; or, if more convenient, for the first place, at the commencement—for the third place, at the end, of the group-sign ; thus, ⌐ require, ⌐ feature, ⌐ quality, ⌐ figures.

ISS PREFIXED TO AN EL-HOOK SIGN.

§ 170. Iss may be prefixed to an El-hook sign ; thus, ⌐ supply, ⌐ civil, ⌐ cycle, ⌐ saddle, ⌐ disclose.

REM. *Caution.*—It should be particularly observed that a loop or a large circle is never prefixed to an El-hook sign.

---

§ 169. Can a vowel be written so as to be read between the consonants denoted by an El or Ar hook sign ? For this purpose, how should you write a long dot-vowel ? a short dot-vowel ? When is the vowel-circle written before the group-sign ? when is it written after ? May it, in any case, be written on either side, without regard to the length of the vowel ? Give some words in which it is not convenient to place the vowel-circle before the group-sign, for a long vowel ; or after the group-sign, for a short vowel. Write ' dark, term, engineer, paralyze.' How should a parallel-dash vowel be written so as to read between the consonants denoted by an El or Ar hook sign ? Write ' germ, calcine.' How should a vowel-dash standing at an oblique or right angle with the consonant-stroke be written so as to read between the consonants denoted by an El or Ar hook sign ? How, for this purpose, should an angle or semicircle be written ? When an angle or semicircle of the first or third place can not be conveniently written through the group-sign, how else may it be written ? Write ' portray, burst, school, correct, require, feature, quality, figures.'

§ 170. Can Iss be prefixed to an El-hook sign ? Write ' supply, civil, cycle, saddle, disclose.' [Rem.] Is it allowable to prefix a loop or a large circle to an El-hook sign ?

ISS, SES, AND STEH PREFIXED TO AN AR-HOOK SIGN.

§ 171. (*a*) Making an Ar-hook into a small circle, prefixes *s ;*—into a large circle, prefixes *ss*—

1. To any one of the straight-line Ar-hook signs when preceded by no stroke; thus, ⟋ spray, ⟍ sober, ⌐ straw, ⌐ cider, ⟍ scrape, ⟍ sister.

2. To any one of the straight-line Ar-hook signs preceded by a stroke in the same direction ; thus, ⟍ prosper. ⟍ destroy, ⟍ execrable, ⟍ disaster.

3. To Ker or Ger preceded by a straight stroke in the direction of Pee, Tee, or Chay ; thus, ⟍ subscribe, ⟍ describe, ⟍ disagree.

4. To Per or Ber preceded by a straight stroke in the direction of Chay or Jay ; thus, ⟍ Jasper.

(*b*) In all other cases, the circle is prefixed by writing it distinctly within the hook ; thus, ⟍ express, ⟍ extreme, ⟍ is there, ⟍ sinner.

REM. 1. *Syllable-Names of the Per-Signs Preceded by the Circles and Loop.*— (*a*) Per, Ber, etc., in connection with a preceding Iss, may be named by prefixing to their names the syllable *Iss*, or, if convenient and certain, the sound of *s ;* thus, Iss-Per or Sper, Iss-Ber, Iss-Ger, etc. (*b*) In connection with a preceding Ses, by prefixing the syllable *Ses ;* thus, Ses-Per, Ses-Ter, Ses-Cher, etc. (*c*) In connection with a preceding Steh, by prefixing the syllable Steh ; thus, Steh-Per, Steh-Ger, Steh-Ter, etc. (*d*) The Ar-hook signs preceded by Iss, Ses, or Steh, when spoken of as a class, may be denominated respectively the Iss-Per, Ses-Per, and Steh-Per signs.

REM. 2. The junction of Iss-Ker and Iss-Per with the strokes to which it is allowable to attach them, is effected by joining the circle on the right-hand side of the preceding stroke, and then writing, from the point at which the circle is completed, the stroke of the Ker or Per.

REM. 3. It is the common practice of good phonographers to omit *r* from *scribe* in ' describe, subscribe, prescribe, proscribe, superscribe,' and from *scrip-* in their derivatives, ' descriptive, subscription,' etc.

---

§ 171. To what signs may *s* or *ss* be prefixed by making an Ar-hook into a small or large circle ? How must the circle be written in other cases ? How and when may Iss or Sez be prefixed to any one of the straight-line Ar-hook signs ? Write ' spray, sober, straw, cider, scrape, sister, prosper, destroy, execrable, disaster, subscribe, disagree, Jasper, express, extreme, is there, sinner.' [Rem.] How are the Per-signs named when Iss is prefixed ? when Ses is prefixed ? when Steh is prefixed ? How are the signs named, when spoken of as a class ? How is Iss-Ker joined to a preceding straight stroke in the direction of Pee, Tee, or Chay ? How is Iss-Per joined to a preceding straight stroke in the direction of Chay or Jay ? How do good phonographers frequently contract *describe*, etc. ?

CAUTION.

§ 172. (*a*) The Ster-loop is never prefixed to an Ar-hook sign; (*b*) and the Steh-loop is prefixed, only to the straight-line Ar-hook signs when preceded by no stroke, by making the hook into a small loop; thus, ⟍ stupor, ⟋ stager.

SPER. DISTINGUISHED FROM SPEE.

§ 173. The use of the loops and circles to imply an Ar-hook may be readily distinguished from their ordinary use, by observing that in the former case they are required on the side of the stroke contrary to that for the simple circles and loops; thus, ⟍ spr, ⟍ sp ; ⟍ pspr, ⟍ psp ; ⟍ stpr, ⟍ stp ; ⟋ sspr, ⟋ ssp ; ⟍⎯ pskr, ⟍⎯ psk ; ⎣⎯ tskr, ⎣⎯ tsk ; ⟨ chspr, ⟨ chsp. See §§ 27, 28, 29.

3. THE HOOK FOR IN, UN, OR EN.

§ 174. The syllable *in*, *en*, or *un* may be expressed by a back hook—

1. At the beginning of a straight-line Iss-Per sign; thus, ⟍ inseparable, ⟍ inscribe, ⟍ unscrupulous, ⟍ unscrew, ⟍ unstrung, ⟍ insecure.

2. At the beginning of any other stroke, to avoid turning a circle on the convex side of En; thus, ⟍ insoluble, ⟍ unseemly, ⟍ enslave.

Rem. 1. *Name.*—This hook may be called the In-hook.
Rem. 2. The In-hook may be used for the syllable *on* in *onslaught.*

---

§ 172. Is it allowable to prefix a Ster-loop to an Ar-hook sign? To what Ar-hook signs may the Steh-loop be prefixed? Write 'stupor, stager.'

§ 173. How may Iss-Per signs be distinguished from the Iss-Pee signs? Make and compare Iss-Per, Iss-Pee—Pee-Sper, Pee-Spee—Steh-Per, Steh-Pee—Ses-Per, Ses-Pee—Pee-Sker, Pee-Skay—Tee-Sker, Tee-Skay—Chay-Sper, Chay-Spee.

§ 174. In what cases may the syllable *in*, *en*, or *un* be expressed by a back hook? Write 'inseparable, inscribe, unscrupulous, unscrew, unstrung, insecure, insoluble, unseemly, enslave.' What is avoided by the use of the back hook in writing 'insoluble, unseemly, enslave?' [Rem.] How may this hook be named? In what word may it be used for the syllable *on?*

4. REPORTING LER AND REL HOOKS.

§ 175. The reporter occasionally enlarges the small El or Ar hook, to add to an El-hook sign the sound of *r*—to an Ar-hook sign the sound of *l;* thus, ⟍ bl, ⟍ blr, ⟍ pr, ⟍ prl; ⌒ secular, ⌒⟍ corporal.

REM. 1. This principle can not be employed to add *r* to Mel, Nel, Rel; for the hooks of these signs are already large, and it would not be allowable to make them still larger.

REM. 2. *Syllable-Names.*—(*a*) The enlarged Ar-hook may be called the Rel-hook; (*b*) the enlarged El-hook may be called the Ler-hook. (*c*) The Rel-hook signs may be named Prel, Trel, Krel, etc.; (*d*) and the Ler-hook signs, Pler, Tler, Kler, Fler, etc. (*e*) When spoken of as a series, they may be named the Pler and Prel signs.

VOCALIZATION OF THE PLER AND PREL SIGNS.

§ 176. (*a*) A vowel is read before all the consonants indicated by a Pler or Prel sign, if written before it; (*b*) but if written *after* such sign, it is read before the *l* or *r* added by the enlargement of the hook; thus, ⌒ ocular, ⎸ trial.

PLER AND PREL SIGNS PRECEDED BY ISS.

§ 177. S may be prefixed to a Pler or Prel sign by writing a circle within the hook; thus, ⌒ scholar, ⎸ sideral.

WORD-SIGNS AND CONTRACTIONS.

§ 178. LIST OF INITIAL-HOOK WORD-SIGNS.

⟍ ⸨ ---⸨--- ⟋ ⌒ ⌣

able, t$_i^e$ll *or* it will, until, at all, which-will, call *or* equal-ly, difficult-y,

⟍ ⸨ ⸨ ⸨ ⟍ ⟍ ⟍

full, [fully,] value, they will, princip$_{al}^{le}$, surprise, member, remember,

---

§ 175. What is added to an El-hook sign by enlarging the hook? to an Ar-hook sign? Write ' bl, blr, pr, prl, secular, corporal.' [Rem.] Why can not this principle be employed to add *r* to Mel, Nel, Rel? What is the name of the enlarged Ar-hook? of the enlarged El-hook? What are the names of the Rel-hook signs? of the Ler-hook signs?
§ 176. Repeat the rule for vocalizing a Prel or Pler sign. Where does a vowel read when placed after a Prel or Pler sign? when placed before? Write ' ocular, trial.'
§ 177. How can Iss be prefixed to a Pler or Prel sign? Write ' scholar, sideral.'
§ 178. Cover the word-signs given in § 178 and write the proper signs for the words below them. Cover the sign-words and read the word-signs. [Rem.] Write

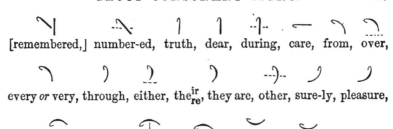

[remembered,] number-ed, truth, dear, during, care, from, over,

every *or* very, through, either, the$_{re}^{ir}$, they are, other, sure-ly, pleasure,

Mr., mere, remark, [remarked,] more, near, nor, manner.

REM. 1. *Derivatives.*—Derivatives from the words of this list may be written according to the principle of § 40, Rem. 2. For example, join Lay-Iss to *Care* for *careless;* Bel to *Remark* and *Pleasure* for *remarkabl-e-y, pleasurabl-e-y;* En-Iss or Ar to *Full* for *fullness, fuller;* Lay to *Mere* for *merely;* El to *Near* for *nearly* (§ 156, 3); En-Iss to *Near* for *nearness;* Ar to *Near* for *nearer.*

REM. 2. *Distinctions.*—(*a*) If it is deemed necessary, *equal-ly* may be distinguished from *call* by writing ĕ in *equal* and ĭ in *equally;* (*b*) *very* from *every* by writing ĭ in the former; *surely* from *sure* by writing Lay near *sure* for *surely.* (*c*) With very little practice in reading phonography, these distinctions become entirely unnecessary.

REM. 3. *Miss, Misses, Mrs., Messrs.*—Miss is written with Em-Iss; Misses, with Em-Ses, in the first position. (*b*) Mrs., pronounced Missess, is written with Em-Iss-Ess, in order to distinguish it from Misses, the plural of Miss. (*c*) Messrs. is written with Em-Iss-Ray-Iss.

REM. 4. *All, Will Added.*—On the principle of adding *will* to the sign for *they,* and *all* to the sign for *at,* the reporter prefixes an El-hook to the simple-consonant, and dash-vowel, word-signs, and to the horizontal *and*-tick, to add *all* or *will;* thus, ＼ by all, (for all, ＼ of all ＼ to all, ⌒ who will, ⌒ and all, *or* and will. (*b*) The reporter occasionally adds *all* or *will* to a full-length Ar-hook sign, by enlarging the hook; thus,) there will *or* they are all, ⌐ during all.

REM. 5. *Are, Our Added.*—In the reporting style, *are* or *our* may be added to the simple-consonant, and the dash-vowel, word-signs, and to the horizontal *and*-tick, by prefixing an Ar-hook; thus, ＼ by our, ⌐ of our, ＼ to our, ⌒ and are *or* and our. (*b*) The reporter occasionally adds *are* or *our* to a full-length, small-Elhook sign, by enlarging the hook; thus, (for all are *or* for all our. (*c*) To these signs *self* may be added by a small circle; *selves,* by a large circle; thus, ⌒ to ours *or* to ourself, ⌒ to ourselves, ＼ by ourself, ＼ by ourselves. See § 38, 5. (*d*) The circles added to the dashes should, of course, be properly proportioned to the size of those signs.

' careless, remarkable, remarkably, pleasurable, pleasurably, fullness, fuller, merely, nearly, nearness.' How may *equal-ly* be distinguished from *call?* *very* from *every?* *surely* from *sure?* To what signs may *will* be added by an El-hook? What word may the reporter add to a full-length Ar-hook sign by enlargement of the hook? To what signs may *are, our* be added by an Ar-hook? by enlarging a hook? How may *self* or *selves* be added to signs thus formed?

§ 179. It is found convenient to contract six words containing Pel or Per signs; namely,

⌐ capable	⌣ influential	⌐ remarkable
＼ capability	＼ probability	⌐ transgress.

§ 180. LIST OF WORDS REPRESENTED BY INITIAL-HOOK SIGNS.

A.	M.	S.
able	manner	sure
at all	member	sure-ly
	mere	surprise
C.	more	
call	Mr.	T.
care		tell
	N.	their
D.	near	there
dear	nor	they are
difficult	number	they will
difficulty	numbered	through
during		till
	O.	truth
E.	other	
either	over	U.
equal—§ 178, R. 1.		until
equally—do.	P.	
every—§ 178, R. 2.	pleasure	V.
	principal	value
F.	principle	very
from		
full	R.	W.
[fully]	remark	which will.
	[remarked]	
I.	remember	
it will	[remembered]	

(b) WORDS MENTIONED IN REMARKS UNDER § 178.

and all	merely	remarkable
and will	Messrs.	remarkably
by all	Miss	there will
by our	Misses	they are all
by ourself	Mrs.	to all
by ourselves	nearer	to our
careless	nearly	to ours
for all	nearness	to ourself
for all are	of all	to ourselves
for all our	of our	who will.
fullness	pleasurable	
fuller	pleasurably	

§ 179. Repeatedly write the contractions containing Pel or Per signs.
§ 180. Repeatedly write the proper signs for the words of this list.

II. FINAL HOOKS.

1. HOOKS FOR F, V, AND N.

§ 181. *On the Straight Lines.*—*F, v,* or *n* may be added to any straight line (with, or without, an initial hook, loop, or circle), by a small final hook; written for *f* or *v,* on the circle side (§ 27, 1), and for *n,* on the contrary side; thus, ⟍ puff, ⟍ pun; ⌈ deaf, ⌡ den; ⟋• chafe, ⟋• chain; ⟶ cave, ⟶ cane; ⟋ rove, ⟋ roan; ⟋ heave, ⟋ hewn; ⟍ brief, ⟍ brain; ⟍ bluff, ⟍ blown; ⌠ stove, ⌠ stone; ⟨ strife, ⟩• strain.

REM. When preciseness of representation is required, the Ef-hook may be made heavy for *v;* thus, ⟍ proof, ⟍ prove.

§ 182. *N Added to Curves.*—*N* may be added to any curve-sign by a small final hook on the concave, or circle, side; thus, ⟍ fine, ⟍ flown, ⟍ frown, ⟍ main. See § 27, 3.

REM. (*a*) The Ef-hook is never written on the curves, except in the Reporting Style. (*b*) The reporter derives advantage occasionally from representing *f* or *v* on the circle-side of a curve by a small final hook, made, for the sake of distinction, somewhat longer than an En-hook; thus, ⟨ they have.

SYLLABLE-NAMES OF THE SMALL FINAL HOOKS.

§ 183. *Hook for F or V.*—(*a*) This hook may invariably be called the Ef-hook, notwithstanding it frequently represents the sound of *v.* In those instances, however, in which it represents *v,* it may be properly denominated the Vee-hook. (*b*) The signs with an Ef-hook, when spoken of as a class, may be called the Ef-hook signs. (*c*) The simple, or group, signs, with an Ef-hook, are named by prefixing the sounds they represent to the syllable Ef, if this can be done conveniently; if not, add the sound of *f* to the syllable-name of the stroke; thus, Pef, Chef, Ref, Plef, Tlef or Telf, Chref or Cherf, Prelf, Plerf, Chlerf.

---

§ 181. What sounds may be added to straight lines by a small final hook? On which side is the hook for *f* or *v* written? On which side is the hook for *n* written? To what signs may the Ef-hook be added? To what straight lines may the En-hook be added? Write ' puff, pun, deaf, den, chafe, chain, cave, cane, rove, roan, heave, hewn, brief, brain, bluff, blown, stove, stone, strife, strain.' [Rem.] How, with the use of a hook, may *v* be distinguished from *f?* Make this distinction in writing ' proof, prove.'

§ 182. What sound is added to a curve-sign by a small final hook? On which side of the curve-sign should the hook be written? Write 'fine, flown, frown, main.' [Rem.] Is a hook for *f* or *v* ever written on a curve-sign? When used on curves, how can it be distinguished from the En-hook?

§ 183. What is the hook for *f* and *v* called? How are the Ef-hook signs named?

§ 184. *Hook for N.*—(*a*) This hook is named the En-hook. (*b*) The signs with the En-hook, when spoken of as a class, are called the En-hook signs. (*c*) The simple, or group, signs with the En-hook, are named by prefixing the sounds they represent to the syllable En, or, if more convenient, by prefixing the syllable-name of the stroke to the syllable En or to the sound of *n*, the accent being placed upon the name of the stroke; thus, Pen, Ken, Plen, Chlen or Chélen, Pren, Chren, Chern, Prélen, Plern, Chlern.

VOCALIZATION OF THE EF AND EN HOOK SIGNS.

§ 185. (*a*) A vowel after a stroke with an Ef or En hook, is read before the hook; thus, Ј . den, ＼ pun. (*b*) Hence, a stroke-sign must be employed for *f, v*, or *n*, whenever it is followed by a vowel which can not be written before a following consonant; as in ＼ penny, ⌒ money, ⋀ terrify, ＼ profess.

ISS ADDED TO THE EF-HOOK SIGNS.

§ 186. *S* or *z* may be added to an Ef-hook sign by a small circle, written within the hook; thus, ＼ proves, ｜ strifes, ⌐ scoffs.

REM. A loop or the large circle is never added to the Ef-hook.

ISS, SES, STEH, AND STER ADDED TO STRAIGHT-LINE EN-HOOK SIGNS.

§ 187. Making the En-hook on a straight line—

1. Into a small circle, adds *s*; thus, ＼ pens, Ј tense, Ј dense, ／ chance, ⌐ cans, ／ runs.

2. Into a large circle, adds *ss*; thus, Ј condenses.

3. Into a small loop, adds *st*; thus, Ј condensed.

4. Into a large loop, adds *str*; thus, ＼ punster.

REM. 1. To signs thus formed, it is allowable, especially in the reporting style, to add a *stroke*, provided the circle or loop would not thereby be placed in the position

---

§ 184. What is the name of the hook for *n* ? How are the En-hook signs named?

§ 185. Where does a vowel read when placed after an Ef or En hook sign? Write 'den, pun.' How must *f, v*, or *n* be expressed when followed by a vowel which can not be written before a following stroke? Why may not the hook be used in such a case? Write 'penny, money, terrify, profess.'

§ 186. How, with the use of a circle, may *s* or *z* be added to an Ef-hook sign? Write 'proves, strives, scoffs.' [Rem.] Is it allowable to add a loop or a large circle to an Ef-hook?

§ 187. What is added to a straight-line En-hook sign, by making the En-hook into a small circle? into a large circle? into a small loop? into a large loop? How may *s, ss, st, str* be added to a straight-line En-hook sign? To what final-hook signs may *s, ss, st, str* be added by making the hook into a circle or loop? Write 'pens, tense, dense, chance, cans, runs, condenses, tenses, chances, condensed, chanced, punster.' [Rem.] When may a stroke be affixed to signs formed by making an of a simple circle or loop; or, an Ens or Enses circle, in the situation of a circle including the Ar-hook. See Rem. 3, below. The reporter, for instance, writes

⌐ᵖ for *begins a;* —ᵪ for *against the.* (*b*) It is sometimes more convenient, when a stroke follows, to write the circle distinctly within the hook: thus, ⟋°

ransom, ˙.⟍ gainsayed. (*c*) *S* or *z* may be added to the Enses-circle, and the Enst and Enster loops, by a circle turned on the opposite side of the stroke; thus, ⟍ᵔ punsters.

REM. 2. *Syllable-Names.*—(*a*) The En-hook made into a small circle is called the Ens-circle; into the large circle, the Enses-circle; into the small loop, the Enst-loop; into the large loop, the Enster-loop. (*b*) The signs formed by the attachment of these circles and loops may be named Pens, Penses, Penst, Penster; Plens, etc.; Prens, etc.

REM. 3. *Caution.*—The Ens and Enses circles are never used between crossing lines, or between straight lines in the same direction; for, between crossing lines, they are in the situation of simple Iss and Ses; and if used between straight lines in the same direction, the second line would be read, in connection with the circle, as an Iss-Per or Ses-Per sign. Hence, ⟍— is *psk,* not *pnsk* (see § 27, 4); —⟋ *kssr,* not *knss-r;* ⟍ *p-spr,* not *pns-p* (see § 171, *a,* 2); ○⟍ *d-sstr,* not *dnss-t.*

ISS ADDED TO THE EN-HOOK ON CURVES.

§ 188. *S* or *z* may be added to an En-hook on a curve, by a small circle written distinctly within the hook; thus, ⟋° lines, ˙ ° means.

REM. A loop or the large circle is never added to an En-hook on a curve.

THE HOOKS FOR F AND N IN THE MIDDLE OF WORDS.

§ 189. The Ef and En hooks, when more convenient than a stroke, are occasionally used in the middle of a word; thus, |ᵥ⟍ define, ↑ᵥ⟍ contrivance, ⟍—ı provoke, ⟍⟋ proverb, |⟍˳ defense, ⟋⟍ furnish, ⟍ punish, ⟍⟍ finish.

REM. 1. *The Ef-hook in the Middle of Words.*—The following is a partial list of the

---

En-hook into a circle or loop? Write 'begins a, against the.' Is it ever more convenient to write the circle within the En-hook of a straight line? Write 'ransom, gainsayed.' How may a small circle be added to the group-signs for *pnst, pnstr, pnses,* etc.? Write 'punsters.' What is the name of the En-hook made into a small circle? into a large circle? into a small loop? into a large loop? What are the signs for *pns,* etc., called? May or may not the Ens-circle be used between strokes? If not, why? Write 'psk, kssr, pspr, dsstr.'

§ 188. How, with the use of a circle, may *s* or *z* be added to an En-hook on a curve-sign? Write 'lines, means.' [Rem.] Is it allowable to join a loop or the large circle to an En-hook on a curve-sign?

§ 189. May or may not an En or Ef hook be used in the middle of a word? Write 'define, contrivance, provoke, proverb, defense, furnish, punish, finish.' Write the words given in the lists in § 189, Rems. 1, 2.

words in which the Ef-hook may be advantageously employed between two strokes: Paver, prefer, proffer, perverse, briefer, braver, believer (Blef-Ray), befog, soporific (Spref-Kay), province, profane, buffoon, prophet, profit, diver, driver, contriver, deliver (Delf-Ray), traffic, extravagance, advance, defense, divinity, divide, devote, deviate, chaffer, juvenile, river (Ref-Ray), rougher, rover, reverence, reveal (Ref-Lay), rival, cover, discover, coffer, giver (Gef-Ray), graver, clever, heaver (Hef-Ray). (b) The sound of *r* after an Ef-hook is almost invariably represented by Ray, because it can be usually employed in this case more conveniently than Ar.

REM. 2. *The En-hook in the Middle of Words.*—The following is a partial list of the words in which the En-hook may be advantageously employed between two strokes: Banish, finish, gainsay, vanish, convenience (con-Ven-Ens), finance, lonely, linear, replenish, French, furniture (Fren-Tee-Ray), Francis, princess (Pren-Ess-Iss), finery, keen-eyed, openness (Pen-Ens), evenness (Ven-Ens), thinness (Then-Ens), vacancy, millennium (Em-Len-Em), millionaire, turnkey (Tee-Ren-Kay), Spanish, pecuniary.

---

2. LARGE HOOKS FOR SHON AND TIV.

§ 190. *Shon and Tiv Added to Straight Lines.*—The syllables *shon* and *tiv* may be added to any straight line (with or without an initial hook, loop, or circle) by a large hook; written for Shon on the circle-side; and on the contrary side, for Tiv; thus, ﹨ passion, ﹨ combative, ⁀ operation, ⁀ operative, ⌣ intrusion, ⌣ nutritive, ﹤ provocation, ﹤ provocative.

REM. The hook for *shon* may be used for any syllable of similar sound, however spelled, as for the final syllables of 'magician, Persian, tertian, suspicion, fashion, passion (phonetic *pacon*), derision (ph. *derijon*), flexion (ph. *flekcon*).' (b) Care must be exercised lest the spelling should lead to the employment of this hook for syllables whose consonants are not *shn* or *zhn*, as for the *tion* of *question* = *kwestyon*.

§ 191. *Shon Added to Curves.*—The syllable *shon* may be added to curve-consonants by a large final hook on the concave, or circle, side; thus, ⌒ motion, ⌒ fashion, ⌒ allusion. See § 27, 3.

REM. 1. If it should be thought necessary or desirable to distinguish, with the use

---

§ 190. What syllables may be added to straight lines by a large final hook? On which side of the straight line is the hook for *shon* written? On which side of the straight line is the hook for *tiv* written? Which of the Tiv or Shon hooks is written on the circle-side of straight lines? which on the contrary side? Write 'passion, combative, operative, intrusion, nutritive, provocation, provocative. [Rem.] What syllables besides *shon* may be represented by the Shon-hook? When is it disallowable to represent the syllable *tion* by the Shon-hook? Give some word in which the consonants denoted by *tion* are not *shn* or *zhn*.

§ 191. What syllable may be added to a curve-sign by a large final hook? On which side of the curve-signs is the Shon-hook written? Write 'motion, allusion, fashion, vision.' [Rem.] How, with the use of the Shon-hook, may *zhon* be dis-of the hook, between *zhon* and *shon*, the hook may be made heavy for the former; thus, |⟋⟍ delusion.

Rem. 2. *Shon Represented by Shen.*—Shon or a similar syllable is usually represented by Shen in the following cases:

(*a*) When this syllable contains the only consonants in a word; as in ⟍⟋ ocean.

(*b*) When this syllable is preceded by initial *s* only; as in ⟍⟋⁻ session.

(*c*) When this syllable is preceded by two vowels in a word requiring to be distinguished by outline from another of the same consonants; as in Con-Tee-En-Shen, *continuation*, which requires to be distinguished from 'contention.'

(*d*) In derivatives from words ending with Ish, as in *diminution* from *diminish*.

Rem. 3. *Tiv Following Curves.*—The Tiv-hook is never written upon a curve-consonant. (*b*) The syllable *tiv*, when it can not be represented by a hook, is usually best represented by Tef. Hence, write En-Tef for 'native,' Em-Tef for 'motive,' Vee-Tef for 'votive,' En-Kays-Tef for 'inquisitive.'

SYLLABLE-NAMES OF THE LARGE FINAL HOOKS.

§ 192. *The Hook for Shon.*—(*a*) This hook is named the Shon-hook, or simply Shon. (*b*) The strokes with the Shon-hook, when spoken of as a class, are called the Shon-hook signs. (*c*) The simple, and group, consonants, with a Shon-hook, are named by adding the syllable *Shon* to the syllable-names of the strokes; thus, Pee′shon, Dee′shon, Ray′shon, Pel′shon, Per′shon, Pler′shon, Prel′shon, Wer′shon, Rel′shon.

§ 193. *The Hook for Tiv.*—This hook is denominated the Tiv-hook, or simply Tiv. (*b*) The strokes with a Tiv-hook, when spoken of as a class, are called the Tiv-hook signs. (*c*) The simple, or group, consonants, with a Tiv-hook, are named by adding the syllable Tiv to the syllable-names of the strokes; thus, Pee′tiv, Dee′-tiv, Chay′tiv, Pel′tiv, Rel′tiv, Per′tiv, Cher′tiv, Pler′tiv, Prel′tiv.

ISS ADDED TO SHON AND TIV.

§ 194. *S* or *z* may be added to the Shon or Tiv hook by a small circle written within the hook; thus, ⟍⟋ passions, ⟋⟍. operatives, ⟍⟋ fashions.

---

tinguished from *shon?* Make that distinction in writing 'delusion.' Specify the cases in which Shon or a similar syllable should be represented by Shen. Write 'ocean, session, continuation, contention, admonish, admonition, diminish, diminution.' Is it allowable to write a Tiv-hook on a curve-consonant? How, for the most part, should *tiv* be represented, when it can not be represented by a hook? Write 'native, motive, votive, inquisitive.'

§ 192. What is the name of the hook for *shon?* How are strokes with that hook attached, named? What are such signs called, when spoken of as a class? Make 'Peeshon, Rayshon, Pelshon, Pershon, Wershon, Relshon.'

§ 193. What is the name of the hook for *tiv?* How are strokes with that hook, named? What are such signs called, when spoken of as a class? Make 'Peetiv, Deetiv, Peltiv, Pertiv, Wertiv.'

§ 194. How, with the use of a circle, may *s* or *z* be added to Shon or Tiv? Write passions, operatives, fashions.'

SHON AND TIV IN THE MIDDLE OF WORDS.

§ 195. The Shon and Tiv hooks are sometimes used in the middle of a word; thus, ⟨ visionary, ⟨ auctioneer, ⟨ attractiveness, ⟨ activity.

REM. The junction between Shon and a following stroke is sometimes rendered easier by an incurvation of the point of the hook; thus, ⟨ conditional. See § 25, c.

VOCALIZATION OF THE SHON AND TIV HOOK SIGNS.

§ 196. A vowel after a stroke with a Shon or Tiv hook is read before the hook; thus, ⟨ condition, ⟨ notion, ⟨ consecutive.

REM. 1. When a third-place vowel and a large final hook occur on the same side of a stroke, the vowel may be written within the hook. See in § 190, 'passion, intrusion, provocative;' in § 191, 'fashion, allusion;' in § 194, 'passions, fashions;' in § 196, 'consecutive.'

REM. 2. A vowel after Shon or Tiv must be written before a following stroke; as in 'visionary, auctioneer, activity,' in § 195; (b) or written after a stroke for the final consonant of *shon* or *tiv*.

---

3. SMALL HOOK FOR SHON.

§ 197. The syllable *shon* may be added by a small hook—

1. *To a Circle or Loop;* thus, ⟨ decision, ⟨ position, ⟨ possession, ⟨ persuasion, ⟨ transition, ⟨ condensation, ⟨ administration.

2. *To an Ef-Hook;* thus, ⟨ division, ⟨ devotion, ⟨ diffusion.

REM. 1. This hook may be named the Small Shon-hook; or, for the sake of distinction, and with reference to its being always preceded by a vowel, it may be called the Esh'on-hook, or simply Esh'on.

REM. 2. The principle of writing *f-shn* with two small hooks is of but little service comparatively, and should be very sparingly used, since most words ending

---

§ 195. May or may not Shon or Tiv be used in the middle of a word? Write 'visionary, auctioneer, attractiveness, activity.' [Rem.] How may the joining of Lay and Shon be rendered easy? Write 'conditional.'

§ 196. Where does a vowel read when placed after a stroke with a Shon or Tiv hook? Write 'condition, notion, consecutive.' [Rem.] When may a third-place vowel be written within a large hook? Write 'fashion, intrusion, provocative, delusion, passions, fashions, consecutive.' How must a vowel be written when it occurs after *shon* or *tiv?* Write 'visionary, activity, auctioneer, conditional.'

§ 197. To what signs may the syllable *shon*, etc., be added by a small hook? Write 'decision, position, possession, persuasion, transition, condensation, administration.' [Rem.] What is the name of the small hook for *shon?* What is said of the use of two small hooks for *f-shn?* What usually is the best mode of writing *f* or *v* followed by *shon?* Write 'diffusion, privation, devotion, division.' How, with

with these consonants are more easily written, more legible, and can be more distinctly and readily vocalized, when written with an Ef or Vee stroke; thus, privation, diffusion; than when written with two small hooks.

REM. 3. The Eshon-hook may be made heavy for *zhon;* but this is not considered necessary in practice.

REM. 4. The reporter derives advantage occasionally from omitting one or more consonants preceding Iss-Eshon, or the consonants occurring between Iss and the syllable *shon;* writing 'täsätion,' for instance, for 'taxation;' 'spesätion' for 'specification;' 'jusation' for 'justification;' 'transätion' for 'transaction;' 'prosution' for 'prosecution.' In accordance with this principle is formed the contraction for 'investigation,' which is given at § 202.

VOCALIZATION OF ESHON.

§ 198. Eshon may be vocalized—

1. *When Joined to a Circle or Loop*—by writing a first-place vowel before the hook; a second-place or third-place vowel, after the hook. See 'decision, transition, persuasion, administration,' in § 197, 1.

2. *When Joined to an Ef-Hook*—by writing the vowel, of whatever place, beside the hook. See 'division, devotion, diffusion,' in § 197, 2.

REM. 1. A third-place vowel never occurs before Eshon, except in some contractions made in accordance with the principle of Rem. 4 under the preceding section.

REM. 2. The Eshon-hook after a loop or circle may usually be left unvocalized without endangering the legibility of the writing.

ISS ADDED TO ESHON.

§ 199. Iss may be added to the Eshon-hook, thus, possessions, physicians.

ESHON IN THE MIDDLE OF WORDS.

§ 200. Eshon may occur in the middle of a word; thus, transitional, devotional, conversational.

REM. Words of the class of *conversational, transitional, devotional,* etc., will be found sufficiently legible, even though the vocalization in some cases should be purposely or necessarily imperfect.

---

the use of a hook, may *zhon* be distinguished from *shon?* How does the reporter sometimes contract words ending in *shon* preceded by Iss, with or without an intervening consonant? Write the reporting contractions for 'taxation, specification, justification, transaction, prosecution.' What contraction of the Corresponding Style is formed in accordance with this principle?

§ 198. How is Eshon vocalized when it is joined to a circle or loop? when joined to an Ef-hook?

§ 199. Is it allowable to add Iss to the Eshon-hook? Write 'positions, physicians, transitions, administrations, persuasions.'

§ 200. May the Eshon-hook be used in the middle of a word? Write 'transitional, conversational, devotional.' [Rem.] What is said with respect to the legibility of the words of the class of 'conversational,' etc.?

WORD-SIGNS AND CONTRACTIONS.

§ 201. LIST OF FINAL-HOOK WORD-SIGNS.

Before, [above,] whatever, differ-${}^{ent}_{ence}$, truthful-ly, whichever, careful-ly,

gave, I have, whoever, upon, been, remembrance, done, down,

general-ly, can, again—often, phonography—Standard Phonography,

even, within, then, than, alone, men, man, opinion,

none, known, objection, objective, subjection, subjective.

REM. 1. *Often, Even.*—*Often* is written in the second position, notwithstanding its accented vowel is first-place, in order to distinguish it more certainly from *even*, with which, in rapid writing, it is found to conflict, if both are written in the same position.

REM. 2. *I have.*—These words are usually written with the first form given for them in the preceding list.

REM. 3. *Derivatives.*—(a) ' Objectionable,' *objection* with Bel disjoined, or, what is better, with Bce joined ; (b) 'generalize,' *general* with Zee disjoined ; 'generalization,' *general* with Zee'shon disjoined, or, what is preferable, with Iss-Eshon joined ; (c) 'objectively, subjectively,' *objective, subjective*, with Lay disjoined, or with El joined. Other derivatives may be formed in accordance with the principle of § 40, Rem. 2.

REM. 4. *Have, Of, and If Added.*-   the principle of adding *have* to the abbreviated *I* (see § 103), and *ever* to the signs for *which* and *who*,—*have* or *of* may be added, by an Ef-hook, to any full-length straight-line, to the dash-vowel word-signs, and to the horizontal *and*-tick; thus, out of; it will have; each of;

all of, all have; to have; or of, or have; but of, but have;

who have, who of; should have; *and of*, but not *and have*. This is a principle of the corresponding style, and may be freely and advantageously used.

§ 201. Cover the sign-words of § 201 and read the word-signs above. Cover the word-signs and repeatedly make the proper signs for the words below. [Rem.] Why is *often* written in the second position ? How is *even* distinguished from *often* ? What is the usual form for ' I have ?' Write ' objectionable, generalize, generalization, objectively, subjectively.' To what signs may *have* or *of* be added by an Ef-hook ? Write ' out of, it will have, each of, all of, all have, to have, or of, or have, but have, but of, who have, who of, should have, and of.' Is it allowable, in the (*b*) The reporter does, and the advanced writer of the corresponding style *may*, apply this principle for the addition of *if*, when it can not be more conveniently expressed by its usual sign. For example, the sign for *or* and *but*, with the Ef-hook, may be used respectively for *or if*, *but if*.

REPORTING PRINCIPLES.

REM. 5. '*Not*' *Added.*—The reporter adds *not* to the signs for *but* and *or*, by an En-hook; thus, ⌡ but not, ⌄ or not, ꝯ but are not.

REM. 6. *What or Would Added.*—The reporter joins a brief Way like an En-hook to the dash-vowel word-signs in the direction of Pee, and to the horizontal *and*-tick, to add *what* or *would*; thus, ⟋ of what, ⟍ to what, ⟋ all would, ⟋ and what, ⟋ and would. (*b*) This hook may be made into a circle, to add *s*; thus, ⟍ 'to what is, to what has, etc. See § 88, 3. (*c*) *What* or *would* may be added to *any* curve by a small hook turned on the convex side; thus, ⟍ for what, for would.

REM. 7. *Own Added.*—*Own* may be added by an En-hook (when the stroke is not more convenient) to the full-length consonants expressing *our;* and to the dash-vowel word-signs, and the horizontal *and*-tick, to which *our* has been added by an Ar-hook; thus, ⟍ by our own, ⟋ of our own, ↪ and our own.

REM. 8. ' *Than*' *added to Comparatives.*—Any comparative without a final hook, loop, or circle may have 'than' added to it by an En-hook. Mern, for instance, **may** be written for 'more than;' Iss-Nern for 'sooner than.'

2. LIST OF CONTRACTIONS CONTAINING FINAL-HOOK SIGNS.

§ 202. It is found convenient to contract five words whose outlines contain final-hook signs; thus,

⟋ investigation ⟋ phonographer ⟍ phonographic

⟍ representation ⟋ representative.

§ 203. LIST OF WORDS REPRESENTED BY FINAL-HOOK SIGNS.

[above]	done	objection	than
again	down	objective	then
alone	even	often	truthful-ly
before	gave	opinion	upon
been	general-ly	phonography	whatever
can	I have	remembrance	whichever
careful-ly	known	Standard Pho-	whoever
differ	man	nography	within.
difference	men	subjection	
different	none	subjective	

Reporting Style, to add *if* by an Ef-hook? Write 'or if, but if.' With the use of the reporting principles explained in Rems. 5, 6, 7, and 8, write ' but not, or not, but are not, or are not, of what, to what, all would, and what, and would, to what is, to what has, for what, for would, by our own, of our own, and our own, our own, more than, sooner than.'

§ 202. Repeatedly write the contractions containing final-hook signs.

§ 203. Repeatedly write the proper signs for the words in § 203.

III. WIDENING.

P OR B ADDED TO EM.

§ 204. Em may be widened; thus, ⌒ ; to indicate the addition of the sound of *p* or *b*; thus, ⌒ lamp, ⌒ swamp, ⌒ rcmp, ⌒ impose, ⌒ impostor, ⌒ embezzle, ⌒ humbug, ⌒ ambition. (*b*) This sign may take an En or Shon hook, but no initial hook.

REM. 1. *Syllable-Name.*—The widened Em may be called Emp, when it represents *mp;* and Emb, when it represents *mb*.

REM. 2. Mer, ⌒ (in which the stroke is widened, to distinguish Mer from Wem), can not be mistaken for Emp or Emb with an Ar-hook, for this sign never takes an initial hook.

REM. 3. The advanced writer may use Emb in the second position as a sign for 'may be.'

REM. 4. *P Omitted.*—P is usually omitted when immediately preceded by *m* and immediately followed by *t, sh,* or *k;* as in *temptation, consumption, pumpkin;* for words of this class are sufficiently legible without the expression of the *p*.

VOCALIZATION OF EMP OR EMB.

§ 205. A vowel written beside Emp or Emb should not be read between the two consonants, but *before* or *after* both, according as it is written above or below; thus, ⌒ impósed, ⌒ ímpost, ⌒ impugn. See 'ambition, embezzle,' in § 204.

§ 206. WORD-SIGNS CONTAINING EMP.

⌒ ⌒ ⌒
import$_{ance}^{ant}$, improve-ment, impossib$_{il}^{le}$ty.

REM. *Derivatives.*—'Improved,' *improve* with Dee below it. The advanced writer, however, usually omits the Dee, 'improved' being readily distinguished from 'improve,' by reference to the context. (*b*) 'Impossibilities,' Empses.

---

§ 204. For what purpose may Em be widened? How, without joining Pee or Bee, may its sound be added to Em? What hooks does the sign for *mp* or *mb* take? Does it take an initial hook? What final hooks does it take? Write 'lamp, swamp, romp, impose, impostor, embezzle, humbug, ambition.' [Rem.] What is the name of the sign for *mp*? for *mb*? How is the widened stroke of Mer to be distinguished from Emp or Emb? How may the advanced writer write *may be*? Specify the cases for the omission of *p*. Give some words from which *p* may be omitted.

§ 205. Where does a vowel written beside Emp or Emb read? Write 'impose, impost, impostor, impugn.'

§ 206. Write 'important, importance, improve, improvement, impossible, impossibility' Write 'improved.' How is this word written by the advanced writer?

IV. LENGTHENING.

LENGTHENED CURVES.

§ 207. Doubling the length—

1. *Of Ing*, adds *kr* or *gr*; thus, thinker, hunger, longer.

2. *Of any other curve*, adds *tr, dr,* or *thr*; thus, letter, winter, older, mother, father.

REM. 1. *Syllable-Names.*—The lengthened curves may be named by prefixing the syllable-name of the stroke to the sound denoted by its lengthening; thus, Lay'ter, Way'ter, Wen'ter, En'ther, Fel'ther, Fer'ther, Fler'ther, Frel'ther, Ing'ker.

REM. 2. The reporter may distinguish words, in which a vowel precedes a lengthened curve, as in *older*, from words in which a vowel follows, as in *later*, by making the stroke, in the former case, considerably curved; and less curved, in the latter case; thus, older, elder, etc., later, letter, etc.

REM. 3. In the Reporting Style, it is allowable to lengthen a final Ing, to add *their, they are,* or *there;* thus, among their.

REM. 4. The past tense or perfect participle of a verb ending in Lay'ter, En'ter or Ing'ker, is usually formed best by adding Dee to the primitive; thus, slaughtered, rendered, anchored.

REM. 5. Shel'ter, if written quite slanting, may, unlike Shel (§ 161, *b*), stand alone and be used with advantage for *shelter, shoulder.* (*b*) Dee may be added for *sheltered, shouldered.*

VOCALIZATION OF THE LENGTHENED CURVES.

§ 208. (*a*) Sounds added by lengthening a curve should be read—

1. After the vowel following the stroke; thus, water, neither.

---

§ 207. What sounds are added to Ing by doubling its length? What sounds are added to any other curve-sign by lengthening it? Write 'thinker, longer, letter, winter, older, mother, father.' [Rem.] How are the lengthened curves named? How, in the Reporting Style, may words in which a vowel precedes a curve, as *older*, be distinguished from words in which a vowel follows a lengthened curve, as in *later?* Write 'older, elder, later, letter, latter.' What is said of adding *their* to a final Ing? How is it best to form the past tense or perfect participle of verbs ending in Lay'ter, En'ter, or Ing'ker? Write 'slaughtered, rendered, anchored.' May Shel'ter stand alone? Write 'shelter, shoulder, sheltered, shouldered.'

§ 208. Are the sounds added by lengthening read before or after a vowel after the lengthened stroke? before or after a sound expressed by a final hook, loop, or circle? Write 'water, neither, modern, lanterns.' What is said as to the expression of a vowel following the sounds added by lengthening? Write 'alteration, eccentric, angry, ultra.'

2. Before any sound expressed by a final hook, loop, or circle; thus, ⌒ modern, ⌒ lanterns.

(b) Hence, a vowel following the consonants denoted by lengthening must be omitted, as in ⌒ alteration; written before a following stroke-consonant, as in ⌒ eccentric; or written after an Ar-hook sign; thus, ⌒ angry, ⌒ ultra.

POSITION OF LENGTHENED CURVES.

§ 209. In determining the position of a lengthened curve, regard the second half as a distinct sign, and place the first half in its proper position, according to the rules previously given. See §§ 52, 53.

(b) If a lengthened Way, for example, is to be written in the second position, let the first half, or Way proper, rest on the line, and the addition for *tr*, *dr*, or *thr* extend below the line. See examples in the next section.

§ 210. LIST OF LENGTHENED-CURVE WORD-SIGNS.

| ⌣ entire | ⌣ another | ⌒ matter |
| ⌣ rather | ⌣ whether | ⌣ f$_u^a$rther. |

REM. *Entirely, Material-ly.*—*Entirely* is formed from the sign for *entire*, in accordance with § 40, R. 2, by adding El; and *material* or *materially*, from the sign for *matter*, by adding Lay.

'THEIR,' 'THEY ARE,' OR 'THERE' ADDED.

§ 211. A curve-sign without a final hook, loop, or circle may be lengthened to add *their, they are,* or *there;* thus, ⌣ in there, *or* in their; ⌣ if there, if their, *or* if they are; ⌣ for there, for their, *or* for they are; ⌣ when there, when their, *or* when they are; ⌣ through there, *or* through their.

REM. *Own Added.*—*Own* may be added to these or any other signs expressing *their*, by an En-hook, when the stroke for *own* is not more convenient; thus, ⌣ from their own.

---

§ 209. How is the position of a lengthened curve determined?

§ 210. Repeatedly write and read the lengthened-curve word-signs. [Rem.] How are *entirely* and *material-ly* written?

§ 211. To what signs may *their, they are,* or *there* be added by lengthening? Write 'in there, in their, if there, if their, if they are, for there, for their, for they are, when there, when their, when they are, through there, through their.' [Rem.] How may *own* be added to signs expressing *their?* Write 'from their own, for their own, in their own.'

V. HALVING.

1. HALVING TO ADD EITHER T OR D.

§ 212. Either *t* or *d* may be added to certain signs, by halving them :

1. *To Any Unhooked Consonant-Stroke*, except El, Lay, Em, En, Ar, Ing, Way, Yay, Emp or Emb; thus, ⟍ pay, ⟍ pate, paid, ⟍ bee, ⟍ bead, beat, ⌊ vie, ⌊ vied, — get, ⟍ bowed, ⌊ doubt, ⟋ rapid, ⌐ credit.

2. *To Any Hooked Consonant-Stroke;* thus, ⟍ pray, ⟍ prayed, prate, ⌐ᵛ dry, ⌐ᵛ dried, ⟍ play, ⟍ played, plate, ⌐ glow, ⌐ glowed, gloat, ⟋ reply, ⟋ replied, ⌣ wind, ⌣ went, ⌐ wield, ⌣ ward, wart, ⌐ drift, ⌐ contrived, ⟍ paint, pained, ⟍ bent, bend, ⌐ gained, ⌐ find, ⟍ patient, ⌐ ancient.

Rem. 1. Way, Yay, Emp, and Ing are never halved *for any purpose;* but El, Lay, Em, En, and Ar *are* sometimes halved, as will appear from § 213.

Rem. 2. Hooked Way, Yay, Emp, unlike simple Way, Yay, Emp, may be halved; thus, ⌐ swooned, ⌐ yield, ⌐ impugned.

Rem. 3. *T Distinguished from D.*—If it should be deemed desirable, *d*, when added by halving to an Ef, En, or Shon hook sign, may be distinguished from *t*, by widening the hook; thus, ⌐ proved, ⟍ pained, ⌐ fashioned. (*b*) But this distinction is, for the most part, unnecessary.

Rem. 4. In other cases, when *t* and *d* would not be sufficiently distinguished if both were added to the same kind of line, *t* should not be added by halving, except to a light line; nor *d*, except to a heavy line. If, for instance, *bead* requires to be distinguished from *beat*, write Bed for the former and Bee-Tee for the latter. For corresponding reasons, write Pret for *prate*, but Per-Dee for *prayed;* Gled for *glowed*, but Gel-Tee for *gloat;* Wert for *wart*, but Wer-Dee for *ward;* Bred for

---

§ 212. To what signs by halving them may either *t* or *d* be added? What un-hooked consonant-strokes do not admit of halving for the addition of either *t* or *d*? Write 'pay, pate, payed, bee, beat, bead, vie, vied, get, doubt, rapid, credit, pray, prayed, prate, dry, dried, play, played, plate, glow, glowed, gloat, reply, replied, wind, went, wield, ward, wart, drift, contrived, paint, pained, bent, bend, gained, find, patient, ancient.' [Rem.] What unhooked consonant-strokes are never halved for any purpose? May El, Lay, Em, En, and Ar be halved for any purpose? Do Wayn, Yel, and Emp'en admit of halving? Write 'swooned, yield, impugned.' How may *d*, if it is deemed desirable, be distinguished from *t* when it is added by halving to an Ef, En, or Shon hook sign? Is this distinction often needed? Write 'proved, pained.' In what case should not a *t* be added by halving to a heavy line, nor *d* to a light one? How, if it were necessary, could you make a distinction be-tween 'bead, beat; prate, prayed; glowed, gloat; ward, wart; bride, bright; broad, *bride* or *broad*, but Ber-Tee for *bright* or *brought*. (*b*) But when the aid of the context can be availed of, these distinctions are seldom required.

REM. 5. *Ret, Red.*—The shortened Ray is never used alone; hence, 'rate, root, wrought, write, wrote, etc.,' are written with Ray-Tee; and 'reed, rod, road, rode, red, rĕad, rood, rude,' etc., are written with Ray-Dee.

REM. 6. *Past Tense, etc.*—The syllable *ted* terminating adjectives and the past tense or perfect participle of a verb, is usually written with Ted; thus, $\vee$ part, $\diagdown\!/$ parted. (*b*) The vowel of this syllable may usually be omitted without impairing the legibility of the writing.

---

2. HALVING TO ADD T TO A LIGHT, OR D TO A HEAVY SIGN.

§ 213. By halving the curve-signs for *l, m, n,* or *r,*—*t* or *d* is added, according as the shortened letter is made light or heavy; thus, $\frown$ lt, $\frown$ ld; $\frown$ mt, $\frown$ md; $\smile$ nt, $\smile$ nd; $\frown$ rt, $\frown$ rd; $\frown$ late, $\frown$ loud, $\frown$ meet, $\frown$ mode, $\smile$ need, $\smile$ night, $\frown$ art, $\frown$ erred, $\frown\!\cdot$ candidate, $\smile\!\cdot$ undoubted, $\smile\!\cdot$ indicate, $\smile\!\cdot\!\frown$ indicated. (*b*) Let $\frown$ when standing alone, is invariably written upward, and usually, when joined to other strokes. (*c*) Eld $\frown$ is always written downward.

REM. 1. *Final rd.*—Final *rd* preceded by Kay, Gay, Ef, Veé, or Lay, as in 'cured, cord, geared, fired, ford, veered, lured, lard,' may be written with Ard by careful writers; but for the majority of writers, and especially in rapid writing, it will be more convenient in these cases to write *rd* with *Red,* that is, with a shortened Ray.

REM. 2. The strokes of shortened Wem and Wen must not be widened when *d* is added; for these signs could not then be distinguished from $\frown$ Merd and $\smile$ Nerd. See § 168, Rem. 1.

---

brought?' What is said as to the use of these distinctions when the aid of the context can be had? Is shortened Ray ever used alone? Write 'rate, root, wrought, write, wrote, reed, rod, road, rode, red, rĕad, rood, rude.' What is said as to the mode of writing the syllable *ted?* Write 'part, parted.' Is it allowable to omit the vowel of this syllable?

§ 213. For what purpose may the curve-signs for *l, m, n,* and *r* be halved? When is *t* added to these shortened letters? When is *d* added to them? Write, with shortened signs, 'lt, ld, mt, md, nt, nd, rt, rd; late, loud, meet, mode, need, night, art, erred.' Write 'candidate, undoubted, indicate, indicated.' (*b*) What is the direction of Let? of Eld? [Rem.] What is said as to the mode of writing final *rd* preceded by Kay, Gay, Ef, Vee, Lay? Write, first with Ard, and then with Ret, the following words: 'cured, cord, geared, fired, ford, veered, lured, lard.' Is it allowable to widen the strokes of Wem and Wen when halved for the addition of *d?*

REM. 3. Since Yay, Emp, Ing, Way aré never halved, Eld can not bo read for *yd;* Med for *mpt;* Ned for *ngd;* Ard for *wd.*

REM. 4. In a very few cases when Eld can not be conveniently used, Let is employed for *ld;* as in 'muzzled, embezzled.'

REM. 5. The words 'undoubted; indicate, indicated,' in § 213, illustrate the principle of § 212, Rem. 6.

SYLLABLE-NAMES OF THE SHORTENED LETTERS.

§ 214. The halved letters, when spoken of as a class, may be called Shortened, or Short Letters; Half-Length Signs ór Letters; or simply Half-Lengths. (*b*) The different half-lengths are named by adding the syllable *et* or *ed* to the sound of the full-length, except when it is more convenient, or better for distinction's sake, to add the sound of *t* or *d* to the syllable-name of the full-length; thus, Pet or Ped, Bet or Bed, Let, Eld, Met, Med, Net, Ned, Art, Ard, Ret, Wemt or Wemd, Wert or Werd, Plet or Pled, Blet or Bled, Tlet or Teld, Delt or Deld or Dled, Pret, Bred or Bret, Mert or Merd, Pee'shont or Pee'shond, Dee'shond, etc.

§ 215. READING AND VOCALIZATION OF SHORTENED LETTERS.

1. Read a shortened letter (with the vowel or vowels beside it, if any; but *without* a final circle or loop) precisely as though it were a full-length sign.

2. Add the sound denoted by halving.

3. Add the sound of the circle or loop, if any.

Thus: tau-t = taught, fee-t = feet, tauk-t = talked, drif-t-s = drifts, plan-d = planned, complain-t-s = complaints, studen-t-s = students, ar-t = art, mĭ-d-st = midst, stāt-d = stated.

REM. From the preceding paragraph the following propositions are derived: (*a*) A shortened letter is vocalized precisely as though it were a full-length. (*b*) The *t* or *d* added by halving reads *before* a final circle or loop, but *after* all the consonants of the shortened sign, and after the vowels, if any, beside it. Hence the following rule respecting

A VOWEL AFTER T OR D.

§ 216. When a vowel occurs after a consonant which may be added by halving, the vowel must be omitted; as in anticipate; (*b*) written before a following stroke-consonant; as in wisdom; (*c*) or

---

Why not? Why can not Eld, Med, Ned, Ard be read as 'yd, mpt, ngd, wd?' Is Let ever employed for *ld?* Write 'muzzled, embezzled.'

§ 214. How are the shortened letters named?

§ 215. What is the proper method of reading a shortened letter? Write 'taught, feet, talked, drifts, planned, complaints, students, art, midst, stated.' [Rem.] Like what is a shortened letter vocalized? Where does the *t* or *d* added by halving read?

§ 216. What is said as to a vowel occurring after a consonant which may be added by halving? Write 'anticipate, wisdom, unity, notice.'

the consonant must be expressed by a stroke, and the vowel written after it ; as in ᒿ unity, ᒣ notice.

OF JOINING SHORTENED LETTERS.

§ 217. A shortened letter must not be joined to another stroke, except when it would be easy, by reference to their junction, length, width, curvature, or some other particular, to distinguish the joined signs from any other letter or letters ; as in ᒣ. portrait, ᒧ hated, ᒣ midnight, ᒧ sentiment, ᒧ named, ᒧ maiden. Hence, write ᒧ not ᒧ for *effect* ; ᒧ not ᒧ for *liked*.

Rem. It is not allowable to join a shortened Kay to Ef or Lay, or to make similar junctions of a straight line with a curve-sign, one or the other being short ; for such forms would be liable to be mistaken for lengthened curves, or for curves with a full-length straight line joined. Nor would it be allowable to join a half-length straight sign to another straight sign in the same direction ; for the two letters could not be certainly and readily distinguished from a single straight line or from two straight lines. (*b*) It should not be inferred from the example of *named* in the preceding paragraph, that a light full-length and a light half-length may be similarly joined, except by a very careful writer ; for, unless the half-length were heavy, the joined letters would be more readily mistaken for two full-length strokes. If Met, for instance, were joined to En, the two letters might very easily be mistaken for En-Em.

SHORTENED LETTERS DISJOINED.

§ 218. When it would not be allowable to join a shortened letter, it is occasionally better to detach it than to write its equivalent full lengths ; as in ᒣ dated, ᒣ treated, ᒣ dreaded, ᒣ freighted.

Rem. In a few cases, when it would be inconvenient to join a downward Est to a preceding hook, the inconvenience of disjoining a letter, or of a change of outline, may be avoided by writing Est upward ; thus, ᒧ opinionist, ᒧ factionist

POSITION OF WORDS WITH HALF-LENGTH LETTERS.

§ 219. When the first, or only, inclined or perpendicular stroke of a word is a half-length letter, that letter should be written—

1. Half the height of a Tee above the line, that is, in the first position, when the accented vowel is first-place ; as in ᒧ esteem, ᒧ bottom, ᒣ needed, ᒣ tried, ᒧ void.

---

§ 217. When may a shortened letter be joined to another stroke ? [Rem.] May Ket be joined to Ef or Lay ? a shortened straight sign, to another straight sign in the same direction ? Met to En ?

§ 218. Does an advantage sometimes result from disjoining a short letter ? When, and for what purpose, may Est be written upward ?

§ 219. Repeat the rule for the position of words whose first, or only inclined consonant is a half-length. Write, in proper position, ' esteem, bottom, needed,' etc.

2. On the line, that is, in the second position, when the accented vowel is second-place or third-place; as in ⌄ fate, ⌐ estimate, ⌐ abundant, ⌐ sent, ⌐ loud, ⌐ knowest.

REM. Words composed entirely of horizontal consonants, whether full-length or half-length—one or many—are, of course, written in accordance with § 52—

1. The height of a Tee above the line, that is, in the first position, when the accented vowel is first-place; as in ⌢ meet.

2. On the line, that is, in the second position, when the accented vowel is second-place or third-place; as in ⌐ met, ⌐ impugned.

USE OF THE HALVING PRINCIPLE.

§ 220. *T* or *d*, when it can not be allowably and more conveniently expressed in some other manner, may be added by halving to any consonant which it is allowable to shorten.

(*b*) Except usually in the following cases:

1. When the *t* or *d* is followed by a vowel which can not be safely omitted or written before a following stroke; as in 'motto, needy, notice, equity, veto, into, window.'

2. When the *t* or *d* is final, and is preceded by a vowel and a consonant which follows an initial vowel; as in 'unite, avowed, abed, acute.'

3. When the *d* is preceded by *l, r,* or *n,* preceded and followed by a vowel; as in 'hallowed, allied, elude, solid, rallied, married, borrowed, narrowed, torrid, tarried, moneyed, monad, renewed, annoyed, accompanied.' (*b*) This rule does not apply to *t* in a similar situation.

4. When the *t* or *d* is preceded by two vowels; as in 'quiet, poet, Jewett, naiad.'

5. When the only consonant preceding the *t* or *d* is initial *r*; as in 'write, rate, root, wrought, reed, road, red.' See § 212, Rem. 5.

6. When it would not be allowable to join a half-length, nor advantageous to detach it; as in 'liked, effect, cooked, gagged, judged, roared.'

REM. 1. The effect of the above rule and the first exception is to distinguish by outlines between such words as 'need, needy; wind, windy; might, mighty; fat, fatty.'

REM. 2. The effect of the above rule and the second exception is to distinguish by outlines between such words as 'void, avoid; bed, abed; foot, afoot.'

REM. 3. The preceding rule and the third exception secure a distinction by out-

---

[Rem.] Repeat the directions for determining the position of words composed entirely of horizontal signs. Write, and place according to directions, the following words: 'meet, mate, mode, night, need, indicate.'

§ 220. Repeat the general rule for the use of the halving principle. Specify the general exceptions. Write the words given to illustrate the exceptions.

lines between such words as 'fold, fallowed; lied, allied; sold, solid; rolled, ral-lied; marred, married; barred, borrowed; tarred, torrid; tired, tirade; ruined, renewed.'

REM. 4. The above rule and the fourth exception secure a distinction between certain words of a single syllable, as *quite,* and other words of two syllables, as *quiet.* So also 'Jude, Jewett.'

§ 221. LIST OF HALF-LENGTHS USED FOR WORD-SIGNS.

put, about, quite, could, God, good, if it, after, thought, that,

without, astonish-ed ment, establish-ed ment, is it, h-as it, used, wished, let,

let us, world, Lord, rēad, heard, word, might, immediate-ly,

made, somewhat, not, nature, [natural-ly,] under, is not, h-as not,

want, till it, told, until it—called, equaled—valued, particular-ly,

opportunity, spirit, toward, according-ly, cared, great, throughout,

in order, did not, do not, had not, gentlemen, gentleman—kind, cannot,

account, will not, we will not, are not, we are not, were not,

mind—may not, am not—we may not, it will not, which will not.

REM. 1. When all the consonants of a regular verb are expressed by a full-length word-sign, the past tense should be indicated by that word-sign made half-length. For example, see *use* in § 37; *equal, value,* and *care* in § 178, and the past tenses—

§ 221. Cover the word-signs in § 221, and repeatedly write the proper signs for the words below them. Next cover the sign-words and repeatedly read the signs above them. [Rem.] How is the past tense of a verb to be expressed when all the conso-nants of the present tense are expressed by a word-sign? Write 'use, used; equal, equaled; call, called; value, valued; care, cared.' Is the halving principle *used, equaled, valued,* and *cared*—in the above list. (*b*) The halving-principle may be employed, in some other cases, to add a *t* or *d*, to form a derivative from a word-sign or contraction; but very rarely, unless the word-sign or contraction contains the last consonant of the primitive word; hence, Mer, the sign for *remark*, should not be halved to add *t* for *remarked;* but, if preferred to writing a disjoined Dee, Ber, the sign for *remember*, may be halved, to add *d* for *remembered.*

REM. 2. *Derivatives.*—Derivatives from the sign-words of the preceding list may be written in accordance with the principles of § 40, Rem. 2. Thus: to the sign for *World* add El for *worldly;* El-En-Iss for *worldliness;* to the sign for *Read* add Ar for *reader*, and the *ing*-dot for *reading;* to the sign for *Nature* add El for *natural-ly;* El-Steh for *naturalist;* to the sign for *Spirit* add Lay for *spiritual-ly;* Lay-Tee for *spirituality;* to the sign for *Great* add Lay for *greatly;* Ray for *greater;* Steh for *greatest;* En-Iss for *greatness;* to the sign for *kind* add Lay for *kindly;* En-Iss for *kindness;* and prefix En for *unkind;* below the sign for *Astonish* or *Establish* write the *ing*-dot for *astonishing, establishing;* near the sign for *Particular* write Tee or Zee for *particularity, particularize;* near *Lord* or *Gentleman* write Lay for *lordly, gentlemanly.*

REM. 3. *Distinctions.*—If it should be deemed desirable to distinguish by signs between *particular* and *particularly*, etc., Lay may be written near the end of the signs for ' immediate, particular, according,' for ' immediately, particularly, accordingly.'

REM. 4.—' *It, Had, What, Would, Not,' Added.*—The reporter occasionally shortens a stroke to add *it, had, what,* or *would;* thus, _____ in it *or* in what; ⌐̈ had it *or* had had; ⌐̈ it would, it had, at it, at what; --(--- they had, they would. (*b*) To signs thus formed for *it would* or *it had; they would, they had,* etc., the word *not* may sometimes be added by an En-hook; thus, ---|-- it would not, it had not; ---(--- they would not, they had not.

§ 222. LIST OF WORDS REPRESENTED BY HALF-LENGTH SIGNS.

about	can not	good
according-ly	cared	great
account	could	had not
after	did not	has it
am not	do not	has not
are not	equaled	heard
as it	establish-ed	if it
as not	establishment	immediate-ly
astonish-ed	gentlemen	in order
astonishment	gentleman	is it
called	God	is not

employed in other cases to add *t* or *d* to form a derivative? Write, with the use of that principle, the word ' remembered.' How may ' particularly' be distinguished from ' particular ?' ' immediately' from ' immediate ?' ' accordingly' from ' according ?' What words does the reporter occasionally add to others by the use of the halving principle? Write ' in it, in what; had it, had had; it would, it had; at it, at what; they had, they would.' To signs thus formed how may *not* be added? Write ' it would not, it had not; they would not, they had not.'

§ 222. Repeatedly write the contractions given in § 222.

it will not	put	valued
kind	quite	want
let	rĕad	we are not
let us	somewhat	we may not
Lord	spirit	we will not
made	that	were not
may not	thought	which will not
might	throughout	will not
mind	till it	wished
nature	told	without
[natural-ly]	toward	word
not	under	world.
opportunity	until it	
particular-ly	used	

§ 223. LIST OF CONTRACTED WORDS CONTAINING HALF-LENGTHS.

acknowledged, afterward, forward, inconsistent, indiscriminat$^e_{ion}$,

indispensable, intelligence, intelligent, intelligible, interest,

manuscript, onward, practicab$^{le}_{ility}$, transcript, understand, understood.

REM. 1. *Derivatives.*—(*a*) '*Acknowledgment*,' Kay-Jay-Ment; (*b*) '*forwarded*,' Ef-Wer-Ded; 'forwarder,' Ef-Wer-Der; (*c*) 'inconsistency,' Enses-Ten-Ess; 'inconsistently,' *inconsistent* with Lay disjoined, or with El joined; (*d*) 'indiscriminately,' *indiscriminate* with Lay written near the end of the Kay; (*e*) 'intelligencer,' Net-Jay-Iss-Ar; 'intelligibility,' Net-Jay, with Bee written near the Jay; 'intelligently,' *intelligent* with Lay disjoined, or with El joined; (*f*) 'interested,' Net-Stet (see § 221, R. 1, *b*); 'disinterested,' Dees-Nets-Ted; 'disinterestedness,' *disinterested* with Ens joined, or with the beginning of Ens written under the Ted. (*g*) 'Transcribe-r, transcription, understanding, interesting,' and other derivatives, may be formed in accordance with the principle of § 40, Rem. 2.

§ 224. LIST OF CONTRACTED WORDS CONTAINING HALF-LENGTHS.

acknowledged—§ 223, R., *a.*; 221, R. 1, *b.*	intelligible—§ 223, R., *e.*
afterward	interest— do., *f.*
forward— § 223, R., *b.*	manuscript
inconsistent— do., *c.*	onward
indiscriminate—do., *d.*	practicable
indiscrimination	practicability
indispensable	transcript
indispensably	understand
intelligence—§ 223, R., *e.*	understood.
intelligent— do.	

§ 223. Write frequently the signs for the words of § 223.
§ 224. Repeatedly write the words given in § 224.

CONTRACTIONS AND EXPEDIENTS.

§ 225. Aside from the most advantageous use of stenographic *materiel* for the expression of sounds—speed and ease of writing are derived chiefly from the use of certain expedients, and principles of contraction, which may be presented under four heads:

      1. The imperfect expression of words.

      2. Joining parts of words.

      3. Joining words—Phrase-writing.

      4. Omission of words.

I. IMPERFECT EXPRESSION.

---

1. WORD-SIGNS AND CONTRACTIONS.

§ 226. For the sake of uniformity of practice and for ease of reading it is established that certain words, because of their frequent occurrence, or for other sufficient reasons, shall be expressed by a portion of their signs. These contractions, for the sake of distinction, are divided into Word-Signs and Contractions, as explained at § 104, Rem. 2.

For the partial lists of contractions and word-signs, and the remarks concerning them, see the portions of this work which are indicated by the following references: § 33–40; 54–55; 68–74; 102–104; 140–143; 178–180; 201–203; 206; 210; 221–224.

Complete lists of the contractions and word-signs presented in preceding sections will be furnished in a subsequent portion of this work, and accompanied by a synopsis of the principles pertaining to them.

---

2. CONTRACTED PREFIXES.

§ 227. The labor of writing may be materially diminished by the employment of contractions for those prefixes which it would be difficult or tedious to write in full. (*b*) The contractions are called Prefix-Signs, and the prefixes represented by them are denominated Sign-Prefixes.

---

§ 227. What is a prefix-sign ? What is a sign-prefix ?

§ 228. LIST OF PREFIX-CONTRACTIONS.

1. *Accom*—expressed by a heavy dot written at the beginning of the remainder of the word; thus, ⌐· accommodate, ⤺ accompany.

2. *Circum*—indicated by Iss written beside the first stroke of the re mainder of the word; thus, ⁰ʃ circumstances, ⤻ circumference.

3. *Con, Com, Cog*—denoted by a light dot written at the beginning of the remainder of the word; thus, ⤸, conscience, ⌐ commit, ⤹ comply, ⤻ cognate.

4. *Contra, Contro, Counter.*—When these prefixes can not be more conveniently expressed otherwise, they may be indicated by a tick written at the beginning of the remainder of the word; thus, ⌐ contradict, ⤺ controvert, ⤻ countersign.

5. *Decom, Discon, Discom*—expressed by Dee written near the remainder of the word; thus, ⤻ decompose, ⤻ discomfort, ⤻ discontinue.

6. *For-e.*—When this prefix can not be more conveniently written otherwise, it may be expressed by Ef written near the remainder of the word; thus, ⤻ foreknowledge.

7. *Incon, Incom, Incog*—expressed by En written above the line, and near, or partially over, the remainder of the word; thus, ⤻. inconstant, ⤻ incomplete, ⤻ incognito.

8. *Inter, Intro*—expressed by Net written in any position before the remainder of the word; thus, ⤻ interchange, ⤻ introduce.

9. *Irrecon*—expressed by Ar written near the remainder of the word; thus, ⤻ irreconcilable.

10. *Magna, Magni*—expressed by Em written over the remainder of the word; thus, ⤻ magnanimous, ⤻ magnify.

11. *Miscon, Miscom*—expressed by Em-Iss written above the remainder of the word; thus, ⤻ misconduct, ⤻ miscompute.

---

§ 228. How is *accom-* expressed ?—con, com, cog ?—contra, contro, counter ?—decom, discon, discom ?—for-e ?—incon, incom, incog ?—inter, intro ?—irrecon ?—magna, magni ?—miscon, miscom ?—noncon, noncom ?—recon, recom, recog ?—

12. *Noncon, Noncom*—expressed by Nen written over or through the first stroke of the remainder of the word; thus, ⌐ʝ. noncontent, ⌐↳ nonconducting, ⌐↰ noncommittal.

13. *Recon, Recom, Recog*—expressed by Ray written near the remainder of the word; thus, ↗⌐ reconcilable, ↗⌣ recommend, ↗⌢ recognize.

14. *Self*—expressed by Iss written beside the first stroke of the remainder of the word; thus, ○↖ self-respect, ○ʝ selfish, ○| selfhood.

15. *Uncon, Uncom*—expressed by En written on the line, near the remainder of the word; thus, ⌣⌐ uncontrolled, ⌣↘ uncombined.

16. *Unrecon, Unrecom, Unrecog*—expressed by Ner written partly over the remainder of the word; thus, ⌐↶ unreconciled, ⌐↘ unrecompensed, ⌐↶ unrecognized.

REM. 1. *Licenses in the Use of the Prefix-Signs.*—(*a*) One or more initial syllables resembling a prefix given in the preceding list, may be represented, if it can be advantageously, by the sign of such prefix. Hence, (*b*) *enter* may be expressed by the sign of *inter;* thus, ⌣ʝ• entertain; (*c*) *incum* or *encom*, by the sign of *incom;* thus, ⌣↘ incumbent; (*d*) *recum* by the sign of *recom;* thus, ↗↘ recumbent; (*e*) *con ÷ cong*, by the sign of *con;* thus, ⌐ conquer=congker; (*f*) *magne*, by the sign of *magna;* thus, ⌐↖ magnetism, ⌐⌐ magnesia.

REM. 2. *Prefixed Syllables.*—When any one of the prefixes given above is preceded by a syllable, as *in* or *un*, such syllable may be expressed by the proper letter or letters joined to, or written near, the prefix; thus, ⌐↘ uncircumscribed, ⌣ʝ unselfish, ⌐↖ undecomposed, ⌐↳ uncontradicted, ⌐↘ uninterrupted, ⌐↶ unforeseen, └↘ disencumber, └↗ disinterested, ⌣↘ unaccomplished. (*b*) The prefixed syllable, in such a case, may usually be left unvocalized. (*c*) To preserve lineality of writing, it is occasionally necessary that a prefix-sign, when joined to a preceding syllable, should be brought out of its usual position; as in 'disencumber.'

self?—uncon, uncom?—unrecon, unrecom, unrecog? [Rem.] How may initial syllables resembling a prefix be represented? How may *enter* be represented? incum? encom? recum? con = cong? magne? Write 'entertain, incumbent, encompass, recumbent, conquer, magnetism, magnesia.'—How may a syllable be prefixed to a prefix-sign? Write 'uncircumscribed, unselfish, undecomposed, uncontradicted, uninterrupted, unforeseen, disencumber, disinterested, unaccomplished.'—From

REM. 3. *Accom.*—The reporter usually omits the dot for *accom* from 'accomplish, accompany,' and their derivatives; but it should usually be inserted in 'accommodate, accomplice,' and their derivatives.

REM. 4. *Circum.*—(a) The advanced writer of the Corresponding Style may omit the sign for *circum* in writing 'circumstance' and its derivatives. (b) The practiced reporter may omit it in writing 'circumscribe, circumspect,' and their derivatives. (c) In the Reporting Style, 'circumference' and its derivatives may be written without the sign for *circum*, or, what is better, with that sign joined to the remainder of the word. (d) The experienced reporter will join the sign for *circum* in writing 'circumnavigate, circumvent,' and their derivatives.

REM. 5. *Cog.*—(a) The sign for *cog* should never be omitted. (b) When it is desired to distinguish this prefix from *con*, the latter is written with the dot, and *cog* with Kay-Gay. But this distinction is considered wholly unnecessary.

REM. 6. *Con, Com, Concom.*—(a) The reporter usually omits the sign of *con* or *com* from most common words. (b) *Con, com* in the following words and their derivatives is best written in the manner indicated by the syllable-names:—*conic*, Kay-En-Kay—*comity*, Kay-Em-Tee—*commissary*, Kay-Ems-Ray—*commiserate*, Kay-Ems-Ret—*commotion*, Kay-Emshon—*commerce*, Kay-Mers—*comrade*, Kay-Merd. (c) *Concom* occurs in *concomitant* and its derivatives. It may be represented by two light dots, one above the other, or, if more convenient to the writer, these dots may be united to form a perpendicular dash; thus, ⌡ or ⌡. *concomitant.* (d) The writer should accustom himself to make the sign for 'accom, cog, con, com, concom,' before commencing the remainder of the word.

REM. 7. *Con, Com, Cog, Contra, etc., Preceded by In.*—(a) The prefix *con, com*, or *cog* is sometimes expressed in connection with the preposition *in*, by the sign for *incon*, etc.; thus, ⌒ in conjunction, ⌄ in comparison. (b) The reporter may indicate this prefix, in other cases, by commencing the remainder of the word, when convenient, under the last stroke of the preceding word; thus, ⌐ᴗ common consent. (c) The prefix *contra, contro*, or *counter* may, in like manner, be expressed in connection with the preposition *in*, by the sign for *uncontra* (see Rem. 2, above); thus, ⌐⌒ in contradistinction.

REM. 8. *Contra, etc.*—The sign for *contra* may be used by way of license for *contri* in *contribute* and its derivatives. (b) But this prefix should not be employed for *contra* or *contro* when it is not a prefix, as in *contract, control*. (c) The tick for *contra*, etc , is usually best written at right angles with the following stroke; but any slight variation from that direction, which may seem convenient, will not impair the legibility of the writing.

---

what words may the sign for *accom* be omitted by the reporter? in what words should it be inserted? From what words may *circum* be omitted by the advanced writer of the Corresponding Style? by the reporter? In what words may the reporter join it? May the sign for *cog* be omitted? How may *cog* be distinguished from *con*? Make the distinction in writing *cognate, connate*. Is this distinction usually necessary? May the reporter omit the sign for *con, com*? Write the words mentioned in Rem. 6, b. How may *concom* be expressed? Write *concomitant.* How may *con, com*, or *cog* be expressed in connection with a preceding *in*? How may the reporter express this prefix in connection with a preceding word? How may *contra*, etc., be expressed in connection with a preceding *in*? How may *contri* be sometimes expressed? Write *contribute.* What is the usual

REM. 9. *For-e.*—(*a*) When the junction would be easy and the outline formed distinct, it is sometimes allowable to join Ef, the sign for *for-e*, to the remainder of the word; thus, ⟍⟋ forward, ⟍ forever. (*b*) This prefix is invariably joined when represented by other signs. (*c*) Ef, as a sign for *for-e*, is joined in the following words and their derivatives: Forever, forewarn, forsooth, forswear, forward— by the reporter in the following words: Foreclose, forefather, foreknow, forenamed, foresee, foreshow, forethought, forgery. (*d*) Write *for-e* with Fer in the following words: Foretell, forgave, forget, forsake; with Ef-Ar in the following words: Foreland, forelock, foreman, foremast, foremost, forerun, foresale.

REM. 10. *Inter, Intro, Enter.*—(*a*) The advanced writer very frequently joins the sign for these prefixes to the remainder of the word; thus, ⎿ interdict, ⎾ introduce, ⏋ entertain, ⌐ intercourse. (*b*) It may be joined in the following words and their derivatives: Enterprise, entertain, interchange, intercourse, interdict, interest, interfere, interjacent, interjection, interpolate, interpose, interpret (Net-Pret), interrogate, interrupt (Net-Pet), intersect, intertwine (Net-Tee-Wen), interval, intervene, interview, interweave (Net-Weh-Vee), introduce, introspect, introvert.

REM. 11. *Incon, Incom.*—(*a*) The sign for this prefix is occasionally joined to the remainder of the word; thus, ⌣ inconsistent, ⌢ incomplete, ⌣ inconvenient. (*b*) *Incom-n* or *in com-n* is sometimes joined to a following stroke by an In-hook; thus, ⌡ *inconsiderable* or *in considerable*. (*c*) The sign for *in-con* or *in-com* may be joined in the following words: Incompetent, incomprehensible, inconceivable, in consequence (Ens-Kens), inconsiderable, inconsistent, inconvenient.

REM. 12. *Miscon, Miscom.*—The sign of this prefix may be joined to the remainder of the word in writing 'misconduct, misconjecture,' and their derivatives.

REM. 13. *Noncom.*—(*a*) The sign for this prefix is never joined. (*b*) Non, written as it frequently is with Nen, is distinguished from Noncom, by being written *near* but not *over* the first stroke of the remainder of the word.

REM. 14. *Self, Self-contra.*—(*a*) The reporter very frequently joins the sign for *self* to the remainder of the word; thus, ⌐ self-esteem, ⌐ selfish. (*b*) *Self* may occasionally be joined by the reporter to a following Iss, by enlarging it; thus, ⌐ self-same. 'Self-sufficient,' etc., may be written in like manner. (*c*) *Self-con-m* may be expressed by writing the sign for *self* in the place for the *con* or *com* dot; thus, ⌐ self-conceit. (*d*) *Self-contra* may be expressed by the sign for *contra* with Iss prefixed.

REM. 15. *Uncon, Uncom.*—(*a*) The experienced writer may join the sign for this

direction of the tick for *contra* ? When is it allowable to join Ef as a sign for *for-e* ? Write 'forward, forever.' Write the words mentioned in Rem. 9, *c* and *d*.—May the sign for *inter, intro*, etc., be joined to the rest of the word? Write the words beginning with *enter, inter*, etc., in Rem. 10 *b*. — May the sign for *incom-* be joined? Write the words beginning with *incom-n-* in Rem. 11.—Is it allowable to join the sign for *miscon-m* ?—How is *non-* distinguished from *noncon-m* ?—Does the reporter ever join *self* to the remainder of the word? How may he join it to a fol-

prefix in the following words, and their derivatives: Unconcern, unconditional, un-constitutional (Ens-Teeshon-Lay, the first *t* being omitted, according to § 236, 3). (*b*) *Uncon* or *uncom*, like *incom*, may sometimes be joined to a following stroke by an In-hook.

REM. 16. *Unrecon, Unrecom, Unrecog.*—(*a*) The practiced writer always joins the sign for this prefix to the remainder of the word. (*b*) The sign for *unrecon* may be used disjoined for *in* and a following prefix *recon, recom, recog,* or *recum.*

WORD-SIGNS USED FOR PREFIX-SIGNS.

§ 229. Word-signs are sometimes used as signs for prefixes; thus, ⌣ altogether, (although, ⌢⌣ to-morrow, ⌣ to-night, ⌣/ underrate, ⌐· undertake, ⌣ understand, ⌣— undergo, ⌣ afternoon.

REM. 1. *Position of Word-Sign Prefixes.*—(*a*) All word-signs (except *under*), *when used as prefix-signs*, always retain the position they have as word-signs. (*b*) In a few words, *under*, when joined, adapts its position to that of the remainder of the word; as in 'undertake, understand.'

REM. 2. *'All, To, After, Under' Joined.*—Whenever the junction would be convenient and allowable, the signs for 'all (*al-*) to, after, under' may be joined to the remainder of the word; as in 'altogether, although, almighty, almost, all-sufficient, to-day, to-night, to-morrow, afternoon, afterthought, undertake, undersigned, understand, undergo,' etc. (*b*) *All* is represented by Lay in 'also, alway, always,' because in these words that prefix can be more readily written with Lay than with the word-sign for *all.* These words are sufficiently legible without vocalization.

§ 230. LIST OF SIGN-PREFIXES.

Accom	incog	recom
after	incon	recum
circum	in con, etc.	self
cog	incontra, etc.	self-con
com	in contra, etc.	self-contra
con	incom	uncon
con = cong	incum	uncom
concom	inter	under
contra	intro	unaccom
contro	irrecon	uncircum
counter	magna	uncontra
decom	magne	undecom
discom	magni	unfore
discon	miscon	uninter
disencum	miscom	unself
disinter	noncon	unrecog
encum	noncom	unrecon
enter	recog	unrecom.
for-e	recon	

lowing *Iss?* How may *self-con* be expressed? *self-contra?* May the sign for *uncon-m* be joined? Write the words beginning with *uncon-m* in Rem. 15.

§ 229. Are word-signs ever employed as prefix-signs? Write 'altogether, although, to-morrow, to-night, underrate, undertake, understand, undergo, afternoon.' [Rem.]

OTHER PREFIXES AND THEIR USUAL SIGNS.

REM. 1. The prefixes and initial syllables in the following list are always joined to the remainder of the word, and it is usually most convenient to write them with the signs indicated by the syllable-names placed after them:

Prefix.	Usual Sign.	Examples.
Amb, ambi	Emb or Em-Bee	ambiguous, ambition, ambulate
ante	Net	antedate, antecedent, antepast
ant, anti	Net	antidote, antipathy, antagonist
astro	Est-Ray	astrology, astronomy
bene	Bee-En	bènefit, benevolent, benediction
cata	Ket	catalogue, catalysis
cent, centi, centu	Iss-Net	centiped, centage, centennial
chiro	Ker	chirography, chirology, chironomy
còl	Kel	collect, college, colleague
cor	Ker	correct, corrupt, correspond
hepta	Pet	heptachord, heptarchy
hydro	Der	hydropathy, hydrometer
hyper	Hay-Per	hyperbole, hypercritic
juris	Jer-Iss	jurisdiction, jurisconsult
meta	Met	mętathesis, metaphysics
multi	Em-Let	multiply, multitude
octo, octa, oct	Ket	octennial, October, octant
philo, phil	Fel	philippic, philosophy
para	Per	paragraph, paradox
per	Per	perfection, perfume
peri	Per	periphery, periscopic
poly	Pel	polyglot, polygamy
retro	Art-Ray	retrospect, retrograde
stereo	Ster	stereotype, stereometer
subter	Sbed-Ray	subterfuge, subterranean
super, supra	Sper	superfine, superlative, supramundane
sus	Ses	suspect, sustain, susceptible
sys	Ses	system, systole, systemize
with	Theε	withdraw, withhold, withstand.

REM. 2. *Trans and Post.*—These prefixes may usually be contracted to *tras* and *pòs;* thus, ⌐ transact, ⌐ postpone.

REM. 3. *Trans-* in the following words and their derivatives is written with Ters, unless otherwise noted: Transact, Transalpine, transanimate, Transatlantic (Ters-Lent-Kay in the Reporting Style), transcend, transcendant (Ters-Ned-Net in the Corresponding Style; in the Reporting Style, Ters-Nent, that is, 'trăs-énant'), transcribe (Ters-Kay-Bee), transfer (Ters-Ef in the R. S.), transfigure, transfix, transform, transfuse, transgress, tranship (Ter-En-Ish-Pee), transient (Tershont,

---

What is the position of word-signs when used as prefix-signs? Does *under* ever adapt its position to that of the remainder of the word? Write 'understand, understood.' What word-sign prefixes are sometimes joined to the rest of the word? Write 'almighty, almost, all-sufficient, to-day, after-thought, undertake, undersigned,' etc. Write the words in which *all* is written with Lay?

§ 230. Write the words given in § 230, Rem. 1, with the usual signs for the prefixes, as explained. How are *trans-* and *post-* usually written? Write 'transact, postpone.'

that is *trá shent*), transit, transition-al (Trens-Eshon-Lay), translate, translucent (Ters-Els-Net), transmarine, transmigrate, transmit, transmute, transparent, transpire, transplant, transplendent, transport, transpose, transubstantiation (Ters-Bees-Tee-En-Shayshon; in the R. S., Ters-Bee), transverse (Ters-Vee-Ar-Iss).

---

3. CONTRACTED AFFIXES.

§ 231. The speed and ease of writing are considerably increased by the employment of contractions for certain affixes which it would be inconvenient and tedious to write in full. (*b*) The contractions are denominated Affix-Signs; and the affixes which they represent are called Sign-Affixes.

§ 232. LIST OF AFFIX-CONTRACTIONS.

1. Bl_y^e—expressed by Bee joined, when Bel can not be conveniently employed; thus, ⤳ sensibl$_y^e$, ⤳ profitabl$_y^e$. (*b*) Lay may be added to the Bee, when the legibility of the writing seems to require it.

2. *Bleness, Fulness*—expressed by a small circle written at the end of the preceding part of the word; thus, ⤳₀ serviceableness, ⤴ teachableness, ⊤ questionableness, ⤳ indispensableness, ⏉ doubtfulness, ⤳₀ mindfulness, ⟋₀ carefulness, ⟨ faithfulness.

3. *For-e*—expressed by Ef, joined whenever it can be conveniently, to the preceding part of the word; thus, ⟩ therefore.

4. *Ing*—expressed by a light dot at the end of the preceding part of the word; thus, ⸳| eating, ⸳⟍ keeping, |ᵛ dying. For the uses of this affix-sign, and the mode of expressing -*ing the* and -*ing a-n-d*, see §§ 112–114.

5. *Ingly*—expressed by a heavy tick written in the direction of Pee or Chay, at the end of the preceding part of the word; thus, ⟋⟍ lovingly, ⟍ knowingly.

6. *Ings.*—When this affix can not be more conveniently written with Ing-Iss, it is expressed by a heavy dot at the end of the preceding part of the word; thus, ⟋⸳ meetings, | doings, ⟍⸳ prancings.

---

§ 231. What is an Affix-Sign? What is a Sign-Affix?

§ 232. What is the sign for -*ble* or -*bly?* bleness, fulness? for-e? ing, ing a-n-d,

7. *Lessness*—expressed by a large circle written at the end of the preceding part of the word; thus, ⌒○ carelessness.

8. *Lty, Rty*—with any vowel preceding or following the *l* or *r*—may be added to any simple, or group, consonant sign, by disjoining it from the preceding part of the word; thus, ⌐\ instability, ⌐⌢ formality, \⌐ popularity, \⌐\ prosperity.

9. *Ly.*—When this termination can not be more conveniently written by an El-hook; as in 'nobly, feebly;' or by an El or Lay joined; as in ⌐⌐ homely, ⌐ completely; it may be expressed by Lay written near the end of the preceding part of the word; thus, ⌐⌐ manly.

10. *Mental, Mentality*—expressed by Ment written near the end of the preceding part of the word; thus, ⌐ instrumental *or* instrumentality, ⌐ fundamental.

11. *Ology.*—Jay written partially under, or joined to, the preceding part of the word, may be used as a sign for *ology*, when it can not be more conveniently expressed otherwise; thus, ⌐ zoology, ⌐ physiology, ⌐ theology.

12. *Rty.*—See subsection 8, above.

13. *Self, Selves.*—*Self* is usually expressed by a joined Iss; *Selves*, by a joined Ses; thus, ⌐ myself, ⌐ himself, ⌐ thyself, ⌐ ourself, ⌐ ourselves, ⌐ yourselves, ⌐ themselves. (*b*) But when the junction would be inconvenient or disallowable, the circle should be written beside the last stroke of the preceding part of the word; thus, ⌐ man's self, ⌐ our own selves.

14. *Ship*—expressed by Ish written near the preceding part of the word, or joined, if it can be conveniently, and without sacrifice of legibility; thus, ⌐ lordship, ⌐ friendship.

15. *Someness*—expressed by a small circle written at the end of the preceding part of the word; thus, ⌐○ irksomeness.

16. *Soever*—usually expressed by Iss-Vee joined; thus, ⌐ whatsoever, ⌐ whensoever, ⌐ whencesoever, ⌐ whereso-

---

ing the? ingly? ings? lessness? How may it be indicated that *-L-ty -r-ty* is to be added to a sign? What is the sign for *ly?* mental, mentality? ology? self, selves?

ever, $\big($ whosoever; (b) but when it would be inconvenient or disallowable to join Iss-Vee, -*soever* is represented by Iss written beside
the last stroke of the preceding part of the word; thus, $\diagdown^{\text{o}}$ whithersoever, ℓ_{o} whosesoever, $_{\wedge \text{o}}$ howsoever.

REM. 1. *Bleness, Fulness, Someness, etc.*—No confusion results from employing
the same sign for -*bleness,* -*fulness,* and -*someness;* -*self* and -*soever;* -*ment* and
-*mentality;* *ly* and *lrty.* (b) The sign for -*bleness,* -*fulness,* and -*someness* may be
regarded as Iss—the sign of their last sound. (c) The sign for -*lessness* is *Ses,* representing the final sounds of the two syllables.

REM. 2. *Derivatives.*—Derivatives from -*ology,* -*lty,* -*rty,* etc., may be expressed
by adding to the primitive the proper signs for the additional sounds of the derivative; thus, to Jay, the sign for *ology,* add Kel, to express *ological-ly;* and add Steh
to express *ologist.* (b) To express *lties* or *rties,* add Iss to the sign which is disjoined to denote the addition of *lty* or *rty.*

REM. 3. *Ly.*—This termination is usually expressed by an El-hook in words like
'feebly, nobly, visibly, sympathetically, legally;' (b) and in other words by Lay or
El joined; as in 'homely, completely, mostly (Ems-Lay), sweetly, bodily, rudely,
actually (Ket-Lay), honestly (Ens-El), suddenly (Sden-El), wantonly (Went-En-El).'
(c) In many cases when *ly* can not be conveniently or allowably joined, it may be
omitted without endangering the legibility of the writing; as in 'actively, objectively, subjectively, carefully, usually, surely.'

REM. 4. *Lty, Rty, Joined.*—The signs formed, according to § 232, 8, for -*bility,*
-*perity,* -*parity,* etc., may be joined occasionally; thus, $\diagdown\!\!\diagdown$ possibility, $\diagdown\!\!\curvearrowright$
sensibility, $\big\downarrow$ disparity.

REM. 5. *Mental Joined.*—Ment for -*mental* may usually be joined to the preceding part of the word; thus, Snet-Ment, 'sentimental.' (b) The reporter writes Ment
on the line for the words 'mental' and 'mentality;' writing, for instance, Ment-
Kayshon for 'mental action.'

REM. 6. *Alogy.*—The termination *alogy* in 'genealogy, mineralogy,' etc., may be
expressed by Jay written the same as for *ology.*

REM. 7. *Self, Selves.*—(a) *Self* may be added to a word ending in Iss not joined
to a hook, by enlarging the circle; thus, $\curvearrowright\!\!\!O$ one's-self; (b) but since Iss in the
word *man's* is joined to an En-hook, it would not be allowable to enlarge it for the
addition of *self.* See § 188, Rem. (c) *Self* might be added to 'our own' by a small
circle joined; but since it is not allowable to join a large circle to the En-hook, 'our
own selves,' and similar phrases, must be written with the sign for *selves* disjoined.
(d) *Self* and *selves,* even when separate words, are usually best written with the
affix-signs. *Self* occurs as a separate word in the following sentence from Pope:

---

ship? someness? soever? [Rem.] How may the sign for *bleness, fulness* be regarded? the sign for *lessness?* How are derivatives from *ology, lty,* etc., formed?
May the sign for *ly* be omitted? If so, in what cases? Is it ever allowable to join
the signs for *bility, perity,* etc.? Write 'possibility, sensibility, disparity.' Is the
sign for -*mental* ever joined? How does the reporter write the words *mental, mentality?* How may -*alogy* in *mineralogy,* etc., be indicated? When and how may
the sign for *self* be added to a preceding circle? Why must 'our own selves' be
written with a disjoined *selves?* How are *self* and *selves* usually written when

"A man's self may be the worst fellow to converse with in the world;"—and in such phrases as the following: 'our own self, my own self, his own self, my single self.'

Rem. 8. *-Ful-ly.*—The advanced writer may frequently add *-ful-ly* to a full-length straight-line consonant by an Ef-hook; thus, � truthful-ly, ⎯⎯ careful-ly. (*b*) If legibility should seem to require it, *ly* may be added by a disjoined Lay. (*c*) But in such cases, when it seems necessary to distinguish by signs between *-ful* and *-fully*, it is better to write the Ef-hook for *-ful*, and Fel for *-fully*.

Rem. 9. *Tive-ly.*—When it can not be added by a Tiv-hook, the termination *tive* is usually best written with Tef; thus, En-Tef, 'native;' Pees-Tef, 'positive;' (*b*) and the termination *tively*, with Tef, with El-joined, or with Lay disjoined. (*c*) The advanced writer, however, usually writes *-tive* for both *-tive* and *-tively*.

Rem. 10. '*Ancy,*' etc., *Implied by a Disjoined Letter.*—The advanced writer may sometimes disjoin a letter to express *-ancy, -ency, -idity,* etc.; thus, ⎝⎯ vagran-cy, ⎣\ despondency, ⎵⎛ validity, ⎯⎤ Christianity, ⎞\ verbosity.

WORD-SIGN AFFIXES.

§ 233. A word-sign may be used as an affix-sign; thus, ⎓⎓ here-after, ⎞ thereto, ⎞ ⟋ thereon, ⎞ ⟍ thereof, ⎴⎧ when-ever, ⟋⎦ wherever.

Rem. 1. *After* may be joined to 'there' for 'thereafter.'

Rem. 2. *To.*—The word-sign for *to* may be joined to Wer for *whereto;* to 'hither' for *hitherto;* and to 'on,' thus, ⎴⎓, for *onto,* which sometimes occurs. (*b*) *To* is expressed by Tee joined to the preceding part of the word in 'into, hereinto, there-into, whereinto; unto, hereunto, thereunto, whereunto; thitherto.' (*c*) 'Into, here-into,' etc., may usually be left without vocalization; but, for the sake of distinction, 'unto' and its compounds should have the vowel of its first syllable inserted.

Rem. 3. *On.*—The advanced writer may join *on* by an En-hook, in writing the following words: Hereon (Arn in the first position), thereon (Thern [2]), whereon (Wern [2]), hanger-on (Ing-Arn), looker-on (Lay-Kren).'

Rem. 4. *Of.*—(*a*) *Of* is joined by an Ef-hook in 'whereof.' (*b*) It is written with the disjoined sign for *of* in the following words: 'Untalked-of, unheard-of, hereof, thereof, unthought-of.'

Rem. 5. *In.*—This affix is usually written with En joined; being thus distinguished from *on,* which is usually added by an En-hook. (*b*) *In* may be added by an En-hook in 'herein, hereinafter, hereinbefore,' etc.

---

separate words? Write 'man's self, our own selves.'—How may *ful-ly* be added to a full-length straight line? Write 'truthful-ly, careful-ly.' How, if desired, in such cases, may *fully* be distinguished from *ful?*—How is *-tive* best written when it can not be written with a Tiv-hook? How does the advanced phonographer write *-tively?*—How may the advanced writer imply the terminations *ancy, idity,* etc. ? § 233. May a word-sign be employed as a sign for an affix? Write 'hereafter, thereto, thereon, thereof, whenever, wherever.' [Rem.] Write 'whereto, hitherto, unto,' and the other words ending with *to,* in Rem. 2, *b*. How are words ending with *unto* distinguished from those ending with *into?* Write the words ending with *on,* in Rem. 3. How is added *in* usually distinguished from added *on?* How

REM. 6. *Ever.*—The affix *ever* is always joined to the preceding part of the word; usually with an Ef-hook, as in 'whatever, whichever, whoever;' but with Vee in 'whenever, wherever, forever,' and a few other words.

§ 234. LIST OF SIGN-AFFIXES.

Alogy—§ 232, R. 6.	ing	parity—§ 232, R. 4.
ancy—§ 232, R. 10.	ing a-n-d—§ 114.	perity— do.
bility—§ 232, R. 4.	ing the—§ 113.	rity— do.
ble	ingly	self—§ 232, R. 7.
bleness—do., R. 1.	ings	selves— do.
bly	lty— § 232, R. 4.	someness—§ 232, R. 1.
ency—§ 232, R. 10.	mental— do., R. 5.	soever— do.
fulness—§ 232, R. 1.	mentality—do., R. 5.	sty—§ 232, R. 10.
ful-ly— do., R. 8.	ology	tive-ly—§ 232, R. 9.
for-e	nty—§ 232, R. 10.	

4. OMISSION OF CONSONANTS.

§ 235. The omission of consonants may be treated under the heads of Syn'co-pe, Apher'esis, and Apoc'o-pe.

Syn'co-pe is the elision of some of the middle letters of words; as 'desk-ibe' for 'describe;' 'in—tial' for 'influential.'

A-pher'esis is the elision of some of the initial letters of a word; thus, '—ber' for 'member, remember;' '—plish' for 'accomplish;' '—stance' for 'circumstance.'

A-poc'o-pe is the elision of some of the final letters of a word; as 'tr—' for 'truth; 'fr—' for 'from;' 'impos—' for 'impossible, impossibility;' 'pract—' for 'practicable, practicability.'

REM. Two or more of these principles may be employed in writing the same word; as of apheresis and apocope in writing '—cul—' for 'difficulty;' of apheresis and syncope in writing '—mar-able' for 'remarkable;' of apocope and syncope in writing 'f—ev—' for 'forever.'

1. SYNCOPE.

§ 236. Of medial consonants, it is allowable to omit—

1. P—when it is immediately preceded by *m*, and immediately followed by *t, sh*, or *k*; as in ⌊ tempt, consumption, pumpkin.

2. K—when it occurs between *ng* and *s* or *z*; or between *ng* and *sh*; as in ⌐ anxiety, ⌐ anxious, ⌐ sanction.

3. T—when it occurs between *s* and another consonant; as in ⌐ mostly; (*b*) also in a few words with a vowel between the *t*

may *in* be joined in 'herein,' etc. ?—How is -*ever* joined to the preceding part of the word?

§ 235. What is Syncope? Apheresis? Apocope?

§ 236. When is it allowable to omit *p? k? t?* Write 'tempt, consumption, anxiety, anxious, sanction, mostly, mistake, domestic.' What is the general rule for and the following consonant; as in ⌒ mistake, domestic, destitute.

4. *Generally*, any consonant whenever its expression would necessitate a tedious or difficult outline, and its omission would not endanger legibility; as—

K—from 'instruction, construction, destruction, refraction, infraction, restriction.'

L—from 'intelligence, intelligent, knowledge.'

N—from 'atonement, husbandman, transpose, merchandise, demonstrate, identical.'

P—from 'capable, capability.'

R—from 'describe, surprise, transcribe, manuscript.'

TG—from 'investigation.'

For instances of the omission, in the Reporting Style, of various consonants preceding Shon or Iss-Eshon, see § 197, R. 4.

REM. 1. *Trans.*—The n may usually be omitted from this syllable. The mode of writing it in most of the words in which it occurs, is indicated at § 230, Rem. 3.

REM. 2. In the Corresponding Style, when an En-hook has been omitted, as in writing 'atonement, attainment' (Tee-Ment), the hook may be added after lifting the pen.

REM. 3. The contractions for the following words are instances of syncopation: ac*know*ledge, dis*advanta*ge, ca*pa*ble, in*flu*ential, trans*gr*ess, sub*j*ection, sub*j*ective, inves*ti*ation, phon*ograph*er, repre*senta*tion, inte*lli*gence.

2. APHERESIS AND APOCOPE.

§ 237. It is occasionally allowable to omit some of the initial or final consonants of a word; thus, ＼ remember, ／ advantage, ⌒ remark, ⌒ impossible, ＼ indispensable, ＼ practicability.

REM. 1. The advanced writer may, in a few cases, extend the practice of apheresis and apocope beyond the established word-signs and contractions for the Corresponding Style; writing, for instance, 'Stens' for 'circumstance,' Ef-Ret for 'comfort,' Pel-Ish for 'accomplish' (see § 223, Rems. 3 and 6), Ray-Spens, for 'responsible,' Pers-Dee for 'proceeding,' Rayses-Tee for 'resisting,' Pee-Bee for 'public.' (*b*) An affix-sign, especially when it can not be conveniently joined, may be omitted by the reporter, whenever its omission would not seriously endanger the legibility of his writing; thus, com-Ens, 'commenc*ement*'—Ray-En-Jay, 'arrange*ment*'—Ned-Stend, 'understand*ing*'—Iths[3]-Gay, 'thanksgiv*ing*'—Fer-Gay, 'forgiv*ing*'—Lev-Kend, 'lov*ing* kind*ness*' (see § 182, R. 1, *b*).

REM. 2. *Special Contractions.*—(*a*) Sometimes a contraction which is suggestive and legible in one kind of subject-matter would not be legible, and therefore not allowable, in another kind. The practical reporter, understanding this, not unfre-

---

omitting medial consonants? Write the words given as examples of the rule of § 230, 4. [Rem.] When must the n of *trans-* be written? What is said as to writing an En-hook in 'atonement,' etc.?

§ 237. Give some examples of the omission of initial or final letters. [Rem.] What is said as to the use of the principles of apheresis and apocope by the advanced writer of the Corresponding Style? What is the reporter's practice as to the omission of affixes? What is said as to contractions for special uses? With reference quently, to meet the wants of the occasion, devises, for words and phrases of fre-quent occurrence, contractions which, though legible and proper for his present purposes, would not be legible, and would not therefore be used, in reporting of a kind differing materially from that for which such contractions were devised. He will, for instance, when reporting an anatomical lecture, use such contractions as Skel for 'spinal column,' En-Vee-Kay for 'inferior vena cava,' Pel-Em or Pel for 'pulmonary,' Lay-Ster-Tees for 'lower extremities,' Lay-Em for 'lymphatic,' Decs-Eshon for ' dissection ;'—when reporting a sermon or theological lecture, such con-tractions as Jays-Ef for 'justification by faith,' Sel³-Sel for 'salvation of the soul,' Jay-Cher for 'Jewish Church,' Jers-Em for 'Jerusalem,' En-Jays-Em for 'New Je-rusalem,' Trets-Em for 'Trinitarianism,' Vers-Em for 'Universalism,' Spers-Em'for 'Spiritualism,' Ar-Kay for 'Roman Catholic,' Wers-Ged for 'works of God ;'—most of which contractions it would obviously be unsafe to employ for the same words and phrases when introduced rarely, and as it were casually, into discourses of a differ-ent kind. (b) The experienced reporter's favorite mode of forming contractions for long compound names or phrases of frequent occurrence, is to join one or two let-ters (usually the initial ones) of two or more parts of the name or phrase ; thus, En-Ems-Kay, 'United States Mail Steamship Company'—En-Rel, 'New York and Erie Railroad'—Ens-Rel, 'New York Central Railroad'—Layter-Iss-Per, 'literal sense of prophecy'—Sper-Bee, 'Supreme Being'—En-Pee-Spet-Ter, 'in the popular ac-ceptation of the term'—En-Vee-Kay, '*inferior vena cava*'—Met-Pels-Yayn, 'may it please your Honor'—Met-Pels-Kay, 'may it please the Court'—Pees-Kay-Pee, 'party of the second part'—Jers-Kay, 'jurisdiction of the Court'—En-Dees-Kay-Kret, 'in the discretion of the Court'—Pers-Em, 'President's Message'—Kay-Ef-Rels, 'Committe on Foreign Relations'—Pee³-Iss-Tee, 'patent suit'—Ish-Ner-Pee, 'Commissioner of Patents'—En-Enses-Pee-Efs, 'in the United States Patent Office' —Iss-Dent, 'substantial identity'—Dees-Em, 'defendant's machine'—Plets-Em, 'plaintiff's machine'—Vee-Jet-Kay, 'vegetable kingdom.'

REM. 3. *How to Form a Contraction.*—(a) When it seems necessary or desirable for any reason to shorten the expression of a word, the best contraction for it is to be devised with reference to four particulars, which are here stated in the order of their importance :

1. Distinctness and suggestiveness, that is, legibility. 2. Brevity, and ease of formation. 3. Convenience of forming the derivatives from it. 4. The convenience of joining it with other words.

REM. 4. *Legibility of Contractions.*—In cases of contractions settled and memor-ized as the signs of words, the requirement of suggestiveness is not so imperative as in other cases. Ber, for instance, though not of itself very suggestive of *remember*, becomes sufficiently suggestive and legible when memorized as a sign for that word. Sometimes a contraction, which is not sufficiently distinct from other outlines, when placed in a given position, may meet the requirement for distinctness when written in some other position, though it should be one not indicated by the accented vowel of the word. (b) The legibility of several adjacent contractions is frequently in-creased by joining them ; because, in this manner, peculiar outlines are usually secured, which are easily distinguished from outlines for other words or phrases.

REM. 5. The importance and frequency of the use of the three principles of con-traction—Apheresis, Syncope, and Apocope—in forming phonographic contrac-tions, is nearly in the proportion of 8, 22, 70.

REM. 6. For remarks respecting the omission of sign-prefixes (which comes under

---

to what considerations should a contraction be formed ? What is said respecting the legibility of contractions ?

apheresis), refer to § 228, Rems. 3, 4, 6, 14. For remarks as to the omission of sign-affixes (which comes under apocope), see § 232, Rems. 3, 8, 9.

---

5. OMISSION OF VOWELS.

§ 238. Since the majority of words are distinct from others in their consonant-sounds, and since in most cases where this distinction and that of the context are not sufficient, an equivalent one is provided, namely, that of outline or of position—it is evident that as soon as the phonographer has become familiar with the outlines of words, the vocalization may, to a considerable extent, be dispensed with, without materially diminishing the legibility of the writing. And there are several reasons which should induce phonographers to hasten to acquire such a familiarity with phonographic outlines as will enable them to omit the majority of the vowels. These reasons may be stated as follows:

1. The unvocalized style will secure advantages, in respect to the speed of writing, over the fully vocalized style, nearly equaling those secured by the latter style over the common longhand.

2. Judging of words by reference to the context, as is necessary to some extent when reading unvocalized phonography, leads to a careful observation of the grammatical relations of words, the construction of sentences, the signification of words and phrases, and the natural sequence of ideas; and thus are secured mental benefits which could hardly be obtained so well in any other manner.

3. Having acquired the ability to read unvocalized phonography, you will be able to release your correspondents from the drudgery and loss of time imposed by full vocalization. Remember that to save time is to lengthen life;—that to save unnecessary labor is to contribute in effect to the spiritual and material wealth of the human race.

4. The practice of omitting most of the vowels in writing the Corresponding Style will cultivate habits which are of great importance to the successful use of Phonography for reporting purposes.

§ 239. After the student has become conversant with the principles of vocalization, and tolerably familiar with consonant-outlines, he may omit—

1. Unaccented vowels; as from 'rot*a*ry, capt*ai*n, capit*a*l, doubtless, *a*natomy, *u*ndoubted.'

2. Even accented vowels from words of peculiar outlines; as 'beautiful, distinction, necessary, intended, always, certain, convenience, exercise, better.'

REM. 1. Usually the need of vocalization is inversely proportioned to the number of the consonants. (*b*) Words containing a single consonant with a vowel before and after it, should, if possible, have both vowels written; at least the accented one; thus, $\diagdown$ or $\diagdown$ for *obey.*

---

§ 238. What are the advantages of the unvocalized style of Phonography?
§ 239. What vowels may the practiced writer omit? [Rem.] To what is the need of vocalization inversely proportioned? Upon what principle may unvocalized

REM. 2. Vowels may usually be omitted with entire safety from outlines whose syllable-names make the required words, or closely resemble them; as from Kayses for *cases*, Es-Ens for *essence*, Lay-Ber for *labor*, Lay-Dee for *lady*, Ray-Dee for *ready*, Deest-Ingshon for *distinction*, Dred for *dread*, Layter for *later*, Enter for *enter*. (*b*) The vocalization of a portion of a word may be omitted in like case; as from the syllables denoted by *italics* in the following words: '*Scie*nce, pre-*emp*tion, *arg*ument, con*q*uer, e*v*il, inte*n*tion.'

REM. 3. A final unaccented vowel, especially ĭ, may usually be omitted with en-tire safety, when preceded by Lay, Ray, or *any* consonant *which, if not followed by a vowel, would be expressed by a hook, loop, or circle, or by lengthening or short-ening;* as the final vowels of 'fancy, rosy, penny, many, chaffy, bevy, body, pity, mighty, hungry, angry, entry, ultra, needy, windy.'

REM. 4. An initial vowel may usually be omitted, whether accented or not, *when the form of the word implies an initial vowel;* as from 'ask, assign, awake, oyer, argue, alum, older, avoid, annoyed.' See §.60; 117, 4; 118, 3; 152, 1; 156, 1; 185; 207, R. 2; 220, R. 2. (*b*) And in *other* cases, an *unaccented* initial vowel may usually be omitted, unless needed to distinguish the word from another not commencing with an initial vowel; as in *immeasurable*, to distinguish it from *measurable; immate-rial*, to distinguish it from *material*. (*c*) Words of the classes just mentioned are usually distinguished, in the Reporting Style, by difference of position, when they can not be distinguished by difference of outlines.

REM. 5. A simple vowel-sign may usually be omitted with greater safety than a diphthong or detached Way or Yay; and the latter, therefore, are rarely omitted, and are sometimes inserted in preference to an accented simple vowel; as in

❙ idea, ＼＿ argue.

II. JOINING PARTS OF WORDS.

1. CERTAIN VOWEL-SIGNS JOINED TO CONSONANTS.

§ 240. Whenever the junction would be convenient, it is allowable, and usually advantageous, to join—

1. *Initial I, Oi, Wĭ*—to a following stroke; thus, ❙ eyed, ❙ hide, ╱ highly, ╱ oil, ❙ wide. See § 101; 104; 139, 1.

2. *Final Ew, Ow, Yŭ, Yoo*—to a preceding stroke; thus, ＿ cue, ⌐ glue, ＼ new, ＼ bow, ＼ bowed, ⌊ doubt, ＼ now, ～ ammonia, ＼ nephew. See § 101; 104; 139, 2.

REM. In writing the derivatives from such words as 'cue, doubt, new, nephew' —for instance, 'cues, doubtful, news, newly, nephews'—the vowel-sign must be written separately.

Lay-Dee be written for *lady*, Ray-Dee for *ready?* What is said as to the omission of a final vowel occurring after a consonant which might be expressed by a hook, loop, or other mode of abbreviation? What is said as to the omission of an initial vowel? as to the omission of diphthongs and detached Way or Yay?

§ 240. What initial vowels are joined to a following stroke? what final ones to a preceding stroke? How are the final joined vowels written in derivatives?

2. JOINING AFFIX AND PREFIX SIGNS.

§ 241. The speed of writing is considerably increased by joining prefix or affix signs, whenever it would be allowable, to the other part of the word. The general cases in which such junctions are allowable have already been specified in the chapters treating of the prefix and affix signs.

REM. Several of the contractions given in preceding sections were formed by uniting a prefix or affix sign to the other portion of the word; as, 'understand, understood, inconsistent, forward, afterward.'

III. JOINING WORDS—PHRASE-WRITING.

§ 242. The speed and legibility of writing may be considerably increased by the judicious use of Phrase-writing, that is, by joining words occurring together in phrases or clauses; as, 'it-is-quite-necessary, we-are-very-sure, we-may-be-told, it-is-not-so.'

REM. The novitiate writer should, for a considerable time, confine his use of phrase-writing to joining sign-words. Experience will gradually teach him in what cases he may safely depart from this limit.

§ 243. *Phrase-Sign, Sign-Phrase.*—Two or more word-forms joined are termed a Phrase-Sign, or Phrā′se-o-gram; (b) and the words represented by such sign are denominated a Sign-Phrase, or Phrā′se-o-graph.

CAUTIONS.

§ 244. To guard against the disadvantageous use of phrase-writing, the following cautions are given:

1. Do not join words which are not united in a phrase or clause.

2. Do not join words when the junction would be difficult or disallowable.

3. Do not employ phrase-signs which extend an inconvenient distance above or below the line of writing.

4. Do not employ phrase-signs of inconvenient length.

REM. 1. The object of Caution 3, above, is to guard against the use of phrase-signs whose advantage would be more than counterbalanced by the loss of time in the pen's return to the line of writing, and by their interfering with the writing above or below.

REM. 2. Caution 4, above, would apply to a phrase-sign like that for the following phrase: 'I wish you could make some other arrangement.' This phrase would require a sign of inconvenient length; and it should, therefore, be divided into con-

---

§ 242. What is phrase-writing? [Rem.] To what extent should it be carried by the novitiate writer?

§ 243. What is a phrase-sign? a sign-phrase? What is an equivalent term for phrase-sign? for sign-phrase?

§ 244. What cautions are given as to phrase-writing? [Rem.] What is the object venient parts; thus, 'I-wish-you-could-make some-other-arrangement,' or I-wish you-could-make some-other-arrangement.'

REM. 3. *General Rules for Joining Words.*—For the purpose of reference, a few general rules for joining words are here stated:

1. A common substitute, or a noun of frequent occurrence, is frequently joined to a following verb; thus, 'he-had, it-may, they-were, they-shall, we-think, you-are, each-may, such-can, who-make.'

2. A defining, limiting, or modifying word is usually joined to the word defined, limited, or modified; thus, 'a-man, that-time, this-day, no-one, some-one, long-ago, recent-date, as-well-as (Iss-Lay-Iss), as-soon-as (Ses-Ens), so-as, great-advantage, as-great-as, as-much-as, very-much-more, a-very-important-matter, enter-upon, go-forward, come-into.'

3. A simple or compound auxiliary verb, with or without *not*, is frequently joined to the principal verb; thus, 'shall-be, will-have, will-be-seen, will-not-be-seen, may-not-be-seen, does-know, does-not-know, may-be-expected.'

4. A common verb is occasionally joined to a common word following it; thus, 'does-it, give-me, give-some, do-this, make-it.'

5. A preposition is usually joined to a following word; thus, 'to-the, to-him, of-my, for-this, in-that, in-which, by-which, upon-that, from-this.'

6. A common conjunction or adverb is usually joined to a following word of frequent occurrence; thus, 'when-shall, if-this, if-they, if-we, since-that, since-then, since-this, when-the, so-as, nor-is-it, nor-can, neither-this, as-well-as, and-this, because-it-is, though-they, there-are.'

POSITION OF PHRASE-SIGNS.

1. DETERMINED BY THE FIRST WORD.

§ 245. Usually the first word of a phrase-sign is written in its proper position, and the other word or words follow without regard to position; thus:

and a-n		but the—§ 70, R. 1.
and the		could not
as h-is, etc.—§ 38, R. 4.		for a-n
as the		for h-is
as a		for the
as well as		has been
as soon as		I am, I may
but a-n		I do

of Caution 3? How and why should be divided this phrase: "I wish you could make some other arrangement?" Repeat the general rules for joining words.

§ 245. By what usually is the position of a phrase-sign governed? [Rem.] How is the tick *a-n-d* written in phrase-signs?

(	I think		on a-n
	I will		on account of
	if a-n		on the
	if his		on the contrary
	in a-n		or a-n-d
	in his		or the—§ 70, R. 1
	in order that		should be
	in order to		should do
	in the		should a-n
	into a-n		should the
	into the		that h-is
	is a-n		to a-n
	is as, etc.—§ 38, R. 4.		to the
	is the		we have
	is to		we have no
	it is		we have seen
	it is not		which the
	it is said		you can
	it is the		you may
	it should be		you must
	of a-n		you must not
	of course		you will,
	of his		you will do.
	of the		

REM. 1. (a) The tick for a-n-d, when joined to a following tick a, an, or the, is written on the line. (b). In other cases, it is adapted to the position of the following words as provided in the next section.

2. DETERMINED BY THE SECOND WORD.

§ 246. The position of a phrase-sign is determined by the second word in the following cases :

1. When the first word is represented by a dash, or by a horizontal stroke, of the first position, and it can be joined to the second word without being brought down to or below the line ; thus, ⌐ in these, ⌐ in this, ⌐ in those ; so also ' of these, of this, of those ;' ' of each, of which, of much ;' ' I did not, I do not, I had not.'

2. When the tick for *a-n-d* or *the* is the first portion of the phrase-sign, and the second word is not *the* or *a-n-d ;* thus, ⌐ and it, ⌐ and for a, ⌐ and but, ⌐ and should, ⌐ and in a, ⌐ the first, ⌐ the way.

3. Occasionally, to distinguish one phrase-sign from another ; as, ⌐ his own, thus distinguished from ⌐ is no.

4. Occasionally, when the legibility of the second word depends considerably on its position ; as, ⌐ as if, ⌐ as much as.

REM. 1. The effect of the rule of § 245, Rem. 1, and of § 246, 2, is to secure a distinction by position between ' and a' and ' and but'—' and the' and ' and should.' See § 71, Rem. 2.

REM. 2. The position of the signs for *I am* and *I will* are determined by the first word, because the *I* could not be adapted to the position of the second word, without being brought down to the line. (*b*) For this reason *I will* is distinguished from *he will; I am*, etc., from *he may;* the latter commencing on the line, and the former commencing above it. See § 146, Rem. 5.

IV. OMISSION OF WORDS.

§ 247. The speed of writing may be considerably increased, without sacrifice of legibility, by omitting certain words, which may be intimated by the manner of writing the adjacent words, or readily supplied by a reference to the context.

' OF THE' OMITTED.

§ 248. *Of the*, connecting words, may be omitted, and be intimated,

---

§ 246. In what cases is the position of a phrase-sign governed by the second word ? [Rem.] How is *and the* distinguished from *and should? and a* from *and but?* How is *I will* distinguished from the reporting phrase-sign for *he will?*

§ 248. When may ' of the' be omitted ? When omitted, how are these words inti-

usually by writing the adjacent words near to each other; thus, ⌐ₒ|· close of the day; but occasionally by joining them; thus, ᴄ⌒ᴠ one of the most.

REM. *Of the* is usually represented by ⌐ when it is preceded or followed by a vowel-wordsign, as that for *eye* or *awe;* lest such vowel-wordsign should be mistaken for the vocalization of the word near which it is placed.

'HAVE' OMITTED.

§ 249. *Have* preceding *been* and *done* in phrase-signs, may be omitted, when it can not be more clearly or easily expressed by an Ef-hook; thus, ⟨ shall have been, ⟍ to have been ⅂, can not have done; but, ⟍ I have been, ⟨ which have been.

OMISSION OF WORDS IN THE REPORTING STYLE.

§ 250. The reporter, and the advanced writer of the Corresponding Style, may omit other words, as specified below·

1. *Of* may be omitted when it occurs between two nouns which can be joined to indicate the omission; thus, ⟋‾ Word of God, ⟍ kingdom of heaven.

2. *To* may be omitted when followed by an infinitive which can be joined to the preceding word, to indicate the omission; thus, ⌒⟍ I intend to be.

3. Generally, it is allowable, in the Reporting Style, to omit *any other word which must, and may readily, be supplied,* to complete the sense or construction; as—

A—from signs for such phrases as the following: 'for a moment, such a one, in a word, for a long time, in such a case.'

And—as in ⟍⟍ by and by; or, with the adjacent words joined, ⟍ wise and good; Mer-Mer, 'more and more;' Ver-Ver, 'over and over;' Ver-Bee-Vee, 'over and above;' Ray-Chay-Pee-Ar, 'rich and poor; Ther-Ther, 'through and through.'

From—to—as in writing ‖· from day to day; ‖ from time to time; or, sometimes with the adjacent words joined; thus, Ar³-Ar, 'from hour to hour;' Pels-Pels, from place to place.'

In—as in writing ⌣ hand in hand.

On the—as in writing ᴄ on the one hand,) on the other hand; Wens²-Dee, on the one side;' Thers-Dee, 'on the other side.'

---

nated? [Rem.] How usually should 'of the' be written when one of the adjacent words is a vowel-wordsign?

§ 249. What is the rule for the omission of *have?*

§ 250. What is the rule for omitting and implying *to* and *of* in the Reporting Style? What is the general rule for omitting words in the R. S.? Give examples of the omission of 'a, and, from—to, in, on the, or, or the, to, of.' [Rem.] How may a

Or—as in writing ⌒ more or less; Sner-Lay′ter, ‘sooner or later:’ Gret-Lays, ‘greater or less.’

Or the—as in writing Wen²-Ther, ‘one or the other.’

The—as in ⅃/ on the contrary; En¹-Eld, ‘in the world.’

To—as in writing ⌐ ‘according’ for ‘according *to*;’ ‘in relation’ for ‘in relation *to*;’ ‘in regard’ for ‘in regard *to*;’ Tees-Ems-Em, ‘it seems me,’ for ‘it seems *to* me;’ Tees-Med-Em, ‘it seemed me,’ for ‘it seemed *to* me.’

With—as in writing ⟍ ‘in conjunction,’ for ‘in conjunction *with*.’

Rem. 1. *Of.*—Instead of omitting *of* and implying it by joining the adjacent words, it is sometimes better to express it by an Ef-hook; thus, ⟍⟋⌒ variety of causes.

Rem. 2. *To.*—The omission of *to*, when it precedes a stroke to which it could not properly be joined, may be intimated, in the Reporting Style, by commencing that stroke at the line of writing; thus, ⟍ to us, *or* to say; *provided*, that the word so written would not be liable to be mistaken for some other word in the third position. (*b*) It is safe to write ‘you, whom, him, come’ under the line to indicate a preceding *to*; thus, ˑˑˑ to you, ˑˑˑ to whom, ˑˑˑ to him, ˑˑˑ to come.

---

word be written to imply a preceding *to*, when it could not properly be joined? Write, according to the principle stated, ‘to us, to say, to you, to whom, to him, to come.’

LISTS

OF

WORD-SIGNS AND CONTRACTIONS.

§ 251. LIST OF WORD-SIGNS.

P.
- up
- hope
- princip$^{le}_{al}$
- surprise
- upon
- put
- particular-ly
- opportunity
- spirit.

B.
- by
- be
- to be
- subject
- able
- member, remember
- number-ed
- before
- *above*
- been
- remembrance
- objection
- subjection

- objective
- subjective
- about.

T.
- it
- at, out
- its
- itself
- t$^{e}_{i}$ll, it will
- until, at all
- truth
- whatever
- truthful-ly
- till it
- told
- until it
- toward
- it will not.

D.
- do
- had
- dear
- during

- differ-$^{ent}_{ence}$
- done
- down
- did not
- do not
- had not.

CH.
- each
- which
- much
- which will
- whichever
- which will not.

J.
- advantage
- general-ly
- gentlemen
- gentleman.

K.
- kingdom, common
- *commonly*
- come
- because

(sign)	word	(sign)	word	(sign)	word
	call, equal-ly		*fully*	**TH.**	
	difficult-y		from		th$_y^{ee}$
	care		Phonography, often		the$_y^m$
	can		Standard Phon.		though, thou
	careful-ly		f$_u^a$rther		these, thyself
	quite		if it		this
	could		after.		those, thus
	called, equaled				themselves
	according-ly	**V.**			they will
	cared		ever		either
	can not, kind		have		the$_{re}^{ir}$, they are
	account.		however		other
G.			several		within
	give-n		value		then
	together		over		than
	gave		every, very		that
	again		even		without
	God		valued.	**S.**	
	good	**Th.**			see
	great.		think		so
F.			thank-ed		us, use — *yuus*
	if		through		astonish-$_{ment}^{ed}$
	for		thought		establish-$_{ment}^{ed}$
	few		throughout.		
	full				

Z.			let us		myself
)	was		world		himself
..-)-..	use = *yuz*		will not		we may
)	is it		we will not.		Mr., mere, remark
)	h-as it				more
...)...	used	**R.**			men
	is, his		her, he$_{re}^{ar}$		man
	as, has		are		importan$_{ce}^{t}$
	first.		our		improve-$_{ment}^{d}$
SH.			hers, herself		impossib$_{ility}^{le}$
	wish, she		ours, ourself		matter
	shal$_t^l$		ourselves		might
	sure-ly		we are		somewhat
	wished.		where		immediate-ly
ZH.			aware		made
	usual-ly		rather		mind
	pleasure.		Lord, rēad		may not, am not
L.			heard		we may not.
	wil$_t^l$		word	**N.**	
	whole		are not		in, any
	while, we will		we are not		no, know
	well		were not.		own
	alone	**M.**			influence
	let		me, my		when
			am, may, him		

	one.		away		an, and
	near, nor		whether		all
	manner		we		of
	opinion		with		too, two
	none, known		were		to
	not		what		awe, already
	nature		would.		or
	natural-ly				owe, oh
	entire	**Y.**			but
	another		your		ought
	under		yours, yourself		on
	is not		yourselves		who, whom
	h-as not		ye		whose
	want		yet		whoever
	in order.		beyond		should
			you.		ay, aye
NG.					I, eye, high
	thing	**H.**			how
	language.		he.		I have.
W.		**Vowels.**			
	why		the		
	way		a		

§ 252. LIST OF SIGN-WORDS.

	A.		at all
•	a—§ 71 ; 114		aware
	able		away
	about		awe
	above		ay, aye—102, R. 3.
	according-ly		**B.**
	account		be
	advantage		because
	after		before
	again		been
	all—178, R. 4.		beyond
	alone		but
	already		by.
	am		**C.**
	am not		call
•	an-d—71 ; 114 ; 246, 2		called
	another		can
	any		can not
	are—37, R. 2		care
	are not		cared
○	as—252, R. 7		careful-ly—232, R. 8
)	as it		come
	as not		common
	astonish-ed/ment—221. R. 2		*commonly*
	at		could.

	D.	⌒	from
⌉	dear	⌣	full
⌄	did not	⌣	*fully.*
⌊	differ-ent/ence		**G.**
⌐	difficult-y	⟶	gave
⌶	do	╱	general-ly—201, R. 3, *b*
⌡	done	╱	gentleman—221, R. 2
⌡	do not	╱	gentlemen— do.
⌶	down	═	give-n
⌶	during	─	God
	E.	▬	good
╱	each	⌐	great—221, R. 2
⌐	either		**H.**
⌣	entire—210, R. 1	⌐	had—221, R. 4
⌐	equaled	⌐	had not
⌐	equal-ly—178, R. 2, *a*	o	has—37, R. 1
⌐	establish-ed/ment—221. R. 2	)	has it
⌣	even	⌣	has not
⌣	ever	⌣	have—182, R. 1 ; 201 R. 4.
⌐	every	╱	he—146, R. 5
v	eye.	⌐	hear
	F.	⌐	heard
⌐	fu·rther	⌐	her, here
⌐	few	⌐	hers, herself
⌀	first	v	high—252, R. 8
⌣	for		

⌢	him		**K.**
⌢	himself		kingdom
∘	his—37, R. 1; 252, R. 8		kind
⟍	hope		know
⋀	how		known.
⌣	however.		**L.**
	I.		language
∨	I—103		let
∪ ⊂	I have—201, R. 2		let us
⟍	if		Lord.
⟍	if it		**M.**
⌢	immediate-ly		made
⌢	importan$_{ce}^{t}$		man
⌢	impossib$_{ility}^{le}$—206, R. 1, b		manner
⌢	improve-$_{ment}^{d}$—206, R. 1, a		may
⌣	in		may not
⌣	influence		matter
⌣	in order		me
∘	is—252, R. 7		member
)	is it		men
⌣	is not		mere—178, R. 1
|	it—221, R. 4	do.	Mr.—178, R. 3
⌊	its		might
⋮⌊⋮	itself		mind
⌠	it will		more
⌡	it will not.		much

⌒	my	⌒	ourselves
⌒	myself	-·|·-	out
	N.	⌒	over
⌣	nature	---	own—201, R. 7; 211, R. 1.
⌢	natural-ly		P.
⌣	near—178, R. 1	⌢	particular-ly—221, R. 3
⌣	no	⌣	phonography
⌣	none	⌒	pleasure
⌣	nor	⌒	princip_{le}^{al}
⌣	not—201, R. 5; 221, R. 4	---	put.
⌐	number-ed—252, R. 6.	=	Q.
	O.		quite.
⌐	objection—201, R. 3, a		R.
⌐	objective—201,R.3,c; 232,R.9	⌐	rather
⌐	of—201, R. 4	⌐	rĕad—221, R. 2
⌣	often—201, R. 1	⌒	remark
❘	oh, owe—252, R. 5, c	⌐	remember
╱	on	⌐	remembrance.
⌣	one		S.
⌣	opinion	⌐	see
⌐	opportunity	⌐	several
❘	or	⌐	shal_t^l
⌐	other	⌐	she
╱	ought	⌐	should
⌐	our—178, R. 5	⌐	so
⌐	ours, ourself	⌐	somewhat

	spirit—221, R. 2		through
	Standard Phonography		throughout
	subject—252, R. 5		thus
	subjection		thy
	subjective - 201, R. 3, c		thyself
	sure-ly—178, R. 2, b ; 232, R. [3, c		till
	surprise.		till it
	T.		to—229
	tell		to be
	than—201, R. 8		together—229
	thank-ed		told
	that		toward
	the—70, 113		truth
	thee		truthful-ly—232, R. 8
	them, they		too, two.
	the$_{rc}^{ir}$, they are—211		**U.**
	themselves		under
	then		until
	these		until it
	they will		up
	thing		upon
	think		us
	this—252, R. 7, b		usual-ly—232, R. 3, c
	those .		use = yus
	thou, though—229		use = yuz
	thought		used.

	V.		which will
	value		which will not
	valued		while
	very—178, R. 2, *b.*		who-m
	W.		whoever
	want		whose—69, R. 3
	was		whole
	way		why
	we		wil^l_t
	we are		will not
	we are not		wish
	we may—140, R. 2		wished
	we may not		with
	we will—140, R. 1		within
	we will not		without
	well		word
	were		world
	were not		would—201, R. 6, *c*; 221, R. 4.
	what—201, R. 6, *c*; 221, R. 4		**Y.**
	whatever		ye
	when		yet
	where—233, R. 2 3 4		you—140, R. 3
	whether		your
	which		yours, yourself
	whichever		yourselves.

REM. 1. *Word-Signs and Contractions Distinguished.*—For the distinction be-tween word-signs and contractions, see § 104, Rem. 2.

REM. 2. *Double Terminations, etc.*—In the lists of word-signs and contractions, a word is occasionally printed with a hyphen; thus, *give-n, h-as;* with double termina-tions; thus, *the$_{re}^{ir}$;* or with a hyphen and double terminations; thus, *differ-$_{ence}^{ent}$;* to intimate that the corresponding signs represent *give* and *given; as* and *has; their* and *there; differ, different,* and *difference.*

REM. 3. *Dot-lines, etc.*—The dot-lines in the lists of word-signs and contractions indicate the line of writing, and serve to show the position of the accompanying word. When a word-sign or contraction is printed without such a line, it is under-stood to belong to the second position.

REM. 4. *Italics, etc.*—Words not strictly belonging to the list of sign-words, but whose signs are inserted to guard against incorrect modes of writing, or for some other reason, are printed with *italics.* In the partial lists they were inclosed in brackets. (*b*) 'Object,' if written without the vowel 'ŏ,' belongs to the list of word-signs.

REM. 5. *Derivatives.*—(*a*) One or more sounds prefixed or affixed to a word to form a derivative may be denominated a *formative sound*, or simply a *formative.* (*b*) A derivative from a word-sign may almost invariably be formed by adding, by some convenient sign or mode of writing, the formative sound; thus, ⌐ com-monly, ⌣ uncommon, ⟍| remembered, ⟩ eyed, ! owing, ⌣ things, ⌐ kingdoms, —ᵒ comes (see § 38, 1 and 2), ⋯⌐⋯ ours, ⎰ whose, ⌐ great-est, ⌣ influences, ⌣ influenced (see § 38, Rem. 2), ⟶ careful, ⌐ cared, ⌐ valued. (*c*) Some of the derivatives from sign-words denoted by a vowel-sign—as 'awes, awful; owes, owed'—must be written with the proper consonant-signs vocalized, precisely as though they were not derived from sign-words; for in-stance, vocalize Zee with *au* for *awes;* Dee with *au* for *awed;* Zee with *ō* for *owes;* Dee with *ō* for *owed.* See § 69, R. 3 and 4; § 102, R. 1 and 2. (*d*) The sign of the formative is usually disjoined when any of the sounds adjoining the formative are not indicated in the word-sign; as in ⟍| subjected, ⟍⟍ objector, ⟍| ob-jected: but ⋯⌐⋯ naturally. (*e*) In other cases, the formative is usually joined, if it can be conveniently. (*f*) For convenience of reference, several derivative word-signs are included in the preceding list. Such are the signs for ' ours, our-self, themselves,' etc.

REM. 6. *Past Tense and Perfect Participle.*—When a verb is represented by a word-sign, and an additional stroke is necessary to write the past tense or perfect participle—as 'remembered, subjected, objected'—the advanced writer may employ the primitive word-sign for both the present and past tense; the tense or time in most cases being readily distinguished by a reference to the context.

REM. 7. '*Is, His, As, Has*' *Added.*—Any word denoted by the circle-wordsign—is, his, as, has—may be added—

(*a*) To any word-sign not terminating with Iss, by adding a circle; thus, ⌐ it is, it has; ⋯⌐⋯ at his, at as; ⌐ that h-is, that h-as; ⌣ if his, if as; ⌐ for h-is, for h-as; ⌣ in his, in as; ⌐ so h-as, ⟍ upon his.

(*b*) To the circle-wordsign, and to word-signs terminating with Iss, by enlarging the circle; thus, ◯ is his, is as, his is, his has; ◯ as h-is, as has, has his, has as; ◖ this is, this has; ◯ because his.

REM. 8. *Distinctions.*—If deemed desirable or necessary for sake of distinction, *his, has*, and *high, when written separately*, may be written with an h-dot before the signs for *is, as*, and *eye*. See § 146, Rem. 3. For remarks as to other distinctions, see § 178, Rem. 2; 201, Rem. 1: 206, Rem. 1, *a;* 221, Rem. 3.

REM. 9. For the different classes of the word-signs, and for various remarks concerning word-signs and their derivatives, see the portions of the Compendium indicated by the following references:

§ 253. LIST OF CONTRACTIONS.

	acknowledge—§ 228, R.1,*a*		nevertheless
	acknowledged—221 R.1,*b*		new—104
	afterward		now—104
	anything		notwithstanding
	become		object—142, R. 1
	capable		onward
	capability		peculiar-ity
	disadvantage		phonographer
	familiar-ity		phonographic
	forever		practicab*le*ility
	forward		probab*le*ility y
	highly		refer-red
	inconsistent		refer*s*ence
	indiscriminat*on*ion		regular-ity—153, 2
	indispensable—231, 2		remarkable
	influential		represent
	intelligence—223, R. 1, *e*		represented
	intelligent— do.		representation
	intelligible		representative
	interest—223, R. 1, *f*		something
	investigation—197, R. 4		transcript
	irregular-ity—152, 1.		transgress
	knowledge		understand—229, R. 1, *b*
	manuscript		understood— do.
	never		whenever
			wherever

Rem. 1. The derivatives from contractions are formed in accordance with a rule substantially the same as that for writing derivatives from word-signs (see § 252, Rem. 5); thus, ⟋| represented, ⟍⟋ objector, ⟍| objected—Kay-Jay-Ment, 'acknowledgment,' ⌐| interested, ⌐ɾ disinterested—En-Kay-Bel, 'incapable.'

Rem. 2. *Past Tense, etc.*—Rather than add a stroke to a verb-contraction, to form the past tense or perfect participle, the advanced writer will employ the primitive contraction for either the present or past tense; as, Ray-Pee for *represent* or *represented;* depending upon the context for distinction between the tenses or times.

Rem. 3. *Object*, if written without the vowel (see § 142, Rem. 1), is properly classed with the word-signs.

Rem. 4. *Whatsoever, etc.*—A number of contractions are formed by the use of the affix-signs for *soever*, which are not included in the preceding list. See § 232, 16.

Rem. 5. For partial lists of the contractions, and for various remarks as to contractions and their derivatives, see the portions indicated by the following references:

Contractions with Diphthongs .... § 104
Simple-Consonant Contractions............................ 142
Contractions with Initial-Hook Signs........................ 179
Contractions with Final-Hook Signs 202
Contractions with Half-Length Signs 223
Contractions Distinguished from Word-Signs............ 104, R. 2
Formation of Derivatives from Contractions............... 221, R. 1, *b*

---

§ 254. EXERCISE ON THE WORD-SIGNS AND CONTRACTIONS.

1. *Word-Signs.*—Be, each, language, under, ye, quite, good, beyond, already, call, careful, could, do not, gave, may not, together, yourselves, who, until, rather, let, member, because, alone, common, differ, give, has it, let us, man, one, over, she, remembrance, toward, told, we will, whole, wish, well, thyself, they will, thank, Standard Phonography, thanked, too, on, matter, if, I, his, kingdom, Lord, can, of, out, to be, want, we are, world, either, are not, been, heard, given, different, establish, may, we, yet, tell, none, even, advantage, pleasure, opinion, nor, during, manner, was, yours, in order, cared, another, carefully, is it, remark, not, way, yourself, me, even, farther, a, full, immediate, no, than, till, valued, whose, your, might, called, had, equaled, if it, naturally, remember, why, natural, gentlemen, who, would, somewhat, immediate, word, will not, first, about, entire, further, objection, made, is not, however, the, two, we may, you, which, until it, themselves, subjective, in, men, it will, no, number, own, put, Mr., I have, it will not, or, ours, were not, us, those, surprise, subject, often, oh, kind, word, up, will, opportunity, itself, established, care, but, am not, dear, myself, is, read, himself, objective, other, are, great, did not, ay, aware, has not, *commonly*, near, nature, phonography, ourselves, its, ourself, improve, immediately, my, particular, shall, our, near, shalt, every, before, *fully*, do, again, awe, down, God, from, eye, hear, come, any, few, her, general, difficult, away, first, here, herself, difficulty, at all, difference, *above*, for, high, gentleman, done, establishment, had not, by, an, have, and, he, able, according, known, accordingly, principal, ought, more, it, how, am, see, mind, account, much, all, improved, particularly, after, should, impossible, so, as it, influence, as not, impossibility, truth, we will not, these, sure, value, would, usual, thing, astonish, truthful.

very, then, astonished, were, usually, astonishment, till it, their, subjection, thy, at, we will, whether, as, they, surely, to, we are not, equal, with, thus, equally, when, use=yuuz, that, spirit, him, hers, generally, principle, hope, important, numbered, importance, thee, we may not, them, where, use=yuus, they are, whatever, truth- fully, wished, there, what, used, think, particularly, improvement, this, whichever, thou, aye, though, which will, thought, within, has, which will not, through, while, whom, throughout, will not, without, whoever, wilt.—Advantages, cares, has his, goods, if his, truths, thinks, manners, is as, because his, as it is, minds, tells, uses, wishes, wants, spirit's, man's, men's, improvements, out of, each of, eyed, uncom- mon, whose, influences, subjected, upon his, greatest, influenced, owing, in his, so as, this is, that is, at his, for his, it is.

2. *Contractions.*—Onward, influential, transgress, refer, disadvantage, forever, represented, transcript, highly, intelligible, indispensable, inconsistent, peculiar, become, new, representation, knowledge, afterward, object, representative, phono- graphic, familiar, intelligent, capability, something, wherever, never, familiarity, phonographer, refers, forward, capable, practicable, peculiarity, understood, intelli- gence, any thing, investigation, regular, nevertheless, irregular, interest, acknowl- edge, acknowledged, manuscript, represent, understand, practicability, notwith- standing, indiscriminate, irregularity, reference, regularity, whenever, probable, referred, probability, indiscrimination.

REM. 1. Let the preceding exercises be written till the words can be expressed with their correct signs, and in their proper positions as rapidly as they would be uttered by a good reader.

THE REPORTING STYLE.

§ 255. THE Corresponding Style contains, in germ at least, nearly every principle of the Reporting Style. The latter is distinguished from the former, principally by its extension of the use of three positions for outlines; its additions to the word-signs and contractions of the Corresponding Style; and its use, to the utmost extent consistent with legibility, of the other time-and-labor-saving expedients explained in the chapter entitled "Contractions and Expedients."

THE REPORTER'S RULE OF POSITION.

§ 256. (a) The reporter writes all words of distinct outlines in the positions assigned them in the Corresponding Style; (b) but when a word is not sufficiently distinguished by outline, the entire word, if composed wholly of horizontal lines—in other cases, its first perpendicular or sloping *stroke*—is written in the first, second, or third of the positions defined in the following sections, according as the word's accented vowel is first, second, or third place.

THE FIRST POSITION.

§ 257. The first position is—

1. *For Horizontals and Vowel-Signs*—the height of a Tee-stroke above the line of writing; thus, `all`, `already`, `we`, `my`, `in`, `sign`, `honor`, `cause`, `seem`, `sing, song`, `meek`.

2. *For All Other Signs*—with the bottom half the height of a Tee-stroke above the line of writing; thus, `by`, `each`, `if`, `chief`, `void`, `try`, `tried`, `bottom`, `esteem`, `needed`, `talk`.

REM. With double-line paper, for the first position, horizontals and vowel-signs should be written so that they will barely touch the lower side of the upper line; (b) perpendicular and sloping full-lengths are written half above and half below it; (c) and half-length sloping and perpendicular letters commence at the lower side of the upper line and descend half the distance to the lower line.

---

§ 255. What are the principal characteristics of the Reporting Style?
§ 256. What is the reporter's rule of position?
§ 257. What is the first position for horizontals and vowel-signs? for all other signs? [Rem.] How are signs of the first position written, when double-line paper is used?

THE SECOND POSITION.

§ 258. The second position for signs of any kind is on the line of writing; thus, | but, . a, | owe, ⊂ were, ⋀ how, ⌐⌐ may, ⌣ no, ·⌣ one, — go, ⌣ none, —⌐ came, | day, ⌐ low, lay, ail, ╱ ray, rōw, ⌡ show, |⌐ dwell, ⋀ rate, wrote, ╱— rogue, rug, ⌐⌐ male.

THE THIRD POSITION.

§ 259. The third position is—

1. *For Horizontals and Vowel-Signs*—just below the line of writing; thus, ⎯⎯ coo, ⎯⎯ áct, ⎯⎯⎯ mew, ⌣⎯· soon, ⎯⎯⎯ mount, ⎯⎯ to whom.

2. *For Perpendicular and Inclined Half-Lengths*—through or just below the line of writing; thus, .⌐. valued, ..)... used, ..⋀... proud, ⎯⎯⎯ put, ⎯⎯⌣ about, ·⎜· doubt.

3. *For All Other Signs*—through the line of writing; thus, --⎜-- dew, ../.. hue, ·/·· chew, --⌐-- sat, soot, -⌐- value, --⎤-- true, --⎤-- drew, --⋀-- prow, ⎯⎯/⎯ cool, ⎯⎯⎤-- acute, -⌣⎯ badly.

Rem. 1. Straight perpendicular and straight inclined half-lengths, without attachments, and of the third position, are usually best written just *below* the line of writing, as they are thus more certainly distinguished from the dash-vowel word-signs of the second position. (*b*) A careful writer, however, may safely write such half-lengths *through* the line.

Rem. 2. *Position of Lengthened Curves.*—In determining the position of a lengthened curve, regard the second half as a distinct sign, and place the first half in its proper position, according to the rules just given. See § 209.

POSITION DENOTED BY FIGURES.

§ 260. The figures 1, 2, 3 may be used to denote respectively the first, second, and third position; as in the lists of Reporting word-signs and contractions. To illustrate, "Pel—1 comply, 3 apply"— indicates that Pel in the first position represents *comply*; in the third position, *apply*. These figures are sometimes printed with "superior" types; thus, Ten[1], Ten[2], Ten[3]. (*b*) The figure 4 may be employed to indicate that the sign denoted by the syllable-name is to be written in

§ 258. What is the second position?
§ 259. What is the third position for horizontals and vowel-signs? for perpendicular and inclined half-lengths? for all other signs? [Rem.] What perpendicular or sloping letters are usually written just below the line? How is the position of a lengthened curve determined?
§ 260. What position is denoted by the figure 1? 2? 3? 4?

the position to imply a preceding *to*, according to § 249, R. 2 ; for instance, Es[4] indicates Es commencing at the line of writing ; thus, ⌐⌐ to say.

§ 261. A violation of the rule of position is occasionally necessary for the sake of distinction in some cases when the strict observance of the rule would have the effect to place in the same position two or more words of the same outline ; thus, Pee[1]-Tee, piety—Pee[2]-Tee, pity ; Ned[1]-Kayshon, indication—Ned[2]-Kayshon, induction ; En[1], any—En[2], no—En[3], own ; Per[1]-Met, prompt—Per[2]-Met, permit—Per[3]-Met, promote.

REM. 1. (*a*) In such cases, it is usually best to write the most frequent word in the position it would have in the Corresponding Style, and the other word or words in some other position, either arbitrarily; according to the ordinarily accented vowel, or according to the distinguishing accent (that is, the accent which some words take when contrasted with words from which they are to be distinguished ; as, "I did not say 'portion,' but '*ap*'portion ;' not 'prove,' but '*ap*'prove") ; thus, Peeseshon[2], position—Peeseshon[1], opposition—Peeseshon[3], possession ; Per'shon[2], operation—Per'shon[3], oppression ; Sper'shon[2], separation—Sper'shon[3], suppression ; Per[2]-Met, permit—Per[1]-Met, prompt—Per[3]-Met, promote ; En[2], no—En[1], any—En[3], own ; Perf[2], prove—Perf[3], approve ; Fel[2]-Ent, fluent—Fel[3]-Ent, affluent. (*b*) When, for the sake of distinction, a derivative must be written out of its natural position, and that position is different from that of the primitive, it is usually best to write the derivative in the position of the primitive ; as, Ned[1]-Kayshon, *indica'tion* (in the position of *indicate*, Ned[1]-Ket), in order to distinguish it from *induction*, Ned[2]-Kayshon ; Kayseshon[3], *accusa'tion* (in the position of *accuse*, Kays[3]), in order to distinguish it from *accession*, Kayseshon[2].

REM. 2. *Derivatives Following the Position of the Primitive.*—Legibility demands that in most cases a primitive word-sign depending considerably on position for legibility should, when a formative sign is added, retain its position, without regard to the general rule ; hence, Net[2], nature—*Net*[2]-El, not Net-*El*[2], natural; Preft[1], prophet—*Preft*[1]-Kay, not *Preft*[2]-Kay, prophetic ; Ken[2], question—*Ken*[2] Bee, not Ken-*Bee*[2], questionable.

ENLARGED WAY AND YAY.

BRIEF WAY ENLARGED.

§ 262. A brief Way may be enlarged—

1. *In its Natural Direction*—to add a Brief-Way sign-word ; thus, ⊂ we were, we would, ⊂ with what, ⊂ were we, ⊃ what we-re, what would, ⊃ would we.

---

§ 261. When is a violation of the rule of position necessary ? [Rem.] In such cases, where is the most frequent word written ? How is the position of the other word or words determined ? What usually should be the position of a word-sign, when a formative sign is added ?

§ 262. What is the effect of enlarging brief Way in its natural position ? inclined

2. *Inclined in the Direction of Chay*—to add any Brief-Yay sign-word ; thus, ⌒ with you, ⌒ would you.

Rem. 1. *Name.*—Brief Way enlarged may be called Enlarged Way ; or, when opening to the east, Weh'weh ; to the west, Wuh'wuh ; to the north-east, Weh'yeh ; to the south-west, Wuh'yuh. (*b*) ' Way' may be substituted for the first syllable of these names, if the sign is heavy ; for instance, the first illustration in § 262. 1, may be called Way'weh.

Rem. 2. If it is deemed desirable for distinction's sake, the use of enlarged Way may be restricted to its substitution for two semicircle-signwords whose signs can not be easily joined ; as for *we would, what we-re, you were,* but not for *we wer*, *what would, you would.* (*b*) For the practiced Reporter, however, this distinction is unnecessary.

Rem. 3. *Weh'weh Joined as a Hook.*—Weh'weh may be joined as a hook to Rent, thus ⌒, for *we were not.*

BRIEF YAY ENLARGED.

§ 263. Brief Yay may be enlarged, in its natural direction, to add a Brief-Way sign-word ; thus, ∪ ye were, ye would, ∪ you were, ∩ you would.

Rem. 1. The Brief Yay enlarged may be called Enlarged Yay ; or, when opening upward, Yeh'weh ; when opening downward, Yuh'wuh. (*b*) When the sign is heavy, ' Yay' may be substituted for the first syllable of these names ; for instance, the sign for *ye would* may be called Yay'weh.

Rem. 2. ' *Have, Ever, Of, If* ' *Added.*—A hook may be written within an enlarged Way or Yay to add *have, ever, of,* or *if,* when not better expresed otherwise ; thus, ⌒ we were of, we were to have.

LENGTHENED STRAIGHT LINES.

§ 264. The reporter may derive great advantage from doubling a full-length straight line, without a final attachment, to add *thr* for *there, their,* or *they are* ; the heavy lines being tapered toward their termination ; thus, --⌐··· till thr, ¯¯⌐ had thr.

Rem. 1. The lengthening of a straight line to repeat a consonant, especially in the Reporting Style, is of rare occurrence. On the contrary, the lengthening of a straight line to add *thr*, can be made of frequent service and decided advantage to the reporter; and since the repeated lines, as Bee-Bee, may be readily distinguished, by the context and by occasional vocalization, from the lengthened lines, as Bee′-ther—the propriety of the use of the latter is sufficiently established.

Rem. 2. *Names and Position.*—The lengthened straight lines are named by add-ing *ther* to the syllable-name of the stroke lengthened; thus, Bee′ther, Tee′ther, etc. Place the first half of a lengthened straight line in the required position. See § 209; 259, R. 2.

Rem. 3. '*Other*' *Added to Lengthened Curves or Straight Lines.*—Certain Nu-meral and Pronominal Adjectives, and Pronouns—as, 'one, three, four, five, eight, any, each, enough, every, few, many, only, several, some, such, sundry, which, my, our, your, their—rarely if ever followed by *their*, and whose final sign is a curve or straight line, may have *other* added to them, by lengthening such sign; thus, Wen′-ther[2], one other, one another—En′ther[1], any other—En′thern[1], any other one—En′-ther[3], no other (in the third position, to distinguish it from *another*, En′ther[2])—Ver′-ther[2], every other—Iss-Vee′ther[2], several other—Sem′ther[2], some other—Chay′ther[1], each other—Iss-Chay′ther[2], such (an)other—Em′ther[1], my other—Ar′ther[3], our other —Yay′ther[2], your other. (*b*) In a few other cases, to secure a special advantage, *other* may be added by lengthening a curve; as in En′ther[1]-Werds, in other words.

Rem. 4. *Within Thr, Been Thr, etc.*—As a sign with a final attachment can not be lengthened, the addition of *thr* to the signs for *been, within*, etc., is precluded; but the advantage of the principle may be secured to add *thr* (= there, their, they are) to 'upon, been, done, down, can, within, then, than,' and a few other words, by omitting the En-hook; thus, Pee′ther[2], upon thr (*up thr*, Pee′ther[2], voc. with ŭ) —Bee′ther[2], been thr—Dee′ther[2], done thr—Dee′ther[3] (voc. with ou), down thr—Kay′ther[2], can thr—Thee′ther[1], within thr—Thee′ther[2] (voc. with ĕ), then thr—Thee′ther[3] (voc. with ă), than thr.

Rem. 5. To a lengthened straight line there may be added—

1. *Own, Not, or One*—by an En-hook; thus, Tee′thern[3], at their own—Dee′thern[3], had there not—Kay′thern[2] (when Kay′ther-Net is not better for phrase-writing), can there not—Iss-Chay′thern[2], such (an)other one.

2. *Have, Ever, Fore, or Of*—by an Ef-hook; thus, Kay′therf[2], can there have, can there ever, can therefore—Tel′therf[3], until they are of.

Rem. 6. To a lengthened curve—

1. *Expressing Their*—*Own* may be added by an En-hook; thus, Ef′thern[2], for their own.

2. *Expressing There*— -*fore* may be added by an Ef-hook; thus, Em′Therf[2], may therefore. See § 182, R. 1, *b*.

Rem. 7. *To Their*—may be advantageously written with Tee′ther[2], as it is thus written in analogy with *of their*, Vee′ther[1]—within their, Thee′ther[1]—with their, Way′ther[1].

Rem. 8. '*Thr*' *Added to Verbs.*—A *t* or *d* sound expressed by halving may be omitted in many cases, principally from verbs, to permit the use of the lengthening

lines named? To what words may *other* be added by the use of the lengthening principle? Why can not a sign with a final attachment be lengthened to add *thr*? See § 208, 2. How may *thr* be added to *been, done*, etc.? How, to a lengthened straight line, may Own, One, or Not be added? Have, Ever, Fore, Of? When and how may *own* be added to a lengthened curve? When and how may -*fore* be added to a lengthened curve? How may *to the′r* be best expressed? How may *thr* be principle, to add *thr;* thus, Rays[1]-Deether, reside(d) thr—Dee-Peether, adopt thr—Steh-Teether[2], state(d) thr.

REM. 9. *Consonant-Strokes Trebled.*—The reporter may occasionally treble a stroke, to add *thr-thr;* thus, Way'therther[2], whether thr—Chay'therther[1], each other thr—Wen'therther[2], one (an)other thr.

REPORTING WORD-SIGNS AND CONTRACTIONS.

§ 265. All the word-signs (except that for *he*), and all the contractions, belonging to the Corresponding Style, are employed without change in the Reporting Style ; and, in addition, those indicated in the following lists of Reporting word-signs and contractions. Special word-signs and contractions may be devised in accordance with the principles of § 237, Rems. 2 and 3.

---

§ 266. REPORTING WORD-SIGNS.

P.

Pee	3 patent-ed (Pee[3]-Bel, patentable), party, happy
Pees	1 possible-ility, 2 posterior
Peeses	1 possibilities, 2 possess (Pee'ses-Tee, possessed—Pee-ses-Vee, possessive—Pee'ses-Ray, possessor)
Peest	3 happiest
Spee	1 speak (Spee'-Ker, speaker—Spee'-Bel, speakable), superior-ity, 2 expect-ed-ation (En-Spee, unexpected), 3 special-ty-ity (Es[2]-Pee, especial)
Ses-Pee.	1 suspicion, suspicious, 2 suspect-ed, 3 exasperate-a ation
Steh-Pee-Steh. .	2 step by step
Pel	1 comply, 2 people-d, 3 apply (Pel[3]-Kay, applicable-ility)
Spel	2 supply
Spels.	1 explicit-ness, 2 supplies
Spler.	2 explore-d-ation
Per	1 appear, proper, propriety (Em-Per[1], improper, impropriety), 3 practice, practica˜ (Per[3]-Ket, practicable-ility)
Pers	1 appears, 2 présent, 3 practices

---

added to such words as ' adopt, resided ?' For what purpose may the reporter treble a stroke? Write ' adopt their, resided there, each other their, whether they are, one another their, etc.

§ 265. Are the word-signs of the C. S. employed in the R. S. ?

Perst..........	3 practiced
Sper	1 spiritual-ity (Spers[1]-Em, spiritualism—Spers[1]-Kay, spiritualistic), 2 supreme, supremacy
Spers	1 express-ive, spiritualize, 3 suppress
Sperst	1 expressed, spiritualist
Prel	1 preliminary, 2 parallel, 3 parliament-ary
Sperl..........	2 superlative-ness
Pef	1 poverty, 3 hopeful-ness, hope to have
Pen	2 punish-ed-ment
Pens	2 punishes-ments, 3 happiness
Spen	1 spoken, 2 expensive-ness, 3 expansion-sive
Spens	2 expense, 3 expanse-ible (Spees[3]-Bee, expansibility)
Ses-Pen	2 suspension-sive
Spee'shon	2 exception-al (Spee'shon[2]-Bee, exceptionable)
Pees-Eshon	1 opposition, 2 position, 3 possession
Plens	1 compliance, 3 appliance
Splen	2 explain, explanatory, explanation (Splen-Bee, explainable)
Pref	1 perfect (Perf[1]-Ket, perfected), 2 Professor, prove, proof, 3 approve-al
Pren	1 pernicious-ness, 2 comprehensive-sion, 3 apprehensive-sion
Prens	1 appearance, 2 comprehensible-ility, 3 apprehensible-ility
Spren	3 supernatural-ness (Sprenst[3], supernaturalist—Spers[3]-Em, supernaturalism)
Sprens	2 experience (Sprenst, experienced)
In-Sprens	2 inexperience, in (the) experience
Pel'shon.......	1 completion, 2 complexion, 3 application
Spel'shon......	2 supplication
Per'shon	1 perfection, 3 oppression
Sper'shon......	1 expression, 3 suppression
Spers-Eshon ...	1 spiritualization
Pee'ther.	2 upon thr, up thr (voc. with ŭ)
Iss-Pet	2 except-ed, 3 accept-ed-ation (Spet[3]-Bel, acceptable)
Steh-Pet	3 stupid-ity
Plet...........	1 complete (Plet[1]-El, completely), complied, 3 applied
Pret	1 appeared, 2 pretty
Pent	2 upon it
Spent	1 spontaneous-ity, 2 expend-iture (Spen[2]-Ded, expended), 3 expand (Spen[3]-Ded, expanded)
Ses-Pend	2 suspend (Ses-Pen[2]-Ded, suspended)
Steh-Pend	2 stupend ous-ness

Plent	1 compliant, 2 plaintiff (sometimes Plet in phr.), plenty-iful, 3 applicant
Splent	2 explained, splendor, 3 supplant
Preft..........	1 profit-ed-able, prophet (Preft¹-Kay, prophetic), 2 provident-ce (Preft²-En, providential-ly)
Prent	2 comprehend (Pren²-Ded, comprehended), 3 apprehend (Pren³-Ded, apprehended)
Sprent	3 superintend-ed-ence-ent

B.

Bee	2 object—see § 142, R. 1
Iss-Bee........	1 subordinate-d-ion
Yuh²-Bee......	you be—see Rem. 2
Bel ,..........	1 belong-ed, by all, 2 believe-d, (Blef²-Ray, believei)
Iss-Bel	1 sublime, sublimity
Ber	1 liberty, by our, 3 brother-hood (Bren³, brethren)
Ben...........	1 combine, combination, 3 to have been
Yuh²-Ben......	you have been—see Rem. 2
Sbee′shon	1 exhibition
Blef...........	2 belief, able to have
Bel′shon	2 obligation
Bee′ther.......	2 been thr—§ 264, R. 4
Bet	1 by what, by it, body (voc.), 2 be it, be had, beauty-iful
Sbet	1 exhibit-ed
Bled	1 build-ing, built, 2 bold-ness, behold, beheld
Bred	1 a-broad, 2 remembered—see § 221, R. 1, b
Beft	2 before it—§ 221, R. 4
Bend..........	1 combined, behind, 2 be not, abundant, abundance, 3 bounty-iful

T.

Tee	1 time (usually Tee-Em in phr.), 2 take (Tee²-Ket, take it—Vert¹-Kay, overtake—Pret²-Kay, partake—Ned-Tee², undertake—Art²-Kay, retake—Bed²-Kay, betake—Ems¹-Kay, mistake), 3 took (but it ‾⎸‾), 4 to it
Teest	3 at first
Iss-Tee........	1 citizen, 3 satisfy-ied, satisfactory, as to it (Iss²-Tee)
Ses-Tee........	1 consist, 2 system-atic (Ses-Tees², systemize), exist
Steh-Tee	2 state (sometimes Stet in phr.)
Ter	1 internal, 2 contráct-ed (cóntract, Ter²-Ket—Ter′-tiv², contractive), 3 it were, at our, attract-ed
Iss-Ter	1 external-ity, 2 construct-ed, extreme (Ster²-Tee,

	extremity), 3 extract-ed (Ster'tiv³, extractive), as it were (Iss²-Ter)
Ses-Ter........	2 sister
Ins-Ter........	2 instruct-ed, (In-Ster-Ter, instructor)
Tler	2 tolerate-d-ion (Tler-Bel, tolerable—Net-El¹, intolerable)
Trel	1 trial, 2 control-led
Tef	1 it ought to have, 3 it would have
Iss-Tef........	1 set off, 2 set forth
Ten	1 contain, 2 taken, 3 attain (Tee³-Ment, attainment —Ten³-Bee, attainable), at one
Tens	3 at once
Iss-Ten........	1 constancy, 2 extension-sive, 3 circumstantial
Iss-Tens	2 extensible (Stees²-Bee, extensibility), 3 circumstance
Ses-Ten	1 consistency, 2 sustain
Ses-Tens	1 consistence, 2 existence
Tee'shon	1 tuition
Stee'shon	1 situation, 2 station, 3 satisfaction
Steh-Tee'shon..	2 constitution-al
Steh-Tee'tiv ...	2 constitutive
Telf..........	2 twelve-fth, it will have—§ 201, R. 4
Tlen	3 at length
Tlern	2 tolerant (intolerant, Net-El¹-Rent)
Tlerns	2 tolerance
Tref	1 contrive-ance, 3 attractive
Stref..........	2 constructive-ness, 3 extravagant-ce
In-Stref	2 instructive-ness
Tren	2 eternal, eternity, 3 at our own
Stren	1 extrinsic-al, 2 strange-ness (Ster²-Jer, stranger)
Ter'shon	2 contraction, 3 attraction
Ster'shon	2 construction, 3 extraction
In-Ster'shon ...	2 instruction, in (the) construction
Tee'ther.......	2 to their (Steether², as to their)
Tet	1 it ought, 3 it had, it would, at it—§ 221, R. 4
Iss-Tet	1 as it ought, 2 stood, 3 as it would, as it had
Ses-Tet........	1 consisted, 2 existed
Steh-Tet	1 constitute-d, 2 stated
Teft	1 it ought to have had, 3 it would have had
Tent..........	1 it ought not, contained, 2 it not, tend-ency, 3 attained, it had not, it would not
Iss-Tent.......	1 constant, 2 extent, extend (Sten²-Ded, extended)
Ses-Tent	1 consistent, 2 sustained, existent
Steh-Tent	1 constituent

Tleft..........	2 it will have had
Treft..........	1 contrived
Ter'shont......	2 transient

D.

Dee...........	1 dollar, contradict-ed (Dee¹-Ket, contradictory—En-Dee¹, uncontradicted), 2 defendant, 3 advertise-d-ment
Yuh²-Dee......	you do, you had
Deest	1 contradistinct-ion (Deest¹-Ing, contradistinguish-ed —Deest¹-Vee, contradistinctive—En-Deest¹, in contradistinction), 2 distinct, distinction (Deest²-Ing, distinguish-ed—Deest²-Ing-Bee, distinguishable—Deest²-Vee, distinctive)
Ses-Dee	2 is said
Del...........	1 idle-ness, 2 deliver-ed, delivery
Der...........	1 doctor, 2 direct-ed (Der-Ket, directory—Der-Ter, director), 3 dark
Sder	2 consider-able-ness
In-Sder	2 inconsiderable-ness
Def	1 divine-ity (Def¹-Ray, diviner—Def¹-Est, divinest—Def¹-Eshon, divination), 2 defense-sive, 3 advance-d (Dees³-Ment, advancement)
Sdef	2 said to have
Ses-Def.......	2 is said to have
Den	1 denominate-d, denomination
Yuh²-Den	you have done—see R. 2
Sdens	3 saddens, sadness
Dee'shon	1 contradiction, 2 condition-al, 3 addition-al
Dlen..........	1 delinquent-cy
Dlens	1 delinquents, delinquencies, 2 deliverance
Dref	1 derive, derivation
Dren..........	3 darken-ed
Drens	2 directness, 3 darkens, darkness
Der'shon	1 derision, 2 direction, 3 duration
Sder'shon......	2 consideration (In-Sder'shon, in (the) consideration)
Dee'ther	2 done thr, 3 down thr (voc. with ou)
Ded..........	1 did, 3 had had, had it—§ 221, R. 4
Yuh²-Ded	you did, you had had—see R. 2
Dlet	1 delight ed
Dred..........	1 deride-d, 2 dread-ed, 3 during it
Sdred	1 considered, considerate-ness
In-Sdred	1 inconsiderate-ness

Sdent	2 accident-al
Yuh²-Dent......	you did not, you do not, you had not--see R. 2
Dee'shond	1 conditioned
Dreft	1 derived, derivative

CH.

Chay...........	2 change-d, (Chay²-Bel, changeable) 3 charge-d (Chay³-Bel, chargeable)
Chel	1 each will, 2 children, 3 much will
Cher	1 cheer, each are, 2 chair, which are, 3 which were
Scher	2 such are, 3 such were
Chler	3 bachelor
Chef	1 which ought to have, 2 which have, 3 which would have
Iss-Chef	1 such ought to have, 2 such have, 3 such would have
Chen	1 each one, 2 which one
Schen..........	2 such a one
Cherf	1 cheerful-ness, 2 which are to have, which are of, 3 which were to have, which were of
Iss-Chay'ther ..	2 such (an)other—§ 264, R. 3
Chet...........	1 which ought, which it, 3 which had, which would
Iss-Chet	1 such ought, 3 such would, such had
Chelt	1 child-hood, which will it
Chert	1 cheered, 2 which are had, 3 charity-able
Cheft	1 which ought to have had, 2 which have had, 3 which would have had
Iss-Cheft	1 such ought to have had, 2 such have had, 3 such would have had
Chent..........	1 which ought not, 3 which would not—(when Chet-Net would not be more convenient)
Iss-Chent......	1 such ought not, 3 such would not, such had not—(when Iss-Chet-Net would not be better)

J.

Jay	2 Jesus, 3 large (En-Jay³, enlarge-ment—En-Jed³, en larged)
Jays	1 religious (Ar¹-Jays, irreligious)
Jayst	2 just-ice (sometimes Jays in phr.) 3 largest
Jay'ses	2 just as
Iss-Jay	2 suggest-ed, suggestion
Jel	2 angel (Jel-Kay, angelic--Ar²-Jel, archangel), 3 evangel-ical
Jels...........	3 evangelize
Jer	2 danger (En-Jer, endanger), 3 larger, jury

Jers	2 dangers-ous, jurisdiction
Jef ....:......	1 Jehovah, 2 Jove, 3 juvenile-ity
Iss-Jef	2 suggestive-ness
Jen	1 religion (Ar¹-Jen, irreligion), 3 junior, imagine-ary-ation (Jen²-Bee, imaginable—En-Jen³, unimagin-able)
Jens	2 generalize
Jenst	1 religionist, 2 generalized
Jay'shon	2 generation (Dee-Jay'shon, degeneration—Ray-Jay'-shon, regeneration)
Jay'tiv	3 imaginative-ness (En-Jay'tiv³, unimaginative)
Sjer'shon	2 exaggeration
Sjert	2 exaggerate-d (Sjert²-Ray, exaggeratory)
Jend	3 imagined (En-Jend³, unimagined)
Jays-Esh'on ...	2 justification
Jens-Esh'on ...	2 generalization

K.

Kay	2 country, 3 to come
Kayst	1 commonest, 2 exterior
Skays	1 exquisite-ness, 3 excuse-able
Skay'ses	2 success-ful
Kel	3 calculate-d-ion (Kel³-Bel, calculable)
Kels	3 conclusive-ness
Skel..........	1 skill, 2 scale, 3 school
Skels	2 exclusive-ness, 3 seclusive, secluseness
Ker	1 correct-ed-ness, 2 occur, 3 cure, accuracy
Kers	1 corrects, 2 occurs, course, 3 cures, curious
Sker	1 scripture-al, describe-d, 3 secure
In-Sker	1 inscribe-d, 3 insecure
Kler	1 clear-ed-ness, 2 clerk (Kler-Kel, clerical), color-ed
Skler	1 scholar, 2 secular
Ken	2 question-ed (Ken²-Bee, questionable), countrymen, 3 countryman
Sken	1 consequential-ness
Skens	1 consequence
Weh-Ken	1 we can—see R. 2
Kef	2 cover-ed
Skay'shon	3 exaction
Kay'tiv	3 active-ity
Kays-Esh'on ...	1 acquisition, 2 accession, 3 accusation
Klef	1 call forth
Sklef..........	1 skillful

Kref	1 corrective
Skref	1 descriptive-ness
In-Skref	1 inscriptive
Kren	1 Christian-ity
Krens	1 Christians-ize, 2 occurrence
Klerf	1 clairvoyant-ce, 2 colorific
Kel'shon	3 conclusion
Skel'shon......	2 exclusion, 3 seclusion
Ker'shon	1 correction, 2 creation
Sker'shon	1 description
In-Sker'shon ...	1 inscription
Ker'tiv........	2 creative
Kay'ther	2 can thr—§ 264, R. 4 ; could thr (voc.)—§ 264, R. 8
Sket	2 sect-arian (Skets-Em, sectarianism), 3 exact-ed-ness
Weh-Ket.......	1 we could—see R. 2
Klet	1 quality-ative, 3 conclude (Kel³-Ded, concluded)
Sklet	1 skilled, 2 exclude (Skel-Ded, excluded), 3 schooled, seclude (Skel³-Ded, secluded)
Kret	1 creature, 2 occurred, court (sometimes Kay in phrase-writing), 3 cured, accurate-ness
Skret	3 secured-ity
In-Skret.......	3 unsecured, insecurity
Kent..........	2 county (sometimes Kay in phr.), 3 countenance-d
Skent	1 consequent
Weh-Kent.....	1 we can not—see R. 2

G.

Gay...........	2 go, ago, 3 to go, to give
Sgay	1 signify-ied, significant-ce
Weh-Gay	1 we give, we have given, we go (voc.)—see R. 2
Gel	2 glory, glorify-ied
Gels	2 glorious
Sgler	1 singular-ity
Ger	1 degree
Gef	2 govern-ed-ment (Gef²-Ray, governor)
Weh-Gef	1 we gave—see Rem. 2
Gen	1 begin-ning, organ (Gen¹-Kay, organic), 2 begun, 3 began, to have gone
Gens	1 organs-ize (Genst¹, organized—Gen¹-Iss-Em, organism—§ 185, R. 1, b)
Sgen	1 significancy
Weh-Gen......	1 we have gone
Sgay'shon	1 signification

Sgay′tiv	1 significative
Gens-Esh′on ...	1 organization
Gel′shon	2 glorification
Glet	1 guilt-y
Gret	1 degreed
Geft	2 gave it
Grend.........	3 grand-eur

F.

Ef	2 fact, 3 half, affect-ed (effect-ed, Ef²-Kay)
Fel	1 feel, fall, fill, follow-ing, 2 fail, fellow, for all, 3 fool
Fels	1 false
Fler	1 if all are, if all our, follower (Fel¹-Ar, feeler), 2 fail-ure, for all are, for all our, fuller
Fer	1 if our, form-ed (Fer¹-Ar, former-ly—Fer¹-Lays, formless—Fer¹ with the *con*-dot, conform-ed—Fer¹-Bee, conformable—Fer¹-Lay, formal-ity—En-Fer¹, inform-ed-ant—Ray¹-Fer, reform-ed—En-Fer³, uniform-ity—Dee¹-Fer, deform-ed-ity—Per²-Fer, perform-ed-ance—Ters²-Fer, transform-ed), 2 free (Fer²-Lay, freely—Fred¹-Em, free-dom), 3 for our
Frel	2 from all
Fen...........	1 if one, 2 for one
Ef′shon	1 fiction, 2 fashion (Ef′shon²-Bee, fashionable), 3 affection-ate
Flen	1 fallen, fall in, 2 fell in, 3 philanthropy-ic-ist
Fren	1 frequency, 2 from one, furnish-ed, furniture
Fel′shon	1 affliction, 2 flexion
Fer′shon	1 formation, 2 fraction, 3 fruition
Fet	1 feature, 2 for it, for what (§ 221, R. 4), 3 future-ity
Fet-Steh	3 footstep
Flet	1 fault-y, filled, followed, feel it, 2 failed, felt, for all it, for all had
Fret	1 from what (from it, Fer²-Met)
Fend.........	3 found-ed-ation
Frent	1 frequent

V.

Vee	3 halve
Vees	1 visible-ility (En-Vees¹, invisible-ility)
Iss-Vee........	2 Savior

Yuh²-Vee......	you have—see R. 2
Ver	3 favor-ed (Ver³-Bee, favorable—Ef²-Vert, favorite)
Vers	1 converse-ant, 2 universe-al (Vers²-Tee, university —Vers²-Em, Universalism), 3 averse
Ven..........	1 evening, 2 have-ing been (when *have* preceding *been* can not be omitted according to § 249)
Vee'shon	1 conviction (with the *con*-dot), 2 vocation, 3 avocation
Vren..........	2 every one
Ver'shon	1 conversion, 2 version, 3 aversion
Vee'ther	1 of thr
Ved	1 of it, a-void-ed-ance, 2 have had, have it, evi-dent-ce, 3 halved
Vert	1 over it (§ 221, R. 4), convert-ed, 2 virtue (Vert²-Lay, virtually—Vert²-Es, virtuous—Verts²-Lay, virtuously), 3 avert-ed
Vent.........	2 have not (when Vee²-Net is not better)

Th.

Ith	3 thousand-th
Iss-Thest	2 south-east (Iss-Thes²-Ren, south-eastern)
Yuh²-Ith	you think—see R. 2
Thef	3 thankful-ness
Thren........	2 through one
Thet.........	2 think it
Thret	1 authority-ative, 2 through it

TH.

Thel	3 thou wilt
Threl	2 there will, they are all
Thef	1 they ought to have (Thef¹-Dee, they ought to have had) 2. they have (Thef²-Dee, they have had), 3 they would have (Thef³-Dee, they would have had)
Iss-Then	2 southern (Iss-Then²-Ray, southerner)
Thlef	2 they will have, 3 thou wilt have
Thref	1 there ought to have (Thret¹-Ben, there ought to have been), 2 they are to have, there have (Ther²-Ben, there have been), 3 there would have (Thred³-Ben, there would have been)
Threlf........	2 they are all to have, there will have (Threl²-Ben, there will have been)
Thet	1 they ought, 3 they would, they had, though it
Thred	1 there ought, 2 there it, 3 there would, there had

Thent	1 they ought not, 2 then it, then had, 8 they would not, they had not, than it (221, R. 4)
Thlent	1 they will not, 3 thou wilt not
Thrent	1 on either hand, there ought not, 2 on th other hand, 3 there would not, there had not
Thee'ther......	1 within thr, that thr (voc. with ă), 2 the other, the thr (voc. with ĕ), 3 than thr (voc. with ă) without thr (voc. with ou)
Thee'thern	2 the other one

S.

Es-Steh	2 assist-ed-ance (Es²-Stent, assistant)
Yuh²-Es	you see, you say (voc.)—see R. 2
Es'ef	3 useful-ness
Ess-Iss-Eshon ..	2 cessation, 3 secession
Est	1 east, 2 so it, so had
Es'tern	1 eastern

Z.

Zef	2 was to have, 3 used to have
Zee'ther	1 is thr, 2 was thr, 3 h-as thr
Zed	2 hesitate-d-ation
Zeft..........	2 was to have had

SH.

Ish	3 issue (Ish³-Dee, issued)
Yuh²-Ish	you shall—see R. 2
Sher	1 wisher, she were, 2 assure (Sher²-Ens, assurance), 3 share (Sher³-Ar, sharer)
Shef.	1 wish to have, she ought to have (Isht¹-Ben, she ought to have been), 2 shall have (Ish²-Ben, shall have been), 3 she would have (Isht³-Ben, she would have been)
Isht	1 she ought, wish it, 2 shall it, 3 she would, she had
Shred	2 assured, 3 shared
Sheft	1 she ought to have had (Isht¹-Net, she ought not), 2 shall have had (Ish²-Net, shall not), 3 she would have had (Isht³-Net, she would not)

ZH.

| Zher .... | 3 measure (Em-Zher³, immeasurable) |
| Zherd .... | 3 measured (En-Zherd³, unmeasured) |

L

Lay...........	2 will-ing
Iss-Lay........	3 salvation
Lef...........	2 will have, willing to have (sometimes *love-ing* in phr. ; as Lef-Ged, love of God—Lef-Kend, loving-kindness)
Welf.........	1 we will have
Lay'ther......	2 let thr—264, R. 8
Let...........	1 little, 2 will have had
Iss-Let........	1 as little
Iss-Led........	2 seldom
Welt..........	1 while it, we will have had
Lay'shon......	2 revelation, 3 revolution

R

Wer..........	2 work-ed, 3 with our
Rel...........	1 real-ity, 2 relate-d-ion-ive (Rel'tive for *relative* when a noun), 3 rule-d (Rel³-Ray, ruler)
Rels..........	1 realize
Ref...........	1 arrive-al, reveal-ed, 2 are to have, are of, revolve-d
Werf.........	1 we are of, we are to have, 2 whereof, 3 aware of
Sarn..........	2 concern (sometimes Iss-Ren in phr.)
Wern.........	1 we are in, 2 workman, 3 with our own
Ray'shon.......	1 irrational-ity, 2 reformation (Ray¹-Fer, reform-ed), 3 ration-al-ity
Ren-Esh'on....	1 ornamentation
Ard..........	1 ordinary (Ster²-Ard, extraordinary)
Iss-Ret........	2 certain-ty (sometimes Iss-Art in phr.)
Wert..........	2 were it, where it, where had
Reft..........	1 arrived, 2 hereafter
Sarnd........	2 concerned (sometimes Iss-Rend in phr.)
Weh'wernt....	1 we were not
Arder.........	1 order (sometimes Ard in phr.)

M

Em...........	3 home (Em³-Lay, homely), to him
Iss-Em........	1 similar-ity, 2 some, 3 consume
Wem.........	1 with me, with my, 2 with him
Mel..........	1 million-th, 2 promulgate-d-ion, 3 family
Mer..........	2 mercy-iful
Merl.........	1 immoral-ity, 2 moral-ity
Smen.......	2 examine-ation (Ker²-Smen, cross-examine-ation), some one

Wem'en........	1 women, we mean, 2 woman
Em'shon	2 mention (Wem'shon[1], we mention)
Iss-Em'shon ...	2 consumption
Emb	2 may be
Iss-Emp[b].......	1 simple-icity (Iss-Emp[1]-Ray, simpler—Iss-Emst[1], simplest), 2 somebody, exemplify-ied-ication, 3 example
Stemp	2 extemporaneous-ness (extemporary, Stemp[2]-Ray-Ray—extemporize, Stemp[2]-Rays)
Wemb	1 we may be
Emb'en	2 may have been
Wemb'en......	1 we may have been
Emp'shons	2 impatience
Em'ther.......	1 might thr—§ 264, R. 8
Sem'ther	2 some other
Sem'thern	2 some other one
Met..........	1 might-y
Smet.........	2 some time
Smed	3 consumed
Wemt.........	1 we might, we met, we made, 2 were made, were met
Mert.........	1 immortal-ity (Mert-Lays[1], immortalize), 2 mortal-ity
Ment	2 amount-ed, mental-ity, 3 movement
Sment	2 examined (Ker[2]-Sment, cross-examined)
Wem'ent	1 we may not, we meant, 2 were meant
Em'shond	2 mentioned
Wem'shond....	1 we mentioned, 2 were mentioned
Emp'end	1 imponderable-ility, 2 impenetrable-ility
Emp'shont ...,	2 impatient, 3 impassioned (Emp-Ish[3], impassionate)

N.

En........	1 never—see Rem. 15
Ens	2 commence-ment
En'ses........	1 United States, 2 commences-ments, necessary
Enst	1 instinct-ive, 2 commenced, next (sometimes Ens in phr.)
Steh-En	2 stenography-er-ic
Ses-En	1 season-ed, 2 as soon
Wen	1 we know, with no, 2 were no, were any (voc.)
Nel	1 in all, 2 only, 3 annual
Nels	1 unless, 2 only as, no less
Ner	3 owner, in our
Nerl	1 nearly, nor will

Nen	1 in one, any one, 3 no one
Snen	1 synonym-ous, is known (none), 2 has known (none)
Wen'en	1 we have known, we have none, 2 were known, were none, 3 were no one
En'shon	1 information (En-Fer[1], inform-ed-ant)
Nerns	1 ignorance
En'ther	1 any other, 2 another, 3 no other—§ 264, R. 3
Wen'$_{th}^{d}$er	2 wonder-ful, one (an)other
En'$_{th}^{t}$ern	1 intrinsic-al, any other one, 2 another one, 3 no other one
Net	1 in it, in what, interior (Net-El[2], interiorly), 3 anterior
Nets-Eshon	2 intercession
Ned	2 hundred-th, 3 owned
Went	1 when it, when had, 2 went, one would, one had
Neft	1 infinite-ty (*infinitude*, Neft[1] with Dee disjoined)
Wen'ent.......	2 on (the) one hand
Nernt	1 ignorant

NG.

Ing	1 English, 3 a-long, length (Ing[3]-Ith, lengthy)
Iss-Ing	1 single-d, 2 as long (see § 245)
Ing'en	3 lengthen
Iss-Ing'en	2 sanguine (Iss-Ing'en-Ray, sanguinary)
Ing'ger........	3 longer
Ing'end	1 England, 3 lengthened

W.

Wayf	1 why have
Way'ter	1 water, with thr
Way'therther ..	2 whether thr—§ 264, R. 9
Waynd........	3 wound (to hurt)
Way'weh	1 we were, we would, we with
Weh'weh	1 with what, 2 were we, were with, were what
Wuh'wuh	1 what we-re, what with, what would, 2 would we, would what
Way'yeh	1 we yet,
Weh'yeh	1 with you, 2 were you, were yet
Wuh'yuh......	1 what you, what yet, 2 would you, would yet

Y.

Yeh	1 year-s

Yeld	1 yield-ed
Yuh	2 you (sometimes Yeh in phr.), 3 to you
Yay'weh	1 ye were, ye would
Yeh'weh	2 you were
Yuh'wuh	2 you would
Hay	2 eh, 3 ah, holy (Hay³-Ray, holier—Hayst⁻, holier . . Hay³-Ens, holiness)
h-tick	2 he—see § 146, R. 5
ι (downward)	2 he have
⌐ (upw'd) or ⌐	he would

Vowels.

···ɪ···	to a
--ρ--	as to a-n (ꞇ as a-n)
ꞇ	and all, and will—178, R. 4
ꞇ	and are, and our—178, R. 5
ꞎ	and of, and if—201, R. 4
ꞎ	and what—201, R. 6
ꞎ	and would— do.
ꞎ	and our own—201, R. 7
···ꞃ···	to the
···ꞃ--	as to the (ꞃ as to)
ꞃ	as the
ꞃ	all of, all have—201, R. 4
ꞃ	all would—201, R. 6
ꞃ	of all—178, R. 4
ꞃ	to all— do.
ꞃ	of our—178, R. 5
ꞃ	to our— do.
ꞃ	to ours—178, R. 5, *c*
ꞃ	to ourselves—do.
ꞃ	to have
ꞃ	of what—201, R. 6

` `	....	to what—201, R. 6
` `	....	to what h-is, to what has—201, R. 6, b
` `	....	of our own—201, R. 7
` `	....	awful-ness, awe of—201, R. 4
` `	....	or of, or have, or if—201, R. 4
` `	....	but of, but have, but if—201, R. 4.
` `	....	or not—201, R. 5.
` `	....	but not— do.
` `	....	but are not—201, R. 5
` `	....	who will—178, R. 4
` `	....	who are—178, R. 5
` `	....	ought to have—201, R. 4
` `	....	who have, who of—201, R. 4
` `	....	on all—178, R. 4
` `	....	on our—178, R. 5
` `	....	should have—201, R. 4.

REM. 1. In the Corresponding Style, a number of word-signs are formed by the omission of vowels simply; but, in the Reporting Style, in which the omission of vowels is the general rule, such imperfection is not regarded as constituting a word-sign; and no word is properly included in the list of sign-words, whose sign has not some imperfection of consonant expression, or peculiarity of outline or position. Ter[1] for *tree* or *try*, unlike Ter[1] for *internal*, is not a word-sign, but merely an unvocalized outline. A principle of classification which would include, in the list of word-signs, Jen[3] for *June*, Pen[3] for *happen*, Jay[1] for *joy*, would very unnecessarily enlarge the list. A large number of word-signs, such as those for ' by all, for their, more than,' etc., might have been indicated in the preceding list; but it has seemed best to omit such signs, except when their insertion was required for special reasons. For the principles governing the formation of such signs, see the portions of the Compendium indicated by the following references: § 178, R. 4 and 5; 201, R. 4-8; 211; 221, R. 4; 232, 13. It has also seemed best to omit many signs which, in due time, the student will naturally form in analogy with some of the signs of this list. For instance, in analogy with Pef[3] for *hopeful-ness*, *hope to have*, the reporter will naturally write Tref[2] for *truthful-ness*, Tref[1] for *try to have*, Tref[3] for *it were to have*, Jef[1] for *joyful-ness*, Kref[2] for *careful-ness*. For the principles governing the formation of derivatives from word-signs, see § 252, R. 5.

REM. 2. ' *You' Joined as a Hook.*—(a) In phrase-writing, the sign for *you* may sometimes be joined as an initial hook on the left-hand side of a descending letter; thus, ⌐ you have been, ⌐ you do, you had, ⌐ you shall, ⌐ you have, ⌐ you think. (b) When *you* commences a phrase, its sign, according to § 245, rests on the line, and thus serves to distinguish the Yuh-hook signs, when standing alone or commencing a phrase-sign, from the Ar-hook signs. In Yuh-Vee and Yuh-Ith there is an additional distinction arising from joining the hook on the convex side of the curve. (c) Even when a Yuh-hook is taken from the position on the line; as in such phrase-signs as Ef[1]-Yuh-Ben, if you have been; Ef[1]-Yuh-Dee, if you do; it is easily distinguished from the Ar-hook by a reference to the context and the other portions of the phrase-sign.

Rem. 3. '*We*' *Prefixed by a Hook.*—(a) It is allowable in a few cases to represent *we* by joining Weh as a hook to Kay and some other horizontal letters which, according to the general rule, would not take the Way-hook; thus, ‿ we can, ⌐ we could, ‿ we give, we have given, ⌐ we go, ⌢ we may be. Signs thus formed do not in practice conflict with corresponding El and Ar hook signs. (b) *We* is generally joined by the Way-hook to a following word commencing with Em, En, Lay, or Ray; thus, Wer[1]-Ker, we require—Wens[1]-Ray, we answer—Wel[1]-Kay, we like—Wemst[1], we must.

Rem. 4. *Eshon Added to the En-Hook.*—The reporter occasionally adds Eshon to an En-hook; as in Ren[1]-Eshon, ornamentation.

Rem. 5. *Termination Ly.*—An adjective-signword may usually be written for an adverb formed from it by the addition of *ly*; as *spiritual* for *spiritually*; *particular* for *particularly*; unless the expression of the termination is found to be necessary for the sake of distinguishing between different words, as in writing *interiorly* to distinguish it from *not*.

Rem. 6. *The Ef-Hook on Curves.*—In several of the word-signs of the preceding list it is indicated that an Ef or Vee hook should be written on a curve; as in the signs for 'thankful-ness, they ought to have, they will have, was to have, will have,' etc., and the student should carefully distinguish Thef, Shef, Neft, etc., which indicate single signs, from Ith-Ef, Ish-Ef, En-Fet, etc., which denote two signs joined.

Rem. 7. *Art, Hast, Wert, Shalt*, etc., belonging to what is called the solemn style, may be expressed the same as the corresponding *are, has, were, shall*, etc., belonging to the usual style of speech.

Rem. 8. *Past Tense.*—It is usually allowable and advantageous for the reporter, when a stroke or more can be saved thereby, to represent the past tense of a verb by the form of the present tense; writing, for instance, Ses-Pend instead of Ses-Pen-Ded, for *suspended;* Stend, instead of Sten-Ded, for *extended;* and depending upon the context for the distinction between the tenses. (b) This principle may be employed in very many cases in representing the past tense of verbs not belonging to the list of sign-words; as in writing Net[1]-Met for *intimated*, Ent[2]-End for *intended*, Ter[2]-Ment for *tormented*, Ray[2]-Gerd for *regarded*, Kay[2]-Net for *acquainted*, Rays-Ret for *resorted*.

Rem. 9. *Distinctions.*—(a) A word whose outline, when unvocalized, would be liable to be mistaken for a word-sign, should have at least its accented vowel inserted. (b) As a sloping or perpendicular half-length can be written through or just below the line, a distinction may be made between 'it had,' 'it would.' etc., by writing the signs for 'it had, they had,' etc., through the line, and the signs for 'it would, they would,' etc., below the line. For the practiced reporter, however, such a distinction is unnecessary.

Rem. 10. *In, In As, In His*, etc., *Prefixed.*—(a) The In-hook may frequently be joined to a word, in its natural position, to prefix *in* (and sometimes *in the* or *in a-n*); thus, In-Sem[1], in similar—In-Sem[2], in some—In-Spret[1], in (the) spirit—In-Skret[1], in (the) secret—In-Semb[2], in (an) exemplification. (b) *In his* or *in as* may, in a few cases, be prefixed by an In-hook and the circle; thus, Ins-Ker'shon[2], in his creation—Ins-Prens[1], in his appearance—Ins-Gret[2], in as great.

REM. 11. *'One' Added.*—One may be added to a considerable number of words, by an En-hook; thus, Smen[2], some one—Nen[1], any one—Nen[3], no one (in the third position, to distinguish it from *none*, Nen[2])—Ten[3], at one—Thee'thern[2]; the other one—En'thern[2], another one—En'thern[3], no other one—En-Ten[2], into one—Bet[1]-Wen'en, between one—Bee[2]-En-Then, beneath one.

REM. 12. *Hooks Omitted.*—The hook of the signs for *been, can, there, their, they are,* or *other* may be omitted when, if written, it would prevent the formation of a desired phrase-sign; thus, Tees[2]-Bees-Dee, it has been said—Ment[2]-Ther (like Ment[2]-Zee), may not thr—Tee-Kay-Nel, it can only—Bee-Bel, been able—Bef[2]-Ther (like Bef-Zee), before their, *or* before other. (*b*) A hook is occasionally omitted from other outlines, to secure a special advantage in phrase-writing; thus, Thee[1]-Yuh, within you—Art[3]-Yuh, around you—Em[3]-Slay, human soul-Em[3]-Mend, human mind—Men[3]-Kay-Kay, instead of Men Ker[2]-Kay, human character.

REM. 13. *'It Ought to Have, It Would Have,' etc.*—(*a*) The outlines Tef[1], Tef[3], for 'it ought to have,' 'it would have,' are regarded as unvocalized Tauv, Twoov; in the first case, *it* being represented by *t;* *ought* by *au;* and *have* by *v; to* being omitted, according to § 250, 2. In the case of Twoov, *it* is represented by *t; would* by *wŏŏ;* and *have* by *v.* Upon the same principle are formed the signs for 'they ought to have, they would have; which ought to have, which would have,' etc. (*b*) *Did have,* which occurs rarely, may, in like manner, be written with Def[1], that is, 'di' have.' (*c*) *Could have* may be written Kef[2] when Ked-Vee is not better, as in 'could have had,' Ked[2]-Ved; or as in 'could have been,' Ked[2]-Ben.

REM. 14. *'To' Added by Halving.*—Bled may be written for 'able to;' as preceding 'understand;' when *to* can not be better implied according to § 250, 2; as in writing 'able to be,' Bel-Bee—able to make, Bel[2]-Em—able to have, Blef[2].

REM. 15. *Never.*—(*a*) In phrase-writing, *never* may always be represented by En, being written in the first position when it commences a phrase-sign; thus, Wen[1]-Ben, we never have been—Ken[2]-En-Bee, can never be—Ther[2]-En-Ken, there never can—En[1]-Ish, never shall—En[1]-Ken, never can. (*b*) Even when *never,* for any reason, is written separately, it may be represented by En[1], instead of En-Vee[2], in the writing of the practiced reporter.

REM. 16. *Forth.*—Forth, when following a verb ending in a straight full-length line, may be represented by an Ef-hook; thus, Steh-Pef, step forth—Klef[1], call forth. (*b*) In other cases, it may be written with Ef-Ith; thus, Kels[1]-Ef-Ith, calls forth—Send[2]-Ef-Ith, send forth. (*c*) The practiced reporter, in many cases, when *forth* can not be expressed by an Ef-hook, will not hesitate to represent it by Ef, trusting to memory and the context to distinguish it from *for.*

REM. 17. *T or D Omitted.*—A *t* or *d* sound expressed by halving may be omitted in some cases, principally from verbs, to secure advantages which would otherwise be lost; as of adding *have* by an Ef-hook; thus, Tref[1] for 'tried to have' as well as 'try to have;' the difference of time being distinguished by the context.

REM. 18. *Ef-Hook on Brief Way and Yay.*—The careful writer may, if he prefers, add 'have' to a brief Way or Yay, by an Ef-hook; as, Wehf[1], we have—Wehf[2], were to have—Yuhf[2], you have. *Of* or *If* may be added in the same manner; as, Wehf[2], were of-Wuhf[1], what if—Yehf[2], yet if.

REM. 19. *Sign-Words Sometimes Written in Full.*—A sign-word is sometimes written in full, if the full form secures a convenience in phrase-writing which could not be secured otherwise; thus, Em[2]-En·Tee-Ems, many times—Ver[2]-Em-Chay, very much—Def[1]-Kay'ses-Tens, divine existence.

REM. 20. *Order of the Word-Signs.*—The preceding list of word-signs is calculated for the use of the reader, while the following one is designed for the use of the writer. In the preceding list, the word-signs are presented in the following general order:—1. Simple Signs. 2. Simple Signs with their various modifications in the order of their explanation in the Compendium; namely, Circles, Loops, Yuh and Weh Joined, Initial Hooks, Final Hooks, Widening, Lengthening, and Halving.

REM. 21. In the preceding and the following list, " phr." = " phrase-writing;" and " voc." (= vocalize) is used to denote the insertion of the vowel of the word, or, of several vowels, the most prominent one.

---

§ 267. REPORTING SIGN-WORDS.

A.

able to—§ 266, R. 14
able to have, Blef²
abroad, Bred¹
abundant-ce, Bend²
accept-ed-ation, Spet³
acceptable, Spet³-Bel
accession, Kays²-Eshon
accident-al, Sdent²
accuracy, Ker³
accurate-ness, Kert³
accusation, Kays³-Eshon
acquisition, Kays¹-Eshon
active-ity, Kay'tiv³
addition-al, Dee'shon³
advance-d, Def³
advancement, Dees³-Ment
advertise-d, Dee³
advertisement, Dee³
affect-ed, Ef³
    effect-ed, Ef²-Kay
affection-ate, Ef'shon³
affliction, Fel'shon¹
ago, Gay²
ah, Hay³

all have, all of, ⟍ ......
all would, ⟍ ....
along, Ing³
amount-ed, Ment³
and all, and will, ⌐
and are, and our, ⌐
and if, and of, ⌐
and our own, ⌐
and what, ⌐ ......

and would, ⌐
angel, Jel²
    archangel, Ar²-Jel
angelic, Jel²-Kay
annual, Nel³
another one, En'thern²
    no other one, En'thern³
anterior, Net³
any one, Nen¹
any other, En'ther¹
any other one, En'thern¹
appear, Per¹
appearance, Prens¹
appeared, Pert¹
appears, Pers¹
appliance, Plens³
applicable-ility, Pel³-Kay
applicant, Plent³
application, Pel'shon³
applied, Pelt³
apply, Pel³
apprehend, Prent³
apprehended, Pren³-Ded
apprehensible-ility, Prens³
apprehension, Pren³
apprehensive, Pren³
approval, Pref³
approve, Pref³
are of, Ref²
are to have, Ref²
arrive-al, Ref¹
arrived, Reft¹
as it had, Iss-Ted³
as it ought, Iss-Tet¹
as it were, Iss²-Ter
as it would, Iss-Ted³
as little, Iss-Let¹
as long, Iss°-Ing

, as soon, Ses-En²
. as thr, Zee'ther³
as to a, --ρ-
as a-n, ᷓ
· as to it, Iss²-Tee
us to the, ...ᷓ--

   as to, ᷓ

   as the, ᷓ

as to their, Iss-Tee'ther²
assistance, Es²-Steh
' *assistant,* Es²-Stent
assist-ed, Es²-Steh
assurance, Sher²-Ens
assure, Sher²
; assured, Shert²
| at first, Teest³
, at length, Tlen³
, at one, Ten³
| at once, Tens³
| at our, Ter³
| at our own, Tren³
, at it, Tet³
; attain, Ten³
| *attainable,* Ten³-Bee
' attained, Tend³
,*attainment,* Tee³-Ment
; attract-ed, Ter³
; attraction, Ter'shon³
; attractive, Tret³
' authoritative, Thret¹
' authority, Thret¹
' averse, Vers³
| aversion, Ver'shon³
| avert-ed, Vert³
| avocation, Vee'shon³
; a-void-ed-ance, Ved¹
' aware of, Werf³

| awe of,   ᷓ

| awful-ness, do.

     B.

; bachelor, Chler³
; be had, Bed²
| be it, Bet²
; be not, Bent²
; beauty-iful, Bet²
' been thr, Bee'ther²

before it, Beft²
began, Gen³
begin-ning, Gen¹
begun, Gen²
behind, Bend¹
beheld, behold, Beld²
belief, Blef²
believe-d, Bel²
believer, Blef²-Ray
belong-ed, Bel¹
body, Bed¹ (voc.)
bold-ness, Bled²
bounty-iful, Bent³
brethren, Bren³
broad, Bred¹
brother-hood, Ber³
build-ing, Bled¹
built, Blet¹

but are not, ᷓ

but have, but if, but of, ᷓ

but it, ᷓ

but not, ᷓ

by all, Bel¹
by it, Bet¹
by our, Ber¹
by what, Bet¹

     C.

call forth, Klef¹
calculable, Kel³-Bel
calculate-d-ation, Kel³
can thr, Kay'ther²
certain-ty, Iss-Ret²;   sometimes
   Iss-Art in phr.
cessation, Ess²-Iss-Eshon
chair, Cher²
changeable, Chay²-Bel
change-d, Chay²
charge-d, Chay³
chargeable, Chay³-Bel
charitable, Chert³
charity, Chert³
cheer, Cher¹
cheered, Chert¹
cheerful-ness, Cherf¹
child, Chelt¹
childhood, Chelt¹
children, Chel²
Christian-ity, Kren¹

Christians-ize, Krens[1]
circumstance, Stens[3]
circumstantial, Sten[3]
citizen, Stee[1]
clairvoyant-ce, Klerf [1]
clear-ed-ness, Kler[1]
clerical, Kler[2]-Kel
clerk, Kler[2]
color-ed, Kler[2]
colorific, Klerf [2]
combination, Ben[1]
combine, Ben[1]
combined, Bend[1]
commence, Ens[2]
commenced, Enst[2]
commences, Enses[2]
commencement, Ens[2]
commencements, Enses[2]
commonest, Kayst[1]
complete, Plet[1]
completely, Plet[1]-El
completion, Pel'shon[1]
complexion, Pel'shon[2]
compliance, Plens[1]
compliant, Plent[1]
complied, Plet[1]
comply, Pel[1]
comprehend, Prent[2]
comprehended, Pren[2]-Ded
comprehensible-ility, Prens[2]
comprehension-ive, Pren[2]
concern, Iss-Arn[2] ; sometimes
    Ren[2] in phr.
concerned, Iss-Arnd[2] ; somet
    Iss-Rend in phr.
conclude, Kled[3]
concluded, Kel[3]-Ded
conclusion, Kel'shon[3]
conclusive-ness, Kels[3]
condition-al, Dee'shon[2]
conditioned, Dee'shond[1]
consequence, Skens[1]
consequent, Skent[1]
consequential-ness, Sken[1]
consider-able-ness, Iss-Der[2]
considerate-ness, Iss-Dred[1]
consideration, Iss-Dershon[2]
considered, Iss-Dred[1]
consist, Ses-Tee[1]
consisted, Ses-Ted[1]
consistence, Ses-Tens[1]
consistency, Ses-Ten[1]

cover-ed, Kef²
creation, Ker'shon²
creative, Ker'tiv²
creature, Kret¹
cure, Ker³
cured, Kred³
cures, Kers³
curious, Kers³

D.

danger, Jer²
  endanger, En-Jer²
dangers-ous, Jers²
dark, Der³
darken-ed, Dren³
darkens, Drens³
darkness, Drens³
defendant, Dee²
defense, Def²
defensive, Def²
degree, Ger¹
degreed, Gred¹
delight-ed, Dlet¹
delinquent, Dlen¹
delinquency, Dlen¹
delinquents-cies, Dlens¹
deliver-ed, Del²
deliverance, Dlens²
delivery, Del²
denominate-d, Den¹
denomination, Den¹
deride-d, Dred¹
derision, Der'shon¹
derivation, Dref¹
derivative, Dreft¹
derive, Dref¹
derived, Dreft¹
describe-d, Sker¹
description, Sker'shon¹
descriptive-ness, Skerf¹
did, Ded¹
did have—266, R. 13, *b*
direct-ed, Der²
direction, Der'shon²
directness, Drens²
director, Der²-Ter
directory, Der²-Ket
distinct-ion, Deest²
distinctive, Deest²-Vee
distinguish-ed, Deest²-Ing
distinguishable, Deest²-Ing-Bee

divination, Def¹-Eshon
divine-ity, Def¹
diviner, Def¹-Ray
divinest, Def¹-Est
doctor, Der¹
dollar, Dee¹
done thr, Dee'ther²
down thr, Dee'ther³, voc. with ou
dread-ed, Dred²
duration, Der'shon³
during it, Dred³

E.

each are, Cher¹
each one, Chen¹
each will, Chel¹
east, Est¹
eastern, Es'tern¹
eh ! Hay²
England, Ing'end¹
English, Ing¹
eternal, Tren²
eternity, Tren²
evangel-ical, Jel³
evangelize, Jels³
evening, Ven¹
every one, Vren²
evidence, Ved²
evident, Ved²
exact-ed, Sket³
exaction, Skay'shon³
exactness, Sket³
exaggerate-d, Sjert²
exaggeratory, Sjert²-Ray
exaggeration, Sjer'shon²
examine-ation, Smen²
  cross-examine-ation, Ker²-Smen
examined, Sment²
  cross-examined, Ker²-Sment
example, Iss-Emp³
exasperate-d-ion, Ses-Pee³
except-ed, Spet²
exception-al, Spee'shon²
exceptionable, Spee'shon²-Bee
exclude, Skelt²
excluded, Skel-Ded²
exclusive-ness, Skels²
exclusion, Skel'shon²
excuse-able, Skays³
exemplify-ied-ication, Iss-Emp²
exhibit-ed, Sbet¹

exhibition, Sbee'shon[1]
exist, Ses-Tee[2]
existed, Ses-Ted[2]
existence, Ses-Tens[2]
existent, Ses-Tent[2]
expand, Spend[3]
expanded, Spen[3]-Ded
expanse-ible, Spens[3]
expansibility, Spees[3]-Bee
expansion-sive, Spen[3]
expect-ed, Spee[2]
   unexpected, En-Spee[2]
expectation, Spee[2]
expend-iture, Spent[2]
expended, Spen[2]-Ded
expense, Spens[2]
expensive-ness, Spen[2]
experience, Sprens[2]
   inexperience, In-Sprens[2]
   in (the) experience, In-Sprens[2]
experienced, Sprenst[2]
explain, Splen[2]
explainable, Splen[2]-Bee
explanation, Splen[2]
explanatory, Splen[2]
explained, Splend[2]
explicit-ness, Spels[1]
exploration, Spler[2]
explore-d, Spler[2]
expressed, Sperst[1]
express-ive, Spers[1]
expression, Sper'shon[1]
exquisite-ness, Skays[1]
extemporaneous, Stemp[2]
extemporary, Stemp[2]-Ray-Ray
extemporize, Stemp[2]-Rays
extend, Iss-Tend[2]
extended, Iss-Ten[2]-Ded
extensibility, Iss-Tees[2]-Bee
extensible, Iss-Tens[2]
extension-sive, Iss-Ten[2]
extent, Iss-Tent[2]
exterior, Kayst[2]
external-ity, Ster[1]
extract-ed, Ster[3]
extraction, Ster'shon[3]
extractive, Ster'tiv[3]
extravagant-ce, Stref[3]
extreme, Ster[2]
extremity, Ster[2]-Tee
extrinsic-al, Stren[1]

F.

fact, Ef[2]
fail, Fel[2]
failed, Flet[2]
failure, Fler[2]
fall, Fel[1]
fallen, Flen[1]
fall in, Flen[1]
false, Fels[1]
family, Mel[3]
fashion, Ef shon[2]
fashionable, Ef'shon[2]-Bee
fault-y, Flet[1]
favor-ed, Ver[3]
favorable, Ver[3]-Bee
favorite, Ef[2]-Vert
feature, Fet[1]
feel, Fel[1]
feeler, Fel[1]-Ar
feel it, Flet[1]
felt, Flet[2]
fell, Fel[2]
fell in, Flen[2]
fellow, Fel[2]
fiction, Ef'shon[1]
fill, Fel[1]
filled, Flet[1]
flexion, Fel'shon[2]
follow-ing, Fel[1]
followed, Flet[1]
follower, Fler[1]
fool, Fel[3]
footstep, Fet[3]-Steh
for all, Fel[2]
for all are, Eler[2]
for all had, Flet[2]
for all it, Flet[2]
for all our, Fler[2]
for it, Fet[2]
for one, Fen[2]
for our, Fer[3]
for what, Fet[2]
form-ed, Fer[1]
   conform-ed, *con*-dot-Fer[1]
   conformable, Fer[1]-Bee
   deform-ed-ity, Dee[1]-Fer
   inform-ed-ant, En-Fer[1]
   perform-ed-ance, Per[2]-Fer
   reform-ed, Ray[1]-Fer
   transform-ed, Ters[2]-Fer
   uniform-ity, En-Fer[3]

formal-ity, Fer¹-Lay
formation, Fer′shon¹
former-ly, Fer¹-Ar
formless, Fer¹-Lays
forth—266, R. 16
found-ed, Fend³
foundation, Fend³
fraction, Fer′shon²
free, Fer²
freedom, Fred′-Em
freely, Fer²-Lay
frequency, Fren¹
frequent, Frent¹
from all, Frel²
fuller, Fler²
from one, Fren²
from what, Fret¹
　from it, Fer²-Met
fruition, Fer′shon³
furnish-ed, Fren²
furniture, Fren²
future, Fet³
futurity, Fet³

G.

gave it, Geft²
generalize, Jens²
generalized, Jenst²
generalization, Jens²-Eshon
generation, Jay′shon²
　degeneration, Dee²-Jay′shon
　regeneration, Ray²-Jay′shon
glorified, Gel²
glorification, Gel′shon²
glorify, Gel²
glorious, Gels²
glory, Gel²
go, Gay²
govern-ed-ment, Gef²
governor, Gef²-Ray
grand-eur, Grend³
guilt-y, Glet¹

H.

had had, Ded³
had it, Ded³
half, Ef³
halve, Vee³
halved, Ved³
happy, Pee³

happiest, Peest³
happiness, Pens³
has known (none), Snen²
has thr, Zee′ther³
have-ing been, Ven², when *have*
　preceding *been* can not be omit-
　ted according to § 249.
have had, Ved²
have it, Ved²
have not, Vent², when Vee²-Net is
　not better
he, h-tick—see § 146, R. 5
he have, ⟋ downward
he would, ⟋ (upward) or ⟍
hereafter, Reft²
hesitate-d, Zed²
hesitation, Zed²
holier, Hay³-Ray
holiest, Hayst³
holiness, Hay³-Ens
holy, Hay³
home, Em³
homely, Em³-Lay
hopeful-ness, Pef³
hope to have, Pef³
hundred-th, Ned²

I.

idle-ness, Del¹
if all are, Fler¹
if all our, Fler¹
if one, Fen¹
if our, Fer¹
ignorance, Nerns¹
ignorant, Nernt¹
imaginable, Jen³-Bee
　unimaginable, En-Jen³
imagine-ary-ation, Jen³
imaginative-ness, Jay′tiv³
　unimaginative, En-Jay′tiv³
imagined, Jend³
　unimagined, En-Jend³
immoral-ity, Merl¹
immortal-ity, Mert¹
immortalize, Mert-Lays¹
impassioned, Emp′shond³
　impassionate, Emp-Ish³
impatience, Emp′shons²
impatient, Emp′shont²
impenetrable, Emp′ent²

impenetrability, Emp'ent²
imponderable-ility, Emp'ent¹
in all, Nel¹
in (the) consideration, Ins-Dershon²
in contradistinction, En-Deest¹
in it, Net¹
in one, Nen¹
in our, Ner³
in what, Net¹
inconsiderable-ness, In-Sder²
inconsiderate-ness, In-Sdred¹
infinite-y, Neft¹
infinitude, Neft¹ Dee disjoined
information, En'shon¹
inform-ed-ant, En-Fer¹
inscribe-d, In-Sker¹
inscription, In-Sker'shon¹
inscriptive, In-Skref¹
insecure, In-Sker³
insecurity, In-Skret³
instinct-ive, Enst¹
instruct-ed, In-Ster²
instruction, In-Ster'shon²
instructive-ness, In-Stref²
instructor, In-Ster²-Ter
intercession, Nets²-Eshon
interior, Net¹
interiorly, Net-El²
internal, Ter¹
intrinsic-al, En'tern¹
irrational-ity, Ray'shon¹
is done, Sden²
is known (none), Snen¹
is said, Ses-Dee²
is said to have, Ses-Def²
is thr, Zee'ther¹
issue, Ish³
issued, Ish³-Dee
it had, Ted³
it had not, Tent³
it not, Tent²
it ought, Tet¹
it ought not, Tent¹
it ought to have, Tef¹
it ought to have had, Teft¹
it were, Ter³
it will have, Tlef²
it will have had, Tleft²
it would, Ted³
it would have, Tef³
it would have had, Teft³
it would not, Tent³

J.

Jehovah, Jef¹
Jesus, Jay²
Jove, Jef²
junior, Jer³
jurisdiction, Jers²
jury, Jer³
just as, Jay ses²
just-ice, Jayst²; sometimes Jays
  in phr.
justification, Jays²-Eshon
juvenile-ity, Jef³

L.

large, Jay³
  enlarge, En-Jay³
  enlarged, En-Jed³
  enlargement, En-Jay³
larger, Jer³
largest, Jayst³
length, Ing³
lengthen, Ing'en³
lengthened, Ing'end³
lengthy, Ing³-Ith
let thr, Lay'ther²—264, R. 8
liberty, Ber¹
little, Let¹
long, Ing³
longer, Ing'ger³
love-ing, sometimes Lef in phr.;
  as, Lef²-Ged, love of God—Lef².
  Kend, loving kindness

M.

may be, Emb²
may have been, Emb'en²
measure, Zher³
  immeasurable, Em-Zher³
measured, Zherd³
  unmeasured, En-Zherd³
mental-ity, Ment²
mention, Em'shon²
mentioned, Em'shond²
mercy-iful, Mer²
might thr, Em'ther¹—264, R. 8
might-y, Met¹
million-th, Mel¹
moral-ity, Merl²
mortal-ity, Mert²

movement, Ment³
much will, Chel³

N.

nearly, Nerl¹
necessary, Enses²
never, En¹—266, R. 15
next, Enst²; sometimes Ens in phr.
no less, Nels²
no one, Nen³
no other, En'ther³
    another, En'ther²
no other one, En'thern³
    another one, En'thern²
nor will, Nerl¹

O.

object, Bee²—142, R. 1
obligation, Bel'shon²
occur, Ker²
occurred, Kred²
occurrence, Krens²
occurs, Kers²
of all, ⟍
of it, Vet¹
of our, ⟍
of our own, ⟍
of thr, Vee'ther¹
of what, ⟍
on all, ⌒
on either hand, Thrend¹
on our, ⟋
on the other hand, Thrend²
on (the) one hand, Wen'end²
one (an)other, Wen'ther²
one had (would), Went²
only, Nel²
only as, Nels²
    unless, Nels¹
opposition, Pees¹-Eshon
oppression, Per'shon³
order, Arder¹; sometimes Ard in
    phr.
ordinary, Ard¹
    extraordinary, Ster²-Ard
organ, Gen¹

organic, Gen¹-Kay
organism, Gens¹-Em—185, R. 1, *b*
organization, Gens¹-Eshon
organize, Gens¹
organized, Genst¹
organs, Gens¹
or have, or if, or of, ᰁ
ornamentation, Ren¹-Eshon
or not, ᠌
ought to have, ℓ
over it, Vert¹
owned, Ned³
owner, Ner³

P.

parallel, Prel²
parliament-ary, Prel³
party, Pee³
patent-ed, Pee³
patentable, Pee³-Bel
people-d, Pel²
perfect, Perf¹
perfected, Perf¹-Ket
perfection, Per'shon¹
pernicious-ness, Pren¹
philanthropic, Flen³
philanthropist, Flen³
philanthropy, Flen³
plaintiff, Plent²; sometimes Plet
    in phr.
plenty-iful, Plent²
position, Pees²-Eshon
possess, Pee'ses²
possessed, Pee'ses²-Tee
possession, Pees³-Eshon
possessive, Pee'ses²-Vee
possessor, Pee'ses²-Ray
possible, Pees¹
possibility, Pees¹
possibilities, Pee'ses¹
posterior, Pees²
poverty, Pef¹
practicable-ility, Per³-Ket
practical, Per³
practice, Per³
practices, Pers³
practiced, Perst³
preliminary, Prel¹
présent, Pers²

pretty, Pret²
professor, Pref²
profit-able, Preft¹
profited, Preft¹
promulgate-d-ion, Mel²
proof, Pref²
proper, Per¹
    improper, Em-Per¹
prophet, Preft¹
prophetic, Preft¹-Kay
propriety, Per¹
    impropriety, Em-Per¹
prove, Pref²
provident-ce, Preft²
providential-ly, Preft²-En
punish-ed-ment, Pen²
punishes-ments, Pens²

Q.

quality-ative, Klet¹
question-ed, Ken²
questionable, Ken²-Bee

R.

ration-al-ality, Ray'shon³
real-ity, Rel¹
realize, Rels¹
reform-ed, Ray¹-Fer
reformation, Ray'shon²
relation, Rel²
relative, *adj*., Rel²
relative, *noun*, Rel'tiv²
relate-d, Rel²
religion, Jen¹
    irreligion, Ar¹-Jen
religionist, Jenst¹
religious, Jays¹
    irreligious, Ar¹-Jays
remembered, Bred²—221, R. 1, *b*
reveal-ed, Ref¹
revelation, Lay'shon²
revolution, Lay'shon³
revolve-d, Ref²
rule-d, Rel³
ruler, Rel³-Ray

S.

saddens, Sdens³

sadness, Sdens³
said to have, Sdef²
salvation, Slay³
sanguine, Iss-Ing'en²
sanguinary, Iss-Ing'en²-Ray
satisfaction, Stee'shon³
satisfactory, Stee³
satisfy-ied, Stee³
Savior, Iss-Vee²
scale, Skel²
scholar, Skler¹
school, Skel³
schooled, Sklet³
scripture-al, Sker¹
season-ed, Ses-En¹
secession, Es³-Iss-Eshon
seclude, Skelt³
secluded, Skel³-Ded
secluseness, Skels³
seclusion, Skel'shon³
seclusive, Skels³
sect-arian, Sket²
sectarianism, Skets²-Em
secular, Skler²
secure, Sker³
secured, Skret³
security, Skret³
seldom, Iss-Led²
set forth, Iss-Tef²
set off, Iss-Tef¹
shall have, Shef²
shall have been, Ish²-Ben
shall have had, Sheft²
shall it, Isht²
shall not, Ish²-Net
share, Sher³
shared, Sherd³
sharer, Sher³-Ar
she had, Isht³
she ought, Isht¹
she ought not, Isht¹-Net
she ought to have, Shef¹
she ought to have been, Isht¹-Ben
she ought to have had, Sheft¹
she were, Sher¹
she would, Isht³
she would have, Shef³
she would have been, Isht³-Ben
she would have had, Sheft³
she would not, Isht³-Net

should have ⸱ downward

significance, Sgay[1]
significancy, Sgen[1]
significant, Sgay[1]
signification, Sgay'shon[1]
significative, Sgay'tiv[1]
signify-ied, Sgay[1]
similar-ity, Iss-Em[1]
simple-icity, Iss-Emp[1]
simpler, Iss-Emp[1]-Ray
simplest, Iss-Emp'est[1]
single-d, Iss-Ing[1]
singular-ity, Sgler[1]
sister, Ses-Ter[2]
situation, Stee'shon[1]
skill, Skel[1]
skilled, Sklet[1]
skillful, Sklef[1]
so had, Est[2]
so it, Est[2]
some, Iss-Em[2]
somebody, Iss-Emb[2]
some one, Smen[2]
some other, Sem'ther[2]
some other one, Sem'thern[2]
some time, Smet[2]
south-east, Iss-Thest[2]
south-eastern, Iss-Thes[2]-Ren
southern, Iss-Then[2]
southerner, Iss-Then[2]-Ray
speak, Spee[1]
speakable, Spee[1]-Bel
speaker, Spee[1]-Ker
special-ty-ity, Spee[3]
   especial, Es[2]-Pee
spiritualism, Spers[1]-Em
spiritualist, Sperst[1]
spiritualistic, Spers[1]-Kay
spiritual-ity, Sper[1]
spiritualize, Spers[1]
spiritualization, Spers[1]-Eshon
splendor, Splend[2]
spoken, Spen[1]
spontaneous-ity, Spent[1]
state, Steh-Tee[2]; sometimes Stet in phr.
stated, Steh-Ted[2]
station, Stee'shon[2]
stenography-er-ic, Steh-En[2]
step by step, Steh-Pee[2]-Steh
stood, Iss-Ted[2]
strange-ness, Stren[2]
stranger, Ster[2]-Jer

stupendous-ness, Steh-Pend[2]
stupid-ity, Steh-Pet[3]
sublime-ity, Sbel[1]
subordinate-d-ion, Sbee[1]
success-ful, Iss-Kay'ses[2]
such a one, Schen[2]
such (an)other, Iss-Chay'ther[2]
such are, Iss-Cher[2]
such had, Schet[3]
such had not, Iss-Chent[3], when Schet[3]-Net is not better
such have, Iss-Chef[2]
such have had, Iss-Cheft[2]
such ought, Iss-Chet[1]
such ought not, Iss-Chent[1], when Iss-Chet[1]-Net is not better
such ought to have, Iss-Chef[1]
such ought to have had, Iss-Cheft[1]
such were, Iss-Cher[3]
such would, Iss-Chet[3]
such would have, Iss-Chef[3]
such would have had, Iss-Cheft[3]
such would not, Iss-Chent[3], when Iss-Chet[3]-Net is not better
suggest-ed-ion, Iss-Jay[2]
suggestive-ness, Iss-Jef[2]
superintend-ed-ent-ence, Sprent[3]
superior-ity, Spee[1]
superlative-ness, Sprel[2]
supernatural-ness, Spren[3]
supernaturalist, Sprenst[3]
supernaturalism, Spers[3]-Em
supplant, Splent[3]
supplication, Spel'shon[2]
supplies, Spels[2]
supply, Spel[2]
suppress, Spers[3]
suppression, Sper'shon[3]
supreme-acy, Sper[2]
suspect-ed, Ses-Pee[2]
suspend, Ses-Pend[2]
suspended, Ses-Pen[2]-Ded
suspension-sive, Ses-Pen[2]
suspicion-cious, Ses-Pee[1]
sustain, Ses-Ten[2]
sustained, Ses-Tend[2]
synonym-ous, Snen[1]
system-atic, Ses-Tee[2]
systemize, Ses-Tees[2]

T.

take, Tee²
take it, Tee²-Ket
  betake, Bed²-Kay
  mistake, Ems¹-Kay
  overtake, Vert¹-Kay
  partake, Pret²-Kay
  retake, Art²-Kay
  undertake, Ned-Tee²
taken, Ten²
tend-ency, Tend²
thankful-ness, Thef³
than it, THent²—221, R. 4
than thr, THee′ther³, voc. with ă
that thr, THee′ther¹, voc. with ă
the other, THee′ther²
the other one, THee′thern²
then had, then it, THent²
then thr, THee′ther², voc. with ĕ
there had, THerd³
there had not, THrend³, when
  THerd³-Net is not better
there have, THerf²
there have been, THer²-Ben
there it, THert²
there ought, THert¹
there ought not, THrent¹, when
  THret¹-Net is not better
there ought to have, THref¹
there ought to have been, THret¹-Ben
there will, THrel²
there will have, THrelf²
there will have been, THrel²-Ben
there would, THerd³
there would not, THrend³, when
  THred³-Net is not better
there would have, THerf³
there would have been, THerd³-Ben
they are all, THrel²
they are all to have, THrelf²
they are to have, THref²
they had, THed³
they had not, THent³
they have, THef²
they have had, THef²-Dee
they ought, THet¹
they ought not, THent¹
they ought to have, THef¹
they ought to have had, THef¹-Dee
they will have, THelf²
they will not, THlent¹

they would, THed³
they would have, THef³
they would have had, THef³-Dee
they would not, THent³
think it, Thet²
thou wilt, THel³
thou wilt have, THelf³
thou wilt not, THlent³
though it, THet³
thousand-th, Ith³
through it, Thret²
through one, Thren²
time, Tee¹ ; usually Tee-Em in phr.
to a, ---т---
to all, ᒑ
to come, Kay³
to give, Gay³
to go, Gay³
to have, ᒐ
to have been, Ben³
to have gone, Gen³
to him, Em³
to it, Tee⁴
to our, ᒐ
to ours, ᒐ
to ourselves, ᒐ
to the, ---⊤--
to their, Tee′ther²
to what, ᒐ
to what h-as (h-is), ᒐ
to you, Yuh³
tolerable, Tler²-Bel
  intolerable, Ent-El¹
tolerance, Tlerns²
tolerant, Tlern²
  intolerant, Ent-El¹-Rent
tolerate-d-ion, Tler²
took, Tee³
transient, Ter′shont²
trial, Trel¹
tuition, Tee′shon¹
twelve-fth, Telf²

U.

United States, Enses¹
universe-al, Vers²
Universalism, Vers²-Em

university, Vers²-Tee
unless, Nels¹
  only as, Nels²
unsecured, In-Skret³
upon it, Pent²
upon thr, Pee'ther²
  up thr, Pee'ther², voc. with ŭ
used to have, Zef³
useful-ness, Es'ef³

V.

version, Ver'shon²
virtual, Vert²-Lay
virtue, Vert²
virtuous, Vert²-Es
virtuously, Verts²-Lay
visible-ility, Vees¹
  invisible-ility, En-Vees¹
vocation, Vee'shon²
void-ed-ance, Ved¹

W.

was to have, Zef²
was thr, Zee'ther²
was to have had, Zeft²
water, Way'ter¹
we are in, Wern¹
we are of, Werf¹
we are to have, Werf¹
we can, Weh-Ken¹
we can not, Weh-Kent¹
we could, Weh-Ket¹
we gave, Weh-Gef¹
we give, Weh-Gay¹
we go, Weh-Gay¹, voc.
we have given, Weh-Gay¹
we have gone, Weh-Gen¹
we have known (none), Wen'en¹
we know, Wen¹
we made, Wemt¹
we may be, Weh-Emb¹
we may have been, Weh-Emb'en¹
we may not, Wem'ent¹
we mean, Wem'en¹
we meant, Wem'ent¹
we mention, Wem'shon
we mentioned, Wem'shond¹
we met, Wemt¹
we might, Wemt¹
we were, Way'weh¹

we were not, Weh'wernt¹
we will have, Welf¹
we will have had, Welt¹
we with, Way'weh¹
we would, Way'weh¹
we yet, Way'yeh¹
went, Went²
were any, Wen², voc.
were it, Wert²
were known, Wen'en²
were made, Wemt²
were meant, Wem'ent²
were mentioned, Wem'shond²
were met, Wemt²
were no, Wen²
were no one, Wen'en³
were none, Wen'en²
were we, Weh'weh²
were what, Weh'weh²
were with, Weh'weh²
were you, Weh'yeh²
were yet, Weh'yeh²
what we-re, Wuh'wuh¹
what with, Wuh'wuh¹
what would, Wuh'wuh¹
what you, Wuh'yuh¹
what yet, Wuh'yuh¹
when it (had), Went¹
whereof, Werf²
where it (had), Wert²
whether thr, Way'therther²
which are, Cher²
which are had, Chert²
which are of, Cherf²
which are to have, Cherf²
which had, Chet³
which had not, Chent³, when
  Chet³-Net is not better
which have, Chef²
which have had, Cheft²
which it, Chet¹
which ought, Chet¹
which ought not, Chent¹, when
  Chet¹-Net would not be better
which ought to have, Chef¹
which ought to have had, Cheft¹
which one, Chen²
which were, Cher³
which were of, Cherf³
which were to have, Cherf³
which will it, Chelt¹
which would, Chet³

which would have, Chef³
which would have had, Cheft³
which would not, Chent³,. when
  Chet³-Net would not be better
while it, Welt¹

who are, ⁊

who have, who of, ℓ

who will, ↄ

why have, Wayf¹
will-ing, Lay²
will have, Lef²
will have had, Let²
willing to have, Lef²
wisher, Sher¹
wish it, Isht¹
wish to have, Shef¹
with him, Wem²
with me (my), Wem¹
with no, Wen¹
with our, Wer³
with our own, Wern³
with thr, Way'ther¹
with what, Weh'weh¹
with you, Weh'yeh¹
within thr, THee'ther¹
without thr, THee'ther³, voc. with
  ou
woman, Wem'en²
women, Wem'en¹
wonder-ful, Wen'der²

work-ed, Wcr²
workman-en, Wern²
would we, Wuh'wuh²
would what, Wuh'wuh²
would you, Wuh'yuh²
would yet, Wuh'yuh²
wound (to hurt), Waynd³

Y.

year-s, Yeh¹
ye were, Yay'weh¹
ye would, Yay'weh¹
yield-ed, Yeld¹
you, Yuh²; sometimes Yeh in phr.
you be, Yuh²-Bee
you did, Yuh²-Ded
you did not, Yuh²-Dent
you do, Yuh²-Dee
you do not, Yuh²-Dent
you had, Yuh²-Dee
you had had, Yuh²-Ded
you had not, Yuh²-Dent
you have, Yuh²-Vee
you have been, Yuh²-Ben
you have done, Yuh²-Den
you say, Yuh²-Es, voc.
you see, Yuh²-Es
you shall, Yuh²-Ish
you think, Yuh²-Ith
you were, Yeh'weh²
you would, Yuh'wuh²

REM. 1. *All Thr, With All, etc.*—In analogy with the mode of writing ' of thr, of it, for all, for all it,' Layther¹ may be written for ' all thr;' Let¹, for ' all it;' THel¹, for ' with all;' THlet¹, for ' with all it;' THel'ther¹, for ' with all thr;' THlef¹, for ' with all of;' Ish'ther³, for ' should thr;' Isht³, for ' should it;' En'ther², voc., for ' under thr;' Ar'ther¹, for ' or thr, or (the) other, or another;' Art¹, for. ' or it, or had (would);' Arf¹, for ' or would have;' THet¹, for ' with it;' THret³, for ' thou art.'

REM. 2. ' *Us' Added.*—' Us' may usually be best joined to a preceding word by a circle or by enlarging a circle; thus, Gays¹, give us—Gay'ses¹, gives us—Pens², upon us—Bel'ses², bless us—Es¹-Ses, sees us—Tee¹-Chay'ses, teaches us.

REM. 3. *Our*, in phrase-writing, may be written with Ray, when it can not be more conveniently expressed otherwise; thus, Thee'ses²-Ray, this is our.

REM. 4. ' *Is, As,' etc., Prefixed.*—(*a*) A circle-signword may frequently be prefixed to a word commencing with a circle, by enlarging the circle; thus, Ses²-En, as soon—Ses¹-Emp, is simply—Ses¹-Mets, is sometimes—Ses²-Mets, has sometimes —Ses¹-Lays, his soul's—Ses¹-En, is his own. (*b*). The sign-word thus prefixed usually determines the position of the sign, in accordance with § 245. \

§ 268. REPORTING CONTRACTIONS.

A.

abridge-ment, Ber¹-Jay
abrupt-ness, Bee²-Ray-Pet
abstinent-ce, Bee²-Sten
abstract-ed, Bee³-Ster
abstraction, Bee³-Ster'shon
absurdity, Bees²-Ard
abject, Bee²-Jay
acceptable, Spet³-Bel
acquaint-ed-ance, Kay²-Net
admeasurement, Dee²-Zher
administer, Dee³-Iss-Ter
administration, Dee³-Iss-Ter'shon
admit-ted-tance, Dee¹-Met
admonish-ed-tion, Dee³-Men
advancement, Dees³-Ment
adventure-d-r, Def³-Enter
agency, Jay²-Ess
aggrandize-ment, Grend-Zee²
aggregate-d-ion, Ger²-Gay
agriculture, Ger²-Kel
allegory-ical, El²-Ger
almighty-ness, 'All'-Met¹
ambiguity, Emb¹-Gay
ambitious-ly-ness, Emb-Ish¹
America, Em²-Kay
American, Em²-Ken
Anglo-Saxon, Ings²-En
animal kingdom, En²-Kay
animal nature, En²-Net
animal world, En²-Eld
anniversary, Vers²-Ray
antagonism, Ent³-Gays-Em
antagonist-ic, Ent³-Gay
anticipate-d, Ents-Pet¹
anticipation, Ents-Pee¹
antique-ity, Ent¹-Kay
any body, En¹-Bed
approach-able, Per²-Chay
approximate-d-ion, Per¹-Kays
arbitrary, Ar³-Bet
archangel, Ar²-Jel
archbishop, Ray²-Chay-Bee
architect-ure-ural, Ar²-Ket
aristocracy-tic, Ar²-Stee
arithmetic-al-ian, Ray²-Ith-Met
arrange-ment, Ray²-En-Jay

artificial-ity, Ret¹-Ef
ascend-ed-ancy, Es²-End
ascendant, Es²-Nent
ascribe, Es²-Ker
ascription, Es²-Ker'shon
aspect, Es³-Pee
aspire-ation, Es²-Per
assemble-y-ed, Es²-Em
assignment, Es²-Ment
assimilate-d-ion, Es¹-Em
astronomy-ical-er, Est²-Ren
Atlantic Ocean, Tee²-Lent-Kay'-shon
atmosphere-ic-ical, Tees²-Fer
atonement, Tee²-Ment
attainment, Tee³-Ment
attraction of gravitation, Ter³-Ger
augment-ed-ation, Gay²-Ment
auspicious-ly-ness, Es¹-Pee
authentic, Thent²-Kay, or Thent²
authenticity, Thent²-Est, or Thent⁷
avenge, Vee²-Jay
average, Vee³-Jay

B.

back, Bee³-Kay, or Bee³
backgammon, Bee³-Gay-Men
background, Bee³-Grend
bankable, Bee³-Ing-Bee
bank-rupt-cy, Bee³-Ing
baptize-d-ist-ism, Bee²-Pee
barbarity, Ber²-Bret
barometer-rical, Ber²-Emter
beginner, Gen¹-Ar
benefaction, Ben²-Ef'shon
benefactor, Ben²-Ef
benefactress, Ben²-Ef-Rays
beneficent-ce, Ben²-Ef
beneficial, Bee²-Ef
benevolent-ce, Bee²-En-Vee
benignant, Bee²-En-Gay
Benjamin, Bee²-En-Jay
bespeak, Bee¹-Spee
bigot-ed-ry, Bee¹-Get
billingsgate, Bels¹-Get
biography-er-ic-al, Bee²-**Ger**
bishop-ric, Bee¹-Ish

blindfold, Bled¹-Fled
blind man, Bled¹-Men
British America, Bret¹-Em
broken-hearted, Ber²-Ken-Ret
burdensome, Ber²-Dees-Em, or
  Berds²-Em
burning-glass, Bee²-Ray-Gels
busybody, Bees¹-Bed

C.

calculable, Kel³-Bel
California-n, Klef-Ray¹
canon-ical, Kay²-Nen
capacious-ty, Kay-Pee²
capricious-ly-ness, Kay-Per¹
carpenter-ry, Ker-Pent²
casuist-ic-ry, Kays-Est²
category-ical, Ket³-Ger
catholic-ism, Kay-Ith²
celestial, Slay²-Es
certificate, Iss-Ret¹-Ef
challenge-d, Chel²-Jay
challenger, Chel²-Jer
chamber, Chay²-Ber
changeable, Chay²-Bel
chapter, Chay³-Pet, or Chay³
character, Ker²-Kay
characteristic, Ker²-Kayst
characteristics, Ker²-Kay'ses
characterizes, do.
chargeable, Chay³-Bel
chaste-ity, Chayst²
chemical-ly-istry, Kay²-Em
chimera-ical, Kay¹-Mer
chirography-ical, Ker¹-Ger
collateral, Kay-Lay'ter²
collect-ed-ion, Kel²-Kay
comfort-ed-able, Ef²-Ret
commercial, Kay²-Mer
conformable, Fer¹-Bee
conjecture-d-al, Jay²-Kay
conjunctive-ure, Jay²-Ing
conscientious-ly-ness, Ish²-En
conservative, Iss-Ray²-Vee
conspicuous-ly-ness, Spee¹-Kays
constitutionality, Steh-Tee'shon²-
  Tee
contaminate-d-ion, Tee²-Men
contemplate-d-ion, Tee²-Emp
contiguity, Tee²-Gay
contingency, Tee²-En-Jay

contradictory, Dee¹-Ket
contradistinctive, Deest¹-Vee
contradistinguish-ed, Deest¹-Ing
contumacious-ly-ness, Tee²-Em-Ish
criminate-d-ion-al, Ker¹-Men
cross-examination, Ker²-Smen
cross-examined, Ker²-Sment
culpable-ility, Kel²-Pee
cupidity, Kay-Pet¹

D.

debenture, Dee²-Bee
debilitate-d-ion, Dee¹-Blet
debility, Dee¹-Bee
decapitate-d-ion, Dee²-Kay-Pet
December, Dees²-Em
deceptive-ion, Dees²-Pee
declaim-ation-atory, Dee²-Kel
declare-d-ation, Dee²-Kler
declension, Dee²-Klen
decline-able-ation, Dee¹-Klen
declivity, Dee¹-Kel
defamatory, Dee²-Ef-Met
deficient-cy, Dee²-Ef-Shay
deform-ed-ity, Dee¹-Fer
degeneration, Dee²-Jay'shon
degradation, Dee²-Gred
deject-ed-tion, Dee²-Jay
delicacy, Del²-Kay
delicate-ness, Del²-Ket
democracy-tic, Dee²-Em
Denmark, Dee²-Em-Ray-Kay
denunciatory-ion, Dee²-Nen
depart-ed-ment, Dee²-Pret
depend-ed-ence-ency, Dee²-Pend
deplorable, Dee²-Pler
deponent, Dee²-Pen
depravity, Dee²-Prel
deprecate-d-ion, Dee-Per
deprivation, Dee²-Pref
depth, Dee²-Pee
derange-ment, Der²-En-Jay
derogation, Der²-Gay
derogatory-ily, Der²-Get
descendant, Dees²-Nent
deserve-d, Dees²-Ray
desideratum, Dees²-Dret
designate-d-ion, Dees²-Gay
desirable, Dees²-Ar
despicable-ness, Dees²-Pee-Kay
despondent-cy, Dees²-Pend

despot-ic-ical, Dees²-Pet
despotism, Dees²-Pets-Em
destructible, Dee²-Ster
destruction, Dee²-Ster′shon
destructive-ness, Dee²-Stref
determine-able, Dee²-Tren
determined-ly, Dee²-Trend
determination, Dee²-Ter′shon
detest-ation, Deds²-Tce
detract-or, Dee³-Ter
detraction, Dee³-Ter′shon
detriment-al, Dee²-Ter
develop-ment, Def²-Pee
devolve, Def²-Vee
diameter-rical, Dee²-Emter
dictionary, Dee′shon²-Ray
differential, Def²-Ren
dignify-fied-ty, Dee²-Gay
dilapidate-d-ion, Del²-Pet
diminish-ed-ution, Dee²-Men
diplomat-ic, Dee²-Pel-Met
director, Der²-Ter
directory, Der²-Ket
disadvantage, Dees²-Jay
disagree-able-ment, Dees¹-Ger
disappoint-ed-ment, Dees¹-Pent
disbelieve, Dees¹-Bel
discharge, Dees²-Chay
disclaim-ed, Dees²-Kel
discord-ant, Dees¹-Kret
discountenance-d, Dees³-Kent
discover-ed-y, Dees²-Kef
discrepancy, Dees²-Kay-Pee
discriminate-d-ion, Dees²-Kay
disdain-ful, Dees²-Den
dishonor-able, Dees¹-Ner
disinterested-ly-ness, Dees²-Ents-Ted
disjunctive, Dees²-Jay-Ing
disorganization, Dees²-Gens′eshon
disparage-ment, Dees²-Pee-Jay
displeasure, Dees²-Zher
disqualify-ication, Dees¹-Kel
dissatisfy-ied-faction, Dees³-Tee
disseminate-d-ion, Dees²-Men
dissimilar-ity, Dee′ses²-Em
distinctive, Deest²-Vee
distinguished, Deest³-Ing
distinguishable, Deest²-Ing-Bee
distract-ed-er, Dees³-Ter
distraction, Dees³-Ter

distribute-d, Deester²-Bet, or Dee-ster²
distribution, Deester²-Bae′shon, or Deester²
District of Columbia, Dees²-Kel
divination, Def¹-Eshon
Divine Being, Def¹-Bee
diviner, Def¹-Ray
divinest, Def¹-Est
divulge, Def²-Jay
doctrine-al, Dren¹
domestic, Dee²-Ems-Kay
dominate-d-ion-ant, Dee¹-Men
downcast, Dee³-Kayst
downfall, Dee³-Fel
down-hearted, Den³-Art
downright, Dee³-Ret, voc. with ī
downtrod-den, Dee³-Tred
downward, Dee³-Ard
dramatic, Der³-Met
dwelling-house, Dee²-Lay-Hays
dwelling-place, Dee²-Lay-Pels
dyspeptic-sia, Dees²-Pee-Pee

E.

eccentric-ity, Kays²-Enter
ecclesiastic-al, Kel′ses-Tee²
economy-ical, Ken¹-Em
effect-ed, Ef²-Kay
effeminate-ness-acy, Ef²-Men
efficacious-ly, Ef²-Kay-Ish
efficient-cy, Ef²-Shay
electro-ic-ity, El²-Kay
emblematic, Em-Bel²-Met
emphatic-al, Em-Fet²
endanger, En-Jer²
engagement, En-Gay-Jay²
enlarge-ment, En-Jay³
enlarged, En-Jed³
enormity, Ner¹-Em
entangle-d-ment, Ent²-Ing
entertainment, Ent-Tee²-Ment
enthusiast-ic-m, En-Ith²-Ses
envelope, En-Vee²-Pee
episcopal-ian-cy, Pees²-Kay
equinoctial, Kay¹-En-Kay
equivalent-ce, Kay-Vee²
escape-d, Es²-Kay
especial-ly, Es²-Pee
essential-ly, Es²-En
eternal existence, Ter²-Ses-Tens

eternal life, Tren²-Ef
eternality, Tren²-Tee
evaporation, Vee²-Pee
eventual-ly-ity, Vee²-Net
everlasting, Vee¹-Lays
exaggeratory, Sjert²-Ray
excellency, Kays²-Len
exceptionable, Spee'shon²-Bee
exchange-d, Kays-Chay²
exchanger, Kays-Chay²-Jer
exchangeable, Kays-Chay²-Bel
exchequer, Kays-Chay²
exchequer bill, Kays-Chay²-Bee
exclaim-ed, Kays²-Kel
exclamation-ory, Kays²-Kel
excluded, Skel-Ded²—266, R. 8
executor, Kays²-Ray
executrix, Kays²-Kays
expanded, Spen³-Ded—266, R. 8
expansibility, Spees³-Bee
expedient-ce, Kays-Pet¹, or Spet¹
expeditious-ly, Kays-Pet¹-Ish
expended, Spen²-Ded—266, R. 8
experiment-al, Sper²-Ment
extemporary, Stemp²-Ray-Ray
extemporize, Stemp²-Rays
extended, Sten²-Ded
extensibility, Stees²-Bee
extenuate, Sten²-Tee
extenuation, Sten²-Shen
exterminate-d-ion, Ster²-Men
extinction, Kays-Tee²
extinguish-ed, Kays²-Tee
extraordinary, Ster²-Ard
extremity, Ster²-Tee

F.

facetious-ly-ness, Efs²-Shay
factious-ly-ness, Ef³-Kay
faculty, Ef²-Klet
fainthearted-ness, Fent²-Ret
falsification, Fels¹-Eshon
fanatic-al, Ef³-Net
fanciful, Ef²-Ens-Ef
fashionable, Ef'shon²-Bee
fastidious-ness, Efs²-Ted
fantasm, Fent²-Zee
fantastic-al, Fent²-Est
favorable, Ver³-Bee
February, Ef²-Bee
financial, Fen²-En

flexible-ility, Fels²-Bee
for instance, Ef²-Stens
forge-ry, Ef²-Jay
forger, Ef²-Jer
formal-ity, Fer¹-Lay
former-ly, Fer¹-Ar
formless, Fer¹-Lays
fortune-ate-ateness, Ef¹-Ret
fragment-ary, Fer²-Gay
frank-ness, Fer³-Kay
frankly, Fer³-Kel
Franklin, Fer³-Klen
frantic-ness, Fert³-Kay
fraternal-ity, Fret²-Ren, or Fer'tern¹
frigid-ity, Fer¹-Jed
frontispiece, Frets²-Pees
Fugitive Slave Law, Ef²-Jays-Lay

G.

genera-ic, Jay²-Ner
genteel, Jet¹-El
gentile, Jet²-El
gentility, Jet¹-Elt
gentle-ness, Jay²-Net
geography-ical-er, Jay²-Ger
geometry, Jay²-Met
geometrical, Jay²-Emter
governmental, Gef²-Ment
governor, Gef²-Ray
gracious-ly-ness, Ger-Ish²
grandchild, Gred²-Cheld
granddaughter, Gred²-Ter
grandson, Gred²-Sen
gravitate-d-ion, Ger-Ved²
gravity, Ger-Ved²
Great Britain, Gret²-Bret
Great Britain and Ireland, Gret²-
   Bret-Rel'end

H.

habeas corpus, Hay²-Ker
hazard-ed-ous, Zee²-Ard
henceforth, Ens-Ef²
heretofore, Ret²-Ef
hieroglyph-ic-ical, Ar¹-Glef
history-ical, Est¹-Ray
holier, Hay³-Ray
holiness, Hay³-Ens
Holy Ghost, Hay³-Gay
horticulture, Art¹-Kel

House of Lords, Hays²-Lay
houses of Parliament, Hay'ses³-Pee
House of Representatives, Hays³-Ray
hypocrisy, Pee¹-Ker
hypocritical, Pee¹-Kret

I.

identical, Ded¹-Kel
identification, Dent¹-Ef'shon
idiosyncrasy-tic, Dees¹-En
ignominy-ious, Gen¹-Em
illegal-ity, El²-Gel
illegible-ility, El²-Jay
illegitimate-cy, El²-Jet
illiberal-ity, El²-Brel
illogical-ness, El¹-Jay
imaginable, Jen³-Bee
immeasurable, Em-Zher³
impassionate, Emp-Ish³
imperceptible-ility, Em-Pers²-Pet
imperfection, Em-Per'shon¹
imperfectly, Em-Perf¹
implacable-ility, Em-Pel²-Kay
implicit-ness, Em-Pels¹
impoverish-ed-ment, Emp-Ver²
impracticable-ility, Em-Per³-Ket
impregnate-d-ble-ion,   Em-Per²-Gay
improper-ly-riety, Em-Per¹
in the words of my (the) text, En¹-Werds-Teest
in reference, Ner¹-Ef
in regard, Ner¹-Ged
in respect, Ner¹-Spee
in so far as, Ens¹-Efs
in the first place, En¹-Ef-Pel(s)
in the second place, Ens¹-Kay-Pel(s)
in the mean time, En¹ Men-Tee
inartificial-ity, Nert-Ef²
inauspicious-ly-ness, Ens-Pee²-Ish
inclement-cy, En-Kel²
incline-ation, En¹-Klen
incombustible-ility, 'incom':Beest²
incredible-ility, En¹-Kret
indefatigable, End-Fet²
indefinite-ly-ness, End-Ef²
indemnify-ity, End¹-Em
indemnification, End¹-Em'shon
indenture, End²-Ent

independent-ce, End-Pend²
indescribable, Ends-Kay-Bel²
indifferent-ce, En-Def²
indignant-ly-tion-ity, End¹-Gay
individual, End-Ved¹
individuality, End¹:Ved
indivisible-ility, End-Vees¹
indoctrinate-d-ion, En-Dren¹
indulge, End-Jay²
infer-red, En-Ef²
infers-ence, En-Efs²
inferential, En-Fen²
inferior-ity, En-Ef¹
infidelity, En-Fet¹
infiniteness, Neft¹:Ens
infinitesimal, Neft¹-Es
infinitive, Neft¹:Vee
infinitude, Neft¹:Dee
infirm-ity, En-Fer²
inflict, En-Fel¹
infliction, En-Fel'shon¹
inform-ed-ant, En-Fer¹
informal-ity, En-Fer¹-Lay
infraction, En-Fer'shon³
infringe-d-ment-er, En-Fren¹
ingredient, En-Gred¹
inhabit-ed-ant, En-Bet²
inquire-y, En-Wer¹
inscribable, In-Sker-Bel²
insignificant, Ens-Gay¹
insolvency, In-Slay¹-Ven
inspect-ed-ion, En-Spee²
inspire-ation, In-Sper¹
instructor, In-Ster²-Ter
integrity, Ent²-Gret
intellect-ual-ity, Ent¹-Ket
intelligible-ility, Ent-Jay²
intemperate-ance, Ent²-Emp
interdiction, Ent-Dee'shon¹
interiorly, Ent-El²
intermingled, Ent¹-Em-Ing
interpret-ed-ation, Ent-Pret²
intestate, Ents-Tet², voc. with a
intestine, Ents-Ten²
intimidate-d-ion, Ent¹-Med
intolerable, Ent-El¹
introduction, Ent-Dee'shon²
introspect-ion, Ent-Spee²
invent-ed-or, En-Vent²
invention, En-Ven²
invisible-ility, En-Vees¹
invite-ation, En-Vet¹

involve, En-Vee[1]
irrecoverable-ness, Ar[2]-Kef
irrefragable-ility, Ar[2]-Fer
irrelevancy, Rel[1]-Ven
irreligion, Ar[1]-Jen
irreligious, Ar[1]-Jays
irresistible-ility, Ar[2]-Scs-Tee
irrespective-ly, Ar[2]-Spef
irresponsible-ility, Ar[2]-Spens

J.

January, Jay[2]-En
Jefferson, Jay[2]-Fer, or Jef
Jesus Christ, Jay[2]-Kay
Jesus of Nazareth, Jay[2]-Ens
joint stock, Jed[1]-Stee-Kay
judicature-ory, Jed[2]-Kay
judicial, Jed[1]-Ish
  judiciary, Jed[1]-Sher
judicious-ly-ness, Jed[1]-Shay
jurisconsult, Jers[2]-Kays-Let
jurisprudence, Jers[2]-Pce
justify-iable, Jays[2]-Ef
juxtaposition, Jays[2]-Pces'eshon

K.

kingdom of Christ, Kef[1]-Kay
kingdom of God, Kef[1]-Ged
king's bench, Kays-Bee[2]

L.

labyrinth, Lay[2]-Ber-Ith
landscape, Lends[2]-Kay
languish, El[2]-Ing-Ish
laughing-stock, Lay[2]-Efs-Tee-Kay
learned counsel, Lay[2]-Ar-Kay
learned judge, Lay[2]-(Ar-)Jay
legal-ity, Lay[1]-Gel
legendary, Lay[2]-Jed-Ray
legislate-d-or-ion, Lay[2]-Jay
legitimate-d-ness, Lay[2]-Jet
lengthwise, Ing[3]-Ways
lengthy, Ing[3]-Ith
Leviticus-al, Lay[1]-Vet
lexicography-er-ic, Lays[2]-Kay-Ger
liberal-ity, Lay[1]-Brel
libertine, Lay[1]-Bret
libertinism, Lay[1]-Brets-Em
looking-glass, Lay[3]-(Kay-)Gels

loving kindness, Lef[2]-Kend
luscious-ness, Lay[2]-Ish

M.

machine, Em-Ish[2]; sometimes Em
  in phr.
machinery, Em-Ish[2]-Ray
machinist, Em-Ish[2]-Steh
magnet-ic-ism, Em[2]-Gen
magnificent-ce, Em[1]-Gay
majesty-ic, Em-Jay[3]
majority, Em Jert[1]
malevolent-ce, Mel-Vee[2]
malformed-ation, Mel-Fer[2]
malicious-ly-ness, Mel-Ish[2]
malignant-ce, Mel[1]-Gay
manufacture-r-ory, Em-En-Ef[2]
manifest-ed-ation, Em[1]-Ens
Massachusetts, Ems-Chay[3]
materialism, Emters[2]-Em
materialistic, Emters[2]-Kay
materiality, Em'ter[2]-Let
maxim-um, Ems[2]-Em
meanwhile, Em[1]-Nel
  in the mean time, En[1]-Men-Tee
mechanic-al, Em[2]-Kay
mechanism, Em[2]-Kay
Mediterranean, Med-Tren[2]
melancholy, Mel[2]-Kel
memory-andum, Em[2]-Em
merchandise, Em-Ray[2]-Chet-Zee
merchantable, Em-Ray[2]-Chet-Bel
messenger, Ems-Jer[2]
metaphysical, Met-Efs[2]
method-ical, Em-Thed[2]
Methodist-ic-ical, Em-Thet[2]-Stch
metropolitan, Em'ter-Pel[1]
Mexico, Ems[2]-Kay
microscope, Ems-Kay-Pee[2]
mingle-d, Em[1]-Ing
minimum, Men[1]-Em
ministerial, Em-Ens-Tee[2]
minority, Em[1]-Nert
misconjecture-d, Ems-Jay[2]-Kay
misdemeanor, Ems-Dee[2]
misfortune, Ems-Fret[1]
modification, Med-Ef'shon[2]
monstrous-sity, Mens-Tees[2]
mortgage, Mer[1]-Gay
  mortgagee, Mer-Gay-Jay[2]
mortification, Mert-Ef'shon[2]

my part, Emp¹-Ret
mystification, Ems(t)¹-Esh′on

N.

needful, Ned-Ef ¹
neglect, En²-Gay
neglectful, En²-Gef
negligent-ce, En²-Gel
New Foundland, En-Fed²-El′end
New Jersey, En²-Jay
New Testament, Net²-Steh
New York, En²-Yay
New York City, En²-Yays
New York State, En²-Yay-Steh
nobody, En²-Bed
nocturnal, En²-Ket-Ren
nomenclature, En²-Em-Klet
nonconformist, Nen†Efst²
nonconformity, Nen†Ef ²
nondescript, Nends¹-Kay
non-essential, Nen-Es²-En
North America, Ner¹-Em
North Carolina, Ner¹-Ker
nothing, En-Ith²
notification, Net-Ef′shon²
nourish-able-ment, Ner-Ish²
Nova Scotia, En-Skay-Ish²
November, En-Vee²
noxious-ly-ness, En-Kay-Ish²

O.

obligatory, Bel²-Get
obscure-ity, Bees²-Kay
observant-ce, Bees²-Ray
observe-d-ation, Bees²-Ray
obstruct-ed, Bee²-Ster
obstruction, Bee²-Ster′shon
obstructive, Bee²-Stref
octangular, Ket²-Ing
officious-ness, Ef ¹-Ish
oftentimes, Fent¹-Ems
ofttimes, Fet¹-Ems
Old Testament, Eldst²
Old and New Testament, Let²-Netst
oligarchy-ical, El²-Ger
omnific, Men-Ef ²
omnipotent-ce, Men-Pee²
omnipresent-ce, Em-Per²
omniscient-ce, Men-Ish²
organic, Gen¹-Kay

organism, Gen¹-Iss-Em
original, Ar¹-Jen
orthodox, Ray¹-Ith
ostentatious-ly-ness, Est¹-Ent
overwhelm-ed, Ver²-El

P.

paganism, Pee²-Gays-Em
painful, Pen²-Ef
panegyric, Pee²-Jer
pantomime-ic, Pent²-Em
partial-ity, Per²-Shel
party of the first part, Pee³-Efs-Pee
party of the second part, Pee³-Skay-Pee
passenger, Pees²-Jer
patentable, Pee³-Bel
paternal-ity, Pet²-Ren
patronage, Pet³-Ray-Jay
pecuniary-ily, Pee²-Ken
pedant-ic, Pee²-Dent
pedantry, Pee²-Ded-Ray
pedobaptist, Ped¹:Bee²-Pee
peevish-ly-ness, Pef ²-Shay
penetrable-ility, Pent²-Bee
penetrate, Pent²-Ret
penitential, Pent²-En
Pennsylvania, Pees²-Lay-Vee
perfected, Perf ¹-Ket
perform-ed-ance, Per²-Fer
permanent-ly-ce, Per²-Men
perpendicular-ly-ity, Per²-Pen
perpetual-ate-ion, Pee²-Ray-Pet
person, sometimes Pers in phr.
persons, sometimes Perses in phr.
personification, Pers²-En-Ef′shon
perspective, Pers²-Pef
perspicacious-ly-ness, Pers²-Pee-Kay-Ish
perspicuity, Pers²-Pee-Kay
pertinacious-ly-ness, Pee²-Ret-En-Ish
pestilential, Pees²-Len
phenomena-on-al, Fen²-Em
Philadelphia, Flet²-Ef
philosophy-ic-ical, Fels²-Ef
photography-ic-ist-er, Fet¹-Ger
physical world, Efs²-Eld
physiognomy, Efs²-Gay
piquancy, Pee¹-Ken

platform, Plet²-Fer
placable-ility, Pel²-Kay
plenipotentiary, Plen²-Pee
polygamy-ous, Pel¹-Gay
    ponderous, Pend¹-Rays
    ponder, Pend¹-Ar
ponderable-y, Pend¹-Bee
pontiff-ical, Pent¹-Ef
popularity, Pee¹-Pee
potential-ity, Pee²-Ten
powerful-ness, Pee³-Ref
    power, Pee³-Ray
precious-ness, Per²-Ish
precipitate-d-ion, Pers¹-Pet
predestinarian, Pred²-Stee-Nern
predestinate-d-ion, Pred²-Sten
predestine-ation, Pred²-Sten
predetermine-ation, Pred²-Tren
predicable, Pred²-Kay
predominate-d-ion, Pred¹-Men
predominant-ce, Pred¹-Men
prefigure-d-ation, Pref²-Gay
prejudice-d, Per²-Jed
prejudicial, Per²-Jed-Ish
prepare-ation-atory, Per²-Pee-Ray
    prepared, Per²-Pee-Ret
prerogative, Per²-Ray-Gay
presbytery-ian, Pers²-Bet
presbyterianism, Pers²-Bets-Em
prescribe-d, Per¹-Skay
prescription, Per¹-Skay'shon
prescriptive, Per¹-Skef
presént-ed-átion, Pers²-Ent
preserve-d-ation, Pers²-Ray
presidential, Pers²-Den
pretension-sive, Per²-Ten
pretension, Per²-Ten
priestcraft, Pers¹-Keft
prima facie, Per¹-Ef
prime minister, Per¹-Em-Enster
primogeniture, Per²-Em-Jay
problematical, Per¹-Bel-Met
proclaim-ed-er, Per²-Kel
proclivity, Per¹-Kel
prodigious-ness, Pred¹-Jay
product, Per²-Dee
productive-ness, Per²-Def
proficient, Per²-Ef
prognosticate-d-ion, Per¹-Gay
próject, Per¹-Jay
projéct-ed-ion, Per²-Jay
prominent-ce, Per'-Men

property, Per¹-Pee
propitious-ness, Per²-Pee-Shay
proportion-ed, Per²-Pee'shon
proportionate-ly-ness, Per²-Pee'-shon-Tee
proscribe, Per²-Skay
prospect-ed, Pers¹-Pee
prospective-ly, Pers¹-Pef
prostitute-d, Pers²-Tet
protestant-ism, Pret¹-Stent
protract-ed, Per³-Ter
protraction, Per³-Ter'shon
protractive, Per³-Tref
providential, Preft²-En
provincial, Pref²-En
prudential, Per²-Den
public-ation-ish-ished-isher, Pee²-Bee
pugnacity-ous-ly, Pee²-Gay
pulpit, Pel²-Pee
punctual-ity, Pee²-Ing
punctilious-ly-ness, Pee²-Ing-Ket
pungency, Pen²-Jay
purgatory-ial, Per²-Get
pusillanimous-ity, Pees³-Len

Q.

quadrangular-ity, Ket²-Ray-Ing
qualifications, Kel¹-Ef'shons
questionable, Ken²-Bee
questioner, Ken²-Ar

R.

radiancy, Ray²-Den
ramification, Ar²-Em-Ef'shon
rapacious-ness, Ray²-Pee-Shay
rapid-ity, Ray²-Pet
ratification, Ret²-Ef'shon
rebutting evidence, Ray²-Bet-Ved
recapitulate-d-ion, Ray²-Kay-Pet
reciprocate-d-ion, Ray²-Sper
reclaim-ed, Ray²-Kel
reclamation, Ray²-Kel
recollect-ed-ion, Ray²-Kel-Kay
recover-y-ed-able, Ray²-Kef
rectification, Ray²-Ket-Ef'shon
redound-ed, Red²-End
reduction, Ray²-Dee'shon
redundance-y, Red²-End
redundant-ly, Red²-Nent

reflect-ed-ion, Ray²-Ef-Kay
reform-ed-atory, Ray¹-Fer
refract ed-ion, Ray³-Fer
refractory, Ray³-Fer-Ket
refute-d-ation, Ray²-Fet
regenerate-d, Ray²-Jen
regeneration, Ray²-Jay'shon
regenerative, Ray²-Jay'tiv
reject-ed-ion, Ray²-Jay
relevancy, Rel²-Ven
relinquish-ed-ment, Rel²-Ing
reluctant-ce, Rel²-Ket
remit-ted-tance, Ar¹-Met
remonstrate-d, Ar²-Em-Strct
repeat-ed-tition, Ray¹-Pet
repent-ed-ance, Ray²-Pent
replenish-ed-ment, Ray²-Plen
reprehensible-ility, Ray²-Prens
reprehensive-sion, Ray²-Pren
reproach-able, Ray²-Per-Chay
republic-ation-ish-ished, Ray²-Pee-Bee
republican, Ray²-Pee-Ben
repugnant-ce, Ray²-Pee-Gay
repute-d-ation, Ray³-Pet
resemble-d-ance, Ar²-Sem
reserve-d ation, Rays²-Ray
resignation, Rays²-Gay
respect-ed-ing-ful, Rays²-Pee
respectable-ility, Rays²-Pee-Bee
respective, Rays²-Pef
resplendent-ence, Rays²-Plent
respond-ed-ent-ence, Rays²-Pent
responsive, Rays²-Pen
responsible-ility, Rays²-Pens
restrict-ed, Ray²-Ster
restriction, Ray²-Ster'shon
restrictive, Ray²-Stref
resurrection, Rays²-Ray
retract-ed, Ray³-Ter
retraction, Ray³-Ter'shon
retractive, Ray³-Tref
retrospect-ion, Art²-Rays-Pee
retrospective, Art²-Rays-Pef
revenge-d, Ray²-Vee-Jay
revengeful-ness, Ray²-Vee-Jef
Rev. Dr., Ray²-Vee-Der
reverential, Ref²-Ren
revive-d-al, Ray¹-Vee
revivify, Ray¹-Vee-Ef
revivification, Ray¹-Vee-Ef'shon
rhetor-ic-al, Art²-Ray

Romanism, Ar²-Ems-Em
Roman Catholicism, Ar²-Kay-Ith, or Ar²-Kay

S.

sagacious-ness, Sgay-Ish²
sanctify-ied-ication, Iss-Ing²-Ket
sanctimony-ious-iousness, Iss-Ing²-Em
sanguinary, Iss-Ing'en²-Ray
sanguify, Iss-Ing-Ef²
Secretary of State, Skrets²-Tet
Secretary of War, Skret²-Wer
scientific, Es¹-Ent
scoundrel-ism, Sked'-Rel
sculptor-ure, Skel-Pet²
sectarianism, Skets²-Em
sedentary, Sdet²-Ray
sentimentalism, Sent²-Mets-Em
sentimentalist, Sent²-Ment-Est
September, Spet²-Em
Shakspeare, Ish²-Spee
signature, Sgay¹-Net
simpler, Semp¹-Ray
simplify, Semp-Ef²
simplification, Semp-Ef'shon²
skeptic-al-ism, Skay-Pet²
slumber, Slay² Ber
so far as, Es²-Efs
sober-minded-ness, Sber²-Mend
solvency, Slay¹-Ven
somnambulist-m, Smen-Bee²
South America, Iss-Ith²-Em
South Carolina, Iss-Ith²-Ker
south-eastern, Iss-Thes²-Ren
southerner, Iss-Then²-Ray
south-western, Sways²-Ren
south-west, Swayst²
spacious-ness, Spee²-Ish
speakable, Spee¹-Bel
specify-ic, Spees¹-Ef
specious-ness, Spee²-Ish
speculate-d-or-ory, Spee²-Klet
spendthrift, Sped²-Ther
spiritualism, Spers¹-Em
spiritualistic, Spers¹-Kay
standard, Sted²-Ard
stepping stone, Steh-Pee²-Sten
stopping-place, Steh-Pee¹-Pels
straightforward-ness, Stref²-Ret
stranger, Ster²-Jer

stratify-ication, Ster³-Tee-Ef
strength, Ster²-Ith
strengthen, Ster²-Then
structure-al, Ster²-Ter
subjugate-d-ion, Sbee²-Jay
subserve - d - ient - ience - iency, Sbees²-Ray
substantial-ity, Sbee²-Stee
substantiate-d-ion, Sbee²-Sten
substantive-ly, Sbee²-Stent
substitute-d, Sbees²-Tet
subtract-ed-ion, Sbee²-Ter
subtrahend, Sbee²-Trend
succinct-ly-ness, Ses-Ing¹-Ket
sufficient-cy-ly, Iss-Ef²-Shay
suffocate-d-ion, Iss-Ef²-Kay
suit in chancery, Sten³-Chay
supererogation-tory, Sper²-Ray-Gay
superficial-ity, Sper²-Ef
superincumbent, Spren²-Bent
supernaturalism, Spers³-Em
superscribe-d, Sper²-Skay
superscription, Sper²-Iss-Kay′shon
superstitious-ness, Sper²-Stee
superstructure, Sper²-Iss-Ter
Supreme Being, Sper²-Bee
surreptitious-ly-ness, Iss-Ray²-Pet
survive-d-r, Iss-Ray¹-Vee
swindle-d-r, Sway¹-Del, or Iss-Waynd¹
sympathetic-al, Iss-Emp-Thet²

T.

tabernacle, Tee²-Ber
tachygraphy-ic, Tee²-Kay-Ger
taciturnity, Tees²-Tren
tangible-ility, Tee²-En-Jay
tantamount, Tet²-Ment
technical-ity, Tee²-Kay
telegraph-er-ic, Tel²-Ger
telescope-ic, Tel²-Skay
temperament-al, Tee²-Emp-(Ment)
temperate-ance, Tee²-Emp
temperature, Tee²-Emp′ter
tenement, Tee²-Ment
terminate-d-ion, Ter²-Men
testament, Tees²-Ment
testamentary, Tees²-Ment-Ray
testification, Tees²-Eshon
testify, Tees²-Ef

testimony, Tees²-Em
testimonial, Tees²-Em-Nel
Texas, Tee′ses²
texture, Tee²-Ster
thanksgiving, Thes³-Gay
thankworthy, Ith³-Wer-Thee
thenceforth, Thees²-Ef
thenceforward, Thees²-Ef-Wert
theoretical, Ith²-Ret
thermometer-rical, Ther²-Em
thunder-storm, Ith²-En′derst
timidity, Tee²-Med
to become, Bee³-Kay
torpid-ity, Ter¹-Ped
tragedy-ic-ical, Ter²-Jay
tranquil-ity, Ter³-En, or Ter³-Ing
transatlantic, Ters²-Lent-Kay
transcend-ed, Ters³-End
transcendent-al-ism, Ters²-Nent
transcribe-d-r, Ters¹-Kay
transcription, Ters¹-Kay′shon
transfer-red, Ters²-Ef
transfers ence, Ters²-Efs
transform-ed-ation, Ters²-Fer
transparent-cy, Ters²-Pee
transubstantiation, Ters²-Bee
trigonometry-ical, Ter¹-Gen
tympanum, Tee²-Empen
typography-er-ic, Tee²-Pee-Ger
tyrannic-al, Tee²-Ren

U.

unclaim-ed, En²-Kel
uncontradicted, En-Dee¹
undecided-ly, Ends-Ded¹
undignified, En-Dee²-Gay
undiscoverable, Ends²-Kef
unexpected, En-Spee²
uniform-ity, En-Fer³
unimaginable, En-Jen³
unimaginative, En-Jay′tiv³
unimagined, En-Jend³
unimportant-ce, En¹-Emp
unimproved, En²-Emp
United States of America, Ins-Em¹
Universalism, Vers²-Em
universality, Vers²-Lay
university, Vers²-Tee
unmeasured, En-Zherd³
unquestionable, En²-Ken-Bee
unquestioned, En²-Ken

unwilling-ness, En-Lay²
utilitarianism, Tel²-Ters-Em

V.

vacancy, Vee²-Ken
vainglory, Vee²-Gel
valediction, Vel²-Dee′shon
valedictory, Vel²-Dee
valid-ity, Vee²-Eld
vegetable-rian, Vee²-Jet
vegetarianism, Vee²-Jets-Em
vegetate-d-ion, Vee²-Jet
vengeance, Vee²-Jens
vexatious-ly-ness, Vee²-Kays
vice versa, Vee²:Ver²
vicious-ness, Vee¹-Shay
virgin, Vee²-Jen

Virginia, Vee²-Jay
viva voce, Vee²:Vee²

W.

warrant-ed-able, Wernt¹
worship-ed, Wer²-Ish
worshiper, Wer²-Ish-Ar
wretched-ness, Ray²-Chet

Y.

yes, sir, Yay′ses²
yesterday, Est²-Dee, or Es′ter²

Z.

zigzag, Zees²-Gay
zoography, Zee²-Ger

Rem. 1. From the preceding list there have been excluded many contractions which might, and will in due time, be formed by the reporter, in accordance with the general principles of § 237, R. 3; and also a large number of contractions for past tenses or perfect participles, which will be formed in accordance with the principles of § 266, R. 8. Numerous contractions which are formed by the omission of prefixes or affixes, have, for a corresponding reason, been excluded. On the other hand, several phrase-signs, such as Jay-Ens for 'Jesus of Nazareth,' have been included, because of their involving principles of contraction. The practiced reporter will form, in accordance with § 237, Rems. 2 and 3, numerous special contractions, as they may seem to be demanded.

Rem. 2. *Primitive Words Sometimes Inserted.*—In many cases in the preceding list, where a contraction for a derivative word has happened to be the complete outline for a primitive word, such word has been inserted to indicate that fact; thus, 'En-Vet¹,' the contraction for 'invitation,' is the complete outline for 'invite;' and this word has therefore been inserted.

Rem. 3. In devising the contractions for the words in the preceding list, there has been kept constantly in view the principle of making like contractions for like words; so that one contraction, familiarized, is an index, in almost every instance, of the contractions for words of similar terminations. To illustrate—learning the contraction for 'gracious-ly-ness,' is in effect learning the contractions for the words of similar terminations, as, 'ambitious-ly-ness, contumacious-ly-ness;' except in a few instances where still further contraction may be made, as in the signs for 'capricious-ly-ness, conscientious-ly-ness.' The contractions for 'permanent-ce, dominant-ce, independent-ce, correspond-ent-ence, superintend-ent-ence, repent-ant-ance,' and words of similar terminations, are all formed in analogy. Contractions for words ending in 'graphic-al,' as a general rule, follow the analogy of 'geography-ic-al.' This general rule being borne in mind, not only may the large number of contractions presented in the preceding list be more readily learned than a few abbreviations formed without reference to general principles, but the principle of these contractions being familiarized, the reporter will readily form numerous others as they are needed.

Rem. 4. *'Distract' and 'Administer' Distinguished.*—'Administer' may be distinguished from 'distract' by writing the circle distinctly within the Ar-hook in the

9

sign for the former word, and by implying the Ar-hook in the sign for the latter ' word, by turning the circle on the left-hand side of the Dee.

REM. 5. Derivatives from contractions are generally formed by prefixing or affixing the proper signs for the formative ; thus, to the contraction for 'applicable,' prefix En for 'inapplicable ;' to the contraction for 'changeable,' prefix En for 'unchangeable.' See § 252, R. 5.

REM. 6. *Letters Disjoined, etc.*—(*a*) To indicate that a sign is to be written disjoined near the other portion of the word, it is preceded or followed by a colon ; thus, 'En:Beest' indicates that the sign for 'incom' should be written separate, according to § 228, 7 ; and in 'Neft:Dee' it is indicated that Dee should be disjoined, and written partially under the Neft. (*b*) The dagger (†) is printed between two signs to indicate that the character following it is to be written through the preceding one ; thus, 'En†Ef' indicates that the Ef is to be written through the En. (*c*) By inclosing one or more letters in curves, it is indicated that the writer may, if he choose, dispense with the sign, or signs, for such letters : thus, in 'En-Ef-Pel(s),' it is indicated that the circle for the *s* may be omitted.

REM. 7. The contraction for a verb may, as a general rule, be employed as a sign for the actor; thus, the contraction for 'interpret' may be employed as a contraction for 'interpreter ;' the contraction for 'conjecture' may be employed as a contraction for 'conjecturer ;' the contraction for 'discover,' as a contraction for 'discoverer.'

REM. 8. '*S*' *Sometimes Omitted.*—When several Es-sounds occur together, one or more may be omitted to secure the advantage of a phrase-sign ; thus, Thees²-Tens, this circumstance—Theeses²-Tens, this existence.

REM. 9. -*Ful-ness.*—These terminations may be expressed by Ef joined, when the Ef-hook or a joined Fel can not be conveniently employed ; thus, Sen¹-Ef, sinful—Pen²-Ef, painful-ness.

REM. 10. *Reference, Preference.*—In the Corresponding Style, Ray²-Ef was given as a contraction for 'refer,' and Ray-Efs for 'reference.' The example of that abbreviation was followed in providing contractions for 'inference, in reference,' etc. ; but the reporter may omit the Iss from all these words. He will thereby secure the advantage of lengthening the Ef to add *thr*, and of shortening it to add *it*. See §§ 211 ; 221, R. 4.

REM. 11. *Mode of Learning the Word-Signs and Contractions.*—The word-signs and contractions may be most readily learned in the following manner :—1. Carefully read the lists through several times. 2. Having familiarized a small portion, say one or two pages, have a reader or fellow-student read the words, while you give the name and position of the sign. 3. When the names and position can be accurately given, have the contracted words read to you many times, while you write the signs therefor. This practice should be continued until the word-signs and contractions can be written as fast as the words can be properly spoken by the reader.

DISTINCTIONS.

§ 269. Words of similar or different meanings, and containing the same consonants, are distinguished—

1. By difference in the mode of representing the first consonant; thus, Ray-Spens, responsible—Rays-Let, resolute (see § 153, 2) ; Ar-Spens, irresponsible—Ar-Iss-Let, irresolute (see § 152, 1).

2. By some other difference of outline; thus, Em'der-Tee², moderate—Med-Ret¹, immoderate; Pers¹-Ket, prosecute — Pee²-Rays-Ket, persecute; Bee²-Ray-Ith, berth—Ber²-Ith, breath.

3. By difference in position; thus, Per²-Met, permit—Per¹-Met, prompt—Per³-Met, promote; End¹-Kay'shon, indication—End²-Kay'-shon, induction. (See § 261.)

4. By the vocalization of one or more of the words to be distinguished; thus, Em²-Gret, emigrate—Em¹-Gret, migrate—ĭEm¹-Gret, immigrate.

REM. The mode of distinguishing several of the sign-words has already been exhibited in the table of reporting word-signs. The following table will be useful for reference, and as an extended illustration of the principles of this section.

---

§ 270. WORDS DISTINGUISHED BY DIFFERENCE OF OUTLINE
OR POSITION.

Arranged according to the Phonographic Alphabet.

Pee²-Tee, pity—Pee¹-Tee, piety—§ 261, R. 1.

Pet²-Ren, paternal-ity—Pet³-Ren, patron, pattern

Pee²-Slay, apostle—Pee¹-Slay, epistle

Pee'shont², patient—Pee'shon²-Tee, passionate

Pee²-Pees, purpose—Per²-Pees, perhaps, propose

Per¹-Pee, property—Per¹, proper-riety—Per²-Pret, appropriate

Per²-Pershon, appropriation—Per²-Peeshon, proportion—Per²-Pee-Ray, preparation

Per²-Peeshon, proportioned—Per²-Peeshon-Tee, proportionate.

Per¹-Beeshon, prohibition—Per²-Beeshon, probation—Per³-Beeshon, approbation

Pret²-Kayshon, protection—Per²-Deeshon, production

Pee²-Ret-En, pertain—Per²-Ten, appertain

Per¹-Sket, prosecute-or—Pee²-Ray-Sket, persecute-or

Per¹-Skay, prescribe-d—Per²-Skay, proscribe-d

Pers²-Ar, oppressor—Pee²-Ray-Es-Ar, pursuer

Per³-Ish, Prussia—Pee²-Ray-Ish, Persia

Pershon³, Prussian—Pee²-Rayshon, Parisian—Pee²-Ray-Shen, Persian

Pershon², operation—Pershon³, oppression

Pee²-Rayshon, portion—Pee³-Rayshon, apportion

Per²-Ems, promise—Per¹-Ems, premise

Per²-Met, permit—Per¹-Met, prompt—Per³-Met, promote

Per¹-Men, prominent—Per²-Men, permanent—Per²-Men-Ent, pre-eminent

Pels²-Dee, placid—Pee²-Lays-Dee, pellucid
Bet²-Ef, beautify—Bee²-Tee-Ef, beatify
Bee¹-Slet, obsolete—Bee³-Slet, absolute
Bee²-Ray-Ith, birth—Ber²-Ith, breath
Bend², abundant—Ben²-Dend, abandoned
Tee²-Arter, tartar—Ter²-Ter, traitor—Tred²-Ar, trader
Ter²-Lay, utterly—Ter³-Lay, truly
Tren², train—Tee²-Ren, turn
Ten³-Bee, attainable—Tee²-En-Bel, tenable
Dee²-Ter, editor—Dee¹-Ter, daughter
Ded¹-Ar, auditor—Ded¹-Ray, auditory—Ded²-Ar, debtor—Ded³-Ar, doubter
Dee²-Let-(Ray), adultery—Dee²-Layter, idolater-ry
Dees²-Ten, destine—Deest²-En, destiny
Deeses¹, disease-d—Dees²-Es, decease
Dees²-Let, desolate—Dees²-Elt, dissolute
Dees²-Layshon, desolation—Dees²-Elshon, dissolution
Dee²-Layshon, adulation—Dee³-Layshon, dilution, delusion
Del¹, idleness—Dee²-Lay-Ens, dullness
Dee²-Ems-Tershon, demonstration—Dees³-Tershon, administration
Dee²-Men, diminish-ution—Dee³-Men, admonish-ition
Dee¹-Men, domination—Dee²-Em-Enshon, condemnation—Dee²-Em Enshon, damnation
Dershon¹, derision—Dee²-Rayshon, adoration—Dershon², duration
Jay³, large—h-tick-Jay³, huge (see § 146, R. 4)
Jay²-Net, agent—Jent², gentleman
Jay²-Net, gentle—Jet¹-El, genteel—Jet²-El, gentile
Kayst¹, cost—Kays-Dee¹, caused
(Kay-)Ster²-Ket, extricate—Ster³, extract
Kays¹-Eshon, acquisition — Kays²-Eshon, accession — Kays³-Eshon, accusation
Sten², extension—Sten²-Shen, extenuation
Kelshon¹, collision—Kay-Layshon¹, coälition—Kay-Layshon³, collusion
Ker-Prel², corporal—Ker-Pee²-Rel, corporeal
Kred¹, accordance—Ker-Dens¹, credence
Ged¹, God—Gay-Dee¹, guide
Gret²-Lay, greatly—Gred-Lay³, gradual-ly
Ver³, favored—Ef²-Vert, favorite
Efs²-Kel, physical—Efs²-Kay-El, fiscal
Fel²-Ent, fluent—Fel³-Ent, affluent
Ef¹-Ar-Iss, fierce—Ef³-Rays, furious
Ef²-Werd, forward—Fer²-Ard, froward

Fer²-Em, af-firm—Fer¹, form—Ef²-Ar-Em, farm

Ef²-Em-Lay, female—Mel³, family

Ved¹, avoid—Ved² (voc. with ã), or Vee²-Dee, evade

Vel³-Bel, valuable—Vee²-Lay·Bel, available

Vee¹-Layshon, volition—Vee²-Layshon, violation—Vee³-Layshon, evolution—Velshon³, valuation

Vee²-Lent, violent—Vee²-El′ent, valiant

Ith²-Steh, atheist—Iths²-Tee, theist

Ithst²-Kay, atheistic—Iths²-(Tee-)Kay, theistic

Spee³, special-ly—Es²-Pee, especial-ly

Spee²-Ret, support-ed—Spret², separate-d

Stee³ (voc. with ū), suit—Stee³, satisfy

Steh-Dee², steady, study—Sted²; staid

Stee²-Bel, stable—Stee³-Bel, suitable

Est²-Dee, or Ester², yesterday—Stee², or Stee²-(Ray-)Dee, Saturday

Lays², less—Lays² (voc.), else

Lay²-Bred, labored—El²-Bret, elaborate

Let²-Tet, latitude—Let²-Tee-Dee, altitude

Lay¹-Kay, like—El¹-Kay, alike

El²-Kay-El, alcohol—El²-Kel, alkali

Lay¹-Kel, likely—Lay²-Kay-Lay, luckily

Lay¹-Em, lime—El³-Em, alum

El²-Ment, element—El³-Ment, aliment

Lends¹, islands—Lends³, lands—Lends¹, with the first part of ī joined, highlands

Ray¹-Ter, writer—Ard¹-Ar, or Ar′der¹, reader—Ar²-Ter, orator—Art²-Ray, rhetor

Emp′shont², impatient—Emp′shond³, impassioned—Emp-Ish³, im· passionate

Em-Bel², amiable—Em-Bel³, humble

Ray³-Ned, ruined—Ray³-En-Dee, renewed

Em¹-Gret, migrate—īEm¹-Gret, immigrate—Em²-Gret, emigrate

Mel²-Rayshon, melioration—Mel³-Rayshon, amelioration

Men¹-Net, imminent—Men²-Net, eminent

En¹-Ef, in fact—En¹-Ef-Kay, in effect

En¹-Bed, anybody—En²-Bed, nobody

En-Ded¹, indeed—En²-Det, no doubt

End¹-Kayshon, indication—End²-Kayshon, induction

En-Vee²-Shayn, innovation—En-Veeshon², invasion

End-Ted¹, indicted—End-Ted², indebted—End-Ted³, undoubted

End-Ef¹, needful—End-Ef², indefinite—En-Def¹-End, undefined

End¹-Els, needless—End²-Els, endless

En-Jay²-Ens, ingenious—En-Jay²-En-Es, ingenuous

En-Ved[1]-Bel, unavoidable—En-Vet[2]-Bel, inevitable
In-Sper[1]-Bel, inseparable—In-Sper[3]-Bel, insuperable
En[1]-Zee, noisy—En[1]:Zee[1], uneasy

REPORTING WORD-SIGN FOR 'I.'

§ 271. In the Reporting Style, the pronoun *I*, when standing alone, may be represented by the abbreviated ī, written in the direction of Tee; thus, ⌐ . See § 103.

REM. (*a*) *I* commencing phrase-signs, invariably occupies the first position, and is thus distinguished from *he*, which, when commencing phrase-signs, always rests upon the line of writing. (*b*) *I* and *he* following other words in a phrase-sign, are distinguished by difference of direction of their signs; the tick for *I*, in such case, being vertical or horizontal, while the tick for *he* is inclined. See § 103 and § 146, R. 5.

THE THER-TICK.

§ 272. Thr = 'there, their, they are,' when it can not otherwise be conveniently expressed in a phrase-sign, may be denoted, if the writer choose, by a heavy tick written in the direction of Bee or Jay; thus, ⌐ since thr; ⌐ would thr.

REM. 1. The experienced reporter may use the same tick for *other;* as in writing 'since other, around other,' etc.

REM. 2. This Ther-tick may take an En or Ef hook, or a circle, for the purposes for which they are added in similar cases, as previously specified—as to add 'own, not, have, ever, fore, his, is,' etc.

PHRASE-WRITING.

§ 273. For the principles of phrase-writing, see § 242–250.

REM. 1. If the pupil will familiarize and apply the principles of phrase-writing, which have been, for the first time, presented in this book, while he will save himself from the burden of much empirical and imitative practice, he will find that the largest list of phrase-signs ever published will appear meager indeed as compared with the phrase-signs which he will naturally, easily, and readily form under the guidance of these few and simple principles.

NUMBERS.

§ 274. (*a*) Instead of writing two or more ciphers in succession, phonographically express the denomination they would represent; thus, 2 ⌐ = 2,000; 4 ⌣ = 400; 6 ⌐ = 6,000,000.

(*b*) When convenient, the termination 'ty' in the numbers 20, 30, etc., may be expressed by an upward line written from 2, 3, etc. ; thus,

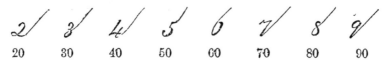

| 20 | 30 | 40 | 50 | 60 | 70 | 80 | 90 |

REM. Phonographic numerals will be found of decided service to the reporter, and they should be thoroughly familiarized.

REFERENCES, REPETITIONS, OMISSIONS, DOUBT, ETC.

§ 275. *References.*—In making references to the larger and smaller divisions of a work of any kind, write the number of the greater division in the first position, and of the minor divisions in lower positions, according to their grade ; thus, $\begin{smallmatrix}1\\2\\3\end{smallmatrix}$ = 1st book, 2d chapter, 3d section ; or, 1st epistle, 2d chapter, 3d verse ; or, 1st volume, 2d book, 3d chapter.

§ 276. *Repetitions.*—(*a*) A clause upon which other clauses or portions of sentences are made to depend, after being written once, may be substituted in the following portions of the sentence by a long straight dash ; thus, "He aspired to be above the people——the authorities ——the laws——his country" = "He aspired to be above the people ; he aspired to be above the laws ; he aspired to be above his country."

(*b*) A comma may be substituted for the long dash when but few words are repeated.

(*c*) When a word of two or more strokes is repeated, with some word intervening which may be readily supplied, write the first syllable of the first word, and near that, or joined to it, write the repeated word in full ; as, Dee[1]:Dee[1]-Per, deeper and deeper—Ster[2]-Ster-Ing'ger, stronger and stronger—Bel[3]-Bel-Ker, blacker and blacker—Der[1]-Der-Pee, drop by drop—Sen[1]-Sen-Tee-Ray, century after century—Kay[1]: Kay[1]-Ker, quicker and quicker—Gret[2]-Gret-Ray, greater and greater— Tee[3]:Tee[3]-Ray-Jay, outrage upon outrage.

(*d*) In a corresponding manner, write words composed of similar parts, and also similar words occurring together, or separated by a word which may be safely omitted ; as, Peel[1]-Pee-Ket, pickpocket— Ef[1]-Ef-Del, fiddle-faddle—Tee[1]-Tee-Tel, tittle-tattle—En[2]:Vee[2]-Lens, *nolens volens.*

§ 277. *Omissions.*—(*a*) When one or more words have been omitted, leave a blank proportionate to the number of words omitted, and write a caret below the line.

(b) When the omission extends to the end of the sentence, write a long period just before the commencement of the next sentence.

§ 278. *Punctuation.*—It is very essential to the correct and easy reading of reports, that the period should be denoted either by greater space than usual between words, or, what is better, by the long mark of the period. Other pauses are usually omitted. See § 78, R. 1, *b.*

Rem. In reporting testimony, an answer should be separated from the preceding question by a long vertical straight line, and from the following question by the long period, or by commencing a new paragraph with the following question.

§ 279. *Doubt.*—When, as it sometimes happens, the reporter fears that he has misheard a word, a letter *d*, made thus, ∂, may be written under the doubtful word, to express his *d*oubt. This character may be written instead of any word which the reporter has entirely failed to catch. Such words may usually be supplied, when transcribing the notes, by reference to the context.

§ 280. *Materials for Writing.*—Various remarks with reference to pens, pencils, reporting paper, the manner of holding the paper, the turning of leaves, and many other matters of use and interest to the phonographer, may be found in the first volume of the "Phonographic Intelligencer."

Questions.—§ 269. How may words of similar or different meanings and th same consonants be distinguished?—§ 271. How may 'I' be represented whe standing alone? [Rem.] How are *I* and *he* commencing phrase-signs distin guished? How are they distinguished when following other words?—§ 272. Wha kind of a tick may be used to represent *thr* when it can not be conveniently ex pressed otherwise? Write 'since thr, would thr.' [Rem.] May the Ther-tick b sometimes employed for *other?* For what purpose may the Ther-tick take an E hook? an En-hook? a circle?—§ 274. How is a numeral denomination, denoted b several ciphers, to be written? Write 2,000; 400; 6,000,000. How may the termin tion 'ty' in 20, 30, etc., be written?—§ 275. How may the greater and smaller div sions of a book be expressed?—§ 276. How may a repeated clause be denoted May a comma be sometimes substituted for repeated words? How are repeate words, separated by a word which may be omitted, to be written? Write 'deep and deeper, century after century,' etc. What other words are written in a corr sponding manner? Write 'pickpocket, fiddle-faddle, *nolens volens.*'—§ 277. Wh is to be done to denote the omission of one or more words? when the omission e tends to the end of the next sentence?—§ 278. What is said as to punctuation i reporting? How is an answer to be separated from questions?—§ 279. How doubt expressed?

APPENDIX.

A.

AN EXTENDED PHONETIC ALPHABET—STENOGRAPHIC, SCRIPT, AND TYPIC.

§ 1. THE vocal elements may be divided into two species:

1. *Vowels*—sounds produced by modifying the current of the voice; as, ā, au, oo, ŏ.

2. *Consonants*—sounds produced by a greater or less interruption of the current of the voice (whispered or sonant); as, p, b, l, r, h.

VOWELS CLASSIFIED.

§ 2. Of vowels, viewed with respect to the number of the organic conformations required for their production, there are two species:

1. *Simple Vowels*—those produced principally by the conformation of the tongue or the lips; as, ē, ā, ō, oo.

2. *Composite Vowels*—those produced by the concurrent conformation of the tongue and the lips; as the German ö and ü, and the English ŭ.

§ 3. Of vowels, considered with regard to the manner of their emission, there are two species:

1. *Oral Vowels*—those emitted entirely through the mouth; as, ā, ō, au, ĭ, ă.

2. *Orinasal Vowels*—those emitted through the mouth and nasal passages simultaneously; as the French *en*, *in*, *on*.

REM. 1. For several reasons depending upon the representation of the vowels, it seems preferable to regard Nasalization as an accident of the vowels rather than as the *differentia* or characteristic of any species.

§ 4. Of the simple vowels there are two species:

1. *Lingual Vowels*—produced principally with the tongue (Lat. *lingua*); as, ē, ā, ah.

2. *Labial Vowels*—produced principally with the lips (Lat. *labia*); as, au, ō, ŏŏ.

REM. 1. In producing *au* there is required the modifying action of the cheeks as well as the lips; but the term 'labial' describes it with sufficient accuracy, since the sound is dependent principally upon the conformation of the lips.

§ 5. (*a*) Vowels, viewed with reference to their property of quantity, may be divided into—

Long Vowels—as, ē, ā, au, ō, ŏŏ.

Short Vowels—as. ĭ, ė, ă, ŏ, ŏŏ.

9*

(*b*) Viewed with respect to the property of quality, into pairs; as, ō (old), ò (whole); â (pâtte, Fr.), ŏ (pot).

§ 6. Vowels may be variously divided with reference to their accidents : with reference to the language in which they occur, into—1. Native. 2. Foreign. With reference to the manner of their representation, into Dots, Dashes, Parallels, etc.

§ 7. *Composite Vowels.*—These vowels are produced by the concurrent conformations of the lips and tongue; that is, by the synchronous utterance of a lingual and labial vowel, as of ē and ōō to produce the German ü=French u; of ō and ē, to produce the Ger. ö = Fr. eu = Eng. e (earn); and of ah and au, to produce the Eng. ŭ.

§ 8. *Order and Relation of the Simple and Composite Vowels.*—The Simple Vowels are divisible into two species—Linguals and Labials—approaching each other most closely, in likeness, or relationship, of sound, at *ah* and *au* (the most perfect vowels); the former series being connected with the consonants by the relationship of ē (the weakest of the lingual vowels) and *y* (the weakest of the lingual consonants); and the latter series being connected with the consonants by the relationship of ōō (the weakest of the labial vowels) and *w* (the weakest of the labial consonants). The natural order and relationship of the Simple Vowels may then be presented in the following manner :

(y) ē, ā, ah | au, ō, ōō (w)

Let the first series be represented by a dot, and the latter series by a dash. Now if these signs are written by the consonants, in the order of the sounds of the different series, a natural representation will be secured. See *Compendium*, § 47. Let the Composite Vowels be arranged in the order of the lingual vowels which enter into their composition; thus, ü, ò, ŭ.

REM. 1. *Order of the Vowels Mechanically Determined.*—"Professor Willis, in experimenting on the nature of sound, discovered that in placing a reed in a common organ pipe, the length of which could be varied at pleasure, and forcing the air through it with a pair of bellows, he obtained, according to the length of the pipe (beginning with the one expressed by the shortest, and proceeding to the one given by the longest), the following series of sounds, as expressed by the italicized vowels of the given words, viz.: 1, m*e;* 2, m*a*te; 3, m*a*r; 4, m*a*w; 5, m*o*w; 6, m*y*rrh; 7, m*oo*d; and that, continuing to lengthen the pipe, the *same* sounds were still heard, but *in an inverse order,* 7, 6, 5, 4, 3, 2, 1; and that, still farther increasing its length, the *same* identical sounds again occurred, but *in the first order;* and so on throughout."—*Cambridge Philosophical Transactions,* vol. iii., pp. 231–262.

REM. 2. "The natural order of the primary vowels, as determined mechanically, is I E A O U or U O A E I [= ē ā ah ō ōō or ōō ō ah ā ē], as heard in the English words *field, vein, far, owe, ooze.* This order should be so well impressed upon the memory that the vowels may be repeated fluently in either direction, as it will be found useful in studying the inflections of words; and on this account the elements are here treated according to the order of their affinities."—*Haldeman's Latin Pronunciation,* § 59.

In the following section Prof. Haldeman says substantially, that the closeness of ē and ōō approximates them to the nearest consonants, into which they are apt to fall, the first into the semivowel *y,* and the last into the semivowel *w.* Ā and ō exhibit, in a less degree, the tendency to become consonants; while *ah,* from its openness, and its want of relation to the extreme vowels, is farthest removed from the consonants, and is consequently the type and most noble of the vowels.

REM. 3. *From Professor Haldeman to the Author.*—"The run of your vowel-scale is close to nature, especially as you do not put *u*rn [ŭ] near the labial vowels *owe* and *ooze* [ōō]. Its improper position [between ō and ōō] arose from the interpretation Prof. Willis put on his experiments, determining *urn* to be the natural vowel of a vocal tube, without giving a guarantee of the accuracy of his ear."

§ 9. *Stenographic Representation of Foreign Vowels.*—A convenient representation of the foreign vowels, without disturbing the representation of native vowels, is secured thus:

1. Represent a foreign lingual vowel by an Arrow-Point (﹀), made heavy or light (according as the vowel is long or short), and in the place of its native mate.

2. Represent a foreign labial vowel, or the lengthened ŭ, by a Lance-Point (﹀), made heavy or light (according as the vowel is long or short), and in the place of its native mate, or nearest relative.

3. Represent a foreign composite vowel (except lengthened ŭ) by a parallel dash, written in the place of the lingual vowel which enters into its composition; thus,

ǀ ŭ, ǀ ŏ. See § 7, above.

REM. 1. The lengthened ŭ, though a composite vowel, is indicated after the manner of representing a foreign labial vowel: thus, ⊣ǀ, so that its sign may correspond to the settled sign for the native mate, ŭ.

REM. 2. The mate of au, though not previously recognized as an English sound, occurs in such words as *lost*, *long*, *cross*, etc.; and may therefore, instead of being represented by a light lance-point in the place of au, be denoted by a light dash, written in the first vowel-place, at an oblique angle with the consonant, in analogy with the method of representing ò (whòle), the mate of ō (old). See Compendium, § 48.

§ 10. *Typic and Script Representation of Foreign and Shade Vowels.*—Regard the vowels as a descending series from ē to ōō; and let an acute accent (′) be placed over a type to make it a sign for a sound next higher in the scale; and let a grave accent (ʻ) be placed over it, to make a sign for a vowel next lower in the natural scale; as, í for the *e* of *befall*, a short vowel next above i (*it*); ℰ̀ for the French é, a long vowel next below ℰ. (*b*) If two vowels occur between any two vowels represented by distinct types, depress the upper type to represent the higher one of the intermediate vowels, and elevate the lower type to represent the lower of the intermediate vowels. To illustrate—say that two vowels occur between ℰ and ꝺ; write ℰ̀ for the higher, and ꝺ′ for the lower, of the two intervening vowels. The same plan of indicating foreign or shade vowels may be pursued in longhand.

REM. 1. For convenience of conversation, let those sounds which are provided with a distinct phonotype be called Type-Sounds or Sign-Sounds, and let the others be called Typeless Sounds.

REM. 2. In some cases in this Appendix, an accent is, in consequence of a lack of the proper types, placed after, instead of over, the type affected by it.

§ 11. *Nasalization of Vowels.*—A Nasalized or Orinasal Vowel is produced by partially opening the nasal passage, while the correct position for the production of an oral vowel is assumed by the tongue or lips.

REM. 1. Prof. Haldeman, in his "Latin Pronunciation," § 100, says: "A nasal vowel, like a nasal consonant, is made by pronouncing the letter with the nasal passage open."

§ 12. *Stenographic Representation of Orinasal Vowels.*—(*a*) In phonetic shorthand, denote the nasalization—

1. *Of a Dot-Vowel*—by a comma-tail appended to the dot; thus, (ʼ).

2. *Of a Dash-Vowel*—by waving the dash; thus, (∼).

3. *Of an Arrow-Point Vowel*—by curving the point downward; thus, (﹀).

4. *Of a Lance-Point Vowel*—by curving the point upward; thus, (⌣).

(*b*) Or the nasalization of the Dash, Arrow-Point, and Lance-Point, Vowels may be denoted by a small circle written beside their signs; thus, ＼○ = Fr. *bon.*

§ 13. *Typic and Script Sign of Nasalization.*—In typography and longhand, let the nasalization of a vowel be denoted by a circle or by a comma-like sign after or below it; thus, e͓—a͓.

VOWEL-DIPHTHONGS.

§ 14. Diphthongs may be divided into Vowel and Consonantal Diphthongs.

REM. 1. For a definition of diphthongs and the condition of their production, see the Compendium, § 87.

§ 15. Vowel-Diphthongs may be divided, with reference to their stenographic signs, into two classes:

Class I.—the first element shown by the direction, and the second element, by the position of the sign.

Class II.—the first element shown by the *general* direction, and the second element, by the particular direction or form of the angular sign.

REM. 1. Class I. may be subdivided into two sections:—Section 1—the direction of whose signs is north or east, and whose first sounds are common elements of diphthongs. Section 2—the direction of whose signs is north-east or south-east, and whose first sounds are denoted by parallel dashes, and are rarely elements of diphthongs.

CONSONANTS.

§ 16. A consonant is a sound produced by the obstruction, to a greater or less degree, of the current of the voice; as, p, b; f, v; s, z; w, wh.

§ 17. Consonants may be divided, with reference to the direction of the breath—expired or inspired—into two species:

1. *Expirates*—as, p, b, and most, if not all, other elements of speech.
2. *Inspirates*—as the sounds produced by sipping, swallowing, snoring.

REM. 1. Expirate consonants are always to be understood as denoted by the term 'consonants,' or by a consonant-sign, unless it is otherwise specified or indicated.

§ 18. Consonants may be divided, with reference to the kind of voice emitted or inspired, into two species:

1. *Spoken, or Sonant, Consonants*—as, b, d, zh, z, g.
2. *Whispered, or Surd, Consonants*—as, p, t, sh, s, k.

§ 19. Consonants may be divided, with reference to the organs *by* which, or the points *at* which, they are produced, into four species:

1. *Labial Consonants*—1′. Outer; as, f, v; 2′. Middle; as, p, b; 3′. Inner; as, w, wh.
2. *Lingual Consonants*—1○. Dentals (1′. Outer; as, th; 2′. Outer-middle; as, dh; 3′. Inner-middle; as, t, d; s, z; 4′. Inner, as, sh); 2○. Palatals (1′. Outer; as, smooth r; 2′. Middle; as, y; 3′. Inner; as, ch in Ger. Ich); 3○. Gutturals (1′. Outer; as, k, g; 2′. Inner; as, k', g').
3. *Glottal Consonants*—as, h, coughing, growling, groaning.
4. *Nasal Consonants*—as the sounds of sneezing, snorting, snoring.

REM. 1. The term 'Nasal Consonants' is here employed to denote certain consonants produced in the nose, in contradistinction from certain oral-consonants which have the accident of nasalization or twanging, and which are properly termed Nasalized Consonants or Twangs. Let the term Narals (formed from the Latin

Nares, nostrils) or the word Myc′trals (formed from the Greek μυχτηρ, a nose) be used to denote the consonants produced in the nose, and then the term Nasals may be employed as usually heretofore to denote the twangs.

REM. 2. A class of sounds, which may be called Lingua-Labials, may be pro· duced by placing the tongue near the lips, or in complete or partial contact with them. Spitting, for instance, is speaking a lingua-labial *t*, which is probably denoted by the first two letters of the Greek πτύω, to spit. These lingua-labials may be denoted by a *p* or *b* (to denote the *point* of obstruction), followed by a smaller dental letter, to denote the *kind* of obstruction; thus, p′, bᵈ; pˢʰ, bᶻʰ; pˢ, bᶻ. In Stenography, the second letter may be written through the first near the end; thus, Pee†Tee, the sound produced by spitting. See the Comp., § 268, R. 6, *b*.

§ 20. Consonants may be divided, with reference to the kind of sound produced, into the following species:

1. *Mutes, or Explodents*—as, p, b; t, d; k, g.
2. *Rough Sibilants, or Hushes*—as, f, v; th, dh; sh, zh.
3. *Smooth Sibilants, or Hisses*—as, s, z, ph = Gr. φ, bh = Ger. w.
4. *Liquids, or Hums*—as, w, wh; l; r; h.
5. *Jarring Consonants, or Trills*—as, the snarling of a dog; the interjection of contempt produced by the trepidation of the lips; a deep growl; hawking; loud snoring.
6. *Orinasals, Nasalized Consonants, or Twangs*—as, m, n, ng.

REM. 1. (*a*) The phonetic student should carefully observe what kind of contact or relation of the organs is required for the production of the different kinds of consonants specified above. (*b*) The Explodents require the organs to be brought into complete contact, or forced from that position, according as the sound is final or initial; and with greater or less suddenness and force, according as the sound is whispered or spoken. (*c*) The Rough Sibilants, or Hushes, require such an appulse of the organs that the voice may be forced through, in a broad, thin sheet, as it were; as in producing sh, zh; f, v. (*d*) The Smooth Sibilants, or Hisses, require the voice to be forced through a small aperture, as it were a small tube decreasing in diameter toward the outer extremity. (*e*) The Hums, or Liquids, require the organs to be in the most open position consistent with the formation of a consonant. (*g*) Trills require the voice to be expired or inspired between the appulsed or approximated organs with sufficient force to cause them to vibrate with greater or less rapidity, according as the sound to be produced is a surd or a sonant. (*h*) The Orinasals, Nasalized Consonants, or Twangs, require the current of voice through the mouth to be partially or completely obstructed, and partially or fully expired or inspired through the nose, according as the sound to be produced requires a complete contact or an approximation of the lips or of the tongue.

§ 21. *Of the Expression of Sibilants, etc.*—The letter *h* has been extensively used in Romanic print to express sibilation or aspiration; thus, kh, gh, to denote the sibilants of k, g; sh, zh, to denote the rough sibilants corresponding to the smooth sibilants, s, z; wh, rh, mh, to express whispered w, r, m. In stenography, h (expressed by a dot, or by a tick joined at the beginning or written through between the vowel-places) may be used for the same purpose, when it would not be better answered by swelling a light line or tapering a heavy line; thus,

w wh; y yh; ng ngh; k kh; g gh; l lh.

§ 22. *Expression of Trilling.*—Let trilling be denoted—in typography, by an inverted colon (⠒) before the letter; thus, :b;—in stenography, by a wave-like sign written through the stroke; thus, ⟍ = :b.

§ 23. *Expression of Inspiration.*—To indicate that a letter is to be inspired—in typography, place a small circle before it; thus, °wh; in stenography, write a perpendicular ellipse before it; thus, 0⟍ = °wh = the sound of sipping.

§ 24. AN EXTENDED ALPHABET.

Lingual Vowels.

1	2	3	4	5	6	7	8	9	10	11	12	13	14	15	16 :—
i	í	ï	i	ɛ	é	ɛ̀	e	ɔ	ɐ	ʁ́	a	ʙ	a̓	ʙ̀=ꙩ	o

Labial Vowels.   **Composite Vowels.**

17	18	19	20	21	22	23	24	25	26	27	28 :—	29	30	31	32	33	34.
ꙩ	o̓	ő	ó	ꙫ	o	e̓	o̓	úi	u	ɯ	u̓	ɯ	u	œ	ʙ	ɯɯ	ɯ

Consonants—Labials.

35	36	37	38	39	40	41	42	43	44	45	46 :—
b	p	v	f	bh	ph	w	q=wh	:b	:p	m	mh
Bee	Pee	Vee	Ef	⟍	⟍	Way	⟍	:Bee	:Pee	Em	Emh

Dentals.

47	48	49	50	51	52	53	54	55	56	57	58
d	t	đ	ð	j	c	z	s	l	lh	:d	:t
Dee	Tee	Thee	Ith	Zhay	Ish	Zee	Es	El	⌠	:Dee	:Tee

Palatals.

59	60	61	62 :—	63	64	65	66	67	68	69	70 :—
ꞅ	ꞅh	n	nh	ɑ	ɹ	ȷ	ç	r	rh	y	yh
:Ar	:Rhay	En	Enh	Dee	Tee	/	/	Ar, Ray	Arh, Rhay	Yay	Yhay

Gutturals.

71	72	73	74	75	76	77	78	79	80	81	82
g	k	g̓	k̓	g=gh	x=kh	g̓	x̓	r	rh	r̓	rh̓
Gay	Kay	Gay	Kay	—	—	Ghay	Khay	Ghay	Khay	Ghay	Khay

83	84	85	86	87	88	89	90	91	92 :—
r̓	rh̓	ɒ	ɒh	:g	:k	:g̓	:k̓	ŋ	ŋh
Ar, Ray	Arh, Rhay	Ar, Ray	Arh, Rhay	:Gay	:Kay	:Gay	:Kay	Ing	Ingh

Glottals.

93	94	95	96	97	98	99	100	101 :—
ʎ	ɾ	rh	ʍ	ʁ	θ ə	h	:ɾ	:ʎ

Nasals.

102	103	104	105	106	107	108	109	110	111.
ʁ	ʁ	ʍ	ņ ņ	h′	:ʁ	dj=ɟ=ɟ	tc=ɡ	dy	tyh
						Jay	Chay		

Close Vowel-Diphthongs.
Class I.—Section 1.　　　　　　　　　　　　　　　　　　　Section 2.

112	113	114	115	116	117	118	119 :—	120	121
ii	iu=ʉ	ei	eu	ai=ị	au	òi=ɵ ou=ʊ		ůi	ůu

Class II.

122	123	124	125 :—	126	127	128	129	130	131	132	133.—
ʁi	ʁu	ai	au	ɵi	ɵà	ɵe	ɵu	ʊi	ʊu	ui	uà

Open Vowel-Diphthongs.—For the distinction between the open and close vowel-diphthongs, and the mode of distinguishing them stenographically, see the Compendium, §§ 88; 95; 98, R. 2.

Rem. 1. *Transition Symbols.*—When setting from the ordinary cases of types, for the new letters of the preceding alphabet, other letters may be substituted; thus,

1	5	7	9	10	13	15	17	21	22	27	29
ʎ	ʊ	ê=ɐ	æ	ă=â	ᴀ=ʌ	â=ɔ′=ʌ‘	ɔ=ô	ɒ=o̬	ɔ=o̬	ɯ=ū	ü

30	31	32	33	34	49	50	75	89	108	109	113	116
ů	ö=œ	ĕ	ū̬	ʊ	dh=tʜ	th	ɡ	ng=ɥ	ɟ	ɢ	ʉ	ị

At Nos. 120, 121, it was necessary to use transition symbols for the first element of the diphthongs, from lack of the proper phonotypes. Some of the transition symbols are formed by inverting types, as will be discovered by turning the page upside down. No. 22 is formed from ɒ (inverted ǫ). ŏ is a well-settled sign for No. 21; but the use of ŏ for the vowel of *not* is as well established. Therefore, to avoid as far as possible the confusion and misunderstanding which would result from a diverse use of letters, ǫ, ǫ, instead of ō, ŏ, have been given as the optional signs of Nos. 21 and 22. No. 79 may be formed from a small-capital ꜰ.

Rem. 2. *Caution.*—In the Compendium it was found convenient to mark the vowels of 'her, ask, whole' thus, è, à, ò. The different use of these letters in the extended alphabet should be carefully noted.

Rem. 3. *Inverted-Type Letters.*—Several of the letters of the preceding alphabet are produced by inverted types, as those for Nos. 59, 93, 94, 98.

Rem. 4. *Long Vowels.*—The preferable way of representing the long vowels is by types distinct from short-vowel types; but when such types can not be procured, a long vowel may be represented by a short-vowel type with the macron over it; thus,

1   5   13   27

ī   ē   ā   ū

(*b*) In English printing, if the author or printer would depart so much from phonetic principles, ē, ā, ī, ū may be employed for ɪ, ʙ, ɪ, ʮ, that is, for the vowels of Dee, day, die, dew.

Rᴇᴍ. 5. *Doubtful Quantity.*—When the quantity of a vowel is doubtful, it is best to use a short-vowel type. In printing English it will be unnecessary to distinguish between the long and the short quantity of ŭ; and thus an inconvenience which might arise from lack of the type of the long quantity, will be avoided.

Rᴇᴍ. 6. *Optional Types.*—(*a*) For the monotypes Ꭰ, ɋ, and their scripts, there may be substituted, if deemed preferable, the following types and scripts: Ɉ ɉ, *Ɉ ɉ*. The type ɋ has the merit of being a combination of dj, the phonotypes for the elements of the diphthong denoted by that monotype; but ɉ has the advantage of being a simpler and more agreeable type, and also of having a good substitute (ɟ, an inverted f) in the common "case." The line crossing ɉ may be regarded as the lower tick, or serif, of d, that is, as a vestige of d, just as the dots of the German ü are regarded as the vestiges of an e. (*b*) Sounds Nos. 65 and 66 may be represented by Ɉ' ɉ', C' c', or, to avoid so far as possible the use of diacritic accents, by Ɉ' ɉ, C' ç.

Rᴇᴍ. 7. *Type-Capitals.*—The type-capitals for the composite vowels and consonant No. 75, are the following:

29   30   31   32   33   34   75

Ꚕ   Ꚙ   Œ   Ᵹ   Ꙍ   Ʊ   ꟃ

Rᴇᴍ. 8. *Scripts*—(*a*) In the preceding alphabet, scripts have been given for every new distinct vowel-type. This having been done, it was of course unnecessary to furnish the scripts of the accented letters. In four instances the scripts of old letters have been given, to show the distinction between them and some of the new scripts. (*b*) The writing letter (small or large) for No. 31 is formed of the scripts of Nos. 21 and 8 closely joined as are the two letters composing the type. (*c*) The script-capitals for Nos. 29, 30, and 33 are respectively 𝒰𝒷, 𝒰𝒻, 𝒰𝒾. (*d*) The scripts of most of the new consonant-types have been presented in the English Phon. Alph. (see Comp., p. 15). The scripts for Nos. 66, 75, and 93 may be the following:

66   75   98

𝒢 ɉ   𝒢 ɉ   ə

(*e*) The small writing letter for the type No. 79 may be 'ℛ,' with the descending stroke running below the line. If preferred, the type 'r,' descending like a 'p,' might be substituted for r, while Γ should continue to be used for the capital. (*g*) If thought necessary to distinguish between Nos. 59, 67; and a better type than that presented above is desired for No. 59,—a reversed r may be substituted for ɹ, with a large and small 𝓇 for the large and small script, and with 𝐈 as the type-capital. The scripts of R r will then be ℛ ℛ. The large and small script for ɑ (the guttural r) may be the script sometimes employed for r, namely, 𝓇 (*h*) The scripts for the remaining new types may be rude copies of the types, as ʌ for ɹ, Γ for ɾ.

Rem. 9. *Phonographs.*—(*a*) The consonant-phonographs have been indicated so far as possible by their syllable-names. (*b*) When the mark of trilling (⫶) is placed before a syllable-name, it is indicated that the stenographic sign of trilling should be written through the phonograph denoted by the name. (*c*) In several instances it was deemed unnecessary to make in stenography as many distinctions as were made in typography. For instance, Tee and Dee may be used for t`, d` and ꓶ, ɑ, two different varieties of t, d; a knowledge of the language in which these occur rendering a distinction by signs unnecessary. So, also, it was deemed unnecessary to make any stenographic distinction between Nos. 71, 72 and 73, 74; or between Nos. 75, 76; 77, 78; 79, 80. (*d*) The signs of Nos. 46, 62, 92 are respectively Emh, Enh, Ingh; that is, Em, En, Ing, with an h-tick written through near the end. Arh, Rhay may be either Ar or Ray, swelled toward the end, or with an h-tick written through near the termination. (*e*) For ordinary purposes no distinction is required to be made by stenographic signs between Nos. 59, 60, 67, 68; and any mode of expressing *r* may be employed for either of them; the reader depending upon the relation of the sound, and a general knowledge of the language, for distinctions which have not generally been made in typography. (*g*) A considerable convenience may be secured, in writing German, by using instead of the signs given above for bh and ph the different signs for w and wh. No error in reading can result from this, if the reader will bear in mind that w and wh, though closely resembling bh and ph, do not occur in that language. (*h*) Where no stenographic sign has been provided for a sound which has been furnished with a type, it has been supposed that a stenographic sign was unnecessary, as there would be no occasion in stenographic writing to represent such sounds, or that the printing sign (abridged if possible) might be used as a stenographic letter. (*i*) The second element of Nos. 110 and 111, and similar combinations, as ny (o*ni*on), ly (Wi*lli*am), may be expressed by brief Yay joined to the sound of the first element, when no vowel follows; or written in the place of a following vowel.

Rem. 10. *Brief Way or Yay in the Vowel-Places.*—When it is desired to write *w* or *y* in the vowel places, lengthen one horn of Weh or Yey to indicate a following arrow-point vowel—of Wuh or Yuh, to indicate a following lance-point vowel; and join at an angle to the brief Way or Yay the signs of vowels denoted by parallel or oblique dashes; thus,

wí	wɪ̀	wé	wê	wæ	wă	wʌ′	wà	wâ	wò	wò′

yí	yɪ̀	yé	yê	yæ	yă	yʌ′	yà	yâ	yò	yò′

wө′	wū	wө̀	wө̀	wɯ′	wù	wü	wù	wö	wë

yө′	yū	yө̀	yө̀	yɯ′	yù	yü	yù	yö	yë

Rem. 11. *Accent.*—The arrow-points (′ `) being required for diacritical purposes, the accent may be denoted by lance-points placed after the accented syllable, and to denote the different inflections, written in different directions; thus,

` falling inflection, ` ` rising inflection, ` rising circumflex, ` falling circum-' flex. These signs may be placed in different positions with reference to the line, to denote the different pitches of the voice; say slightly above, even with the top and bottom, and slightly below, the small letters; thus, a' a' a, a. Instead of lance-points, straight light lines might be employed for accents; the signs of the falling and rising inflection being joined to denote the circumflex; thus, ʌ rising circum-flex; v falling circumflex. The inverted period (˙) may be employed as an indif-ferent mark of accent; that is, to denote stress, but not the inflection, of the voice.

REM. 12. *The Diastole.*—When combinations of two letters (as dh, th, lh, mh, ng) which are sometimes or frequently used for single sounds, are employed for *two* sounds, the letters may be separated by a diastole (.); thus, fut.hŏld, in.got. If the accent should be on the syllable ending with the first of the two letters, the mark of accent will serve the purpose of the diastole; thus, foot˙hold. Experience with the common print shows that it is generally unnecessary to insert the diastole; and it may therefore be usually omitted in phonetic print, the reader being pre-sumed to be sufficiently well acquainted with the language to determine the words in which the diastole, or separation, occurs, even when its sign is omitted.

§ 25. TABLE OF EXAMPLES AND DESCRIPTIONS OF THE VOCAL ELEMENTS.

1. *eel*; Fr., G., L., Gr., l. i.
2. *belong*;   do.,   sh. i.
3. *ear*.
4. *it*, new.
5. *ale*; Fr. é l.; G. *e* l.; I., G., l. cl. e; L. e l.; Gr., η.
6. Sund*ay*; Fr. é sh.; I., G., sh. cl. e; L. sh. e.
7. loc. E. b*ear*; Fr. ê (même); I., Sp., G., l. open e; G., Sw., l. ä; W. e. l.; Gr. η (?).
8. *ell*; Fr. open e unaccented; I., Sp., sh. op. e; G., Sw., sh. ä; W. e sh.; Gr. ε.
9. *care*, b*ear*, f*air*, th*ere*; W. l. a (bâch, *little*).
10. *at*; W. sh. a (bach, a *hook*).
11. *half*, *alms*; loc. p*a*, *ah*.
12. *ago*, *ask*.
13. *arm*, *ah*; Fr., I., G., Gr., L., l. a.
14. h*arrow*; All*ah*; C*u*ba; *ai*sle; Fr., I., G., Gr., L., sh. a.
15. Fr. â (pâte).
16. p*o*t, n*o*t, d*o*t.
17. *all*, f*o*rm; Ga. a.
18. l*o*st, l*o*g, d*o*g, f*o*rbid, *oi*l.
19. loc. E. m*ou*rn; I. l. open o.
20. I. sh. open o.
21. *o*ld, *o*h; L. o l.; Gr. ω; Fr. au, and l. open o; G., D., W., l. o.
22. n*o*ne, *o*bey; L. sh. o; Gr. o; Fr. sh. open o; G., D., W., sh. o.
23. loc. E. s*ou*; I., Sw., l. cl. o; Hu. ó.
24. I. sh. cl. o; Hu. sh. o.
25. long quantity of No. 26; s*oo*n.
26. f*u*ll, c*ou*ld, n*ew*, n*ow*; Fr. sh. ou; W. sh. w.
27. f*oo*d, f*oo*l; Fr. l. ou; I., G., l. u; W. l. w.

28. loc. E. l*oo*k, f*oo*t; I., Sp., G., Hu., sh. u; Gr. υ in diphthongs.
29. G. ü l.; Fr. l. u; L., Sw., D., l. y; Gr. υ l.
30. G. ü sh.; Fr. sh. u; L., Sw., D., sh. y; Gr. υ sh.
31. f*i*rm; G. l. ö; Fr. l. eu; Sw. l. œ.
32. h*er*, *ear*th, s*i*r; G. sh. ö; Fr. sh. eu; Sw. sh. œ.
33. long quantity of No. 34.
34. *u*p, c*u*r.
35. m. l*a*. so. exp.—*b*ay.
36. m. l*a*. wh. exp.—*p*ay.
37. o. l*a*. so. hush—*v*ie.
38. o. l*a*. wh. hush—*f*ie; L. f; G. v and f.
39. m. l*a*. so. hiss—L. *ɟ* = Gr. F (digam-ma); Heb. Bheth.
40. m. l*a*. wh. hiss—L. PH; Gr. φ.
41. i. l*a*. so. hum—*w*ay; L. v; Gr. ου fol-lowed by a vowel.
42. i. l*a*. wh. hum—*wh*ey, *wh*y.
43. m. l*a*. so. trill—a sound made to babies.
44. m. l*a*. wh. trill—an interjection of con-tempt.
45. m. l*a*. so. twang—*m*e, ai*m*.
46. m. l*a*.wh. twang—te*m*pt; Fr. schis*m*e; W. mh.
47. i.-m. d. so. exp.—*d*o, a*d*d.
48. i.-m. d. wh. exp.—*t*o, a*t*.
49. o.-m. d. so. hush—*th*en, brea*th*e; m. Gr. δ̇; Heb. Dhaleth.
50. o. d. wh. hush—*th*in, brea*th*; Gr. Ϧ.
51. i. d. so. hush—*Zh*ay; Fr. j.
52. i. d. wh. hush—*sh*e; Fr. ch; G. sch; P. x, ch.
53. i.-m. d. so. hiss—*Z*ee, i*s*, buz*z*.

54. i.-m. d. wh. hiss—see, hi*ss*.
55. i.-m. d. so. hum—*l*aw, i*ll; B*l*y.
56. i.-m. d. wh. hum—p*l*y; W. ll (*Ll*an-ell*y).
57. i.-m. d. so. trill—
58. i.-m. d. wh. trill—
59. i. d. so. trill—trilled **r** ; L. **r** ; Gr. ρ.
60. i. d. wh. trill—trilled rh ; L. rh ; Gr. ρ́.
61. i.-m. d. so. twang—*n*o, o*n*.
62. i.-m. d. wh. twang—ce*n*ts; W. nh.
63. o. p. so. exp.—Arabic Dâd.
64. o. p. wh. exp.—Arabic Tâ.
65. i. p. so. hush—G. g (kö*n*ig).
66. i. p. wh. hush—G. ch (Ich, welc*h*en); the hiss of a goose.
67. o. p. so. hum—ea*r*, b*r*each.
68. o. p. wh. hum—p*r*each.
69. m. p. so. hum—*y*ou; L., G., j.
70. m. p. wh. hum—in*h*umanity (see L. P. P., § 41) ; L. hj (Hjero).
71. o. g. so. exp.—*g*o, e*gg*; L. *g*.
72. o. g. wh. exp.—*k*ey ; L. c ; Gr. x.
73. i. g. so. exp.—a so. corresp. to No. 72.
74. i. g. wh. exp.—Ar. Qâf; Heb. Qoph.
75. o. g. so. hush—G. g in Tag; Heb. Ghimel.
76. o. g. wh. hush—G. ch in Dach; L. ch; Gr. χ; Heb. Khaph; W. ç.
77. i. g. so. hush—produced farther back than No. 73, and requiring the retraction of the tongue.
78. i. g. wh. hush—Ir. gh in lou*gh*.
79. o. g. so. hiss—probably the m. Gr. γ.
80. o. g. wh. hiss—
81. i. g. so. hiss—
82. i. g. wh. hiss—
83. o. g. so. hum—
84. o. g. wh. hum—
85. i. g. so. hum—the London r.
86. i. g. wh. hum—
87. o. g. so. trill—gargling.
88. o. g. wh. trill—hawking.
89. i. g. so. trill—Newcastle burr (?); Fr. provençal r (?).
90. i. g. wh. trill—hawking.
91. o. g. so. twang—si*ng*; G. ju*ng*; L. n prec. c (q, x), g, ch; Gr. γ prec. γ, x, ξ. χ.
92. o. g. wh. twang—si*n*ks; W. ngh.
93. gl. wh. exp.=coughing; the sudden stoppage of the voice; or sudden expulsion after its retention.
94. gl. so. hush—groaning from excruciating pain.
95. gl. wh. hush—wh. groaning.
96. gl. so. hiss—gentle vocal groaning.
97. gl. wh. hiss—a forcibly uttered h.
98. gl. so. hum—very gentle groaning—an indifferent vowel.
99. gl. wh. hum—*h*e ; a gentle jerk of the breath.

100. gl. so. trill—gentle croaking.
101. gl. wh. trill—a sound produced by stammerers.
102. n. wh. exp.—sneezing.
103. n. wh. hush—inspired, gentle snoring.
104. n. wh. hiss—forcible inspiration ; snuffing.
105. n. so. hum—an indifferent vowel uttered through the nose.
106. n. wh. hum—nasal h.
107. n. so. trill—inspired—loud snoring: snorting.
108. so. cons. di.—e*dg*e, *j*est, *g*em; I. g bef. e or i.
109. wh. cons. di.—e*tch*, *ch*est; G. ts*s*h ; Fr. tch; I. c. before e or i; Sp. ch; Hu. ts.
110. so. cons. di.—ver*d*ure = ver*dy*oor ; Hu. dj, dy, gj, gy.
111. wh. cons. di.—na*t*ure=nä*ty*oor; Hu., Sw., tj, ty.
112. cl.—see Rem. 9. Open—b*ei*ng.
113. cl.—n*ew*, d*ew*, due; Sw. u (?); L. primit*ius*; W. Duw.
114. cl.—loc. E. d*ay*=déi; L ĕi; Gr. ει ; G. ei, ey (?) Open—l*ai*ty; Gr. η.
115. cl.—loc. E. n*ow* = neu; L. ĕu; Gr. ευ. Open—Gr. ηυ; I. *E*uropa.
116. cl.—*ai*sle, *eye*, fine, b*uy*; L. ae; Gr. αι; Du. y; G., D., ai. Open—*a*ye; Gr. ᾳ.
117. cl.—loc. E. now=nau ; L., G., D., au; Gr. αυ ; P. and old L. ao. Open—I. l*au*de.
118. cl.—*oi*l, b*oy*; G. oi, oy. Open—dr*aw*ing.
119. cl.—n*ow*, out; D. ou.
120. cl.—Fr. l*ui* (Ellis).
121. Perhaps this occurs in E. wh*ew*.
122. cl.—Fr. œil (Ellis).
123. cl.—
124. cl.—loc. E. sk*y;* W. ai.
125. cl.—loc. E. n*ow;* the pronunciation usually typified by ' eow ;' "heow."
126. cl.—loc. E. b*y*, g*oi*ng; L. ŏi; Gr. οι. Open—sn*ow*y; Gr. ῳ.
127. cl.—loc. E. sn*ow;* L. ŏu; Gr. ου. Open—Gr. ωυ.
128. cl.—Gr. ό*ε*. Open—*Zo*ë; Gr. ώε.
129. cl.—Gr. ό*α*. Open—*Noa*h; Gr. ώα.
130. cl.—loc. E. *eye*, b*uy;* G. eu.
131. cl.—loc. E. n*ow*.
132. cl.—loc. E. d*oi*ng ; L. ŭi (hui). Open—L*oui*s; G. pfui (Ellis).
133. cl.—Ul*ua*.

REM. 1. *Abbreviations.*—The following abbreviations have been employed in the preceding part of this section.

bef.	before	g.	guttural	m.-G.	modern-Greek
cl.	close	Ga.	Gaelic	n.	nasal
cons.	consonant-al	gl.	glottal	o.	outer
D.	Danish	I.	Italian	op.	open
d.	dental	i.	inner	P.	Portuguese
di.	diphthong	Ir.	Irish	sh.	short
Du.	Dutch .	L.	Latin	so.	sonant
E.	English	l.	long	Sp.	Spanish
exp.	explodent	la.	labial	Sw.	Swedish
Fr.	French	loc.	local	W.	Welsh
G.	German	m.	middle	wh.	whisper-ed.

(*b*) The term "local English" is employed with some latitude of meaning to denote a local, vulgar, peculiar, or individual pronunciation in contradistinction from what is regarded as the general and correct pronunciation. .

REM. 2. *Vowel-Mates.*—The vowels of each pair differ in quantity, but not the slightest in quality. Pronounce a long vowel quickly, *staccato*, and you produce its short mate. Prolong a short vowel, and you produce its long mate. By this method of experiment may be demonstrated the contrary of the following statements, which are substantially made in Mr. Ellis' Alphabet of Nature:

1. That No. 1 and No. 4 are exact mates.
2. That No. 4 and No. 3 are not exact mates.
3. That No. S and No. 5 are exact mates.
4. That No. 7 and No. 8 differ in quality.
5. That No. 13 and No. 10 are mates.
6. That No. 12 and No. 13 are of the same quality.
7. That No. 16 and No. 17 are exact mates.
8. That No. 18 and No. 20 are mates.

In other words, by this method of investigation it may be demonstrated that Mr Ellis has failed in almost every instance to pair the vowels correctly. Having so done, the difficulty of disposing of the true short quantities led to his unfounded and unsupportable distinction of 'long, short, and stopped,' and the bigamous relation of some of the vowels necessarily left others unmated.

REM. 3. *Broadened or Deepened Vowels.*—The vowel-sounds produced with certain positions of the lips or tongue may be modified by drawing back the soft palate, or by otherwise enlarging the cavity back of the vowel-aperture. This modification of the sound may be called *deepening*, or rather *broadening*—for deepening refers rather to pitch, which is not affected by broadening. This modification may be indicated by some diacritic sign, say by the macron (˘), or by a point, under the sign of the vowel modified; thus, ß as a sign for broadened or broad ß. No. 15 is really No. 13 broadened; but as it is generally considered a partially developed au (No. 17), it is accordingly represented by a depressed ah (No. 13) or an elevated au (No. 17). Nos. 15 and 16 then appear merely varieties of Nos. 13 and 14; and, indeed, many who do not attend to the broadening pronounce such words as 'God, not, pot,' etc., with the true short quantity of No. 13, as if spelled Gahd, naht, paht, that is, with No. 14; while others, mistaking this broadened à (No. 14) for No. 17 or 18, pronounce 'Gaud,' etc.

REM. 4. *Of the Vowels.*—(*a*) An instance of No. 7 is afforded when 'bear, fair, care, there,' etc., are pronounced with the long quantity of the vowel of *ell* (No. 8). These words as usually pronounced, contain the long quantity (No. 9) of the vowel of *at* (No. 10). An old Athenian poet, Cratinus, is quoted as saying that the cry of the sheep is Bῆ. "Varro considers [the Latin] e the vowel in the cry of the sheep (BEE), so that it can not be the English ē." (Haldeman's Latin Pron., § 56.) Neither can it be the sound of No. 5, but rather No. 7; and this probably was the sound of the Gr. η; that is, the long quantity of Epsilon, as is indicated by the old form of the letter, and by its substitution for double Epsilon. While it is very probable that the Latin and Greek vowel-letters were employed to represent each a certain *grade* of sound, it is equally probable that they were *not* used invariably for precisely the same qualities. Hence, while the L. e or the Gr. η may have represented at times No. 5, it may also have been used to represent Nos. 7 and 9.

(*b*) An example of No. 11 is afforded when *ah!* is pronounced with a slender, treble sound, closely approaching No. 9. For the position assumed by the tongue for the production of this vowel, see I. P. P., § 146.

(*c*) No. 19 is not unfrequently pronounced instead of No. 17, by persons who neglect to properly open their mouths in pronouncing *all, Gaul,* etc. The word *mourning*, in some mouths, closely approximates *morning*, or, what is the same thing, is pronounced with No. 17 instead of No. 21.

(*d*) No. 23 is produced by placing the lips midway between the positions for Nos. 21 and 27. The author has heard several public speakers substitute this sound for No. 21.

(*e*) The French eu is represented by some phonologists as having two sounds—one of which is No. 31, which is described as *close;* and another, which is described as *open.* The latter, we presume, is composed of Nos. 9 and 21, instead of Nos. 7 and 21. The open eu may then be represented by œ'. This open sound is not distinguished in French orthography, if it is in pronunciation, and a separate stenographic sign seems unnecessary. It might be represented by a lance-point in the second vowel-place.

(*g*) The long quantity of No. 44 occurs perhaps in *urn*, and similar words.

REM. 5. *Of the Consonants.*—(*a*) The sounds 39 and 40 are produced by emitting hissing voice (sonant or surd) between the lips approximated as if about to produce *b*, or as in whistling with the lips kept close to the teeth. In Spanish, b between two vowels has the sound No. 39.

(*b*) Americans generally pronounce r, rh (Nos. 67 and 68) where the English, Irish, and other Europeans pronounce ᴛ, ᴛh (Nos. 59 and 60), trilled with greater or less force. The thick-tongued Londoners either omit r (that is, smooth r) ending a syllable, or substitute for it a guttural hum (ᴀ), that is, *r* produced with the root, instead of the tip, of the tongue, which sound has generally been mistaken for ᴧ or ᴜ.

(*c*) As w is to ᴡ, so is y to ᴊ, and so is ꜱ to ᴧ.

(*d*) Dr. Rapp says in substance, 'To fix the sound of the m.-Gr. Gamma (supposed to be No. 79), pronounce g mute (No. 74), and substitute a soft aspirate,' which is to say, that m.-Gr. Gamma is a smooth sibilant formed at the point for k; in other words, that it is 'an o. g. so. hiss.' He distinguishes this sound from the o. g. so. hush (gh) and hum (r'). He also regards it as belonging to the class of h slightly aspirated, that is, ᴚ, which is a smooth sibilant.

(*e*) The glottis having been closed by the epiglottis, there will be no opportunity for the resonance of the sonant breath prior to the breaking up of the perfect contact thus formed, and hence there is no sonant sound corresponding to ᴀ (No. 93). A grunt, which was at first supposed by the author to be the sonant of ᴀ, was found to be 'ᴚə!' Laughter is a rapid enunciation of syllables composed of some one of the glottal consonants followed by ə, ᴧ, ᴊ, or some other vowel, according to the taste of the performer. Laughter which commences vigorously and gradually subsides may be represented thus: ᴧᴀᴧᴀᴚᴀᴚe.ᴚə.hə.hə.ə.ə.ə.ọ.

(*g*) The glottal sonant **hum** is believed by the author to be that indifferent unac- ʹ cented vowel which occurs in the final syllables of 'able, people, river, paper, open, schism,' and which, in careless or hurried pronunciation, is substituted for most of the unaccented vowels; 'metal, cotton, evil, awful,' for instance, being pronounced 'metəl, kotən, ɪvəl, ɔfəl.' In ordinary printing it will be sufficiently accurate to represent this sound by the sign of the vowel of *met* (e), which vowel more frequently than any other falls into this obscure sound. The sound denoted by h is the substratum of all the whispered consonants; and ə is the substratum of all the sonant consonants. In other words, the different obstructions of the current of voice represented by h produce the different whispered consonants; and the different obstructions of ə produce the different spoken consonants. The different modifications of the current of voice denoted by ə produce the different vowels; and the different modifications of the current denoted by h produce all the vowels whispered.

(*h*) The ordinary gentle breathing, when through the mouth, may be represented by 0; when through the nose, by 8. As such breathings are not sufficiently audible for any purposes of speech, they are not placed among the vocal elements. When the breathing is more or less violent, it produces the sound of some one of the continuous glottal, or nasal, wh. consonants.

REM. 6. *Varieties of the Dental Explodents and Sibilants.*—Several varieties of the dental explodents and sibilants may be produced by making the required kinds of contact back or in front of the points for t, d; th, dh; s, z; c, j. These varieties may be distinguished, if it should be deemed necessary or desirable, in accordance with the principle of § 10. Th`, dh are mates, and the hushes of t′ and d′, of which s′ and z′ are the hisses, or 'lisps,' more properly 'lis′ps.' A strengthened s and z, which may be represented by s` and z`, are produced with a hiss-contact back of the point for s and z. The true hushes of s` and z` are the sounds denoted by the phonotypes c, j. The true hushes of s and z may be denoted by c′, j′, or by sh, zh; to produce which, the upper surface of the tongue, very near the tip, and not the tip itself, must make a sibilant contact with the gums at the point for s. These sounds are very probably those denoted in Polish by s′ and z′. They are a delicate c and j. In the production of c, j, says Dr. Rapp, 'the tongue is broadened and seemingly endeavors to fill the whole palate.' As s and z are to s` and z` so are c′ and j′ to c and j. If the varieties of c and j were to be distinguished by types, the elements of ch in cheer and j in jeer would be given as tc′, dj′. But this would be entirely unnecessary, because the attempt to produce c and j in such connection naturally develops their varieties, c′ and j′. Two varieties of t and d are produced by contacts back of that for t; namely, t``, d``, produced by bringing the tip of the tongue in contact with the outer portion of the hard palate; and t` and d`, produced by a contact midway between the points of contact for t and t``. As t`` and d`` would be inconvenient signs, there have been provided in their stead new types, ɪ, ɑ. An inspired ɪ (○ɪ) is the cluck of a hen.

REM. 7. *Varieties of L.*—A variety of l, which may be denoted by l`, may be produced by bringing the tongue in contact with the palate at the point for *y*. This sound in connection with a following y is the Fr. l *mouillé;* of which more will be said in the following Remark. This *l mouillé* exists in French in theory only; for in practice the sound of the l is always suppressed, and, by many speakers, that of the y also. (*b*) If the tongue is placed in contact with the teeth at the point for th or dh. and the voice be emitted along the sides of the tongue, a variety of l will be produced, which may be represented by l′. This sound is supposed to occur in Polish, where it is represented by l crossed like t or f. (*c*) A trill of l, or lh rather, may be produced in this manner: Having placed the sides and tip of the tongue in close contact with the upper teeth, force the inspired or expired breath between one side of the tongue and the teeth. The inspired trill of lh, that is, ᵒlh, somewhat resembles the cluck of a hen, and is well known to most persons, being frequently used in driving horses.

REM. 8. *Liquid or Softened Consonants.*—(*a*) A sonant or surd y combines with most of the other lingual consonants so readily as to develop consonantal diphthongs. These combinations have usually been mistaken for simple elements, especially when occurring in languages in which orthographical expedients, as gl, ll, gn, lh, etc., have been necessarily resorted to for their representation, or for the purpose of distinguishing a diphthong from a non-diphthongal relation of the elements. (*b*) The term Liquid, or rather Softened, may be usefully applied to a consonant when it has combined with y to form a diphthong; but if so used, the term may be applied as appropriately to t or d as to l or n. (*c*) There may be several modes of distinguishing between the diphthongal and non-diphthongal relation of elements. Some mode is occasionally required, as in distinguishing at times between the diphthongal and non-diphthongal relation of y to a preceding consonant. Almost any method would be preferable to having separate types for diphthongs. To show that a y follows a letter in diphthongal relation to it, various plans have been resorted to; thus, the liquid l is represented by ll in Spanish, lh in Portuguese, gl in Italian. Softened n is denoted by ñ in Spanish, by n′ in Polish, and by gn in Italian. Mr. Ellis proposes to affix an apostrophe in certain cases to liquid letters; thus, l′, t′, k′. (*d*) But the best mode, for all purposes, of distinguishing between the diphthongal and non-diphthongal relation of sounds, is to represent the two elements by their separate signs, and of the two cases of a diphthongal or non-diphthongal relation distinguish the rarer from the more frequent by the diastole. To illustrate—the diphthongal relation of tc being more frequent than the other, let tc represent a diphthong when not separated by the diastole (t.c). On the contrary, y rarely forming a diphthong with preceding consonants, let its relation with them be understood to be non-diphthongal unless followed by the diastole; thus, to distinguish the Italian from the English pronunciation of *bagnio*, write 'bany.o' for the former and 'banyo' for the latter.

REM. 9. *Of the Diphthongs.*—(*a*) It is doubted that ii, ǫe, ǫå, uå comply in every respect with the conditions of a vowel-diphthong; at least, the relation between these elements is not so close as between òi, ou, iu, etc. (*b*) The stenographic sign for ií may be employed for ii as in 'carry*ing*'—in which case the sounds represented do not constitute a diphthong—or for the diphthong constituted by ii or ií. Some of the other diphthongs may be employed with a like latitude. Phonotypes in the representation of diphthongs in ordinary printing may be employed to represent specific and not individual vowel-qualities; thus, ei may be either éi=L. éi=loc. E. ay as in day=déi; or it may be ei=ĕï=Gr. ɛi=G. ei, ey (?)=the slender, pusillanimous pronunciation sometimes given to the English long i. So eu may be éu=the L. ĕu, or eu=ĕu=Gr. ɛυ. The diphthongs of *oil*, *aisle* (=isle=I'll), though strictly òi, åi, may be represented in ordinary printing by oi, ai. However, when individual vowel qualities are to be denoted with precision, and distinguished, every vowel should be denoted by its exact sign. (*c*) In the Introduction to Phonotypy and Phonography, and some other works, the author has spoken of the vowel of *ask* as being the first element of the English long ī, and as the vowel denoted by *a* in *after*, Cuba, particul*a*r, etc. Such statements have been made with the knowledge that they were not the exact truth, but the nearest approximation to it possible without a vocal analysis so discriminating as not to be generally received in the present state of phonological knowledge and education

EXPRESSION OF ASPIRATION.

§ 26. In the Introduction to Phonotypy and Phonography, and in the Phonetic

Quarterly, the author has employed the combination *hw* to express the aspirate of '*w;* but upon a careful review of the questions involved, it seems best that h, *when used as a diacritic sign*, should always be placed after the letter affected by it. If *hw* be used for the aspirate of *w*, consistency requires *ht* instead of *th* for the aspirate of t.

REM. (*a*) If preferred, the Greek spiritus asper (ʻ), an abbreviation of H, may be employed instead of the diacritic h, placed over or after a letter; thus, pʻ, bʻ, ŋʻ. An inverted comma (ʻ) may be used for the same purpose when the type for the spiritus asper is not "in case." (*b*) The whispered ng may be denoted, in transition phonotypy, by ñ; and n simply may be used for ng or ngh, as in the common print, whenever its situation is equivalent to a diacritic mark or a distinct letter: as in 'sink, sankcon, sinks.' In such cases, a law of euphony requires a guttural instead of a dental twang before the k.

PHONOGRAPHIC

READING EXERCISES.

COMPILED BY ANDREW J. GRAHAM.

PHONOGRAPHIC
READING EXERCISES.

EXERCISE I.   C. 1—25.

1.

2.

3.

4.

5. [12, 4, *C*.]

EX. II. C. 26—32.

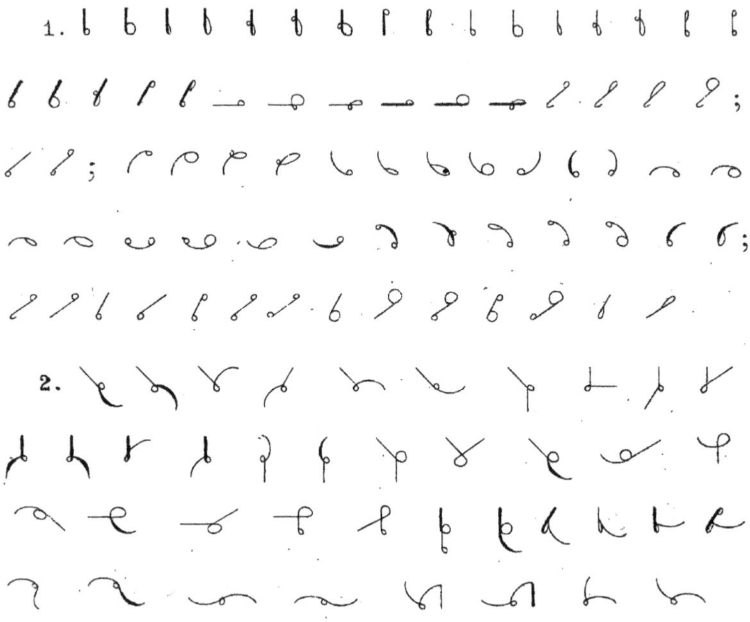

EX. III. C. 33—55.

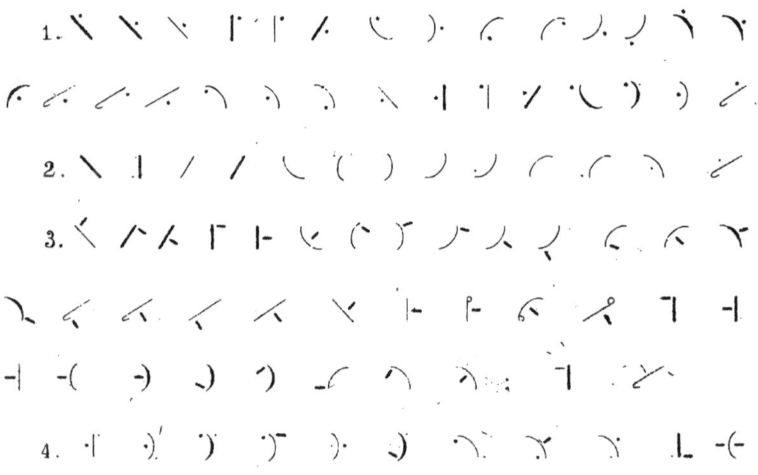

5.

6.

7.

EX. IV. C. 56—77.

1.

2.

3.

4. = Mrs.

5.

6.

EX. V. C. 78–86.

× / ∶ ; , ! (!) [!] ¡ ¿ ? (?) [?]

§ ( ) [ ] { } ‿ " "

☞ ¶ § * † ‡ ‖

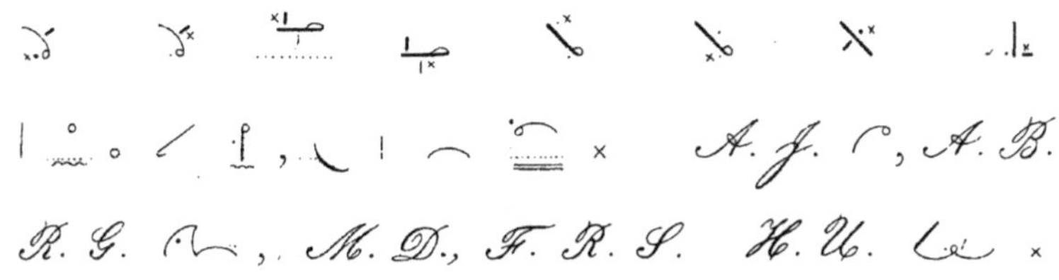
A. J. , A. B.
R. G. , M. D., F. R. S. H. U.

EX. VI. C. 87–104.

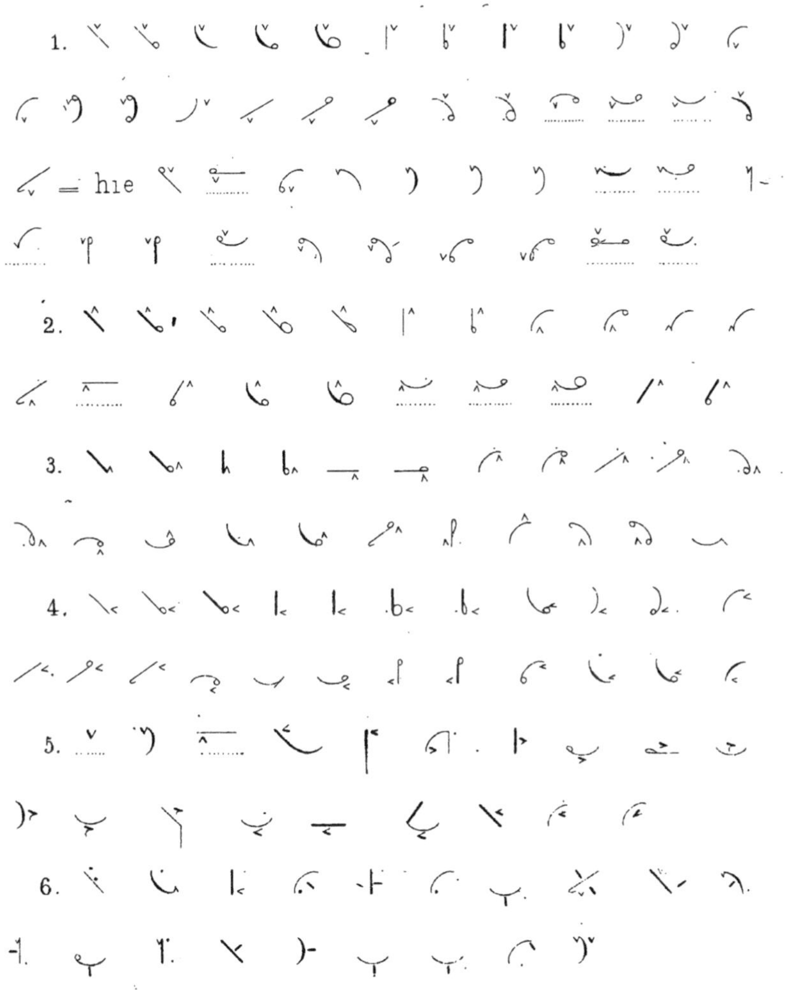
1.
= hie
2.
3.
4.
5.
6.

EX. VII.   C. 105–114.

1.

2.

3.

4.

5.

6

7. [C. 108]

8. [C. 109]

EX. VIII.   C. 115 – 125.

1. ＝ wee

2.

3.

4.

EX. IX.   C. 126–143.

1

2.

3.

4.

EX. X.   C. 144–149.

1.

2.

3.   [C. 147, R. 2]

4.   [C. 148, R. 1]

5.

6.   [C. 148, R. 2]

7. ... ... ; ... ... [C.148, R.2]

8. ...

EX. XI.   C. 151–153.

1. ...

2. ...

3. ...

4. ...

EX. XII.   C. 154–158.

1. ...

2. ...

3.

4.

5.

6.

7.

8.

9.

10.

EX. XIII.　C. 159–169.

1.

2.

14

EX. XIV. C. 170–173.

1.

2.

3.

4.

5.

EX. XV. C. 174–180.

1.

2.

EX. XVI. C. 181–189.

9:

EX. XVII.   C. 190.–196..

1.

2.

3.

4.

5.

6.

EX. XVIII.   C. 197–203.

1.

2.

2.

3.   [C. 197, R. 2]

4.

5. [C. 197, R. 4]

EX. XIX.   C. 204–206.

1.

2.

3.

EX. XX.   C. 207–211.

1.

2.

3.

4.

EX. XXI.   C. 212–224.

1. T Added.

2. D Added.

3. T Added.

4. D Added.

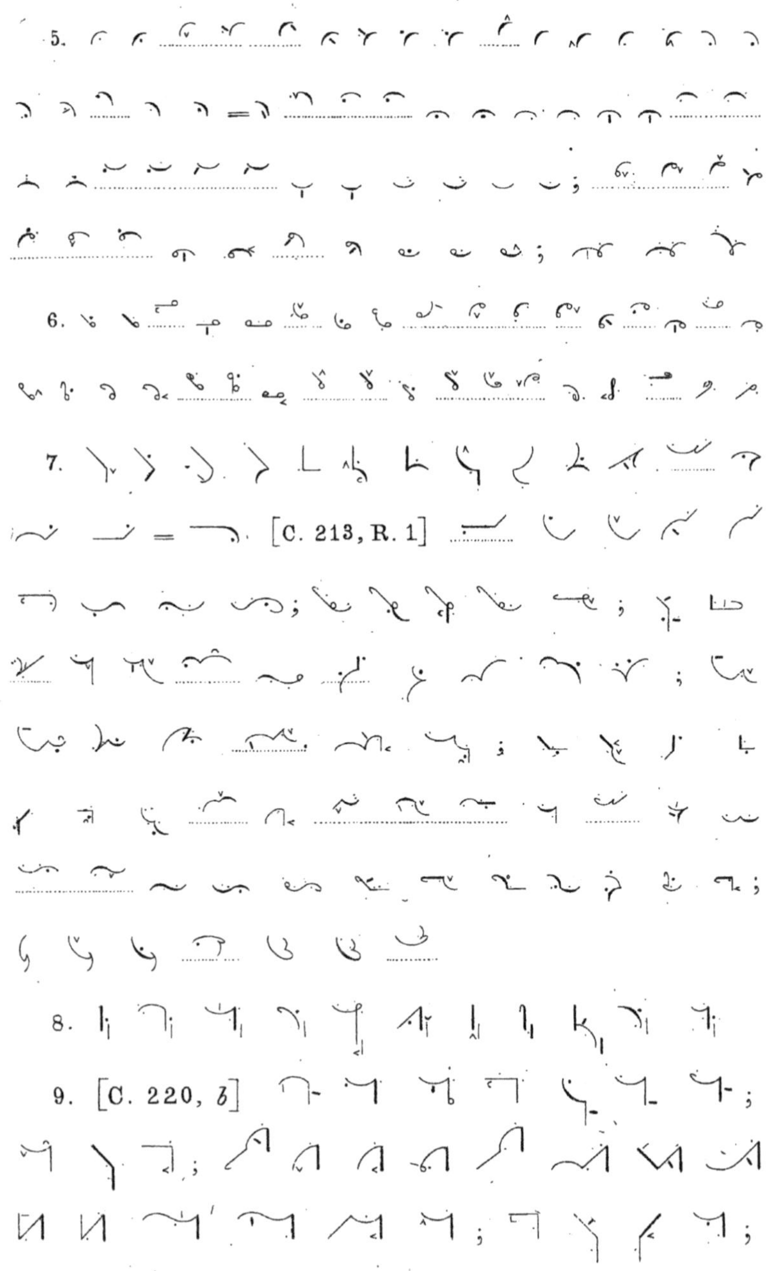
5.
6.
7.
[C. 213, R. 1]
8.
9. [C. 220, b]

10. [C. 149, 5; R. 2]

11. [C 212, R. 6]

EX. XXII. C. 225—230.

1.

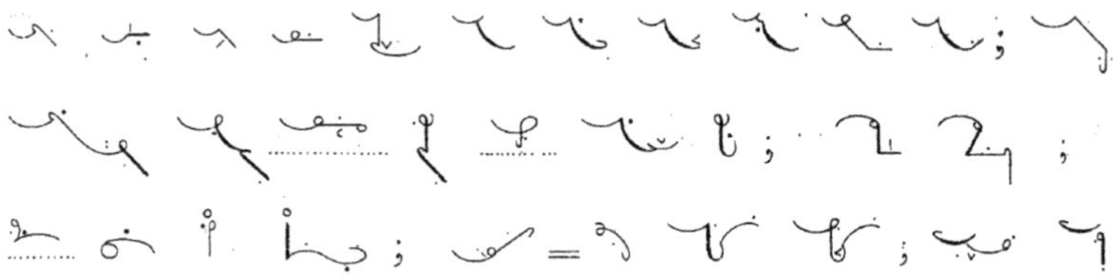

2.

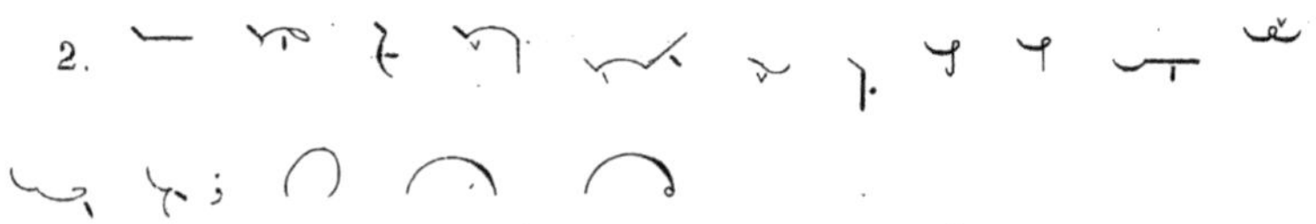

3.

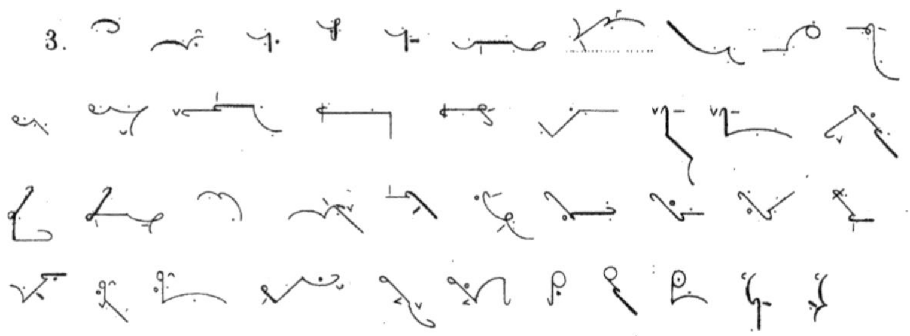

EX. XXIII. C. 231–234.

1.

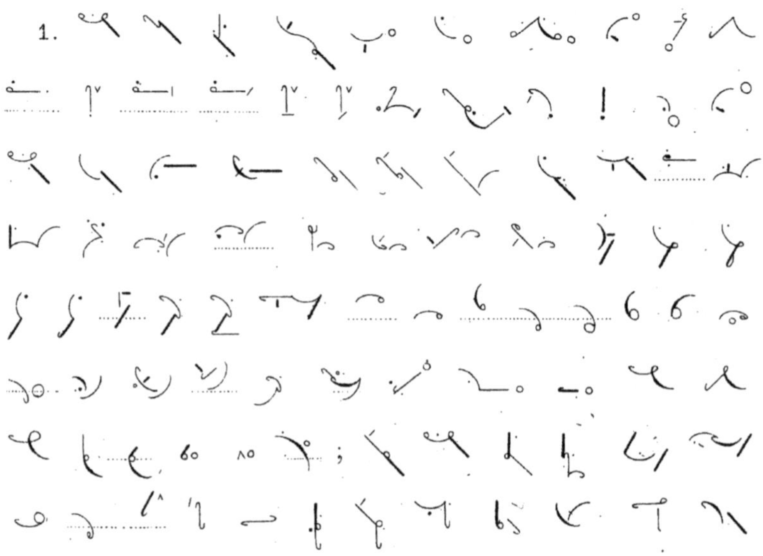

2.

EX. XXIV.   C. 235-241.

1.

2.

3.

4.

5.

EX. XXV.   C. 242-249.

1.

2.

3.

Aphorisms of the Ancients

× Sen.

× Cato

× Cic.

× Cic

× Sen.

× Cic.

× Ter.

× Tacit.

× Cic.

× Ter.

× Cic.

× Sen.

× Cic.

× Cato.

× Cic

× Sen.

× Cic.

× Ad Herrenn

× Cic

× Lucan

× Cic.

× Cic.

× Hor.

× Sen.

× Cic.

× Hor.

× Cic.

× Sen.

× Cic.

× Claud.

× Cic.

× Sen.

× Cic.

× Ter.

× Phœd

× Cic. × Cic.

× Cic. × Plaut

The Fox and the Goat

[Shorthand text]

Damon and Pythias.

[Shorthand text]

The True Philosopher

× Sir John Herschell

The Frost.

Hannah F. Goul

Specimens of the Reporting Style.

The Miseries of War.

x Chalmers.

Defence of Socrates

True Greatness.

PHONOGRAPHIC

WRITING EXERCISES.

~~~~~~~~~~~~~~~~~~~

PART FOURTH

OF THE

Hand-Book of Standard Phonography.

PRELIMINARY REMARKS.

THE object of this work is to furnish a series of progressive exercises in the principles of American or Standard Phonography.

At the head of each exercise, reference is made to certain portions of the Compendium, which should be carefully studied before commencing to write the exercise.

The student who wishes to make sure and rapid progress in Phonography will continue to write each exercise until the form of each word in it can be readily and neatly written, and until the principles referred to are thoroughly understood and impressed upon the memory.

When an exercise is too long to be written out for correction, the student may be directed to write a certain portion of each paragraph; and then the remaining words may be pronounced as it were to a spelling-class, the pupils being required to orally indicate the outlines by means of the syllable-names. This process of indicating outlines may be appropriately called Phonographic Spelling.

When a phonographic class is too large to permit the separate revision of the writing exercise of each pupil, the exercise should be correctly written by the teacher, say on a blackboard, with letters sufficiently large to be readily seen by all the members of the class, who should then compare their writing with the exercise thus presented, and make the necessary corrections.

In most instances where the correct mode of writing is not quite obvious, the outlines of words have been indicated by the mode of printing the words or by syllable names. This plan may seem objectionable, as not demanding sufficiently the exercise of the student's judgment as to the best outlines. But the writer will find that the efforts of memory in recalling consonant-signs, positions of vowels, etc., will leave little opportunity for the exercise of judgment as to outlines, even were he fully acquainted with the principles for the selection of the best word-forms; and the benefits arising from such uncertain exercise of judgment would by no means compensate for the injury resulting from acquiring bad habits of writing. Faulty outlines, once familiarized, not only require considerable time and effort to displace them from the memory, but their analogy, being insensibly or purposely followed, to a greater or less extent, has a constant tendency to vitiate the style of writing. On the contrary, the student having familiarized a considerable number of correct forms, is guided by principles of analogy in the selection of outlines for corresponding words, and rendered practically familiar with principles which relieve him from the necessity of arbitrarily memorizing the forms for the words of the entire language, by enabling him to determine instantly and with great certainty the best outlines for new words as they are presented.

While the plan of indicating outlines in doubtful cases, can not be objected to by pupils, the teacher will find that the judgment of the student is not left without a fair degree of exercise; and if the student should not have the assistance of a teacher, he can but feel thankful that he is by this method guarded from serious errors.

The author deems it so important that the phonographer should not have the injurious example and influence of a bad outline, that from first to last he has used great care to present no word to be written phonographically until the principles in accordance with which it may be correctly written have been explained.

ANDREW J. GRAHAM.

PHONETIC DEPOT, NEW YORK, *July 20th*, 1858.

PHONOGRAPHIC

WRITING EXERCISES.

EXERCISE I. COMPENDIUM, 1-25.

SINGLE CONSONANT-SIGNS.

§ 1. MAKE the signs indicated by the following syllable-names:—Pee, Bee, Tee, Dee, Chay, Jay, Kay, Gay. Ef, Vee, Ith, Thee, Es, Zee, Ish, Zhay, Lay, Ar, Ray, Em, En, Ing, Way, Yay, Hay, Iss, Weh, Wuh, Yeh, Yuh; Pee, Ef, Em, Way, Bee, Vee, Tee, Ith, Es, Lay, Ar, Ray, En, Yay, Dee, Thee, Zee, Chay, Ish, Jay, Zhay, Kay, Ing, Hay, Gay, Weh, Yeh, Wuh, Yuh, h-dot, Iss.

CONSONANT-SIGNS JOINED.

§ 2. Write, as indicated by the syllable-names, the consonants of the words of the following paragraphs;

1. *Straight Lines.*—(a) Peck, pick, Pee-Kay—peg, Pee-Gay—pitch, Pee-Chay—page, Pee-Jay–pity, putty, Pee-Tee—Pedee, pay-day, Pee-Dee—pope, Pee-Pee.

(b) Take, talk, Tee-Kay—Tioga, Tee-Gay—teach, touch, Tee-Chay—tattoo, Tee-Tee—tidy, Tee-Dee–type, top, Tee-Pee—tub, Tee-Bee.

(c) Check, Chay-Kay—Chitty, Chay-Tee—cheap, Chay-Pee—chubby, Chay-Bee.

(d) Cook, cake, Kay-Kay–keg, Kay-Gay—catch, couch, Kay-Chay—cage, Kay-Jay—Cato, Kay-Tee—Cady, Kay-Dee—keep, occupy, Kay-Pee—cub, Kay-Bee.

(e) Rock, Ray-Kay—rag, Ray-Gay—ready, Ray-Dee—haughty, Hay-Tee.

(g) Book, Bee-Kay—beg, Bee-Gay—beach, Bee-Chay—badge, Bee-Jay—beauty, Bee-Tee—body, Bee-Dee–baby, Bee-Bee.

(h) Deck, Dee-Kay—dig, Dee-Gay—ditch, Dutch, Dee-Chay—dodge, adage, Dee-Jay—Deity, data, oddity, Dee-Tee—Dido, Dee-Dee–deep, Dee-Pee—daub, *debut*, Dee-Bee.

(i) Joke, Jay-Kay—jog, Jay-Gay–judge, Jay-Jay—Jeddo, Jay-Dee—Job, Jay-Bee—gew-gaw, Gay-Gay.

2. *Straight Lines and Curves.*—(a) Puffy, Pee-Ef—bevy, Bee-Vee—path, Pee-Ith—bath, Bee-Ith—pious, Pee-Es—bias, Bee-Es–push, Pee-Ish—bush, Bee-Ish—pale, Bee-Lay—ball, Bee-Lay–bear, Bee-Ar—pair, Pee-Ar—palm, Pee-Em—balm, Bee-Em–penny, Pee-En—pang, Pee-Ing—being, Bee-Ing—byway, Bee-Way.

(b) Teeth, Tee-Ith–death, Dee-Ith–dizzy, Dee-Zee—dish, Dee-Shay—deal, doll, Dee-Lay—dare, door, Dee-Ar—deem, Dee-Em—deny, Dee-En—tongue, Tee-Ing.

(c) Chaffy, Chay-Ef—Java, Jay-Vee—Jessie, Jay-Es—chill, Chay-Lay—jail, Jay-Lay—chair, Chay-Ar—jar, Jay-Ar—gem, Jay-Em—China, Chay-En—Jennie, Jay-En.

(d) Coffee, Kay-Ef—Goth, Gay-Ith—chaos, Kay-Es—gauzy, Gay-Zee–cash, Kay-

Ish – coal, Kay-Lay—gale, Gay-Lay—car, Kay-Ar—gore, Gay-Ar—calm, Kay-Em -
gum, Gay-Em—king, Kay-Ing—gong, Gay-Ing

(*e*) Wrath, earth, Ray-Ith—wreathe, Ray-Thee—racy, Ray-Es—rosy, Ray-Zee —
rash, Ray-Ish—rally, Ray-Lay—ruin, Ray-En—ring, wrong, Ray-Ing.

(*g*) Heavy, Hay-Vee—hazy, Hay-Zee—halo, Hay-Lay—honey, Hay-En.

(*h*) Fop, Ef-Pee—fatty, Ef-Tee – veto, Vee-Tee—effigy, Ef-Jay—voyage, Vee-Jay
—fig, Ef-Gay—evoke, Vee-Kay—vague, Vee-Gay—fury, Ef-Ray—vary, Vee-Ray.

(*i*) Ethiopia, Ith-Pee—thatch, Ith-Chay—thick, Ithaca, Ith-Kay—thorough, Ith-
Ray.

(*j*) Asp, Es-Pee—aside, Es-Dee—Osage, Es-Jay--ask, Es-Kay—Isaac, Zee-Kay
—Assyria, Es-Ray-Ezra, Zee-Ray.

(*k*) Shape, sheep, Ish-Pee—shabby, Ish-Bee- shady, Ish-Dee—*chateau*, Ish-Tee
—shock, shake, Ish-Kay-shaggy, Ish-Gay.

(*l*) Leap, Lay-Pee—elbow, Lay-Bee- lady, Lay-Dee—latch, Lay-Chay—ledge,
Lay-Jay—lake, like, Lay-Kay—elk, alike, El-Kay - log, El-Gay—Laura, Lay-Ray.

(*m*) Orb, Ar-Bee—ark, Ar-Kay—Argo, Ar-Gay—aurora, Ar-Ray.

(*n*) Map, Em-Pee—mob, Em-Bee—mighty, Em-Tee – meadow, Em-Dee—match,
Em-Chay—image, Em-Jay—mock, Em-Kay—mug, Em-Gay—merry, Em-Ray.

(*o*) Nip, En-Pee—nib, En-Bee—into, knotty, En-Tee—needy, India, En-Dee—
inch, En-Chay—enjoy, En-Jay—knock, Ionic, En-Kay—narrow, En-Ray—ink, Ing-
Kay.

(*p*) Await, Way-Tee – awoke, awake, Way-Kay.

8. *Curves.*—(*a*) Fang, Ef-Ing—funny, Ef-En—Vienna, Vee-En—fame, Ef-Em—
fear, four, fire, Ef-Ar—veer, Vee-Ar—fallow, Ef-Lay – villa, valley, Vee-Lay- file,
foil, Ef-El—vile, vale, Vee-El—fish, Ef-Shay—fussy, Ef-Es—faith, Ef-Ith—fife, Ef-
Ef—five, Ef-Vee.

(*b*) Thong, Ith-Ing—theme, thumb, Ith-Em.

(*c*) Scion, assignee, Es-En—Zion, Zee-En—assume, Es-Em – assail, Es-Lay – zeal,
easily, Zee-Lay- ossify, Es-Ef.

(*d*) Oshawa, Ish-Way—Shawnee, shiny, Ish-En—shame, chamois, Ish-Em—
shear, shore, Ish-Ar—shawl, shallow, shell, Shay-Lay—sheaf, Ish-Ef-shave, shove,
Ish-Vee.

(*e*) Alway, Lay-Way—long, lung, El-Ing-lion, El-En—lime, loom, Lima, Lay-
Em—alum, elm, Alma, El-Em—lore, liar, Lay-Ar—loll, lily, Lay-Lay—lash, Lay-
Shay—Lucy, Elias, lassie, also, Lay-Es—Louisa, Lizzie, lazy, Lay-Zee—lath, loth,
Lay-Ith—lathe, Lay-Thee—laugh, loaf, leaf, Lay-Ef—live, leave, Lay-Vee.

(*g*) Arm, Ar-Em—error, Ar-Ar—oral, Ar-Lay—Irish, Ar-Ish—heareth, Ar-Ith.

(*h*) Among, Em-Ing—many, money, Em-En—maim, Miami, Em-Em—mill, mail,
mellow, Em-Lay—mush, mash, Em-Ish—massy, Em-Es—mazy, Em-Zee—moth,
Em-Ith—muff, Em-Ef - move, Em-Vee.

(*i*) Name, enemy, En-Em—nail, only, En-El—uneasy, En-Zee—Nassau, En-Es—
'neath, Ianthe, En-Ith—enough, knife, En-Ef—nave, envy, En-Vee.

4. *Ray and Chay.*—Reap, Ray-Pee—cheap, Chay-Pee—rooty, Ray-Tee—chatty,
Chay-Tee—rich, Ray-Chay—chary, Chay-Ray—rage, Ray-Jay—jury, Jay-Ray—
wreck, Ray-Kay—check, Chay-Kay-carry, Kay-Ray—catch, Kay-Chay—parry,
Pee-Ray—peach, Pee-Chay—tarry, Tee-Ray—teach, Tee-Chay—narrow, En-Ray—
inch, En-Chay—Laura, Lay-Ray—latch, Lay-Chay – rear, Ray-Ray—reach, Ray-
Chay—merry, Em-Ray—match, Em-Chay.

5. *Several Consonants.*—(*a*) Party, purity, Pee-Ray-Tee—period, parody, Pee-
Ray-Dee—pink, Pee-Ing-Kay—bearer, Bee-Ray-Ray - bounty, bayonet, bonnet,
Bee-En-Tee—became, Bee-Kay-Em—deputy, Dee-Pee-Tee—damage, Dee-Em-Jay
–tiptoe, Tee-Pee-Tee — tomato, Tee-Em-Tee — Timothy, Tee-Em-Ith — charge,
Chay-Ray Jay—Choctaw, Chay-Kay-Tee—Jamaica, Jay-Em-Kay — Jacob, Jay-

Kay-Bee—Geneva, Jay-En-Vee—cabbage, Kay-Bee-Jay—cubic, Kay-Bee-Kay—camera, Kay-Em-Ray—Canada, Kay-En-Dee—kicked, Kay-Kay-Tee-cogged, Kay-Gay-Dee—Gomorrah, Gay-Em-Ray-gagged, Gay-Gay-Dee—fifty, Ef-Ef-Tee fathom, Ef-Ith-Em—foliage, Ef-Lay-Jay—effect, fact, affect, Ef-Kay-Tee—fagot, Ef-Gay-Tee—variety, Vee-Ray-Tee—avenge, Vee-En-Jay—vacuum, Vee-Kay-Em—vacate, Vee-Kay-Tee—authority, Ith-Ray-Tee—oceanic, Ish-En-Kay—Chicago. Ish-Kay-Gay—shank, Ish-Ing-Kay—Alabama, Lay-Bee-Em—Albany, Lay-Bee-En—Almira, El-Em-Ray—length, El-Ing-Ith—Alleghany, El-Gay-En—lashed, Lay-Shay-Tee—lank, El-Ing-Kay—rebuke, Ray-Bee-Kay—refugee, Ray-Ef-Jay—revenue, Ray-Vee-En—Romish, Ar-Em-Ish—arrange, Ray-En-Jay—melody, Em-Lay-Dee—mi!ch, Em-Lay-Chay—March, Em-Ray-Chay—marriage, Em-Ray-Jay—marsh, Em-Ray-Ish—America, Em-Ray-Kay—monied, Em-En-Dee—month, Em-En-Ith—Mackinaw, Em-Kay-En—monk, Em-Ing-Kay—unpack, En-Pee-Kay-infamy, En-Ef-Em—nominee, pneumonia, En-Em-En—anathema, En-Ith-Em—iniquity, En-Kay-Tee—enigma, En-Gay-Em.

(*b*) Popular, Pee-Pee-Lay-Ar—Pimlico, Pee-Em-Lay-Kay—Poughkeepsie, Pee-Kay-Pee-Es—ophthalmia, Ef-Ith-Lay-Em—effectual, Ef-Kay-Tee-Lay—dignify, Dee-Gay-En-Ef—admirer, Dee-Em-Ray-Ray—orang-outang, Ray-Ing-Tee-Ing--ungenial, En-Jay-En-El—memento, Em-Em-En-Tee—Victoria, Vee-Kay-Tee-Ray—Catholic, Kay-Ith-Lay-Kay.

REM. When the outlines indicated above can be readily and neatly made, the student will derive considerable benefit from translating them into the words for which they were written. From the very outset, he should make it a rule to read over one or more times whatever he phonographs.

EXERCISE II. C., 26-32.

§ 3. Write, as indicated by the syllable-names, the consonants for the words of the following paragraphs:

1. *Circles and Loops on the Straight Lines.*—(*a*) Pace, Pees—base, buys, Bees—toys, Tees—dose, does, Dees—chase, choice, etches, Chays—joys, juice, Jays—case, ax, Kays—guess, gaze, Gays—race, rose, Rays—hiss, Hays.

(*b*) Sip, spy, Spec—sob, Iss-Bee—sit, stay, Stee—said, Iss-Dee—such, Iss-Chay—siege, sage, Iss-Jay—sake, Skay—sag, Iss-Gay.

(*c*) Pieces, Pee'ses—bases, Beeses—teases, Teeses—adduces, Deeses—chases, choices, cheeses, Chay'ses—cases, axes, Kay'ses—guesses, Gay'ses—races, roses, Ray'ses—hisses, Hay'ses.

(*d*) Pieced, paste, Peest—beast, best, based, Beest—test, teased, Teest—adduced, Deest—chased, chest, Chayst—jest, just, Jayst—cased, cast, Kayst—guest, gazed, Gayst—raced raised, rest, Rayst—hissed, haste, Hayst.

(*e*) Step, Steh-Pee--stab, Steh-Bee—state, Steh-Tee—steady, Steh-Dee--stitch, Steh-Chay—stage, Steh-Jay—stake, Skay—story, Steh-Ray.

(*g*) Pastor, Pee'ster—boaster, Bee'ster—taster, Teester—duster, Deester—Ches-ter, Chayster—jester, juster, Jayster—coaster, castor, Kayster—roaster, Rayster—Hester, Hayster.

(*h*) Space, Spees-sobs, Sbees—spaced, Speest—steps, Steh-Pees—states, Steh-Tees—studies, Steh-Dees—sages-Iss-Jays-success, Skayses-Sussex, Ses-Kays—stakes, Steh-Kays—stories, Steh-Rays—Cicero's, Ses-Rays--sorrows, Iss-Rays—sacks, Skays—sags, Iss-Gays—sages, Iss-Jays—suggest, Iss-Jayst.

2. *Circles and Loops on Curves.*—(*a*) Face, Efs—voice, Vees—cease, says, Es-Iss—shows, Ish-Iss—lace, lays, Lays—errs, oars, Ar-Iss—mace, Ems—nose, ounce, Ens—woes, ways, Ways—yeas, Yays.

(*b*) Safe, Sef—save, Iss-Vee—sash, Iss-Ish‐sale, slay, Slay—sore, Sar—size, seize, Iss-Zee—same, Sem—son, sane, Iss En—song, Iss-Ing—sway, Iss-Way.

( ) Faces, Efses—vases, Veeses—ceases, Es-Ses—losses, leases, laces, Layses—masses, Emses—ounces, Enses.

(*d*) Faced, Efst—vest, Veest—ceased, Es-Steh—zest, Zeest—lest, last, Layst—arrest, Ar-Steh—amazed, amassed, Emst—nest, Enst—west, waste, Wayst—yeast, Yayst.

(*e*) Stale, steal, Steh-Iay—stare, store, Steh-Ar—stem, Steh-Em—stung, Steh-Ing.

(*g*) Feaster, Efster—\uster, Veester—Shaster, Ish'ster—Lester, luster, Layster—master, Emster—Nestor, Enster—waster, Wayster.

(*h*) Safes, Sefs—saves, Iss-Vees—sizes, seizes, Iss-Zees—sashes, Iss-Ish-Iss—sales, slays, Slays—steals, Steh-Lays—Sicily's, Ses-Lays‐stems, Stems—sways, Sways—sliced, Slayst—sorest, Sarst—stores, stars, Stars—solaces, Slayses—solaced, Slayst—sources, Sarses‐sums, Sems—sense, Iss-Ens.

3. *Circles and Loops between Strokes.*—(*a*) Passive, Pees-Vee—baser, Bees-Ar—besom, Bees-Em—basin, Bees-En—bask, Bees-Kay—beset, Bees-Tee—beseech, Bees-Chay—dusty, Dees-Tee—deceive, Dees-Vee‐dusk, Dees-Kay—desire, Dees-Ar—cask, Kays-Kay—castle, Kays-Lay‐gossip, Gays-Pee—evasive, Vees-Vee—vessel, Vees-El—society, Es-Stee—necessity, Enses-Tee—necessary, Enses-Ray—exist, Kayses-Tee‐accessory, Kayses-Ray‐decisive, Deeses-Vee‐massive, Ems-Vee—misseth, Ems-Ith—mason, Ems-En‐facility, Ef-Slay-Tee—nasality, En-Slay-Tee—atheism, Ith-Sem.

(*b*) Justify, Jayst-Ef—testify, Teest-Ef—destiny, Deest-En.

4. *Iss Added to Ses, Steh, and Ster.*—Possesses, Peeses-Iss‐diseases, Deeses-Iss—excesses, Kayses-Iss—lists, Laysts—Lester's, Laysters‐masters, Emsters—successes, Skayses-Iss‐fasts, Efsts—vests, Veests—exercises, Kays-Rayses-Iss.

PHONOGRAPHIC TYPE-KEYS.

§ 4. A phonographic type-key is an entire word, or its consonants only, so printed as to indicate the consonant-outline or form. Type-keys, in this work, are formed in accordance with the following plan:

1. A consonant-letter or group of consonant-letters to be represented by a stroke, and the letter or letters to be represented by an attachment (as a circle, loop, or hook), are separated from other consonant-letters by a hyphen or space.

2. Different directions of the same sign, and different signs for the same sound, are distinguished by different modes of printing. For instance, letters to be represented by a circle or loop are sometimes printed with *italics*. El and Ar are distinguished from Lay and Ray by printing them with small capitals—L, R. Other distinctions will be pointed out as they are required.

Examples.—Mason=ms-n=Ems-En ; pu-ri-ty=p-r-t=p r t=Pee-Ray-Tee ; absence=bs-ns=bs ns=Bees-Ens ; low-er=l-r=l r=Lay-Ar ; rai-l=r-l=Ray-El.

EXERCISE III. C., 33–55.

SIMPLE-CONSONANT WORD-SIGNS.

§ 5. Write the sign-words of the following paragraph with their proper signs;

write the outlines for the words preceded by a point (.); and write the remaining words in phonetic or common longhand.

The Whistle.—When I *was* a child about seven years of .age, *my* friends, on a .ho-li-day, filled *my* pocket with halfpence. I went directly towards a .shop (Ish-Pee) where .toys (Tees) were sold *for* children; and being (Bee-Ing) charmed with the sound of a whistle that I met *by* the *way, in* the hands of another .boy, I voluntarily offered *him* all *my* .money (Em-En) *for it.* I then came (Kay-Em) home, and went whistling over the .house (Hays), *much* pleased with *my* whistle, but disturbing all the .f-ami-ly. *My* brothers, and sisters, and .cous-ins, understanding the bargain I *had* made, told *me* I *had given* .fou-r times (Tee-Ems) *as much for it as it was* worth. *This* put *me in* mind of what good *things* I might *have* bought with the .rest of the .money (Em-En); and *they* laughed *at me so much for my* .folly (Ef-Lay) that I cried with vexation. *My* reflections on the *subject* gave *me* more chagrin than the whistle gave *me* pleasure. *This* little event, *however, was* afterwards of *use to me*, the impression continuing on *my* mind: *so* that often, when I *was* tempted to *buy* .some .unnecessary (n-nses-r) *thing*, I .said to *myself,* Do not *give* too *much for* the whistle; and *so* I saved *my* .money. *As* I grew *up*, .came .into the world, and observed the actions of men, I thought I met with .many, very .many, who gave too *much for* the whistle. When I .saw *any* one too ambitious of court-favor, sacrificing *his* .time *in* attendance on .levees, *his* .repose, *his* liberty, *his* virtue, and perhaps *his* friends, to attain *it*, I .said to *myself. This* man *gives* too *much for his* whistle. When I .saw another fond of popularity, constantly employing *himself in* political .bustles (bs-ls), neglecting *his own* .affairs (f-rs), and ruining *them by* that neglect; *He* .pays indeed, .said I, too *much for his* whistle.—*If* I knew a .miser who gave *up* every kind of comfortable living, all the pleasure of *doing* good to others, all the esteem of *his* fellow-citizens, and the .joys of benevolent friendship, *for* the .sake of accumulating wealth; .Poor man, .said I, you indeed .pay too *much for your* whistle. When I met a man of pleasure, sacrificing every laudable improvement of mind, or of fortune, to mere sensual gratifications; Mistaken man! .said I, you *are* providing pain *for yourself*, instead of pleasure; you *give* too *much for your* whistle.—*If* I .saw one fond of fine clothes, fine furniture, fine .equipage (k-p-j), all .above his fortune, *for which he* contracted debts, and ended *his* .career *in* prison; .Alas! .said I, *he has* paid dear, very dear, *for his* whistle. *In* short, I conceived that a great part of the .miseries of mankind *are* brought upon *them by* the false estimate *they* .make of the value of *things*, and *by their giving* (Gay-Ing) too *much for* their whistles.—Dr. Franklin.

As a further exercise on the word-signs, read § 109 of the Introduction to Phonotypy and Phonography, and note the sign-words.

§ 6. Vocalization.

1. Pea, Pee, bee, pay, bay, bey, pa, baa, fee, Vee, fay, fa, tea, Tee, Dee, day, Thee, Cee, say, Zee, lee, Lay, la, lay, Ray, ray, gee (dji), chee, Chay, Jay, Shay, Zhay, Shah, wee, weigh, yea, ha, hey, hay; ape, eve, eat, eight, ait, aid, ace, ease, Aes, eel, ail, ale, ear, air, e'er, Ar, Aar, Aitch, age, ah!

2. Ebb, Ab, Ef, Et, Ed, Ith, Iss, Es, ell, ill, El, err, itch, etch, edge, Ish, ash, eh!

3. Paw, Poe, Po, pugh! pōh! bōw, faugh! foh! foe, toe, tōw, Doe, dough, thaw, saw, sou, law, lo! low, loo, woe, woo, yaw, chaw, jaw, Joe, shoo, show, Shaw, raw, Roe, rōw, haw, hoe, hoo!—ope, oaf, aught, oat, awed, owed, oath, owes, ooze, awl, Orr, oar, o'er.

4. Off, odd, ugh!

5. Opie, abbey, Eva, Effie, eighty, A-te, eddy, Adee, Ada, ădo, Otho, Esau, essay,

1*

Asa, easy, Uzzah, ally, allay, Ellie, Ella, Allah, era, Erie, airy, array, aerie (æri), arrow, itchy, ashy, aha!

6. Maw, May, mōw, ma, knee, gnaw, neigh, nay, key, caw, Kay, Coe coo, gꞷy go; aim, Amy, e'en, awn, eke, ache; Em, Emma, inn, En, Enna, Ann, Anna, Annie, anno, Ing.

7. Lee, chee, law, chaw, jaw, la, Shah, raw, Shaw.

8. *Optional Vowel-Signs.*—Air, airs, Ayers, add, adz, adds, alley, Allah, alley, ash, ashy, abbey, ax, err, errs, Erse, erst, earl, early, earth (Ray-Ith), ergo, myrrh. (Em-Ray), omit, only (En-El), Otho, arrow.

9. Ape, pay, ope, Po, ebb, bay, oaf, foe, eve, Vee, eat, tea, ate, toe, oat, aid, day, oath, thaw, ace, say, ease, Zee, eel, lea, ail, lay, Aitch, Chay, age, Jay, eh, ha; aim, May, e'en, knee, En, neigh, eke, key, ache, Kay, Og, go.

10. *Nominal Consonant.*—ĕ, ā, ah, ĭ, ă, au, ō, ōō, ŏŏ, ŭ, ŏ, ăĭ, ŏĭ, ĭŏŏ, ŏŏŏ, ė, ai(r), ă(t), ŏ, ah! eh!

EXERCISE IV. C., 56–77.

§ 7. INITIAL Iss, Ses, Steh.

1. Sip, steep, step, sop, stop, soap, sup, sap, soup, stoop, sob, stub, stab, seat, settee, sit, city, sought, sot, sate, state, set, stet, sat, soot, sooty, seed, steed, sawed, sod, sowed, sewed, soda, said, steady, study, sad, such, stitch, siege, sage, stage, sedge, seek, sick, stick, sake, stake, sock, stock, stalk, soak, stuck, stucco, sack, stack, soggy, sag, Sarah (Iss-Ray), sorrow, sorry, sirrah, story, starry, sohó.

2. Safe, sofa, save, salve, seam, seem, steam, same, stem, some, sum, Sam., psàlm, stith, seethe, stithy, saith, sooth, soothe, seize, seal, steal, steel, Selah, sill, still, silly, stilly, Sylla, Saul, stall, Sol, sail, stale, sale, solo, stole, sell, cell, Stella, soul, sully, stool, Sally, sallow, seer, steer, sore, store, sir, stir, stare, star, seen, sin, sane, sown, son, sun, sunny, soon, sash, sing, sting, song, sung, stung, sang.

3. Spa, Spee, Smee, sma', Stee, stay, slay, slow, snow, Skay, Schay, sway.

4. System, season, Sussex, Cicero, Sicily, schism, Ses-Tee, Ses-Pee, Ses-Dee sys'to-le, syz'y-gee (siz·idjɪ), Sisyphus (Sisifus), Cæsar, scissors, saucer, Sosthenēs sausage.

§ 8. FINAL Iss, Ses, Steh, Ster.

1. Piece, apiece, appease, peas, pieced, pieces, appeased, appeases, pause, paused, pauses, pays, pace, paste, paces, pester, pesters, oppose, opposed, post, posts, opposes, posies, possess, possesses, poster, posters, pass, passed, past, pest, pests, passes, pastor, pastors, puss, bees, abyss, beast, beasts, abysses, Boz, boss, base, abase, bays, obeys, ebbs, Bess, based, beaux, abased, baste, best, boast, bastes, abscess, basis, bases, abases, Bess's, abscesses, boaster, boasters, odds, dose, doze, dosed, dozed, dust, dusts, dozes, doses, disease, diseases, duster, dusters, tease, eats, toss, oats, toes, Otis, teased, tossed, test, toast, attest, toasts, attests, teases, tosses, taster, tasters, toaster, cheese, chaws, chase, chess, etches, Aitches, chose, choose, chaste, chased, chest, chests, chases, chooses, cheeses, Chester, Chester's, jaws, ægis, ages, Jays, edges, gist, jest, just, jests, Jesus, Jesus's, Jay-Ses, jester, juster, Ross, race, raise, rose, wrist, raised, raced, roast, rest, wrest, rests, roasts, races, raises, roses, roaster, roasters, hiss, hoes, Huss, hawse, haze, Hays, haste, hist, hest, host, hosts, hisses, Huss's, Hester, Hester's, keys, kiss, cause, ox, case, aches, oaks, Cass, ax, kissed, cast, cost, accost, cased, coast, coasts, casts, kisses, cases, Cass's, causes, excess, access, axis, axes, excesses, coaster. caster, castors, geese, gauze, gaze, guess,

eggs, goes, gas, goose, Aug'ust, guest, guessed, ghost, gust, august', agast, ghosts, guests.

2. Fees, phiz, office, face, efface, phase, foes, fuss, fuzz, Fez, feast, faced, effaced, fast, fist, feasts, fists, fasts, faces, offices, phases, fasces, Ephesus, effacés, feaster, foster, fester, faster, eaves, vase, vest, vast, vests, vases, vaster, miss, amiss, maze, maize, amaze, mace, mess, màss, àlms, moss, muss, missed, mist, amazed, mast, amassed, most, must, mists, masts, misses, maces, mazes, amazes, messes, masses, Moses, muster, master, masters, thaws, thesis, theses, cease, saws, sauce, siss, assess, assist, ceased, sauced, assessed, ceases, sauces, lease, Lee's, laws, loss, lace, lays, al-lays, ails, Ellis, else, less, lass, alas, Alice, alleys, loose, lose, least, lost, loosed, last, lest, laced, lasts, losses, looses, loses, laces, lasses, luster, Lester, Lester's, ears, airs, erase, arose, arrows, erased, arrest, arrests, niece, knees, gnaws, neighs, noose, hon-est, nest, noosed, nests, nieces, noses, nooses, Nestor, chaise, shows, ashes, shoes, chaises, Shaster, weighs, wooes, woes, waste, waist, west, wist, wastes, waster, yes, veas, yaws, yeast, yester.

§ 9. Es and Zee.

1. Ace, Asa, Es, asp, Asaph, acid, ask, Osage, Espy; sower, se'eth.

2. Saw, say, essay, posse, pussy, abbacy, fussy, mossy, Macy, màssy, Tasso, Odessa, lessee, also, Lacey, lasso, lassie, racy, Rousseau (Rусsò'), unsay, Nassau, Jesse, gassy Od'yssey, Gussie; Æne'as, chaos.

3. Ease, awes, owes, Ezra, ism, azote, azymous; zany, czar, zeal, zero, Zera, Zeno, Zona.

4. Posy, poësie, busy, boosy, fuzzy, Vesey, mazy, dizzy, daisy, lazy, razee', rosy, cozy, causey, hazy, huzza, huzzy.

§ 10. *Medial Ses.*—Insist, exist, exhaust, necessary, excessive, possessed, rĕsist, dĕsist, accessory, diseased, Mississippi, necessity, possessor (Peeses-Ray), possessive, successive.

§ 11. Vowel Word-Signs.

1. All, of, ought, on, already, or, awe, two, too, who, oh, whom, owe, to, should, but, the, a, and, an; owing, owes, owed, awing, awes, awed.

2. *The The-Tick.*—By the, at the, for the, in the, is the, as the, so the, if the, shall the, may the, know the, why the, are the, think the, have the, because the, give the, though the, which the, to the, of the, on the, all the, or the, but the, should the, ought the; the first, the way.

3. *The A-n-d Tick.*—By a-n, at a-n, for a-n, in a-n, is a-n, as a-n, so a-n, if a-n, shall a-n, may a-n, know a-n, why a-n, are a-n, think a-n, have a-n, be a-n, give a-n, though a-n, which a-n, to a-n, of a-n, on a-n, or a-n, but a-n, should a-n, ought a-n, by and, in and, and the, and a-n, and for, and by, and each, and they, and may, and so, and if, and shall, and should, and but, and who, and ought, and to, and on.

EXERCISE ON THE SIMPLE-CONSONANT AND VOWEL WORD-SIGNS.

§ 12. In the following paragraph, and in other connected reading hereafter pre-sented as writing exercises, an inverted accent (⸜) precedes words to be written in longhand. Of the other words, the sign-words are to be expressed by their signs, and the remainder, by the proper outlines. When sign-words are connected by a hyphen, their signs should be joined.

The ⸜Trap-Door ⸜Spider.—⸜There is-a curious ⸜spider ⸜found in-the south of ⸜France, and some ⸜other ⸜places, which-is ⸜sometimes ⸜called the ⸜trap-door ⸜spider. It hollows out-a ⸜den in-the earth, ⸜generally ⸜about an inch in width (Weh-Dee-Ith), and ⸜from ⸜one to two ⸜feet in depth. The inside of this it first ⸜covers ⸜with a ⸜kind of ‚mortar, and ‚then, as if it ‚meant to ‚paper its ‚walls, hangs (ăIngs) all ‚over them a ‚beautiful ‚silken web (Weh-Bee), which-is said to be smooth as ‚satin, and of dazzling (ds-l-ng) ‚whiteness. But-the most curious ‚part of it is-a ‚trap-door ‚over the ‚entrance, which it ‚perfectly ‚covers. This door is ‚made of ‚different layers of web and earth, and ‚covered ‚with ‚dried leaves ‚closely ‚matted together, and-is so hung (üIng) at-the ‚upper ‚part as to ‚admit of being raised ‚when the animal passes in or out, ‚after which it ‚immediately ‚falls into its ‚place. The edges are curiously ‚fringed ‚with a ‚net-‚work, which ‚conceals the ‚opening, and ‚renders it less ‚liable to be ‚discovered. Along-the edge of this door, on-the inside, are-a ‚number of ‚little ‚holes, which are ‚used by-the animal for ‚holding it ‚down ‚with its ‚claws ‚when it-is ‚attacked by-an enemy.—*Life in-the ‚Insect ‚World.*

EXERCISE V. C., 78–86.

§ 13. Punctuation, etc.

1. *Accent.*—Aróse, árrows, Au′gust, augúst, abyss′, ábbess, obey′, Adee′, éssay, essay′, razee′, rósy, adó, Rousseau′.

2. *Titles.*—A. J. Ellis, A.B. R. G. Latham, M.D., F.R.S. H. U. Janson.

3. *Capitals.*—Rome, America, James, Roscoe, Smith.

4. *Emphasis.*—" Then said the ‚high priest, are these things *so ?*"
" Paul ‚determined to sail *by* Ephesus."
" It is ‚not so ‚difficult to *talk* ‚well as to *live* ‚well." ‚We think less of the injuries ‚we *do* ‚than of those ‚we suffer (sf-r).

EXERCISE VI. C., 87–104.

§ 14. Close Diphthongs.

1. Pie, pies, vie, vies, vice, vices, mice, wise, tie, ties, entice, entices, enticed, die, dye, dies, dice, sigh, sighs, lie, ally, lies, rye, wry, rise, rice, awry (a-rĭ′), arise, arises, nigh, nice, Gneiss, shy, hie, hies, spy, spies, spice, spiced, spices, sky, sly, slice, sliced, slices—ire (C., 101), eyes, ice, icy, eyeing, (h)ighness, (h)eight, (h)igher, ivy, eyed—sight, cite, site, side, sighed, sign, sire, Cyrus, size, sizes, Silas, styles.

2. Boy, boys, Boyce, voice, voices, toy, toys, alloy, alloys, annoy, annoys, noise, noised, noises, Roy, Royce, choice, choices, joy, joys, Joyce, Joyce's, coy, coys, ahoy, hoist, hoists, hoister, Savoy, Sepoy ; oil (C., 101), oily.

3. Bŏw, bough, bŏws, boughs, vow, vows, avows, mŏw, mouse, Dow, Dow's, allow, allows, owl, owls, rŏw, rŏws, rouse, roused, rouses, arouse, aroused, arouses, ounce, ounces, cow, cows, How, How's, house, housed, houses,⁻south, slough, sour, scow.

4. Pew, pews, abuse, abused, abuses, fuse, fused, effuse, view, views, mew, amuse, amused, amuses, dew, due, adieu, deuce, adduce, educe, adduced, adduces, sue, sues, lieu, rue, Luce, Luce's, rues, ruse, news, chew, chews, Jew, Jews, juice, juices, cue, cues, accuse, accused, accuses, yew, hew, hews, Hugh, Hugh's, spew, suit, stew, sued, slew, skew.

OPEN DIPHTHONGS.

§ 15. Deity, laity, aye, ayes, Cairo, Caughey, jawy, rawish, doughy, snowy, stoic, Noah, Goa, Genoa, boa, Alloa, Owen, Zoë, Noë, Louis, Toohey.

CONCURRENT VOWELS.

§ 16. Payee, boa, bayou (bī·ɯ), avowee, iota, Toohey, idea, dewy, doughy, Douay (Dɯ·ɐ), Iowa, Isaiah, Zoë, Leo, Leah, Louis, Owen, Noah, Noë, jawy.

WORD-SIGNS AND CONTRACTIONS.

§ 17. I, eye, aye, [high,] how, highly, now, new, knew ; I am, I will, I shall, I do, I think, I was, I see, I hope, I wish.

EXERCISE VII. C., 105-114.

§ 18. VOWELS BETWEEN CONSONANTS.

1. Pith, peach, pitch, peak, pique, pick, pike, pig, beam, beach, botch, Abijah, big, bog, flp, fop, fib, fob, fief, fife, five, Fitch, Fejee, fish (Ef-Shay), flg, fog, vi've, vim, mob, miff, myth, moth, meek, mock, mica, tip, top, type, team, time, teeth, tithe, teach, tick, talk, deep, dip, deem, dim, dime, ditch, dodge, dish (Dee-Shay), dock, dike, dig, dog, ding, dong, thief, theme, thick, thong, nip, nib, knife, 'neath, niche, notch, nick, knock, cheap, chip, chop, chime, cheek, chick, chalk, gibe, job, jig, jog, sheep (Ish-Pee), shop, Sheba, sheaf, sheath, Shawnee, shiny, shock, keep, Kipp, copy, Cobb, coffee, chyme, kith, king, gang, leap, lip, lobby, leaf, life, leave, live, lime, Le'the, leech, liege, lodge, Elijah, leak, like, ʟike, ʟeague, ʟong, aʟong, ream, ʀim, ʀhyme, reek (Ray-Kay), rick, rig, Riga, reap, rip, ripe, wreathe, peal, Paul, peeʀ, pyʀe, feaʀ, tiʀe.

2. Poach, page, poke, back, both, foam, fame, evoke, vogue, vague, maim, make, tape, tame, tome, take, Davy, dame, tongue, dome, navy, knave, name, choke, shape, shake, cape, cope, came, comb, cage, game, lobe, lave, lame, loam, lathe, loathe, lake, ʀoam, rope, robe, pale, pole, bail, bowl, dale, dole, taʀe, daʀe, dooʀ, tory, Mary.

3. Peck, peg, budge, beck, beg, bug, bung, fudge, muff, mesh, mush, Mecca, mug, among, tub, touch, tug, dum, death, doth, Dutch, deck, duck, thumb, enough, numb, neck, chum, check, chuck, gem, Shem, cup, gum, ledge, luck.

4. Palm, pàth, patch, pouch, push, pack, palm, boom, bàth, batch, Booth, badge, back, book, bag, bang, fume, fag, fang, vouch, Mab, move, mouth, match, mash, tap, tube, tomb, tooth, attach, dupe, dam, dash (Dee-Shay), duke, thatch, nap, Numa, gnash, nook, chap, chaffy, jam, sham, cap, coop, cab, cube, calm, catch, couch, cash, gap, gash, lash (Lay-Shay).

5. Apology, purify, party, parish (Pee-Ray-Ish), package, fifth, baggage, faʀm, fact, effect, mimic, America, magic, topic, outrage, depth, authority, repeal, rebuke, ʟength, rarity, cubic, admirer (Dee-Em-Ray-Ray), dignify, cogency.

6. See C., 109.—Poem, boyish, voyage, Moab, Miami, towage, Tioga, newish, coyish, voweʟ, fueʟ, lōweʀ, coweʀ, dual, duel, toweʀ, feweʀ, avowaʟ, lōweʀ, royaʟ, science, piano, shōweʀ, poet, naiad, riot, Ryan, ʟion.

7. See C., 108.—Pacify, passage, obesity, bask, fasten (Efs-En), effusive, vassaʟ, vesseʟ, muscle, musk, desk, dusk, lesseʀ, looseʀ, rasp, castle, gaspᴘ

8. *Prefixes and Affixes.*—(*a*) Compile, compel, compaʀe, commute (com-Tee), comm-une, compass, compose. (*b*) Conceive, conceit, concede, concise (con-Es-Iss), condemn, conceal, confeʀ, confess, consume, contest, connive, convince (con-Vee-

Ens), console, conscious (con-Ish-Iss), convey, commence, consist (con-Ses-Tee).
(c) Accommodate, accompany. (d) Talking, making, seeking, asking, doing, keeping, lacking, saying, showing, dying. (e) Musings, doings, sayings, facings, risings,
(g) Facing the, facing a-n-d, seeking the, seeking a-n-d, asking the, asking a-n-d,
laying the, laying a-n-d, showing the, showing a-n-d, doing the, doing a-n-d,
making the, making a-n-d, catching the, catching a-n-d.

EXERCISE VIII.   C., 115–125.

§ 19. DIFFERENT MODES OF REPRESENTING W AND Y.

1. Wee, woe, weigh, woo, Wĕh, Wŭh, Wise, weighs, woes, wooes, waist, west,
wist, wast, waster, Wooster, Wistar, wisp, wasp, sway, sways, Swiss, sweep, swap,
swoop, swab, swath, swallow, swell, swim, swum, swam, swing, swung, awoke,
awake, Owego, Owasco, Iowa, await; yaw, yaws, yea, yew, yews, yes, yeas, yeast,
yester, oyer, oyez.

2. Weep, web, wit, wot, wait, wet, weight, weed, widow, wad, weighed, wood,
wade, watch, wage, witch, wedge, walk (Wuh-Kay), week, wake, woke, wax,
waxed, wig, wag, waif, woòf, weave, wave, wavy, wove, withe, wash, wing, unweighed, unweave. [Sweat, sweet, Swede, swayed, switch. See C., § 124, R.]

3. Wemyss (Wɪmz), Wem, win, winnow, wine, wan, wane, wen, weal, wall, wal-
low, wile, wily, wail, wool, woolly, willow, Willis, Wallace, Wells, weary, wary,
war, wear, wore, wire, wiry, worry, ware, swear, swore, twain, twine, Edwin,
quire, choir, query, unwell, unwieldy, unworthy, unwearied, unwary, wince,
winced, winces, wines, wears, worse, worst, Worcester.

4. Yacht, Yates, yawl, yell, Yale, yellow, Yulee, yarrow, Uriah, yore, yawn, yon,
yawns, Eunice, yams, yoke unyoke.

EXERCISE IX.   C., 126–143.

§ 20. DIFFERENT MODES OF EXPRESSING W AND Y.

1. (a) Sweet, sweat, Swede, swayed, switch, suage, switches, Swedish (Iss-Dee-
Shay), suavity, dissuade, Ipswich, unswayed. (b) Twitch, tweak, twig, twang,
thwack, equip, quick, quack, quake, quag, quaggy, equity, acquit, quota, bewail,
dwell, twill, quail, quell, Aquila, quench, equinox. (c) Twist, twists, twisting,
untwist, quest, inquest, bequest. (d) Youth, young, unity, unite, unison; lawyer,
folio, bilious.

2. See C., 134 and 136.—Genii, Honeoye, maniac, ammoniac, insignia, scoria,
opiate, barrier, carrier, superior, interior, anterior, idiom, odious, odium, copious,
furious, various, envious, obvious, notorious, censorious, olio, foliage, Scipio, serious,
studious (Steh-Dees), piteous.

3. Wipe, wight, wide, Dwight, quiet, quietus, quiesce (Kay-Es), quiescence
(Kay-Ess-Ens), quietest, twice, wife, wives, buoy, buoys.

4. See C., 139.—Ammonia, Xenia, scoria, nephew, argue, ague.

§ 21. Determine which of Ew, Yōō, and Yŏŏ is denoted by u, eu, ew, ue, etc., in
the following words.—Dᵤty, union, unite, mute, pure, fury, unity, unique′, u′nison,
universe, usurp, utility, Uto′pia, tune, rude, res′cue, argue, due, sue, rue, rued,
ague, suit, bruise, bruit, feud, euphony, rheum, Eunice, euphonic Europe, eulogy
eulogium adieu, dew, few, Ewing, nephew, Ewell, view, Hugh

§ 22. Write, according to the directions of § 12, the following paragraph :

The ,Good ,Samaritan.—And ,behold, a ,certain lawyer ,stood up, and ,tempted him, saying, "Master, what shall I-do to ,inherit ,eternal life ?" He said unto him, "What is ,written in-the law ? how ,readest thou ?" And he answering, said, "Thou shalt love the ,Lord thy ,God with all thy ,heart, and-with all thy soul, and-with all thy ,strength, and-with all thy ,mind ; and-thy ,neighbor as thyself." And-he said unto him, "Thou hast (¹) ,answered right; this do, and-thou shalt live." But he, willing to justify (Jayst-Ef) himself, said unto Jesus (Jay′ses), " And-who is my ,neighbor ?" And Jesus answering, said, " A ,certain ,man ,went ,down ,from ,Jerusalem to ,Jericho, and ,fell among thieves, who ,stripped him of-his ,raiment, and ,wounded him, and ,departed, leaving him ,half ,dead. And-by ,chance ,there came ,down a ,certain ,priest ,that way ; and when he saw him, he passed by on-the ,other side.—And likewise (Lay-Kay-Zee) a ,Levite, when he was at-the ,place, came and ,looked on him, and passed by on-the ,other side But-a ,certain ,Samaritan, as he ,journeyed, came where he was : and-when he saw him, he had ,compassion on him, and ,went to him, and ,bound up his ,wounds, pouring in oil and wine, and set him on-his own beast, and ,brought him to-an inn, and took ,care of him. And on-the morrow, when he ,departed, he took out two ,pence, and ,gave them to-the host, and said unto him, ' Take ,care of him ; and ,whatsoever thou ,spendest ,more, when I come ,again, I-will repay thee.' Which now of these ,three, thinkest (Ith-Steh) thou, was ,neighbor unto him who ,fell among thieves ?" And he said, "He that ,showed mercy on him." ,Then said Jesus unto him, " Go, and-do thou like-wise."

EXERCISE X. C., 144–149.

§ 23. DIFFERENT MODES OF EXPRESSING H—ASPIRATION.

1. (*a*) Heap, hop, hoop, whoop, half, halve, hem, home, ham, hum, heat, hot hut, hate, height, white, heed, hid, hod, hide, head, hood, heath, hath, heel, hill hall, Hoyle (See C., 101), hull, howl, hear, Horr, hire, hair, hitch, hatch, hutch hedge, huge, hush, hash, hawk, hook, hack, hog, Hague, hoax, hug, hang, hung highway.

(*b*) See C., 146, R. 4.—Hedge, head, huge, horse, hem, hate.

2. Write with the h-tick the following words :—Whiz, whisk, whistle, whist whey, whoa, wheeze, whew, awhile, wheezes.

3. Aspirate the W in the following words by placing the h-tick before the follow-ing vowel :—Whiz, whisk, whistle, whist, whey, whoa, wheeze, whew, awhile, wheezes.

4. (*a*) Whip, whiff, whit, wheat, whig, whack.

(*b*) See C., 148, R. 1.—Whip, whiff, whit, wheat, whig (Wuh-Gay), whack (Wuh-Kay).

5. Wheel, whale, whir, whirl.

6. See C., 148, R. 2.—Wheel, whale, whir, whirl.

7. (*a*) Aspirate the Way-hook in the following words by prefixing the h-tick :—Whence, whin, whine, whim.

(*b*) See C., 148, R. 2.—Whence, whin, whine, whim.

8. Ahoy, hoe, hay, haw, aha, Ohio, Ya′hoo, eh, oh, hue, hew, Hugh, hah, ho, hoy

---

(1) The words ' wert, hast, shalt,' and some other words belonging to what is called the solemn style, may usually be expressed the same as the corresponding ' were, has, shall,' etc., belonging to the usual style of speech.

ugh, Howe, hiss, house, hoist, Huss, hose, hoes, host, hisses, ahead, haughty, holy '
Harry, hairy, hurry, Harris, Horace, hazy, hasten, hasty, hosannah.

EXERCISE XI. C., 151–153.
§ 24. DIFFERENT MODES OF REPRESENTING R.

1. (a) Ear, air, ore, err, Ayr, oar, ere (ɐr), era, Erie, Ira, ire, aura, arise, arisen
(Ar-Sen), arose, erase, Iris, orris, Erse, èrst, orb, harp, hark, ark, argue, harsh (Ar-
Shay), harm, Hiram, aroma, arm, ergo, Oreb, Arab, heareth, Irish (Ar-Ish).

(b) Express R in the following words with Ray:—Arch, urge, aright, arrayed,
earth, hearth. erroneous, arson, orison, Arnos.

2. (a) Ray, raw, wry, rŏw, rye, rue, row, Reese, Ross, rice, rise, race, raise, rose,
rouse, races, raises, roses, raced, rest, roaster; reap, ripe, rob, robe, ruby, review,
wreathe, wretch, ridge, rich, rush, rouge, rash, ready, rode, write, wrote, right,
wrought, root, rude, rack, rock, rogue, ring, wrong, wring, rang; reason, rosin, risk,
rasp, Russell, wrestle.

(b) Ream, Rum, rhyme, Rome, room, rheum, resume.

3. (a) Peer, beer, pair, fire, fear, four, veer, tire, tare, door, easier, essayer,
nigher, ne'er, gnar, newer, cheer, char, jar, giaour (djour), cur, car, bore, gore, lŏwer,
lure, error, sere, seer, sore, sire, source, serious, Cyrus.

(b) Express R with Ray in the following words:—Mar, myrrh, moor, amour,
mire, Thayer, future, futurity, Shakspeare, rare, roar, rear, rarer, barrier, carrier,
courier, wear, swear, yore.

4. Perry, parry, Peru, borrow, bewray, bury, borough, Barry, berry, bureau,
Bowery, fiery, fairy, Pharaoh (Fɐ·rŏ), ferry, furry, furrow, fury, ivory, vary, Imrah,
miry, morrow, Mary, merry, emery, Murray, marrow, marry, Torrey, tyro, terra,
tory, tarry, Tara, diary, dairy, Derry, Darrow, Douro (Dɯ·rŏ), dowry, theŏry,
thorough, Assyria, Ezra, narrow, Henry, Newry, chary, cherry, hedge-row, Jerry,
jury, usury, sherry, Carey, Carrie, Cora, curry, carry, gory, Laura, Ellery, aurora,
sorrow, sorrows, Sarah, yarrow, story, starry, Cicero.

EXERCISE XII. C., 154–158.
§ 25. DIFFERENT DIRECTIONS OF THE STROKE FOR L.

1. Ill, ell, ale, awl, oil, owl, else, loss, losses, last, lists, Lester, Lester's, seal, steel,
seals, slice, solaces, Sicily.

2. (a) Leap, lip, lap, loop, lobby, lobe, leaf, life, loaf, laugh, leave, Levi, live, Livy
love, lava, Lima, limb, lime, lame, loam, lamb, lithe, loath, lath, lathe, loathe, leech,
latch, liege, lodge, ledge, leak, lock, like, lake, luck, Luke, lack, look, lawyer, lyre,
lore, lure, lŏwer, Laura, Lyra, lŏwery, laity, Lodi, lady, laddie.

(b) League, log, lag, leg, long, lung, lion, Lynch, launch, lenity, lounge, luggage,
link, lank, length, listen, lessen, loosen, lesson, Louisiana.

3. (a) Alum, alma, Almira, alumni, alchemy, Hallam, hillock, alike, elk, alack
Alleghany.

(b) El may be used for L in the following words:—Along, Alison, Eleusinia, Illi-
nois, ulna, Helena.

(*c*) Use Lay for L in the following words:—Elope, Aleppo, Elba, elbow, alibi, elf, Alpha, aloof, Olivia, olive, Elva, Alva, health, allege, elegy, alight, elate, alto, allied, alloyed, allayed, allude, allowed, also, allure, Elisha (Lay-Shay), Elias (Lay-Es), always, alliance, illness, Elihu (Lay-Hay).

4. Peal, appeal, appellee, pill, pillow, Paul, Polly, Apollo, Poll, pile, pale, Paley, pole, opal, pool, happily, pull, pulley, bill, billow, billowy, ball, bile, boil, bail, Bailey, belay, bewail, bell, bellow, below, bowl, Buel, Beulah, tall, wittily, whitlow, outlie, tile, toil, tale, toll, tool, towel, tally, tallow, tallowy, outlaw, outlay, deal, Delia, ideal, Adelia, ideally, dill, doll, Dolly, oddly, dial, widely, Doyle, dale, daily, delay, dell, dwell, Headly, dale, dull, duel, duly, dally, dahlia (dá·lia, a plant named from Dahl=DAl, a Swedish botanist), dual, duello, assail, Osceola, Asahel, zeal, easel, easily, thill, Athalia, Thu'le, shawl (Shay-Lay), shallow, loll, lily, lull, Lola, oral, orally, earl, early, meal, mealy, mill, Amelia, Himmaleh, Moll, Molly, mile, Milo, mail, male, Malay, mellow, Emily, homily, mule, mallow, chill, chilly, gill (djil), jail, jolly, July, Joel, jole (cheek), jewel, jelly, Julia, swell, swallow, keel, keyhole, kill, quill, Aquila, chyle, coil, quail, quell, Kelly, coal, cull, cool, cowl, gill, gall, guile, gala, Gollah, gull, gully, ghoul (gœl), galley, hilly, holly, hollow, Hawley, hallow, holy, halloo, hālo.

5. Feel, Ophelia, fill, Philo, folly, foil, fuel, fallow, fowl, veal, villa, vial, viol, volley, vail, avail, valley, vowel, avowal, reel, real, really, rill, royal, royally, rail, Raleigh, Riley, Rolla, roll, rule, rally, ruly, unruly, rely, relay, whirl, wearily, (Wer-Lay), warily.

6. Kneel, anneal, Nile, knell, Nelly, nail, inhale, knoll, null, annul, annual, annually, newly, only, kingly, wrongly, squall, squally, skull, scowl, scholia.

7. Shawl, Shiloh, shyly, shell, Shelley, shale, shaly, shoal, shallow, Ashley, social.

8. Elisha, eyelash, willowish, Walsh, yellowish (Yuh-Lay-Shay), lash, lashed, slash, slush, polish, polished, abolish, abolished, relish, relished.

9. Dash, dish, tissue, whitish, toyish, wettish, tush, sottish, sweetish, Swedish.

10. Ash, issue, Shaw, wash (Weh-Ish), showy, hush, sash, bush, abash, push, Jewish, cash, gush, Irish (Ar-Ish), harsh (Ar-Shay), gnash, mush, fish (Ef-Shay), fishy (Ef-Ish).

EXERCISE XIII. C., 159–169.

§ 26. El, and Ar, Hook Signs.

1. (*a*) Plea, hopple, ply, apply, play, apple, plow, blow, blew, blue, idle, idol, huddle, addle, hatchel, claw, cloy, clay, clayey, Chloe, eclat, clue, eagle, glee, higgle, glow, ogle, ugly, glue, gluey, flee, flea, flaw, offal, awfully, fly, flay, flow, flew, flue, evil, hovel, oval.

(*b*) Please, applause, apples, plus, plays, plies, applies, place, bliss, hobbles, blues, blows, blaze, idols, idles, huddles, addles, hatchels, clause, close, claws, class, clues, higgles, glees, gloss, ogles, glaze, glows, glass, glues, fleece, flaws, flies, flays, flows, flues, evils, hovels, pleases, places, blesses, clauses, classes, glazes, fleeces.

(*c*) Pleased, placed, blessed, blazed, blast, classed, closed, glossed, glazed.

(*d*) Plaster, bluster, blister, cloister, cluster, Gloucester (Glos·ter).

(*e*) See C., 161, R. 2.—Only, analyze, unless, annals, enlist, annalist, analyzed, analogy, analogous, analysis.

2. (*a*) Hopper, pry, pray, pro, prow, bray, brew, brow, tree, trio, eater, otter, try, Troy, hater, tray, trow, utter, hatter, outer, draw, dry, dray, aider, odor, adder, drew, cry, acre, ochre, crow, crew, eager, agree, augur, gray, grow, free, offer, fry,

fray, affray, fro, Ophir, overawe, ether, author, throw, threw, hither, wisher, usher, Asher, azure, inner, honor, Homer, hammer, humor (yumor).

_(b)_ Prize, apprize, price, praise, appraise, press, oppress, prose, prŏws, breeze, brace, brass, bruise, brŏws, trice, tries, trace, truss, truce, dross, dress, address, cross, across, cries, craze, cruise, Greece, grease, egress, grace, grŏss, grows, grass, freeze, offers, fries, phrase, authorize, authors, thrice, honors, hammers.

(c) Priest, priced, apprised, praised, pressed, oppressed, braced, bruised, Trist, traced, trust, dressed, addressed, crossed, Christ, crest, crust, crazed, cruised, grist, graced, grazed, frost, authorized, thrust.

(d) Precise, process, praises, breezes, braces, bruises, brazes, tresses, trusses, dresses, addresses, Crœsus, crises, crisis, crazes, greases, grazes, grasses.

(e) Brewster, truster, thruster.

3. _An El-Hook Sign Followed by a Primary Sign._—(a) Plumb, plume, Platea, Plato, Pluto, play-day, player, Pliny, pledge, plush, pluck, plague, blame, bloom, blithe, blush, bluish, bleach, blotch, oblige, block, bleak, black, idler, clip, club, clevy, climb, claim, acclaim, clam, cloudy, cloth, clothe, clear, Clara (Kel-Ray), clutch, clash, clayish, clique, click, clock, cloak, cluck, clack, clog, cling, clung, glib, globe, gleam, gloom, eagle-eyed, glossy, glassy, glare (Gel-Ar), glory.

(_b_) Flip, flap, flabby, effluvia, flame, phlegm, flume, flighty, fluid, fleecy, flywheel (Fel-El), flail, flier, Flora, flower, flowery, flare, fledge, flesh (Fel-Shay), flush, flash, fleshy (Fel-Ish), flake, flock, fluke, flog, flag, fling, flung.

(c) The following words are written in the Reporting Style with Mel, Nel, Rel. See C., 161, R. 2.—Hemlock, unlatch, unlock, unlike, unlucky, relic, relish, relax, relapse, rail-road (Rel-Ray-Dee).

4. _An Ar-Hook Sign Followed by a Primary Sign._—(a) Prop, apropos, probe, prime, pretty, prowess, prosy, April, prowl, prior, prayer, prairie (pru·ri, not perɐ·ri), preach, approach, Prussia, Prague, ·bribe, bravo, brim, Brahma, broom, ebriety, Brady, broth, breath, breathe, breezy, broil, brier, brewer, brewery, brawny, briny, breach, broach, brooch, bridge, abridge, brush, brick, break, broke, brook, brag, bring, trip, trope, troop, tribe, trophy, trim, treaty, triad, Tracy, utterly, trial, trail, truly, truer, triune, trudge, trash, trachea, track, drip, drop, droop, drab, dream, dram, drouth (drouth, not drout), dressy, drowsy, drill, droll, drily, drear, dreary, drawer, drudge, drake, drug, creep, crop, croop, crib, cream, crime, crumb, create, crazy, crawl, cruel, crier (Ker-Ray), crayon, crouch, crush, crash, creek, croak, crook, crag, grip, grope, group, grab, groom, grotto, greedy, growth, grassy, eagerly, growl, gruel, grower (Ger-Ray), grudge, Greek, grog.

(b) Frame, Friday, froth, freely, frail, friar, Phrygia, fresh (Fer-Ish), freak, Africa, frog, throb, thrill, thrall, thrush (Ther-Shay), throng.

5. _A Primary Letter Followed by an El-Hook Sign._—(a) Papal, people, pupil, employ, imply, maple, tipple, dapple, ripple (Ray-Pel), chapel, couple, payable, pebble, Bible, bubble, feeble, foible, fable, amiable, humble, table, audible, double, liable, lable, allowable, rebel, nibble, noble, enable, quibble, cable, gobble, total, tattle, chattel, shuttle, peddle, fiddle, model, tweedle, Mitchell, pickle, buckle, fickle, vehicle, vocal, Michael, meekly, tackle, tickle, thickly, ethical, likely, oracle (Ray-Kel), knuckle, nickel, chuckle, shackle (Shay-Kel), cackle, ankle, uncle, boggle, bugle, legal, illegal (El-Gel), regal, juggle, goggle, giggle, angle, baffle, muffle, lawful, shuffle, bevel, swivel, devil, youthful, cavil, gav'el, deathly, apishly, boyishly, bushel, facial, officially, rashly (Ray-Shel), harshly, initial, uncial, hoggishly.

(b) _Brief Way and an El-hook Sign._—Whipple (Weh-Pel), whiffle, whittle, wheedle, waddle, weekly, waggle.

(c) The following words are written in the Reporting Style with Mel, Nel, Rel: Pommel-ed (see C., 266, R. 8), enamel, animal, camel, penal, panel, final-ly, venal, tunnel, channel, kennel, barrel, barely, gnarl, coral, thoroughly, purely, son-in-law (Sen-Nel), neuralgia (En-Rel-Jay), manlike (Em-Nel-Kay), comely, calmly, sister-in-law (Ses-Ter-Nel), rural, floral, spiral, New Orleans (En-Rel'ens).

6. (a) Pauper, paper, fiber, vapor, ember, imbrue, taper, Tabor, dipper, lep'er, labor, reaper, robber, harbor (Ar-Ber), neighbor, chopper, jobber, shipper, keeper, copper, sweeper (Sway-Per), poetry, powder, betray, tawdry, tutor, editor, daughter, withdraw, ultra, writer (see Comp., 164, R. 2), entry, Andrew, chowder, equator, accouter, gaiter, pitcher, butcher, badger, voucher, voyager, major, teacher, ditcher, dodger, lodger, ledger, richer, Rodger, archer (Ar-Cher), picker, baker, beggar-y, vicar, vigor, vagary, maker, meager, swagger, taker, Tucker, tiger, decree, dicker, degree, dagger, liquor, looker, leaguer, rigor, roguery, knocker, negro, choker, joker, shaker (Shay-Ker), sugar (Shay-Ger), quicker, quackery, cougar (kuu·gar), angry.

(b) Fifer, favor, Humphrey, mover, laugher, loafer, lever, lover, knavery, Hanover, Shaffer (Shay-Fer), shiver, bather, feathery, Jethro, pusher, fisher, fishery, measure, leisure, rasher (Ray-Sher), harsher (Ar-Sher), erasure (Ar-Zher), Cheshire, Palmer, tamer, dimmer, rumor, rhymer, armor (Ar-Mer), enamor, calmer, banner, Abner, minor, tenor, dinner, ulnar, Eleanor.

(c) Weeper (Wuh-Per), whipper, Webber, wager, watcher, witchery, wisher, winner (Weh-Ner).

(d) Wafer (Weh-Ef-Ar), weaver, waver (Weh-Vee-Ar).

7. See C., 169.—Fail, feel, fill, fell, appear, share, aver, converse, averse, term, firm, germ, shirk, pearl, nerve, person, chair, sharp, shark, dark, charm, barbarous, barbarism, marvelous, calomel, collect, calcine, paralyze, engineer, pioneer, fall, follow, form, former (Fer-Mer), moral, George, Georgia, correct, burst, church, occurs, cursory, vulgar, courage, curb, course, recourse, fool, qualify, quality, deter, figure, require, feature, endure, procure, ignore, territory.

EXERCISE XIV. C., 170–173.

§ 27. A Circle or Loop Prefixed to an El, or Ar, Hook Sign.

1. (a) Supply, supple, Sybil, sable, settle, subtle, sidle, saddle, satchel, sickle, sickly, cycle, suckle, civil, civilly.

(b) Possible, possibly, peaceable, passable, feasible, fusible, visibly, disciple, display, disable, adducible, causable, accusable, paschal, physical, vesicle, phthisical, peaceful, passively, unsocial, unsocially.

(c) Plausible, blissful, briskly, traceable, classical, classically, crucible, graceful, taxable, noticeable, explore.

2. (a) Sipper, spry, spray, supper, sapper, Cibber, saber, sober, Cyprus, cypress, suppress, spruce, straw, satyr, stray, strow, setter, strew, suitor, cedar, cider, sadder, stress, sager, seeker, sicker, sucker, succor, sacker, scarce, Se'gar, Sea'ger, Se'cor, sister, Sestri, Sostra'tus (Ses-Ter-Tees).

(b) Prosper, destroy, destroyer, distress, decider, dissuader, outstrip, outstretch, disaster, disastrous, execrable, excrescence (Kay-Skers-Ens), excursive, excursus, subscribe (Sbee-Sker-Bee), prescribe, proscribe, disagree, descry, discourse, tasker, Jasper.

(c) See C., 171, R. 3.—Subscribe (Sbee-Skay-Bee), subscriber, prescribe, proscribe, describe.

3. A Sper-Sign Preceded by Other Signs.—Caspar, gossiper, disappear, dayspring, lisper, rasper, whisper (Whay-Sper), pastry, pasture, posture, bowstring, shoestring, extreme, gastric, extra, mixture, tapestry, texture (teks-tyur), depositor,

orchestra, apostrophe, mouse-trap, overstrew, beseecher, besieger, massacre, masker, hemisphere (Ems-Fer), atmosphere, passover, dishonor, designer, poisoner, prisoner, listener (Els-Ner), signer (Iss-Ner), sooner, saner.

4. (a) Stopper, stupor, stooper, stabber, stater, stutter, stouter, stitcher, stager, stalker, Stocker, stoker, stagger.

(b) *Stee and an El or Ar Hook Sign.*—Stopple, stipple, steeple, staple, stable, stubble, stickle, stifle, stainer, stunner, stoner.

(c) *Ster and an El or Ar Hook Sign.*—Stripling, strigil (stridj·il), strōcal, straddle, straggle, strickle, strōbil, struggle; stripper, strapper, streamer, strainer, stretcher, striker, stroker, strutter, stridor.

5. *A Sper-Sign Followed by a Primary Letter.*—Supreme, superadd, sprall, soprāno, sprig, spring, sprung, suburb, sobriety, strip, stripe, strap, sătrap, Strabo, stream, strata, stroll, stretch, streak, stroke, struck, string, strong, scrape, scribe, scrub, scream, screech, scrawl, secrecy, scratch, scraggy.

6. *Two El-Hook Signs.*—(a) Pliable, Blakely, blackly, glibly, playfully, flyblow, fulfill, fleshly, flashily, bluishly.

(b) *In the Reporting Style*—Unlikely, unluckily, plural, flannel, colonial, calomel.

7. *Two Ar-Hook Signs.*—Proper, portray, prudery, preacher, perjure, perjury, bribery, breaker, broker, bragger, trooper, traitor, treachery, trickery, draper, drapery, drudgery, creeper, creator, croaker, cracker, Gregory, brother, brasier, abrasure, pressure, frippery, framer, overdraw, overthrow, overgrow, trimmer, tremor, treasure, treasury, dreamer, drummer, shrubbery, crusher, crosier, grammar, grazier.

8. *An El-Hook, and an Ar-Hook, Sign.*—Plummer, apple-tree, plethora, blubber, blamer, blotter, bleacher, obliger, blacker, clipper, clapper, clatter, glitter, flavor, flattery, Fletcher, flicker, clamor, glimmer, glazier.

9. *An Ar-Hook, and an El-Hook, Sign.*—Prickly, briefly, frothily, fragile, freshly, freckle, frugal, verbal, overflow, triple, treble, trouble, trifle, trivial, travel, turtle, treacle, trickle, dribble, drivel, draggle, shrivel, cripple, cradle, crackle, grapple, agreeable.

EXERCISE XV. C., 174–180.
§ 28. In, Ler, and Rel, Hooks.

1. (a) Inseparable, inseparably, insuperable, inspire, unsuppressed, insuppressible, ensober, instructor, unstring, unstrung, unscrupulous, inscribe, unscrew, insecure, insecurity, inscroll.

(b) Enslave, unseemly, unsullied, unsurmised, enslaver, unceremonious, unsolicitous, unsolvable, insoluble, unsalable, insular, unswathe, unswayable.

2. The following words may be written in the Reporting Style with the Ler- and Rel- hook signs:—Blair, abler, April, trial, teller, control, Charles, settler, saddler, sabler, clear, ocular, color, collar, clerk, Clark, caloric, jocular, jugular, scholar, secular, haggler, moral, fuller, traveler, trifler, buckler, smuggler, straggler, cobbler, gambler, tippler, tattler, dabbler, corporal, territorial, editorial, clairvoyance, clergy, tolerable, stickler, sideral, sidereal, mackerel, pastoral, liberal, illiberal (El-Brel).

§ 29. Write, according to the directions of § 12, the following paragraphs:

The ,Discontented ,Pendulum.—An ,old clock ,that had ,stood for fifty years in-a farmer's ,kitchen, ,without giving its owner any cause of ,complaint, early one summer's (Sem-Rays) ,morning, ,before the family (f-m-l) was *s*tirring, ,suddenly ,stopped. ,Upon this, the ,dial-,plate (if we may ,credit the fable) ,changed ,countenance with alarm; the ,hands ,made a ,vain ,effort to continue their course; the wheels ,remained ,motionless with surprise; the weights hung speechless (sp-ch-ls) · each member ,felt disposed to lay the blame on-the others. At length the dial ,instituted a formal (fr-m-l) inquiry as to-the cause of-the ,stagnation, when ,hands, wheels, weights, with one voice, ,protested their innocence (ns-ns).

But now a ,faint tick was ,heard below from-the ,pendulum, who thus spoke :— " I confess myself to be-the sole cause of-the stoppage (stp-j), and I-am willing, for-the ,general ,satisfaction, to ,assign my reasons. The truth is, ,that I-am ,tired of ticking." ,Upon hearing this, the ,old clock became so ,enraged ,that it was on-the very ,point of *striking*.

"Lazy wire !" ,exclaimed the dial-,plate, ,holding up its ,hands. "Very ,good," ,replied the ,pendulum, "it is vastly (vs- L) easy for you, Mistress (ms-trs) Dial, who have always, as every body knows, set yourself up above me—it is vastly easy for you, I-say, to accuse other people of laziness (l z ns) ! You, who have had nothing to do all-the days of your life but to stare (stR) people in the face, and to amuse your-self with watching all ,that goes on in-the ,kitchen ! Think, I beseech you, how you would like to be ,shut up for life in this dark closet, and to wag ,backwards and ,for-wards, year ,after year, as I-do."— *To be continued.*

EXERCISE XVI. C., 181–189.

§ 30. Ef, Vee, and En, Hooks.

1. (*a*) Puff, beef, buff, tough, doff, deaf, chief, chafe, chaff, cough, coif, cuff, calf, quaff, Gough (Gof), reef, rife, rough, roof, huff, hoof.

(*b*) Set-off, staff, stiff, stuff, skiff, scoff, serf, surf.

(*c*) Bluff, belief, cliff, clef.

(*d*) Proof, brief, trough, gruff.

(*e*) Pave, dive, dove, achieve, Jove, gyve, cave, cove, Gove, rive, arrive, rave, rove, heave, hive, hove.

(*g*) Stave, stove, serve, swerve, *starve*.

(*h*) Believe, breve, brave, contrive, twelve, trave, derive, drive, drove, delve, cleave, clave, clove, crave, grieve, groove, grove, glove, glave ; strive, strove.

2. (*a*) Pin, pawn, pine, opine, pain, pen, open, pun, pan, happen, oppugn, bean, bane, ebon, bone, bun, ban, boon, tin, ton, tan, tune, town, dean, Eden, din, hidden, dawn, don, dine, iodine, deign, den, Doane, Dan, chin, chain, Jane, June, John, join, Augean, keen, kin, cane, ken, can, con, cone, coon, kine, coin, rain, wren, ran, roan, run, Rhine, hen, Hun, hone, hewn.

(*b*) Spin, spun, span, spoon, spine, Spain, supine, Sabine, stain, stun, stone, seton, Satan, satin, Sidon, sedan, sadden, sudden, sicken, sequin, skein, scan, Syrian.

(*c*) Plain, plan, blain, blown, clean, clan, glean, glen.

(*d*) Apron, prone, prune, brine, brain, bran, brown, drain, drawn, drone, drown, Adrian, train, crane, crone, crown, Akron, acorn, green, grin, grain, grown, groan.

(*e*) *Brief Way and an En-Hook Sign.*—Weapon, waken, wagon, worn, sworn, warn, Warren, whipper-in (Wuh-Pren).

3. (*a*) *The En-Hook on Curves.*—Fin, feign, fen, fan, fun, fawn, fine, Vaughn (Von),vine, woven (Weh-Ven), oven, heaven, haven, van, Avon, Ethan, thin, thane, heathen, assign, sheen, Ossian, shin, ashen, shône, shown, ocean, shun, shine, lean, Lynn, lane, lawn, loan, loon, loin, line, alien, Ellen, Helen, Eolian, Allen, woolen, horn, iron, arraign, Aaron, earn, urn, mean, main, mane, moan, moon, omen, hu-mane, woman, women, yeoman, non, anon, onion, nine, noon, inane, noun, swain (Iss-Wayn), swine, swoon.

(b) Soften, syphon, seven, saline, slain, Solon, sullen, saloon, serene, syren, concern, seaman, Simon, summon, salmon.

(c) Flynn, flown, Flen, Thlen, throne, shrine, Zhern, Nern, Mern, Thern.

4. See C., 1–5.—Puff, puffy; pen, penny; buff, bevy; ebon, ebony; doff, Duffy, defy; Dane, Dana, deny; chaff, chaffy; chin, China; cough, coffee; kin, Kinney; cone, coney; reef, rive, review; huff, huffy; fin, fun, Finney, funny; vine, viny, vein, veiny; assign, assignee; loan, Olney (El-En); rain, rainy; main, many; moan, money; Swain, Sweeney.

5. Puffs, paves, believes, braves, doves, droves, delves, achieves, Jove's, coughs, caves, cloves, Gove's, groves, gloves, arrives, swerves, heaves.

6. (a) Pens, punster, bans, boons, spins, tense, tenses, dens, dense, condense, condenses, condensed, chance, chances, chanced, John's, trance, entrance', entran'ces, entranced', cans, Kansas, canst, cleanse, cleansed, cleanses, instance, instances, instanced, rains, preference (Pref-Rens), preferences, glance, glances, glanced, appearance, appearances, spinster, spinsters, punsters.

(b) See C., 186, R. 1, b.—Ransom, ransack, gainsayed.

7. Fins, vines, veins, thins, thanes, assigns, shines, shuns, lines, loans, lanes, earns, Aaron's, urns, means, moans, moons, nines, nuns, nonce, swains, swoons.

8. *The Ef-Hook in the Middle of Words.*—Paphian, Buffon, buffoon, toughen, typhoon, Typhon, deafen, dauphin, define, divine, divan, Epiphany, Bavaria, befog, bivouac, outfit, outvote, defied, deified, edified, defer, devote, devotee, deviate, devout, divide, devoid, David, devour, reveal, arrival, rival, revel, revere, river, rover, rougher, reverence, equivoke, heaver, hover, paver, puffer, beaver, tougher, diver, Dover, chaffer, Jeffrey, griever, coffer, cover, quaver, diph'thong, diverge, advocacy, divinity, cacophony, defense, divorce, adverse, advance, roofless, spavin, beverage, believer, deliver, cleaver, clover, clever, prover, approver, brevier, bravery, braver, trover, driver, drover, graver, prophet, profit, grievance, behavior, extravagance, soporific.

9. *The En-Hook in the Middle of Words.*—(a) Panic, penury, pinery, punish, banish, tonnage, tenth, eighteenth, Downing, canopy, coinage, candy, Candia, keen-eyed, Canary (Ken-Ray), quinsy, keenly, keeneR, coineR, economy, Canning, cunning, gunneR, gunnery (Gen-Ray), gainsay, rainbow, Renwick, Rhenish (Ren-Shay), runner, runaway, finer, finery, finely, finish, veneer, vainly, heavenly, vainer, vanish, atheneum, thinner, Athenian, heathenish (Then-Shay), Lenox, Leonora, linear, lonely, lonesome, min'ute, humanity, Monday, manhood, moon-eyed, meaneR, mineR (minor, Em-Ner), nunnery.

(b) *An En-Hook Sign and Two Primary Letters.*—Monomania, mantilla, mental, moonbeam, phenomena, phenomenon (Fen-Em-Nen).

(c) Barnwell (Bee-Ren-Lay), benignly, piquancy, pecuniary, potency, paganish, buttonwood (Bee-Ten-Dee), button-hole, turnkey, diurnal, demeanor, occupancy, cabin-boy, vacancy, organic, millennium, malignly, maligner, milliner, millionaire, envenom, vernal.

(d) Plenty, planet, plunge, blanch, brownish, furnish, French, fringe, frenzy, Greenwood (grn-d), pruner, granary (Gren-Ray), plainer, plenary, planner, cleaner, gleaner, greenly, cleanly, plainLy.

(e) Penurious (Pen-Rays), openness, penance, convenience, finance, evenness, fineness, thinness.

(g) Synonym (Snen-Em), Saranac (Iss-Ren-Kay), seminary (Smen-Ray), sponge, Spanish, spinner, staunch, stench, stingy, stanza, suddenly (Sden-El), schooner (Sken-Ar), scanner.

(h) Moonshine (Men-Shen), organism.

10. *A Primary Letter and an En-Hook Sign.*—Pippin, pinion, pennon, pigeon,

pagan, bobbin, baboon, obtain, button, bidden, beacon, begin, born (Bee-Ren), burn, barn, bourne, Auburn, Byron, Bowman, benign, Bunyan, ottoman, outdone, Italy, turn (Tee-Ren), outrun, taken, token, deepen, domain, demon, adorn (Dee-Ren), deacon, cheapen, chicken, Japan, Julian, cabin, coffin, Koran, cannon, Canaan, kitchen, quicken, gammon, ripen (Ray-Pen), rapine, Reuben, orphan, refine, ruffian, roughen, ravine, raven, renown, region, origin, rejoin, regain, foeman, famine, half-moon, foreign (Ef-Ren), felon, violin, Thorne, Assyrian, aspen, Alpine (Lay-Pen), Albion, leaven, Lyman, lemon, illumine (El-Men), learn (Lay-Arn), linen (El-Nen), legion (Lay-Jen), liken, Arabian, Roman, remain, organ, Oregon, Arragon, muffin, million, minion, imagine, machine, New-Haven, uneven, inhuman, Nathan, enjoin, engine.

11. *A Pel, or Per, Sign and an En-Hook Sign.*—Plebeian, platoon, protean, appertain, blacken, broken, Bremen, Britain, trepan, Tribune, triton, drayman, Dryden, dragoon, chairman, German, chlorine (Kel-Ren), clarion, Griffin, flagon, Phrygian, African, overrun, Mormon, Norman.

§ 31. A final En-Es sound, preceded by a curve-sign consonant, is usually represented by Ens instead of the En-hook and Iss, especially when derivative words require the En-stroke; as, offense, Ef-Ens—offensive, Ef-Ens-Vee—offenses, Ef-Enses—convince, con-Vee-Ens — convinced, con-Vee Enst — convinces, con-Vee-Enses. The following paragraph contains nearly all the words written in accordance with this principle.

(*b*) Fence, offense, evince, convince, lance, lense, mince, immense, announce, enhance, .annoyance, denounce, romance, renounce, assurance (Sher Ens), affirmance (fr-m ns), penance (pn ns), finance (fn ns), .allowance (Lay Ens), .alliance, .conveyance, .affluence, pronounce.

REM. The words in the above paragraph which are preceded by a point (.) require the *n* of the final syllable to be represented by a stroke, not only because the derivatives from them require the stroke, but because two concurrent vowels generally demand that the preceding and following consonants should be represented by a stroke. See the Phonographic Orthographer, § 3, R. 2.

EXERCISE XVII.   C., 190–196.
§ 32. THE SHON AND TIV HOOKS.

1. *The Shon-Hook on Straight Signs.*—(*a*) Passion, potion, option, compassion, Bashan, Titian, tuition, commutation, edition, addition, condition, accommodation, caution, auction, occasion, equation, action, connection, concussion, cushion, Goshen, ration, Hessian.

(*b*) Station, citation, situation, constitution (Steh-Teeshon), section, suction.

(*c*) Collision, completion, conclusion, apparition, operation, oppression, Prussian, compression, abrasion, attrition, contrition, accretion, creation, Grecian, aggression.

(*d*) Seclusion, separation, inspiration, consideration, secretion, consecration.

(*e*) Petition, optician, Parisian, potation, apportion, obtusion, aberration, adoption, diction, education, Egyptian, ejection, occupation, caption, quotation, irritation, Artesian, erudition, radiation, reaction, rogation, fiction, affection, variation, vacation, vocation, assertion, hesitation (Zee-Tee'shon), libation, logician, location, election, elocution, legation, allegation (El-Gay'shon), eruption, irruption, erection, irrigation, arrogation, imitation, mutation, mediation, magician, immersion, notation, intuition, inaction, negation.

(*g*) Dec-eption, ob-trusion, ex-hibition, ven-eration, div-ersion, dis-cussion, expression, co-operation, pro-bation, pro-hibition, dir-ection, attr-action, con-str-uction.

2. (*a*) Combative, commutative, dative, talkative, active, connective, sedative, consecutive, constitutive, ablative, operative, creative, susceptive (Ses-Peetiv).

(*b*) Effective, affective, conductive, adjective, vocative, elective, captive, inac-tive, communicative, negative, inchoative, intuitive, imitative, optative, putative, appetative, fugitive, vegetive, comparative (Pee-Raytiv), abortive, tortive, sport-ive, furtive, commemorative.

(*c*) Applicative, attractive, directive, contractive; significative, justificativc, dupli-cative, explicative, suffocative, prov-ocative, recreative, prerogative (pr-r-g*tv*), speculative (sp-kl*tv*), coagulative (k-gl*tv*), preparative (pr-p-r*tv*), lu-crative, co-operative, re-sto-rative, illus-trative, fi-gurative, rec-itative, autho-ri-tative, pre-sen-tative, t-en-tative, stupef-active, p-ūtref-active, r-efr-active, ab-str-active, def-ective, in-eff-ective, in-f-ective, r-efl-ective, in-fl-ective, coll-ective, re-sp-ective, pros-p-ective, per-sp-ective, corr-ective, in-v-ective, affli-ctive, re-stri-ctive, r-ed-uctive, prŏ-d-uctive, ob-str-uctive, de-str-uctive, instr-uctive, con-str-uctive, ex-pletive, dis-cretive, n-utritive, distributive (Deester-Beetiv), prec-eptive, exc-eptive, perc-eptive, dec-eptive, rec-eptive, ER-uptive, corr-uptive, assertive (Es-Raytiv), div-er*tive*, ex-ecutive, ven-erative, re-sp-ective.

3. *The Shon-Hook on Curves.*—(*a*) Fashion, Phocion, fusion, effusion, affusion, Veeshon, vision, evasion, ovation, confession, confusion, Ith'shon, THeeshon, Es'shon, Zee'shon, Ish'shon, Thee'shon, Lay'shon, elision, Elysian, elation, lotion, illusion, elusion, allusion, halcyon, erasion, oration, erosion, mission, emission, omission, motion, emotion, nation, notion, unction, Way'shon, Yay'shon.

(*b*) Suffusion, solution, consolation, consummation, sanation, sanction, Sway'-shon, con*st*ellation.

(*c*) Afflation, fruition, freshen, version, aversion, conversion, valuation (unvocal-ized Velshon through the line; see the Compendium, § 40, R. 2), convulsion, Thra-cian, cineration (Sner'shon).

(*d*) Palliation (Pee-Lay'shon), pollution, pension, abolition, ebullition, tension, attention, Domitian, admission, dilation, adulation, dilution, delusion, donation, gentian, junction (Jay-Ingshon), coalition, ignition, affiliation, Phœnician, func-tion (Ef-Ing'shon), volition, violation, evolution, Venetian, vitiation (Vee-Shay'-shon), ascension, alienation (Lay-En'shon), monition, munition, mention, mansion, infusion, invasion, animation, inhaLation, inanition, nunnation, initiation (En-Ish'shon).

(*e*) Population, abomination, demolition, domination, dimension, nomination, invention, accumulation, machination, Rumination, iLLumination.

4. Passions, editions, actions, rations, Hessians, stations, sections, collisions, operations, aggressions, considerations, operatives, adjectives, captives, fugitives, prerogatives, restoratives, expletives, perceptives, executives, fashions, visions, illu-sions, orations, emotions, nations, solutions, con*st*ellations, conversions, attentions, donations, functions, revisions.

5. See C., 195.—Optional, passionary, Passion-week (Peeshon-Kay), passionate (Peeshon-Tee), additional, conditional, occasional, auctioneer, rational, missionary, visionary, attractiveness, active-ness, activ-ity, c-aptiv-ity, coh-secutive-ness, ta-lka-tiveness, f-urtive-ly, com-p-arativc-ly.

6. See C., 191, R. 2.—Ocean, ashen, commission, session, scission, concession, attenuation, diminution, admonition.

EXERCISE XVIII. C., 197–203.

§ 33. THE SMALL HOOK FOR SHON.

1. Opposition, possession, position, apposition, abscission, obsession, decision, dissuasion, excision, acquisition, accession, accusation, causation, cassation, recision, recession, physician, secession, cessation, association, incision, compensation, condensation, succession, supposition, precision, procession, persuasion, conversation, authorization, transition.

2. Division, devotion, diffusion, abbreviation, aggravation, profession, derivation.

3. See C., 197, R. 2.—Division, devotion, diffusion, abbreviation, aggravation, profession, derivation.

4. (*a*) Possessions, decisions, acquisitions, accusations, physicians, associations, incisions, persuasions, conversations, successions.

(*b*) Transitional, devotional, professional, conversational.

5. In accordance with the principle of the Compendium, 197, R. 4, write the following words:—Taxation, specification, transaction, prosecution, justification, solicitation, devastation, classification.

§ 34. Write, in accordance with the directions of § 12, the following:

A TEMPERANCE ADDRESS.

BY J. N. HUME, M.D.

Ye ⸝friends of ⸝moderation,
Who think a r-efor-mation,
Or moral r-eno-vation,
Would ⸝benefit our nation;
Who deem ⸝intoxication,
With all its dissipation,
In every rank and station,
A cause of degradation,
Of which your observation
Gives ⸝ample demonstration;
Who see-the ruination,
Distrust and desolation,
The open violation
Of moral obligation,
The ⸝wretched habitation,
⸝Without accommodation,
O any regulation,
For common susten-tation,
A scene of deprivation
⸝Unequaled in creation;
The ⸝frequent desecration
Of Sabbath ordination;
The crime and depredation,
Defying legislation;
The awful prof-anation
Of common conversation;
The mental aberration,
The dire infatuation,
With every sad gradation
Of maniac desperation;—

Ye who with consternation
⸝Behold this devastation,
And utter con-d-em-nation
Of all inebriation,
Why sanction its duration,
Or show disapprobation
Of any combination
For its extermination?
We deem a declaration
⸝That offers no temptation
By any palliation
Of this abomination,
The only sure foundation;
And ⸝under this persuasion
⸝Hold no communication
With noxious emanation
Of brewer's fer-mentation,
Or poisonous preparation
Of ⸝spirits' distillation,
Nor any vain libation
Producing stimulation.
To this determination
We call consideration,
And ⸝without hesitation
⸝Invite co-operation,
⸝Not ⸝doubting imitation
Will raise your ⸝estimation,
And by continuation
⸝Afford you consolation;
For in ⸝participation

2

With this association,
You may by ⸝meditation
Insure the preservation
Of-a future g-eneration
From all con-t-amination.

And-may each ⸝indication
Of such regeneration
Be the theme of exultation
Till its final consummation.

EXERCISE XIX.   C., 204–206.
§ 35. The Widened Em.

1. Imp, hemp, hump, humpy, samp, *stamp*, pomp, Pompey, Pompeii (see C., 134), pump, bump, dump, dumpy, damp, champ, jump, camp, vamp, mump, Limp, Lump, Lamp, Romp, Ramp, shampoo, swamp, swampy, impose, impious, imposed, im′post, imposition, impostor, impatience, impiety, impute, impede, impale, impel, ample, amply, empire, umpire, impair, empower, impure, impeach, impish, imperi-ous, imperative, simple, sample, ensample, example, exemplify, primp, tramp, trump, crimp, cramp, plump, clamp, clump.

2. Emboss, embosses, imbue, imbues, Sambo; ambush, ambitious, ambiguous, imbibe, embalm, embody, somebody, steamboat, embellish, embassy, embezzle, embassador, embarrass, embark, embargo, embank, ambition, humbug.

3. See C., 204, R. 4.—Exemption, assumption, co-emption, presumption, pre-emption, empty, temptation, pumpkin, Sampson, Simpson.

§ 36. Write, in accordance with the directions of § 12, the following paragraphs:

The Discontented Pendulum—Continued from § 29.—" As to ⸝that," said the dial, " is there ⸝not a window in your house, on purpose (Pee-Ray-Pees) for you to look through ?"   " For all ⸝that," ⸝resumed the ⸝pendulum, " it-is very dark here; and, although ('all'-Thee) there-is-a window, I dare ⸝not *stop*, even for-an ⸝instant, to look out at it. Besides, I-am really ⸝tired of my way of life; and-if you wish, I'll tell you how I took this disgust at my ⸝employment. I ⸝happened this morning to be ⸝calculating how many times I should-have to tick in-the course of only the next twenty-four hours; perhaps (pr-ps) some of you above there can give me the ⸝exact sum."

The minute-⸝hand, being *quick* at figures, ⸝presently ⸝replied, " Eighty-six ⸝thou-sand four ⸝hundred [86,400] times." " ⸝Exactly so," ⸝replied the ⸝pendulum. " Well, I appeal to you all, if the very ⸝thought of this was ⸝not enough to fatigue one; and-when I began to ⸝multiply the strokes of one day by those of months and years, really it-is no ⸝wonder if I ⸝felt ⸝discouraged at-the ⸝prospect; so, ⸝after a ⸝great deal of reasoning and hesitation, ⸝thought I to myself, I'll stop." ⸝

The dial ⸝could scarcely (Skers-Lay) keep its ⸝countenance during this harangue (h-r-ng); but resuming its gravity (gr-v-t), thus ⸝replied : " Dear Mr ⸝Pendulum, I-am really ⸝astonished ⸝that such-a useful, industrious person as yourself should-have been overcome (Ver¹-Kay) by this sudden action. It-is true, you have done a ⸝great deal of work in your time; so have we all, and are likely to do; which although it may fatigue us to *think* of, the question (Kays-Ten) is, ⸝whether it will fatigue us to *do*. Would you now do me the favor to give ⸝about half a-dozen strokes to ⸝illustrate my ⸝argument ?"

The ⸝pendulum ⸝complied, and ⸝ticked six times at its usual pace. " Now," ⸝re-sumed the dial, " may I be allowed to inquire if ⸝that exertion (ks-rshn) was at all fatiguing or disagreeable to you?" " ⸝Not in-the least," ⸝replied the ⸝pendulum, " it-is ⸝not of six strokes ⸝that I complain, nor of sixty, but-of *millions*." " Very ⸝good," ⸝replied the dial; " but recollect (r-kl-k-t) ⸝that though you may *think* of-a million strokes in-an ,instant, you are ,required to ,*execute* but one; and ,that, however often·you may here,after have to *s*wing, a ,moment will always (l-w*s*) be given you to swing in." ",That consideration *s*taggers me, I confess," said-the ,pendulum. "Then I-hope," ,resumed the dial-,plate, "we shall all ,immediately ,return to our duty; for-the ,maids will lie in ,bed if we ,stand idling thus."

Upon this the weights, who had never been accused of ,*light* ,conduct, ,used all their influence in urging him to proceed; when, as with one ,consent, the wheels began to turn, the ,hands began to move, the ,pendulum began to swing, and to its ,credit, ,ticked as ,loud as ever; while a red beam of-the rising sun which ,streamed through-a hole in-the kitchen, shining full upon-the dial-,plate, it ,brightened up, as if nothing had been-the ,matter.

When-the farmer came down to breakfast ,that morning, upon looking at-the clock, he ,declared ,that his watch had ,gained half-an hour in the ,night.

Moral.—A ,celebrated ,modern writer says, "Take care of-the *minutes*, and-the *hours* will take care of themselves." This-is-an ad-mi-ra-ble remark, and ,might be very seasonably (ssn-bl) ,recollected when we begin to be "weary in well-doing," from-the ,thought of-having much to do. The ,present ,moment is all we have to do with, in any sense; the past is irrecoverable (R-kv-r-bl), the future is ,uncertain; nor is it fair to bur-den one ,moment with-the weight of-the next. ,Sufficient unto-the ,moment is-the trouble thereof. If we had to walk a ,hundred miles, we should still have to step but one step at a time, and this pro*cess* continued would in-falli-bly bring us to our jour-ney's ,end. Fatigue generally begins, and-is always increased by ,calculating in-a minute the exertion of hours.

Thus, in looking ,forward to future life, ,let us recollect ,that we have ,not to *sus*-tain all its toil, to endure (n-dr) all its sufferings (sf-r-ngs), or ,encounter all its crosses at once. One ,moment comes laden with its own ,*little* burdens, then flies, and-is ,succeeded by ,another no heavier than-the last:—if *one* ,could be borne, so can ,another and ,another.

It seems easier to do right to-morrow than to-day, merely because we ,forget ,that when to-morrow comes, *then* will be *now.* Thus life passes with many, in resolutions for-the future, which-the ,present never fulfills. It-is ,not thus with those who, "*by ,patient conti-n-uance in well-doing,* seek for glory, honor, and ,immor-tality." Day by day, minute by minute, they ,execute the ,appointed task, to which-the requisite measure of time and strength is ,proportioned; and thus, having ,worked while it was ,called day, they at Length rest from their labors, and-their works "follow them." ,Let us then, "whatever our ,hands ,find to do, do it with all our ,might, recollecting ,that *now* is-the proper and ,accepted time."—JANE TAYLOR.

EXERCISE XX. C., 207–211.

§ 37. LENGTHENED CURVES.

1. (*a*) Anchor, hanker, sinker, thinker, winker, rancor, lanker, banker, drinker, clinker, anchorage, handkerchief.

(*b*) Anger, younger, longer, linger, stronger, languor, monger.

2. (*a*) Fitter, fetter, fatter, fighter, voter, theater, Astor, Easter, Esther, oyster, shat-ter, shutter, shooter, litter, letter, latter, later, loiter, lighter, altar, halter, hurter, meter, mater, mutter, miter, enter, hunter, niter, neuter, water, highwater, whiter, waiter, wetter, softer, sifter, psalter, slaughter, Walter, smatter, smiter, center, saunter, winter, neutral, central, concentration, alteration, flatter, filter, falter, fritter, shorter, eccentric, nostrils, nostrum, rostrum, intrinsic, swelter, subaltern, imbitter.

(*b*) Feeder, fodder, shudder, leader, louder, elder, alder, older, holder, ladder, ardor, harder, order, Reeder, madder, wider, wilder, sunder, wonder, molder, smoulder, wilderness, bewilder, modern, moderation, moderate, federal, thunder, tender, slender, slander, render.

(*c*) Luther, lather, Arthur, anther, anthral, phil-anthr-opy, anthracite.

(*d*) Feather, father, thither, the-other, leather, lather, mother, Mather, smoother, neither, wither, weather.

3. See C., 208, 2, *b*.—Angry, hungry, ultra, sultry, feathery, watery, sundry, laundry, sentry, leathery.

4. See C., 211. Let *thr* equal 'there, their, they are.'—If thr, for thr, few thr, have thr, view thr, from thr, over thr, value thr, however thr, think thr, thank thr, they thr, though thr, either thr, they are thr, there thr, other thr, they will thr, see thr, so thr, was thr, use thr, wish thr, shall thr, usually thr, sure-ly thr, will thr, while thr, well thr, hear thr, here thr, may thr, am thr, we may thr, remark thr, more thr, in thr, know thr, when thr, one thr, near thr, nor thr, why thr, way thr, whenever thr, wherever thr, from their own, in their own, when their own, over their own. \

§ 88. Write, according to the directions of § 12, the following paragraphs.

SAYINGS OF CONFUCIUS.

We can ₍not observe the necessary rules of life if there be ₍wanting these three virtues: ₍Wisdom, which makes us discern ₍good from evil; universal love, which makes us love all men who are virtuous; and ₍that resolution which makes us ₍constantly persevere in-the adherence to ₍good, and-in-the aversion to evil. But lest some fearful persons, ₍not well versed in morality, should imagine ₍that it-is impossible for them to acquire these three virtues, they should know ₍that there-is no person incapable of acquiring them; that the impo-tence of man is ₍voluntary. However dull and inexperienced a man may be, if he desire to learn, and grow ₍not weary in-the study of virtue, he is ₍not very far from ₍wisdom. If-a man, although full of ₍self-love, endeavor to per-for-m ₍good actions, ₍behold him already very near ₍that universal love which urges him to do ₍good to all. If-a man feel a ₍secret shame when he hears impure and-unchaste discourses, if he can ₍not forbear blushing thereat, he is ₍not far from ₍that resolution of ₍spirit which makes him ₍constantly seek ₍after ₍good, and have an aversion for evil.

He who in-his studies wholly applies himself to labor and exercise, and neglects (n-gl-k-ts) ₍meditation, loses his time; and he who only applies himself to ₍meditation, and neglects ₍experimental exercise, does only wander and lose himself. The first can never know anything ₍exactly; his knowledge will always be ₍intermixed with ₍doubts and obscurities; and-the last will only p-ur-sue shadows (Shay-Dees); his knowledge will never be ₍certain and solid. Labor, but ₍slight ₍not ₍meditation. ₍Meditate, but ₍slight ₍not labor.

Riches and honors are ₍good. The desire to possess them is ₍natural to all men; but if these agree ₍not with virtue, the wise man ought to contemn, and generously to renounce them. On the contrary, poverty and ignominy (Gen-Em-En) are evils; man ₍naturally ₍avoids them. If these evils attack the wise man, it-is right ₍that he should rid himself of them, but ₍not by-a crime.

Wouldst thou learn to die well? learn first to live well. Acknowledge thy ₍benefits by the ₍return of other ₍benefits, but never revenge injuries.

Labor to purify thy ₍thoughts; if thy ₍thoughts are ₍not ill, neither will thy actions be so.

The ₍great ₍secret to acquire true knowledge is to ₍cultivate and polish the reason, and to ₍get a knowledge of things rather than ₍words, by unceasing (Enses-Ing) per-seve-rance.

EXERCISE XXI. C., 212–224.

§ 39. The Halving Principle.

1. *T Added.*—Peat, pit, pate, pet, pat, apt, aped, pot, pout, beat, bit, bate, bait, bet, bat, habit, bought, boat, Bute, boot, tat, taught, tote, tut, toot, tight, date, debt, dot, dote, doubt, doit, cheat, chit, etched, chat, chit-chat, Choate, jet, jut, jot, kit, eked, quit, coit, kite, caught, act, ached, coat, cut, cute, quote, got, gate, get, goat, gout, feet, fit, fought, oft, fight, fate, fat, aft, foot, vat, vote, east, iced, highest, out, shot, shout, shoot, shut.

2. *D Added.*—Pawed, pod, pied, paid, pad, bead, bid, bade, bed, bad, bide, buoyed, bayed, bode, bud, bowed, Todd, tweed, tide, toyed, towed, did, deed, died, dead, chid, chawed, chide, chewed, jawed, joyed, jade, aged, edged, Jude, kid, quid, quod, Cade, code, cud, cooed, goad, gad, feed, fade, fed, food, feud, vied, avoid, void, vowed, viewed, thawed, eased, oozed, shod, shied, shade, shed, showed, shad, hoed, hied.

3. *T Added to Hook-Signs.*—(a) Wilt, welt, wart, Wirt, went, wont.

(b) Plot, plight, plate, plat, bleat, blot, built, blight, bloat, delight, cleet, clot, guilt, gloat, glut, fleet, flit, flight, fault, felt, flat, flute, flout, athlete.

(c) Operate, prate, Pratt, brought, bright, brat, brute, treat, trite, trait, tret, trout, adroit, drought, Crete, concrete, court, greet, grit, girt, fraught, fright, affright, freight, fret, effort, fruit, overt, threat, throat, shirt.

(d) Puffed, abaft, tuft, doffed, deft, chafed, chaffed, coughed, cuffed, quaffed, gift, reft, raft, heft, hoofed, huffed, bluffed, cleft, profit, prophet (¹), drift, draught, craft, graft.

(e) Pint, point, appoint, paint, pent, pant, bent, tint, taint, tent, content, dint, dent, daunt, chant, jaunt, Kent, cant, rent, rant, faint, fount, font, vent, vaunt, assent, sha'n't, lent, lint, arrant, mint, meant, mount, amount, anoint, warrant, pliant, plaint, plant, blent, blunt, flint, flaunt, print, brunt, Brant, Trent, grunt, grant, front, affront; patient, quotient, ancient, transient (Ter'shont).

(g) Split, sprite, separate, sprout, sprat, street, straight, strut, secrete, consecrate, skirt, spent, stuffed, constant, constituent (con-Steh-Tent¹), consistent (con-Ses-Tent), consequent, scoffed, silent, slant, cement, consonant, sonant, supplant, suppliant.

4. *D Added to Hook-Signs.*—(a) Warred, ward, weird, wired, wield, wild, walled, wailed, weld, willed, wind, wind, waned, wend, wand, wound.

(b) Plead, applaud, plod, plied, applied, played, plaid, ploughed, bleed, build, hobbled, blade, bled, bold, blood, idled, addled, huddled, hatcheled, child, clawed, clod, Clyde, clad, cloud, clewed, higgled, glade, glowed, ogled, glad, haggled, glued, gold, filled, field, followed, flawed, failed, flayed, fled, flowed, flood, yield.

(c) Appeared, prayed, preyed, prude, breed, broad, abroad, bride, braid, bred, brad, bird, brood, brewed, treed, trod, tried, trade, tread, uttered, hatred, dried, deride, dread, cheered, creed, cried, crowed, acrid, occurred, accrued, crowd, crude, agreed, grade, guard, haggard, fraud, freed, offered, afraid, averred, thread, third, shred, ushered, shroud, shrewd, shared, assured, hammered, humored, honored.

(d) Paved, dived, achieved, gyved, caved, arrived, raved, heaved, hived, believed, beloved, approved, proved, braved, delved, derived, contrived, cleaved, gloved, grieved, grooved, craved, staved.

(e) Pinned, pawned, pond, pined, pained, penned, append, opened, happened, pound, compound, oppugned, bond, bind, combined, bend, band, bound, abound, tinned, tined, heightened, attained, tend, attend, toned, atoned, tanned, tuned.

⁽¹⁾ *Prophet* and *profit* may be written by the advanced writer with Preft instead of Preft-Tee, the form given in a preceding section.

attuned, dinned, dawned, donned, dined, deigned, dunned, chained, joined, conned, coined, gained, rind, rained, rend, round, honed, fiend, fawned, fond, find, confined, feigned, fend, offend, fund, fanned, found, confound, convened, vend, thinned, assigned, ascend, shunned, commissioned, leaned, Lind, lined, island, highland, lend, loaned, land, horned, ironed, arraigned, errand, earned, around, mend, amend, moaned, manned, mound, wound (to hurt), impugned, impend, planned, pruned, blonde, blind, blend, brained, brand, trained, drained, drowned, cleaned, crowned, gleaned, gland, grinned, grind, groaned, grand, ground, aground, friend, frowned, throned, warned.

(*g*) Passioned, conditioned, cautioned, occasioned, cushioned, fashioned, motioned.

(*h*) Supplied, sabled, sidled, saddled, sickled, seclude, spread, sabred, sobered stride, strayed, strode, strewed, sodered, sacred, succored, secured, spend, spanned, stand, saddened, sickened, scanned, second, concerned, summoned, swooned, sprained, strained, screened, suspend, sustained, sanctioned, stationed.

5. *T Added to Light, and D to Heavy, Signs.*—(*a*) Lit, lid, leet, lead, light, lied, Lloyd, oiled, hilt, hilled, heeled, lot, laud, halt, hauled, late, laid, lade, Let, led, hailed, held, load, Holt, hold, old, hulled, lad, lute, lewd, jon_t, loud, howled, eared, hurt, erred, art, heart, hard, hired, aired, meat, mete, mead, mit, mid, amid, mite, mate, maid, aimed, hemmed, mote, mode, mud, hummed, mat, mad, moot, mood, mute, mewed, neat, need, knit, hint, naught, nod, gnawed, night, hind, net, end, neighed, note, node, hunt, aunt, ant, gnat, haunt, hand, knout, hound.

(*b*) Slight, slide, styled, sold, concealed, sort, seared, sword, soared, smite, seemed, smote, consumed, saint, send, sand, sound, consent.

(*c*) See C., 213, R. 4.—Muzzled, embezzled, whistled.

6. *Half-Lengths Followed by Iss.*—(*a*) Peats, pits, pates, pets, beads, bids, buds, deeds, cheats, chats, Jude's, kites, quits, acts, goads, fights, fits, fates, shuts, lights, halts, lutes, leads, holds, loads, hurts, meets, maids, nights, notes, needs, ends.

(*b*) Spites, spouts, sects, sifts, slights, slides, swords, smites, cents, saints, sends.

(*c*) Plots, plods, bleeds, blots, clods, clouds, glades, fleets, floods, prates, brides, brutes, treats, trades, dreads, creeds, grades, efforts.

(*d*) Splits, sprites, streets, strides, secludes, secrets.

(*e*) Points, paints, bends, tints, attends, dents, chintz, chaunts, jaunts, counts, rends, rents, finds, vends, ascends, lends, errands, mounts, anoints.

(*g*) Complaints, prints, blends, brands, grinds, grants, glands, warrants, friends, flints.

(*h*) Spends, stands, students, seconds, slants, cements, consonants, sonants.

(*i*) Gifts, tufts, hafts, rifts, rafts.

7. *Half-Lengths Preceded by a Full-Length.*—Appetite, pitched, paged, packed, epithet, pushed, upshot, pelt, polite, appealed, uphold, compelled, part, compared, pumped, bodied, budged, baked, begged, befit, obviate, bethought, bathed, biased, abashed, bullet, ballot, behold, beard, bard, beamed, tipped, outbid, hotbed, touched, attached, ticket, talked, toothed, tithed, tilt, toiled, tart, tarred, outward (Tee-Ard), tempt, dipped, debate, ditched, adequate, conduct dashed (Dee-Shayt), adult, delayed, dulled, dar_t, adored, condemned, chipped, checked, chilled, chimed, Egypt, jobbed, eject, jogged, jilt, jeweled, jarred, gemmed, jumped, kept, occupied, caged, cashed, acquiesced, killed, camped, aconite, gapped, gushed, gummed, fidget, officiate, fort, comfort, fumed, vapid, vouched, vivid, violate, availed, avert, convert, vomit, vamped, thatched, theft, ice-boat, associate, isolate, assailed, assort, assumed, shipped, shocked, shaft, sheared, ashamed, leaped, alleged, Lagged, lift, loved, luLLed, limit, alienate (Lay-Net), repeat, robbed, rigid, requite, ragged, refute, rushed, relate, raiLed, Remit, oRbit, aRmed, matched,

mocked, moved, method, emaciate, malt, mild, melt, mailed, merit, mart, Mahomet, maimed, nipped, notched, hinged, unfit, invade, initiate, knelt, nailed, inurea, named, winked.

8. *Half-Lengths Followed by Full-Lengths.*—Potato, pottage, optic, pótash, aptly, epit'ome, beautify, badly, habitual, bitter, better, bottom, detail, deadly, detach, dotage, detection, deduction, agitate, kettle. cattle, cotton, cottage, Godhead, graduate, graduation (Gred-Shen), fatal, avidity, esteem, history, wisdom (Zed[1]-Em), little, lately, lottery, retail, heartily, written (Ret[1]-En), retain (Ret[2]-En), writing (Ret[1]-Ing), Redeem, hardly, reader (Ard[1]-Ar; Arder in an advanced style), notify, entity, antique, indict, needle, intimation, metal, modify, medium, madam, midway, meditation.

9. *Two Half-Lengths Preceded by a Full-Length.*—Capitulate, candidate (Kend-Det in an advanced style), fortified, fortnight, fortunate, ascertained, legitimate mortified([1]), ascendant (Es-Nent in the Reporting Style), left-hand, rectified, rectitude, inaptitude, infatuated, unindebted, multitude.

10. *Two Half-Lengths.*—Abdicate, abduct, beautified, obdurate, detached, detect, deduct, agitated, actuated, cutlet, affidavit, foothold, evident, estimate, esteemed, eastward (Est-Ard), astound, ultimate, ill-timed, latitude, Retaliate, Retailed, right-hand, redeemed, hardened,· retained, redound, modified, meditate, mitigate, midnight, maddened, sentiment, handmaid, indicted, indebted, undoubted, handled, windward (Wend-Werd[1]), intact, indent, intend, indicate, induct, untold, intimate, entailed, intent, protect, tradewind, chartered, cultivate, curtailed, curtained, gratified, gratitude, graduated, flattened, frightened, verdict, threatened, superintend (Sprent-Ned), inordinate.

11. See C., 213, R. 1.—Lard, lured, allured, lowered, lowered, alert, feared, fared, conferred, suffered, ford, afford, fired, veered, card, cord, curd, cured, geared, gored.

12. See C., 218.—(a) Decded, dated, doubted, situated, unedited, undated, antedated, imitated, meditated, freighted, defrauded, dreaded, instituted, radiated, awaited, escheat, emphatic, methodic, critic, athletic.

(b) See C., 218, R.—Thinnest, finest, vainest, meanest, leanest, keenest, fashionist, visionist, communionist, factionist, elocutionist, canonist.

13. See C., 220, b.—(a) Pity, body, tattoo, duty, Chitty, equity, Cato, gayety, veto, into, notice, window.

(b) Unite, avowed, abed, edit, acute.

(c) Hallowed, allied, alloyed, allude, elude, solid, sallied, rallied, relied, married, borrowed, buried, tarried, torrid, narrowed, moneyed, monad, renewed, annoyed, winnowed, accompanied.

(d) Quiet, poet, Biot, Jewett, naiad.

(e) Write, right, reed, rid, red, réad, wrought, wrote, road, rode, rood, rude, root.

(g) Peeped, popped, piped, judged, kicked, quaked, cooked, gagged, roared, reared, effect, affect, fact, fagot, fagged, evict, convict, vacate, evoked, locate, liquid, propped, bribed, correct, collect, aggregate, afflict, slacked, navigate (Nef-Get in the Reporting Style).

14. *Hay and a Half-Length.*-See C., 149, 5, R. 2.—Heaped, hopped, hoped, hooped, whooped, heated, heeded, hated, headed, hooted, hitched, hatched, hedged hawked, hooked, hacked([2]).

---

(1) The advanced writer of the Corresponding Style and the reporter may write *mortify* and its derivatives thus : Mortify, Mert-Ef—mortified, Mert-Fed—mortification, Mert-Efshon.

(2) In the Reporting Style, it will be better to write this class of words without Hay whenever its use would prevent writing a desirable phrase-sign, as in writing ' it has been hoped,' Tees-Ben-Pet—' has been heaped,' Iss-Ben-Pet.

14. See C., 212, R. 6.—Part, parted; beard, bearded; dart, darted; start, started; melt, melted; mold, molded; rent, rented; land, landed; slant, slanted; paint, painted; bound, bounded; print, printed; brand, branded; plant, planted: blend, blended; treat, treated; dread, dreaded; trade, traded; indicate, indicated; anticipate, anticipated; note, noted; need, needed; mate, mated; locate, located; effect, effected; affect, affected; navigate, navigated; solicit, solicited; elicit, elicited.

§ 40. Write, according to the directions of § 12, the following paragraphs:

ECONOMY OF TIME AND SELF-IMPROVEMENT.

There may be economy of time as well as in spending of money. Time, in fact, is money, or money's worth. Few reflect deeply (d-pl) on this truth. Young persons in particular throw away a vast deal of leisure time in-a way often worse than useless. Much they spend in silly gossip with acquaintances, much in frivolous amusements, much in perfect vacancy of thought. In many country towns, a great amount of time is spent in lounging at doorways or in-the street. If all this idle time, exclusive of what should be properly devoted to open-air exercise, were spent in-the acquisition of some kind of useful knowledge, what-a difference there would be in-the lot of some young persons.

We say to-the young, devote your leisure hours to some useful purpose. And what are your leisure hours? Spare hours in the winter evenings after-the labors of-the day are over, and-also hours in-the morning, particularly during summer. Rising at an early hour—for instance, at 4 or 5 o'clock—may be made-the means of self-culture [see C., 228, 14] to-a very considerable extent. Science or history may be studied; languages may be learned. Early rising is perhaps considered by many to be-a very vulgar practice. Those who say so have perused the biographies of great men with little attention. It is indisputable (nds-pt-bl) that few ever lived to-a great age, and fewer still ever became distinguished, who were not in the habit of early rising. You rise late, and of course get about your business at-a late hour, and-every thing goes wrong all day. Franklin says that "Who rises late, must trot all day, and-not overtake his business at night." Dean Swift avers "that he never knew a-man come to greatness and eminence (Men-Ens) who lay in bed of-a morning." We believe that with other degenerations of our days, history will prove that late rising is-a very prominent (pr-mn-nt) one. There seems to be now a tend-en-cy to turn day into night—to breakfast late, dine late, and go to bed late, and consequently (con-sknt[1]-l) to rise late. All this is most pernicious both to health and morals. To a certain extent, people must do as others do; nevertheless, every one is less or more able to act with something like ind-epend-ence of principle; the young—those who-have every-thing (vr²-n$_z$) to learn—can at least act upon a plan, rising at-an early hour.

In order to arise early, we would recommend an early hour for retiring. There are many other reasons for this; neither your eyes nor your health are so likely to be destroyed. Nature seems to-have so fitted things that we ought to rest in-the early part of-the night. A professor used to tell his pupils that "one hour of sleep before midnight is worth more than two hours after that time." Let it be a rule with you, and-if possible adhered to, that you be at home, and-have your light extinguished by ten o'clock in the evening. You may then rise at-5, and-have seven hours to sleep, which-is about what nature requires. It may be most confidently affirmed that he who from-his youth is in-the habit of rising early, will be much more likely to live to old age, more likely to be-a distinguished and useful man, and-more likely to pass a-life that-is peaceful and pleasant. Read-the life of Franklin, and see what he accomplished, both as respects economizing of time, and-the culti-vation of-his own capacious mind. In connection with self-improvement, let us say a-word on-the duty of professional diligence. It-is-a fact that you can not be too well made aware of, that-a man may distinguish himself, or at least attain great,re-spectability in any profession which-is really honorable and socially useful. What-ever you do,'learn to do it well. Do not be discouraged by difficulties, nor vex yourselves with what may be the final results of your efforts. Just go on quietly and diligently, seizing hold of every occasion for improvement, and acquire habits of industry, which will form your character, and stick to you through life. The likelihood is, that by this simple but persevering course—a course unmarked by any great effort—you will pass the idle, the dissipated, and-the timorous, realizing those rewards which usually wait on well-directed,enterprise.—*Chambers' Miscellany*— *A Present to an Apprentice.*

EXERCISE XXII. C., 225–230.

§ 41. PREFIXES.

1: (*a*) Accommodation, accompany, accomplish.

(*b*) Combat, combative, comfort, comm-and, comm-end, comm-ingle, comm-ence, comm-ission, comm-unicate, comm-ute, com-pare, compassion, compute; conceit, conceRn, conciliate (con-slt), conclusion, confuse, conn-ection, conn-ive ; cognate.

(*c*) Circumference, circumlocution, circumstance, circumscribe, circumvention, circumflex, circumjacent.

(*d*) Contravene, contraband, contradict, contradistinction; controvert, contro-versy; counterfeit, countersign, countermand, countermine, countercheck.

(*e*) Decompose, discomfort, discommode, discontent, discontinue, disconn-ect, disconsolate.

(*g*) Forefather, fore-finger, fore-foot, foreseen, forestall.

(*h*) Incognito ; incommode, incomparable, incompatible, incompressible, incomplete, inconstant, inconclusive.

(*i*) Interpose, interr-upt, interr-ogate, intromission, introduce, interchange.

(*j*) Irreconcilable, irreconciliation.

(*k*) Magnanimous, magnify, magnitude.

(*l*) Miscomputation, miscompute, misconduct, misconstrue.

(*m*) Nonconducting, non$_c$onformis$_t$ (noncon-Fer-Emst), noncompliance (-Plens), noncomm-ittal.

(*n*) Recognize, reconcile, reconciliation, reconn-oiter; recompense, recombine, recomm-end, recomm-it, recomm-ence.

(*o*) Self-respect, self-evident, selfish, self-accused, self-knowledge, self-improve-ment.

(*p*) Uncondemned, unconquerable, unconscious ; uncompressed, uncomm-issioned.

(*q*) Unrecognized, unreconciled, unrecompensed.

2. See C., 228, R. 1-16.—Incumbent, recumbent, compass, conquer, reconquer, magnĕ tic, magnĕ-sia, uncircumscribed, unselfish, undecomposed, uncontradicted, uncontroverted, uninterrupted, uninterpreted, unforeseen, disencumber, disinterested, unaccomplished; accomplish, accompany, accomplice ; circumstance, circumference, circumscribe (Ses-Ker-Bee); conic, comity, commissary, commiserate, commotion, commerce, comrade; concomitant, concomitance ; in conjunction, in comparison, in conclusion, in connection, in conversation, small compensation; common consent; in contradistinction, in countermanding, in countersigning ; contribution, contribute, contributor; forever, forward, forewarn, forsooth, forswear; foretell

2*

(Fer-Tel), forgave, forget, forsake; foreland (f-ʀ-lnd), forelock, foreman, foremast, foremost, forerun, foresale; enterprise, entertain, interchange, intercourse, interdict, interest, interfere, interjacent, interjection, interpolate, interpose, interpret, interrogate, interrupt, intersect, intertwine, interval, intervene, interview, interweave, introduce, introspect, introvert; incompetent, incomprehensible, inconceivable, in consequence, in-considerable, inconsistent, in-convenient, in consideration; misconduct, misconjecture; self-esteem, selfish, unselfish (Ins-Ish), self-same, self-conceit, self-condemnation; unconcern, unconditional, unconstitutional.

8. Altogether, although, almost, almighty, all-sufficient, to-day, to-morrow, tonight, afternoon, afterthought, undertake, undersigned, understand, undergo; always, always, also.

4. Ambition, ambulate, ambiguous, antedate, antecedent, antepast, antidote, antipathy, antagonist, astronomy, benefit, benevolent, benediction, catalogue, catalysis, centiped, centage, centennial, chirography, chironomy, collect, college, colleague, correct, corrupt, correspond, heptachord, heptarchy, hydropathy, hydrometer, hyperbole, hypercritic, jurisdiction, jurisconsult, metathesis, metaphysics, multiply, multitude, octennial, October, octant, philippic, philosophy, paragraph, paradox, perfection, perverse, periphery, periscopic, polyglot, polygamy, retrospect, retrograde, stereotype, stereometer, subterfuge, subterranean, superfine, superlative, supramundane, suspect, sustain, susceptible, system, systole, systemize, withdraw, withhold, withstand, postpone, transact.

EXERCISE XXIII. C., 231–234.

§ 42. Affixes.

1. (a) Sensible, profitable, forcible, insurmountable (Ins-Ar-Ment-Bee), attainable, accountable.

(b) Knowableness, feebleness, teachableness, questionableness, indispensableness, serviceableness; lawfulness, watchfulness, sinfulness, skillfulness, carefulness, faithfulness.

(c) Wherefore, therefore.

(d) Seeking, trying, keeping, eating, dying, doing; seeking a-n-d, trying a-n-d, which having a-n, of having a-n, trying the, seeking the, doing the, of having the, which having the.

(e) Charmingly, lovingly, blushingly, knowingly, amazingly.

(g) Meetings, offerings, doings, prancings, musings.

(h) Artlessness, lawlessness, carelessness, thoughtlessness, groundlessness, boundlessness, harmlessness, listlessness, thanklessness.

(i) Frugality, rascality, legality, prod-igality, congeniality, animality, formality, principality, disability, credibility (Kred-), risibility, expansibility, instability, plausibility; popularity, disparity, prosperity, posterity.

(j) Feeble, feebly, noble, nobly, humble, humbly, sickly, homely, calmly, dimly, completely, keenly, womanly, meanly, manly.

(k) Ornamental (Ren-), supplemental, regimental, elemental, experimental (Kays-Per-), detrimental, monumental (Men¹-), instrumental, fundamental, instrumentality.

(l) Zoology, tautology, osteology, philology, etymology, demonology, phrenology, physiology, theology, chronology.

(m) Myself, himself, ourself, herself, thyself, yourself, themselves, yourselves, ourselves, one's-self, our own self, our own selves, man's self.

(*n*) Hardship, lordship, fellowship (Fel-), apprenticeship, wardship, courtship, friendship, partnership, township (Ten-Ish).

(*o*) Irksomeness, wearisomeness, gladsomeness, fulsomeness, loathesomeness, burdensomeness.

(*p*) Whatsover, whensoever, whencesoever, wheresoever, whosoever, whomsoever; whithersoever, whosesoever, howsoever.

2. See C., 232, R. 1-10.—Theologian, phrenological, phrenologist, principalities, sensibilities; possibility, sensibility, disparity, detrimental; genealogy, mineralogy; one's-self, my own self (Em-En- or Men), my single self; joyful-ly, truthful-ly, careful-ly, deceitful-ly, hateful-ly; native, positive-ly; vagrancy, despondency, validity, verbosity, Christianity.

3. Thereafter, hereafter; thereto, whereto, hitherto, onto, into, unto, hereinto, hereunto, thereinto, thereunto, whereinto, whereunto, thitherto; thereon, hereon, whereon, hanger-on, looker-on; thereof, hereof, untalked-of, unheard-of, unthought-of, whereof; therein, wherein, herein, hereinafter, hereinbefore; whatever, whichever, whoever, whenever, wherever, forever, soever (Es-Vee).

EXERCISE XXIV. C., 235-241.

§ 43. OMISSION OF CONSONANTS.

1. (*a*) Tempt, pumped, bumped, jumped, camped, vamped, thumped, limped, romped, stamped, prompt, cramped, exempt, exemption, consumption, pre-emption, co-emption, pumpkin.

(*b*) P may be sometimes omitted when it precedes *s*.—Sampson, Simpson, Thompson.

(*c*) Anxious, anxiety, sanction, distinction, function, junction, unction, conjunction, injunction, compunction.

(*d*) Mostly, honestly, tasteless, restless, mistrustful, priestly, post-paid, postmark, post-office, postpone, pasteboard (ps-brd), breast-plate, breast-pin, boastful, mistake, testimony, New Testament, destitute, pestilent, combustible, Christopher, contestable, adjustable.

2. (*a*) Instruction, destruction, construction, infraction, refraction, restriction, detraction, reduction, production, affliction, conviction.

(*b*) Intelligent, intelligence, knowledge, indulge, devolve (Def-Vee), develop (Def-Pee), intellect (Net[1]-Ket).

(*c*) Atonement, attainment, husbandman, merchandise, demonstrate, identical, transact, transcend, transfer, transfuse, transient (Tershont), transit, translate, translucent (trs-ls-nt), transmute, transmit, transplant, transport, transpose.

(*d*) Capable, capability.

(*e*) Describe, proscribe, subscribe, surprise, manuscript, priestcraft (Pers-Keft), transcribe, proportion.

(*g*) Investigation, justification. See C., 197, R. 4.

§ 44. OMISSION OF VOWELS.

1. *Unaccented Vowels Omitted.*—Rotary, capital, artless, undoubted, indebted, reasons, possible, traceable, soluble, promised, solitary, America, prominence, anatomy, enemy.

2. *All the Vowels Omitted.*—Length, along, among, beautiful, doubtful, distinction, necessary, expression, forcible, intended, always, into certain convenience

sometimes, harmony, memory, industry, danger, luxury, temperance, indignation, govern, experience, judgment, reflect, sufficient, purpose (Pee-Ray-Pees), reason-áble, sanguine, escape, philosopher, character, inquire, relation, movement, effectúal, change, suddenly, disbelief, proposal, work, honorable, example, moderation, al-teration, collect, correct.

3. See C., 239, R. 2.—Labor, lady, ready, dread, later, enter, essence, pity; sci-ence, pre-emption, redemption (Ard-Em'shon), argument, conquer, intention.

4. See C., 239, R. 3.—Perry, bury, fury, tarry, carry, jury, cherry, folly, valley, fancy, rosy, racy, massy, penny, money, many, chaffy, bevy, body, pity, mighty, hungry, angry, entry, ultra, needy, windy.

5. See C., 239, Rems. 4 and 5.—Ask, assign, awake, awoke, oyer, argue, alum, elm, alike, older (see C., 207, R. 2), elder, avowed, annoyed; idea, argue, nephew.

6.—See C., 240.—Eyed, hide, highly, oil, wide, whiten, white, ivy, ice, hire, bŏw, sprout, trout, loud, glue, ammonia, mania, scoria, nephew, ague, argue, con-tribute.

EXERCISE XXV. C., 242–249.

§ 45. PHRASE-WRITING.

1. The position of the signs for the following phrases is determined by the first word.

All men, all the, and a, and the, are you sure, as it has been, as good as, as great as, as it should be, as soon as, as the, as a, as well as, at last, at one time, at some time, at such, because it is, by every means, by many persons, by me, by my, by some means, by the way, by them, by this time, by which, can do, can not be, could not be, could be, do they, ever has been, every man, every thing, for his own sake, for a-n, for the, for this is the, for which, for you are, for your, from many, from them, from this time, from you, from your, give me, give my, give that, give you, has been, has done, has had, has it been, has made, have been, have done, have not, have they (them), he has, he is, he has been, he has done, he is not, he has not, how could you, how many, how must, how will they, I agree, I am certain, I am glad, I am, I am not, I am quite sure, I am very glad, I am very happy, I can, I can not, I may, I may as well, I may nevertheless, I may not be, I mus(t) be, I mus(t) say, I need, I need not, I will do so, I will not be, I will say, if a-n, if his, if it be, if it had, if it is necessary, if it is not so, if the, if they, if there be, if there should be, if we, if you are, if your, in your own in a-n, in all, in all his, in his, in any, in his opin-ion, in many particulars, in my opinion, in order that, in order to, in the way, into a-n, into the, into this, is-a-n, is the, is to, it is (has), it is (has) a-n, it is (has) the, it is (has) not, it has been, it is (has) always, it is important, it is impossible, it is my opinion, it is necessary, it is not so, it is now, it is plain, it is rather, it is right, it is said, it is (has) the, it may be, it may not be, it will be said, it will do, it would be, it would have, let it be, let us now, let us proceed, manner in which, may ap-pear, may as well, may be, may have, may they, may try, might not be, might seem, mos(t) likely, mus(t) admit, mus(t) be, mus(t) come, mus(t) do, mus(t) not be, never be, never may, nevertheless it is, no man, no more, of a-n, of course, of his own, of importance, of many (of) them, of me (my), on a-n, on account of, on the, on my (me), on you, or a-n, or the, ought not, quite agree, quite as well, should a-n, should be, should not be, should not do, should not have, should the, should they, should think, since a-n, since the, so as to, so as to appear, so as to make, so as to receive, so little, so that, so the, so there is, some one, something has been, such has (is\, such has been, such may be, take care, take occasion, take pains, take part, take place, takes part, takes place, that a-n, that are (Thet[1]-Ray), that are not (Thet[1]-Rent), that has been, that have, that is it, that is so, that may, that might not be, that such, that this, that will, that you are, that your, there are, there can be, there could not, there is nothing, there may be, therefore a-n, therefore the, therefore thr, they do, they had, they may be, they were, they were not, this advantage, this day, this is (has) done, this place, though a-n, though the, to a-n, to as many as, to be a-n, to be the, to his own, to it, to many (of) those who, to some extent, to the, to think, to which you are, to you, to your, under a-n, under his, under that, upon a-n, upon this, upon the, upon them, upon which, very certain, very good, very great, very many, very soon, was as, was good, was not so, we are aware, we are bound, we are never, we have, we have seen, we were, were a-n, were the, were they, were this, what can be, what could be, what the, when we are, when we may, when there is not, whenever a-n, where are they (Wer[2]-Ray-Thee), wherever a-n, wherever the, which a-n, which can be, which could be, which is (has), which may be, which should be; which the, which-may not be, which will be, which you are, which you can, which you will, who are, who can be, who is (has) the, who may be, who may not, will be, will be found, will find, without which, would be the, would come, would do, would have, you are, you are not, you can be, you can not be, you may think, you must, you mus(t) not, you will be, you will find, you will understand, you will do.

2. The position of the signs for the following phrases is determined by the position of the second word.

All its, all which, all principles, all these, all this, all those, all truths, all yours, and as, and but, and should, and who, and were, and with, and do you mean, and if, and for, and few, and ever, and have, and however, and either, and there, and other, and these, and this, and thus, and those, and this is the, and we, and we may, and when the, as if, as if it were, as if there were, as for, as few, as much as, as each, as that, as without, as these, as this, as those, give it, give out, give these, give this, give those, I hope that, I wish, I shall, I think, I thank, I did not, I do not, I had not, I do, I had, I never, I suppose, I shall be, I think there is, I think they, in it, in its, in itself, in each, in which, in much, in every respect, in part, in this instance, in these, in this, in those, in this respect, in your, is so, is that, is without, might be, might think, of its, of each, of which, of much, of these, of this, of those, of which you will, on its, on each, on which, on much, on his part, on her part, on either, on their, on other, the first, the way, the man, what are, what if, what for, with it, with each, with which, with much, with these, with this, with those, with which you are, is no, his own.

§ 46. Words Omitted.

1. (*a*) The loss of the money—the subject of the letter—the day of the week—the advantages of the system—the close of the day—love of the truth—fear of the injury—the meaning of the word—the nature of the subject—one of the most—attribute of the soul—love of the world—in every part of the world—condition of the body.

(*b*) Shall have been, there have been, mus(t) have been, can not have been, we have been, you have been, will have been, never have been, may have been, to have been; can not have done, mus(t) have done, shall have done, may have done, we have done, you have done; which have been, which have done, I have been, I have done, they have been, they have done, they have had.

2. (*a*) Word of God, kingdom of heaven; I hope to be, I wish to be.

(*b*) For a moment, such a one, in a word, for a long time, in such a case, by and by, wise and good, more and more, over and over, over and above, rich and poor, through and through, from day to day, from hour to hour, from place to place, hand in hand, on the other hand, on the one side, on the other side, more or less, sooner or later, greater or less, one or the other, on the contrary, in the world, it seems to me, it seemed to me, in conjunction with, in connection with, variety of causes, to us, to say, to it, to do, to you, to whom, to come, to go, to have gone, to have done, to show.

§·47. If the directions for study and practice should be faithfully followed up to this point, the student can not but be possessed of such a thorough knowledge of principles and also of outlines as to render phonographic writing easy, pleasurable, and useful. The Reading Exercises from the end of Ex. 25 to the Specimens of the Reporting Style, should next be read and copied several times. Thereafter, until your writing becomes faultless, criticise all your writing in accordance with the plan of criticism given in the following sections.

PLAN OF PHONOGRAPHIC CRITICISM.

§ 48. In criticising phonographic writing, let answers be made to questions—

I. As to Contracted Words—

1. Have the primary sign-words been represented by their proper signs in the proper position?

2. Have the derivative sign-words and other contracted words been represented by their proper signs in the proper positions?

II. As to Other Words—

1. Have they, in respect of their consonants, been correctly analyzed?

2. May any of the consonants be omitted in accordance with the general principles for the omission of consonants?

3. Have the consonants to be expressed been written with the best outline and in the proper position?

4. To what extent do they require vocalization? and have the vowels to be expressed been correctly denoted?

5. Have the prefixes and affixes been properly written? or have they been written when they might have been omitted?

III. As to Joining Words or Parts of Words—

1. Have prefixes or affixes been joined in allowable cases?

2. Have initial and final vowel-signs been joined according to § 240 of the Compendium?

3. Have words been joined in phrase-signs when they might be according to § 242-246 of the Compendium?

4. Have the phrase-signs been written in their proper positions?

IV. As to the Omission of Words—

Have words been omitted which might be according to § 245-249 of the Compendium?

V. As to the General Appearance of the Writing—

Can the general appearance of the writing be improved in respect of the size or the junction of the letters, or in any other respect?

Rem. 1. In determining the best outlines for words, reference should be made to The Phonographic Orthographer,' and the portions of the Compendium specifying the cases for the use of the different letters and different principles of writing.

§ 49. KEY TO THE 'SPECIMENS OF REPORTING.

1. Miseries of War.

Oh! tell me, if there be any relentings of pity in your bosom, how could you endure it to behold the agonies of the dying man as, goaded by pain, he grasps the cold ground in convulsive energy, or faint with the loss of blood, his pulse ebbs low, and the gathering paleness spreads itself over his countenance, or wrapping himself round in despair, he can only mark by a few feeble quiverings that life still lurks and lingers in his lacerated body, or lifting up a faded eye, he casts on you a look of imploring helplessness for that succor which no sympathy can yield him. It may be painful to dwell thus in imagination on the distressing picture of one individual; but multiply it ten thousand times—say how much of all this distress has been heaped together on a single field. Give us the arithmetic of this accumulated wretchedness, and lay it before us with all the accuracy of official computation, and, strange to tell, not one sigh is lifted up among the crowd of eager listeners as they stand on t'ptoe and catch every syllable of utterance which is read to them out the registers of death! Oh! say what mystic spell is that which so blinds us to the suffering of our brethren; which deafens to our ear the voice of bleeding humanity when it is aggravated by the shriek of dying thousands; which makes the very magnitude of the slaughter throw a softening disguise over its cruelties and its horrors; which causes us to eye with indifference the field that is crowded with the most revolting abominations, and arrests that sigh which each individual would singly have drawn from us, by the report of the many that have fallen and breathed their last in agony along with him.—*Chalmers.*

2. The Defense of Socrates.

No man knows what death is, yet men fear it as if they knew well that it was the greatest of all evils; which is just a case of that worst of all ignorance, the conceit of knowing what you do not really know. For my part, this is the exact point on which I differ from most other men—if there be any one thing in which I am wiser than they. As I know nothing about Hades, so I do not pretend to any knowledge; but I do know well that disobedience to a person better than myself, either God or man, is both an evil and a shame; nor will I ever embrace evil certain, in order to escape evil which may, for aught I know, be a good. Perhaps you may feel indignant at the resolute tone of my defense; you may have expected that I should do as most others do in less dangerous trials than mine; that I should weep, beg, and entreat for my life, and bring forward my children and relatives to do the same. I have relatives, like other men, and three children; but not one of them shall appear before you for any such purpose. Not from any insolent disposition on my part, nor any wish to put a slight upon you, but because I hold such conduct to be degrading to the reputation which I enjoy; for I *have* a reputation for superiority among you, deserved or undeserved as it may be. It is a disgrace to Athens when her esteemed men lower themselves, as they do but too often, by such mean and cowardly supplications; and you, Judges, instead of being prompted thereby to spare them, ought rather to condemn them the more for so dishonoring the city. Apart from any reputation of mine, too, I should be a guilty man if I sought to bias you by supplications. My duty is to instruct and persuade you, if I can; but you have sworn to follow your convictions in judging according to the laws, not to make the laws bend to your partiality; and it is your duty so to do. Far be it from me to habituate you to perjury; far be it from you to contract any such habit. Do not, therefore, require of me proceedings dishonorable in reference to myself, as well as criminal and impious in regard to you; especially at a moment when I am myself rebutting an accusation of impiety advanced by Melitus.

3. True Greatness.

Grandeur of character lies wholly in force of soul, that is, in force of thought, moral principle, and love; and this may be found in the humblest condition of life. A man brought up to an obscure trade, and hemmed in by the wants of a growing family, may in his narrow sphere perceive more clearly, discriminate more keenly, weigh evidence more wisely, seize on the right means more decisively, and have more presence of mind in difficulty, than another who has accumulated vast stores of knowledge by laborious study; and he has more of intellectual greatness. It is force of thought which measures intellectual, and so it is force of principle which measures moral, greatness—that highest of human endowments, that brightest manifestation of the Divinity. The greatest man is he who chooses the right with invincible resolution, who resists the sorest temptations from within and without, who bears the heaviest burdens cheerfully, who is calmest in storms, and most fearless under menace and frowns, whose reliance on truth, on virtue, on God is most unfaltering. —Channing.

THE

PHONOGRAPHIC

ORTHOGRAPHER:

AN

EXPOSITOR OF PRINCIPLES

FOR THE

ASCERTAINMENT OF THE BEST PHONOGRAPHIC OUTLINES.

~~~~~~~~~~~~~~~~~

PART FIFTH

OF THE

Hand-Book of Standard Phonography.

PRELIMINARY REMARKS.

THE previously unsettled state of phonography, in respect of the outlines oɩ words, may be very properly compared with the chaotic condition of English spelling when each writer spelled to suit his own taste, good sense, or whims. English orthography has finally been made to depend, not upon the observance of natural principles of representing language, but upon the authority of lexicographers. To this method of settling English spelling corresponds precisely the attempted method of settling phonographic orthography by the authority of "phonographic vocabularies." The writer, without the guidance of general principles, feels himself continually subjected to the restraint of authority, even when he has reason to doubt its correctr.ess. Even rules of writing which are dictated by an author's phonographic exper'ence ana taste, are felt to be little better than arbitrary authority, until their dependence upon general principles can be perceived; and even then they must be regarded as statements of their author's opinion of the results or demands of such general principles, rather than as imperative laws.

The object of this treatise is to furnish a statement of certain laws of speed, vocalization, and legibility, by reference to which phonographers will be enabled to determine for themselves the best phonographic outlines, and free themselves from the drudgery of thumbing "vocabularies."

The selection of outlines by reference to these principles, may at first seem slow and irksome; but after a short time, the mind, having become accustomed to the process, seems no longer to consider particulars, to compare different modes of writing and estimate their differences, but it soon arrives, without exertion apparently, at results which will, as a general thing, withstand the severest criticism. The phonographer thus furnished with criteria of judgment and taught self-reliance, is prepared to receive the suggestions of a phonographic vocabulary, or of other phonographers, in respect of phonographic outlines, without liability of injury to his writing.

ANDREW J. GRAHAM.

PHONETIC DEPOT, NEW YORK, *July 20th,* 1858.

THE

PHONOGRAPHIC ORTHOGRAPHER.

§ 1. *Phonographic Orthography Defined.*—The term Orthography (derived from the Greek ὀρθός, correct, and γραφή, writing) is used to signify the writing of words with the proper letters. In the common orthography, the propriety of the use of the letters is determined to a great extent by arbitrary custom, and not, as would be the case in a rational orthography, by the fixed and invariable values of letters. The term Phonographic Orthography is here used to signify the writing of those outlines which, all things considered, are found to be best.

§ 2. *Conditions of Phonographic Orthography.*—A careful investigation has shown that Phonographic Orthography depends upon the requirements or laws of vocalization, speed, and legibility, which will next be considered.

REQUIREMENTS OF VOCALIZATION.

§ 3. The requirements of vocalization are—

1. That, in case of there being an initial or final vowel, the consonant next following the former, or the consonant next preceding the latter, shall be so written as to permit the easy expression of such vowel in its proper order and relation to the consonant; thus, Es-Kay, ask—Zee-Ray, Ezra—Ray-Es, racy—Way-Kay, awake—Yay-Ar, oyer—Hay-Dee, ahead—Pee-En, penny—Chay-Ef, chaffy—En-Ter, entry—Sen-Der, sundry—En-Dee, needy—En-Tee, into.

2. That generally such outlines shall be employed as will permit the easy and distinct expression of the principal medial vowels; thus, Bee-Lay, ball, bail, below, Ballou, etc.—Dee-Lay, deal, dull, dally, dahlia, etc.—Kay-Tee, quiet—Kay-Es, chaos, acquiesce—Es-Ens, science—Tee-En-Shen, continuation.

Rem. 1. The first requirement of vocalization is absolute in the Corresponding Style; and a departure from it in the Reporting Style is allowable in those cases only where a stroke may be saved by, and illegibility not result from, expressing the last consonant so that a final vowel could not be written after it; as in writing Pret[2] for *pretty;* Bed[1] for *body.*

Rem. 2. The second requirement of vocalization demands that a stroke-sign should be used for both the consonant preceding and the one following two concurrent vowels which can not be expressed by a single sign; as ao in *chaos,* io in *lion,* ua in *continuation,* ewe in *Jewett.* This is to secure two strokes between which the vowels may be divided, instead of both having to be written in a confused manner beside one.

REQUIREMENTS OF SPEED.

§ 4. Speed of writing phonographically depends chiefly upon the following-mentioned conditions:

1. The use, if permitted by other principles, of the briefest signs for the expression of sounds.

2. The use, so far as allowed by other principles, of the most readily made junctions.

3. Accordance with the laws of analogy.

4. The use, so far as possible, of signs which can be readily joined to a preceding or a follwing word; that is, accordance with the requirements of phrase-writing.

5. The use of forms favoring lineality of writing.

Rem. 1. By the briefest letters or signs are to be understood those simple or group consonant signs which require for their execution the least time. A following table shows the comparative brevity of different modes of expressing given sounds, by reference to which table, when the opportunity for a choice is presented, the writer may determine with mathematical precision the most rapid signs. Another table furnishes a statement of the comparative speed and ease with which different kinds of joinings between letters may be effected. By reference to that statement a choice as to the best joining may be readily made.

REQUIREMENTS OF LEGIBILITY.

§ 5. Legibility, in addition to good penmanship, depends chiefly upon the following-specified conditions:

1. Writing the consonants, so far as possible, in a manner to denote the vowel-relations of the words.

2. Accordance with the laws of analogy.

3. Distinguishing between words of the same consonants and of like or different significations.

4. The number and relation of the consonants.

5. The relation of the words to the sentence; that is, the context.

REM. 1· ·The first requirement of legibility is complied with to nearly its fullest ex. tent by observing the laws of vocalization and speed; these securing such distinctions as the following: Es-Pee-Shel, especial—Spee-Shel, special ;—Ray-Zee, rosy—Rays, rose ;—Em-Es, massy—Ems, mass ;—Kay-Es, chaos—Kays, case ;—Es-Ens, science, essence ;—Sens, signs, sense, etc. ;—Way-Kay, awoke—Wuh-Kay, woke ;—Yay-Ar, ōyer—Yuh-Ray, yore ;—Hay-Dee, ahead—h-tick-Dee, head ;—Chay-Ef, chaffy— Chef, chaff ;—Pee-En, penny—Pen, pen, pain, etc. ;—Em-Pee, map, etc.—Emp, hemp, etc. ;—En-Ter, entry—Enter, enter ;—En-Dee, needy—Ned, need, etc. ;—En-Tees, notice—Nets, notes. (b) In some other cases, it is necessary, or at least advantageous, to resort to other methods of indicating the different vowel-relations of such words as 'hot, haughty; Hague, Hugo (see the Compendium, § 149, 3); night, unite; bed, abed; foot, afoot; caught, acute (see the Compendium, § 220, b, 2); led, allied, sold, solid; rolled, rallied; marred, married; ruined, renewed (see the Compendium, § 220, b, 3); quite, quiet; pad, poet; Jude, Jewett' (see the Compendium, § 220, b, 4); in which cases a distinction is naturally effected by giving a short form to the shorter word, and a longer form to the word of the greater number of syllables. (c) The fact that the stroke-signs for l and r may or must be written in different directions, may be availed of to considerable advantage, when these consonants are represented by strokes, to indicate the different vowel-relations in such words as ' like, alike ; lime, alum ; rail, rely ; vale, valley ; ark, rack ; air, ray ; fire, fury.' The plan of, and cases for, making this distinction are particularly stated in the Compendium, §§ 152–156, and in general terms, in the following remarks (2 and 3).

REM. 2. *Uses of El and Lay.—L*, when it is the first or last consonant of a word, and when it is to be expressed by a stroke, may be represented—

(a) By Lay, when it commences a word, or precedes a final vowel.

(b) By El, when it ends a word, or follows an initial vowel, and is not the only stroke-consonant in the word.

REM. 3. *Uses of Ar and Ray.—R*, when it is the first or last consonant in a word, and when it is to be expressed by a stroke, may generally be represented—

(a) By Ray, when it begins a word, or precedes a final vowel.

(b) By Ar, when it ends a word, or follows an initial vowel.

REM. 4. The required distinction between words of the same consonants is secured in most cases by the indication of the vowel-relations of words, in accordance with the first requirement of legibility. In other cases, a distinction may usually be made by observing the rule of position, especially in the Reporting Style, though in a very few instances there must be a resort to vocalization. See the Compendium, § 269 ; 256–261.

REM. 5. Analogy of writing is of so much importance as a condition of both speed and legibility, that it will be fully defined and its laws stated in subsequent sections.

REM. 6. As a general rule, the greater the number of consonants in a word, the greater its legibility ; for the number of chances that a given word should contain the same consonants as some other word is inversely proportioned to the number of its consonants. The chances are still further lessened in proportion to the peculiarity of the relation of the consonants. Hence, of words of the same number of consonants, those which are composed in part of common prefixes or affixes are, as a general thing, less legible than the others.

LAWS OF ANALOGY.

§ 6. *Analogy Defined.—Analogy* may be defined as an agreement or likeness between things in certain respects, when they are otherwise entirely different. To illustrate—there is an analogy, in respect of the principal portion of the forms or outlines, between the outline of one and of any other of the following words : Def-En, define—Def-Enshon, definition—Def-En-Tef, definitive—Def-Net, definite—Def-En-Ar, definer ; but there is want of such analogy between Def-Net, definite, and End-Ef-Net, indefinite.   So there is an analogy between Pen-Ens, open*ness*, and Bees-Ens, base*ness*—in respect of the mode of expressing the terminations ; and between Pers-Vee, *per*ceive, and Perf-Ket, *per*fect—in respect of the mode of expressing their initial parts.

§ 7. The laws of analogy are the three following :

1. Derivatives, as a general rule, should be written in analogy with the form of the primitive.

2. Generally, the forms of compound words should follow the analogy of the component words.

3. Generally, classes of words agreeing in certain particulars should be written in analogy in respect of those particulars.

REM. 1. The demands of analogy are so strong that the form of the primitive is sometimes determined with reference to the convenience of writing the derivatives, even in violation of some other principle of speed. To illustrate—to secure an analogical and convenient mode of writing *comforted*, the primitive must be written ' com'-Ef-Ret, instead of Fret, which would be best for speed. The first form is also required by considerations arising from another principle of legibility. In the Corresponding Style, *invert, convert*, must be written En-Vee-Ret, con-Vee-Ret, on account of *inverted, converted*, which are most conveniently written En-Vee-Ray-Ted, con-Vee-Ray-Ted ; but on the other hand, considerations of speed, overruling the law of analogy, require that *inversion, conversion*, should be written En-Vershon, con-Vershon, instead of En-Vee-Rayshon, con-Vee-Rayshon. In the Reporting Style, where the past tense or perfect participle is expressed if more convenient by the form of the present tense, the laws of both analogy and speed are more fully complied with by writing En-Vert, invert-ed—En-Vershon, inversion ;—con-Vert, convert-ed—con-Vershon, conversion.

COMPARATIVE BREVITY.

§ 8. By the comparative brevity of a sign is understood its brevity as compared with another sign of equivalent signification.   The comparative brevity of the Tiv-hook, for instance, is its brevity as compared with equivalent signs for the same sounds, as Tee-Vee, Tee-Ef, Tef, or Ef or Vee with the preceding *t* expressed by halving.

REM. 1. The terms *brief* and *brevity* refer adjectively and substantively to shortness in respect of either space or time. They are here applied to signs with respect to the time occupied in their formation ; and not with reference to the space occupied by them, for it is not invariably true, though nearly so, that the briefest signs in respect of space are also briefest in respect of time. Brief Way and Yay are properly designated thus, because they are briefer than the Way and Yay stroke as to both space and time.

REM. 2. *Faster Than, As Fast As.*—If A can be written once and a half while B is being written once, then A is once and a half *as fast as,* but only one half *faster* THAN, B. If A can be written four times while B is being written once, then A is *four* times *as fast* AS, but only *three* times *faster* THAN, B.

The words *as fast as* express the proportion between the signs, either as to the number of times that each may be written in the same period of time, or as to the amount of time occupied in writing each the same number of times. The words *faster than* express the proportion of gain by the faster over the slower sign, either as to the number of times that the signs may be written in a given period of time, or as to the time occupied in writing them a certain number of times.

REM. 3. (*a*) The first column of figures in the following tables of Comparative Brevity shows in units and hundredths how many times the first sign compared may be written while the second is being written once, or, the separatrix (.) being omitted, how many times the first sign may be written while the second sign is being written one hundred times. The gain in times of the first over the second sign may be ascertained by subtracting from the numbers of the first column 1.00 or 100, according as the numbers are taken with or without the decimal point. (*b*) The second column of figures in the following tables shows in units and hundredths what proportion of the time is required to write the first sign as many times as the second. The percentage of time gained by the first over the second sign may be ascertained by subtracting the numbers of the second column from 1.00 or 100, according as they are taken with or without the decimal point.

§ 9. TABLE SHOWING THE COMPARATIVE BREVITY OF DIFFERENT PHONO-GRAPHS.

	Times.	Time.
Straight and Curved Lines.		
Tee, Chay, Kay—Ith, Es, Ish, Em	1.06	.95
Light and Heavy Lines.		
Tee, Chay, Kay, Ef—Dee, Jay, Gay, Vee...............	1.06	.95
Downward and Upward Lines.		
Chay, Ish, El—Ray, Shay, Lay........................	1.10	.92
Modes of Representing S, St, Str.		
Iss-Tee, Tee-Iss—Es-Tee, Tee-Es.....................	1.14	.88
Ses-Tee, Tee-Ses—Es-Iss-Tee, Tee-Iss-Es, Tee-Es-Iss	1.16	.86
Steh-Pee, Steh-Kay, Steh-Em, Peest, Kayst, Teest—Stee-Pee, Stee-Kay, Stee-Em, Pee-Stee, Kay-Stee, Tee-Stee	1.28	.78
Bee'ster, Dee'ster, Kay'ster—Bees-Tee-Ar, Dees-Tee-Ar, Kays-Tee-Ar	1.46	.68
Bee'ster, Dee'ster, Kay'ster—Bees-Ter, Dees-Ter, Kays-Ter	1.14	.88
Modes of Representing L and Lr.		
Pel, Tel, Fel—Pee-Lay, Tee-Lay, Ef-Lay	1.25	.80
Pler, Tler, Fler—Pel-Ar, Tel-Ar, Fel-Ar...............	1.75	.57
Modes of Representing R and Rl.		
Per, Ter, Ker—Pee-Ar, Tee-Ar, Kay-Ar................	1.31	.76

1*

	Times.	Time
Per, Ter, Ker—Pee-Ray, Tee-Ray, Kay-Ray	1.22	.83
Prel, Trel, Frel—Per-Lay, Ter-Lay, Fer-Lay............	1.75	.57

Modes of Representing Initial Ins, Ens, and Uns.

	Times.	Time
In-Sper, In-Ster, In-Sker—En-Sper, En-Ster, En-Sker ...	1.67	.60
Ins-Lent—Ens-Elent................................	.00	.00
In-Slay-Vee—En-Slay-Vee...........................	1.22	.83

Modes of Representing F and V.

	Times.	Time
Pef, Tef, Chef, Kef—Pee-Ef, Tee-Ef, Chay-Ef, Kay-Ef ...	1.44	.70
Pef, Tef, Kef—Pee-Vee, Tee-Vee, Kay-Vee	1.33	.75

Modes of Representing N, Ns, Nss, Nst, Nstr.

	Times.	Time
Pen, Ten, Chen, Ken, Fen, Len, Men—Pee-En, Tee-En, Chay-En, Kay-En, Ef-En, Lay-En, Em-En	1.37	.73
Pens, Tens, Kens, Fens—Pee-Ens, Tee-Ens, Kay-Ens, Ef-Ens	1.31	.76
Pen'ses, Ten'ses, Ken'ses—Pee-En'ses, Tee-En'ses, Kay-En'ses	1.31	.76
Penst, Tenst, Chenst, Kenst—Pee-Enst, Tee-Enst, Chay-Enst, Kay-Enst................................	1.40	.71
Penster, Tenster, Chenster, Kenster—Pee-Enster, Tee-Enster, Chay-Enster, Kay-Enster................	1.40	.71

Modes of Representing -Tion, Cian, etc.

	Times.	Time
Peeshon, Teeshon, Kayshon, Efshon—Pee-Shen, Tee-Shayn, Kay-Shen, Ef-Shen	1.67	.60

Modes of Representing Tiv.

	Times.	Time
Peetiv, Deetiv, Kaytiv—Pee-Tee-Vee, Dee-Tee-Vee, Kay-Tee-Vee	2.00	.50
Peetiv, Deetiv, Kaytiv—Pet-Vee, Det-Vee, Ket-Vee.....	1.70	.58
Peetiv, Deetiv, Kaytiv—Pee-Tef, Dee-Tef, Kay-Tef......	1.40	.71

Modes of Representing Mp and Mb.

	Times.	Time
Emp—Em-Pee	1.40	.71
Emb—Em-Bee	1.51	.66

Modes of Representing Ter, Der, Ther, and Ther.

	Times.	Time
Layter, Emter, Efter, Enter—Lay-Tee-Ar, Em-Tee-Ar, Ef-Tee-Ar, En-Tee-Ar	2.18	.46
Layter, Emter, etc.—Lay-Ter, Em-Ter, etc.............	2.00	.50
Layter, Emter, etc.—Let-Ray, Emt-Ray, etc.	2.08	.48
Layter, Emter, etc.—Lay-Dee-Ar, Em-Dee-Ar, etc.......	2.32	.43
Layter, Emter, etc.—Lay-Der, Em-Der, etc.............	2.18	.46
Layter, Emter, etc.—Eld-Ar, Emd-Ray, etc.............	1.92	.52
Layther, Emther, etc.—Lay-Ther, Em-Ther, etc.	2.08	.48

	Times.	Time.
Pet, Tet, Ket, Fet, etc.—Pee-Tee, Tee-Tee, Kay-Tee, Ef-Tee, etc.	1.92	.52
Ped, Ted, Ked, Fed—Pee-Dee, Tee-Dee, Kay-Dee, Ef-Dee	2.18	.46
Bet, Det, Get, Vet—Bee-Tee, Dee-Tee, Gay-Tee, Vee-Tee	2.00	.50
Bed, Ded, Ged, Ved—Bee-Dee, Dee-Dee, Gay-Dee, Vee-Dee	1.78	.56

REM. 1. The estimates in the preceding table have been made from the data furnished by numerous and laborious experiments by different writers. Though slight discrepancies may be discovered, it is believed that the estimates are very near the exact truth. The advantages here shown are averages. In some cases they are much greater, and in other cases much less, than here stated.

REM. 2. In accordance with the directions of a following section, the phonographer may determine for himself many other questions of brevity in the Corresponding or Reporting Style. The mode of determining speed here pointed out might be employed to demonstrate mathematically the great superiority of Standard Phonography over any other system of stenography, phonetic or otherwise.

§ 10. TABLE SHOWING THE COMPARATIVE BREVITY OF DIFFERENT JOININGS.

With and Without Angles.	Times.	Time.
Ef-Ar, En-Em, Lay-Ar—Ef-Ef, En-En, Lay-Lay	1.31	.76
En-Ray—En-Kay	1.25	.80
Tee-Tee—Tee-Kay	2.00	.50
Average	1.40	.71
With Acute or Right Angles.		
Ray-Chay, Chay-Ray—Ray-Pee, Chay-Pee	1.44	.70
Ray-Tee, Chay-Kay—Ray-Pee, Chay-Pee	1.22	.83
With Right or Obtuse Angles.		
Tee-Kay—Tee-Chay, Tee-Pee, Pee-Kay	1.31	.76

REM. 1. *Variation of Inclination and Curvature* —The ease of junction may frequently be increased considerably by varying the inclination of the sloping letters and the curvature of the curve-signs. See the Compendium, § 25.

MODE OF DETERMINING COMPARATIVE BREVITY.

§ 11. The comparative brevity of different signs may be determined thus. Determine the utmost number of times that each of the signs to be compared may be written in 100 seconds. Say that the briefer sign is written A times and the other B times. Then B divided by A will give, in hundredths, the proportion of time required for making A as many times as B. And A divided by B will give, in units and hundredths, the number of times that A may be written while B is being written once.

SPECIFIC BREVITY.

§ 12. The specific brevity of a sign is its brevity as compared with that of some other sign, as Pee, Tee, Chay, or Kay, taken as a stand-

ard of measurement.   Specific brevity is determined thus.   Write Tee
or Chay and the sign to be compared with it, each 100 seconds.   Say that
Tee or Chay is written A times, and that the other is written B times.
Then A divided by B gives the specific temporal brevity of the sign
compared with the Tee or Chay ; that is, shows what proportion of
time is required to write it as many times as Tee or Chay.   B divided
by A gives the specific numerical brevity of the sign compared with
the Tee or Dee ; that is, shows how often it may be written while Tee
or Chay is being written once.

§ 13.   TABLE SHOWING THE SPECIFIC BREVITY OF CERTAIN SIGNS.

	Times.	Time
Tee, Pee, Chay, or Kay—the standard of measurement ..	1.00	1.00
Dee, Bee, Jay, or Gay	.95	1.06
Tee-Tee, Pee-Pee	.95	1.06
Tet, Pet, Chet.......................................	1.06	.95
Ith, Es, etc..	.95	1.06

REM. 1. *Large and Small Writing.*—The difference between Tee and Tee-Tee
shows that very much may be lost in respect of speed by making the consonant-
strokes too long.   The best length for the primary strokes (Pee, Tee, etc.) is about
one eighth of an inch.   This enables them to be distinguished easily and certainly
from the half-lengths on one side, and from the double-lengths on the other ; and
without making the half-lengths so short as to render them illegible, and without
requiring inconveniently long and ungainly double-lengths.

REM. 2. The difference between Tee and Dee shows that it is a disadvantage to
write with a heavy hand—that the heavy lines should be barely distinguished from
the light lines, which should be made very light.

ORTHOGRAPHICAL PARSING.

§ 14.   Orthographical Parsing is of two kinds—1. Determining, by
reference to the conditions or principles of Phonographic Orthography,
the best outlines for words.   2. Determining whether a given form
is the best one for the word for which it has been employed. - The
former is called Orthographical Synthesis ; the latter, Orthographical
Analysis.

EXAMPLES OF ORTHOGRAPHIC SYNTHESIS.

§ 15.   Determine the forms for ' bear, brow, burned, blind.

1. *Bear.*—The second principle of vocalization demands two consonant-strokes.   The first principle of speed suggests Ray as the sign of
the *r* as being six per cent. faster than Ar ; but the third principle of
speed and the first principle of legibility require Ar.   Therefore the
best form for this word is Bee-Ar.

2. *Brow.*—The requirements of vocalization are met by any possible

outline; that is, by Bee-Ray, Bee-Ar, or Ber. Speed demands Ber, because of its being faster than Bee-Ar or Bee-Ray, and this form meeting the requirements of legibility, is the best outline for this word.

3. *Burned.*—The second principle of vocalization demands that the second consonant should be expressed by a stroke. The three consonants following the vowel may be most readily expressed by Rend. Therefore, the principles of legibility not contradicting, the best outline for *burned* is Bee-Rend.

4. *Blind.*—The briefest sign for the consonants of this word is Blend. This meets the second requirement of vocalization, and the requirements of legibility, and is therefore the best form for this word.

EXAMPLES OF ORTHOGRAPHIC ANALYSIS.

§ 16. Determine whether or not the best outlines for *indicate, activity, render* are End-Ket, Ket-Vee-Tee, Ray-Ender.

1. *End-Ket.*—This form as an outline for *indicate* consists of the briefest signs of the consonants expressed, permits the proper expression of the vowels, and conflicts with none of the principles of legibility. It must therefore be approved as the outline for the word *indicate.*

2. *Ket-Vee-Tee.*—This form as an outline for *activity* complies with the requirements of vocalization, but it violates analogy, not being analogous to Kaytiv, the best form for the primitive word; and it also violates the second requirement of speed. Kay'tiv-Tee meeting all the requirements of orthographic principles, is the best form for this word.

3. *Ray-Ender.*—This form is the briefest for the consonants of *render,* and complying with the requirements of vocalization and legibility, it must be approved as the best outline for that word.

GRAHAM'S HAND-BOOK

OF

STANDARD OR AMERICAN PHONOGRAPHY.

OPINIONS OF THE PRESS.

From a long review in the New York Evening Post.

"*The system presented in this work is Pitman's Phonography, greatly improved, perfected, and Americanized. Mr. Graham has long been known as an accomplished verbatim reporter, and a successful teacher of Phonography, and he has manifestly bestowed a large amount of labor and research in perfecting this work. He has reduced the art to a complete science, perfect in all its details, having used the English phonography only as a basis for his own system.*"

From the Knickerbocker Magazine.

"*We have found an examination of this book quite as suggestive as the history of the telegraph or of any other of the recent triumphs of art and physical science. It illustrates finely an age which is very* FAST, *in an intellectual, if not in a moral sense. Beginning with first principles, it proposes to write the English language as it is sounded. It then, by a series of most remarkable reductions, which as a matter of intellectual curiosity would delight any man, compresses the written language to such brevity that it can be written as rapidly as spoken. Everything becomes short as well as quick; a dot or a curve takes the place of words; a line contains the printed matter of an ordinary page; and a big old folio tome, such as monks used to spend a lifetime in writing, would, in reporting short-hand style, make a handsome little volume to be carried in the pocket, and to be read of an evening. Every great improvement suggests new ideals. The ideal world of phonography and stenography is a time when written words shall be as obedient to thought as speech is now; when reading shall cease to be slow, and books unwieldy; when all the news of the newspaper can be written on the space of a thumb-nail, and read at a glance; when a scholar shall be able to carry the whole Alexandrian library in his pockets, and when our present fashion of penmanship shall be as antiquated as a stage-coach is now. The work of Mr. Graham contains all the information on the subject, whether for a person desiring to learn the new art, or for one who is only curious about it.*"

From the New York Daily News.

"*The present volume is an* ENCYCLOPEDIA *of the principles and practice of this admirable system of writing Phonography. By easy steps the student is conducted from the elements of Phonography to those refinements and niceties which are required for the purposes of the finished reporter. * * The whole forms an entire system of Standard Phonography.*"

From a very extended and favorable review in the Canadian Phonetic Pioneer.

"*The ' Hand-Book of Standard Phonography,' it will be seen, is a compendium of the whole system.   It commences sooner, and goes farther than any other work ever issued.   It, in fact, begins at the beginning and ends at the ending.* The size of the book results from its completeness—from the plain and familiar manner in which it goes into every principle of the system.''

From the Missouri Republican, *St. Louis.*

" *So manifold are its merits that, within the compass of a book-notice, we can not even enumerate, much less dilate upon them.   The realization in the ' Hand-Book' of all that has been hoped for by the most sanguine adherent of the cause of orthographic and chirographic reform, must be a source of gratification to the phonographic public.''*

From the New York Dispatch.

" *From some knowledge of Phonography and insight into the principles and arrangement of the work before us, we do not hesitate to pronounce it the best and completest yet published.   That it admits of no improvement, as some experienced reporters seem to think, we are not prepared to grant.   A more intimate acquaintance with Phonography might probably make us as enthusiastic as any of them ; but, though it should appear perfect to us, the comparative youth of this science, and the history of everything around us, would cause us to hesitate about pronouncing Mr. Graham's work perfection.   To say it is the best, and is complete, is enough, but no more, perhaps, than it deserves.* It is so simple and thorough that all can understand it, and easily learn from it to successfully write in phonographic characters, *all of which are of the most natural kind.   Children could learn this system much more readily than they can the jagged scrawl in which we pen this note—albeit we write what the compositors call a legible hand.   We hope the merit of Mr. Graham's work may secure it an introduction into all our common schools, so that it may be taught to every child.   Then would follow phonotypy in text-books and newspapers, and then adieu to plodding scribbling and barbarous spelling.   The prospect of the future is decidedly encouraging and refreshing, although we may never live to enjoy its fruits.   Still, let us commend the good and useful, the progressive and harmonizing, and that will make up somewhat for the lack of realization.''*

From the Boston Atlas and Daily Bee.

" *Mr. Graham is widely known as a practical phonographer, author, and teacher.   In each of these departments he has achieved success.   The work which Mr. Graham has now produced is the result of years of labor, study, and practice.   So far as we can judge—and we have examined all the leading works upon the subject—*it is inferior to none extant, and in many respects superior to all other works of this character.   *Hitherto, different authors have had their pet characters and word-letters, each claiming special merit for his* *own distinctive system. The result has been a want of system among those who were pursuing a common subject. Students were perplexed, and many gave up in despair. The need has been for some one competent to the purpose, to introduce a correct system. The Hand-Book of Mr. Graham embraces, in our view, such a system. The fact that it is meeting the approbation of the best phonographers and educators in the country is the best attestation of its merit which can be given."*

From the Scientific American.

" To all who wish to attain a knowledge of the art of Phonography this book will be a valuable companion, and the already proficient will find in it many hints by which they may profit in reporting. It is, we think, a successful attempt to SYSTEMATIZE PHONOGRAPHY, AND PLACE IT BEYOND THE CHANCE OF FUTURE CHANGE, *so that any person acquiring it now will not have to be continually altering, correcting, and unlearning what he has already acquired. This book will, we have no doubt, be largely sold to the flying artillery of the press (reporters), who will thank Mr. Graham for its production and the lessons it teaches."*

From the New York Spiritual Telegraph.

" This is, we believe, the largest and best work upon Phonography ever published. Both the 'Hand-Book' and the system which it explains (and which is said to be a great improvement upon the old phonography) are highly commended by many of the best and most experienced phonographic teachers and reporters; and we are not surprised to learn that the old phonography and the works devoted to it are being rapidly superseded by this excellent work and its American Phonography."

From the New York Christian Intelligencer.

" It would be folly in us to undertake to frame an opinion of a book whose principal parts are to the uninitiated perfectly unintelligible. But, as we know the author of this careful and elaborate work to be one of the best reporters in the world, and that the perfection of his reports is due to the superiority of this very phonographic system which he has now published, we can have no hesitation in recommending it to the attention of all who desire to gain a reliable knowledge of the science and art of Phonography. This Hand-Book is so thoroughly prepared and arranged in every particular, that we should think it a comparatively easy matter for a student of it to master its principles and details without the aid of a private tutor. As an unfolding of the philosophy of verbal sounds and corresponding signs, this manual is worthy the attention of all who are careful to study the structure and capacities of languages."

From the Methodist Quarterly Review, edited by Prof. D. D. Wheedon, D.D.

" This work is the production of a gentleman who is at the head of his profession as a phonographer, and has done much for the diffusion of that beautiful art. It furnishes perhaps the best aid extant for a full acquirement, by easy steps and lucid explanations, of the entire principles. Mr. Graham has furnished some modifications of Pitman's system, by which, as we are informed by

high professional authority, the contractions are rendered more effective, and the rapidity of the reporter's performance is greatly accelerated. If we are rightly informed, the improvements are practically so self-demonstrative as to secure their immediate acceptance by practical reporters.

"*Mr. Graham has, we are gratified to say, established a Phonetic Depot at 348 Broadway, at which the best furnishings for the phonographer, as blank 'note-books,' pens, and books, can be procured.*"

From the Democratic Age.

"*Whoever cares enough about intellectual matters to value ideas, and to value them highly when nobly and pithily expressed, will at once see the benefit of a system with which he can get them down at the spur of the moment, and under the weight of the thought. And after that age in a man's life has arrived when he begins to look back at what he has done, instead of looking with youthful hope into the future, what a field of gratification and sweet remembrance would his note-books afford! We venture there would be less complaining of the time that has fled by, which we know not how to account for, and less wailing over a misspent life.*"

"*In the first place, the author of this book deserves some credit for his perseverance in his cause; and, secondly, the work he has brought out is a comprehensive and able one, and the largest and most exhaustive treatise that we have seen on the subject. So far as the plot of the work and the foundation principles are concerned,* IT IS THE MOST SCIENTIFIC *that we know. Besides being printed in a style that pleases the eye, the engraved portion by Chauncey B. Thorne is very excellent, and the price is quite liberal, when we consider the vast deal of labor that must have been spent upon it.*"

From the New York Atlas.

"*A clear, systematic treatise on the very valuable art of Phonography. Mr. Graham is well known from the many improvements and additions he has made; he has indeed almost elevated short-hand writing to the rank of a science. To professional and literary men, and all others to whom the shortest possible method of committing to writing their own thoughts or the words of others is of importance, this 'Hand-Book' will be of great value, as* GIVING IN THE BRIEFEST SPACE THE FULLEST AND MOST LUCID EXPOSITION OF THE SUBJECT.*"

From the Freeman's Journal.

"*Everybody now-a-days who reads, or who listens—in short, everybody is under obligations to the art of Reporting. The ability to record on the spot uttered thought is the necessary addendum to the art of printing itself, to which it furnishes so considerable a part of its material. As we recollect the old system of short-hand, the characters were of three classes—right lines, sections of a circle, and hooked forms, to which were added a limited number of conventional signs. The principle was, to spell the word after the manner of its sound (paying no attention to its* ORDINARY *spelling), and to employ consonantal elements almost solely. This system was hard to write, and still harder to read. Phonography must be a great expansion and improvement upon the former system; and it has now become so endlessly applied and ramified, that at some future day it seems not an improbability that it will modify and simplify the existing slow and fatiguing 'long-hand'—a system which is very far short of perfection. Without Phonography the knowledge of public affairs in our immense country— a knowledge indispensable to the theory and working of such a government—could not be communicated adequately to the people. Its practice has constituted a new avocation, as the introduction of books, railroads, and the magnetic telegraph have likewise done; and it seems to us that making the art an elementary study would aid materially in the acquisition of language, and forward and facilitate all that belongs to recording and expression.*

"*Mr. Graham's work is the fullest and most thorough exposition of this novel and important art which has ever come under our notice.*"

From the New York Century.

"*The 'Hand-Book of Standard or American Phonography,' by Andrew J. Graham, is an elaborate presentation of this novel science, prepared by the author with no little expenditure of money and brain-work.*

From the Boston Zion's Herald.

"*We are fully persuaded that a thorough knowledge of Phonography is of great value,* AND SHOULD BE REGARDED AS AN ESSENTIAL PART OF A PRAC- TICAL EDUCATION. *To such of our readers as wish to obtain a thorough under- standing of Phonography in its most improved form, we confidently recommend this book.*"

From the New York Tablet.

"*The work is an elaborate exposition of a system of phonetic short-hand, which is regarded by those fully competent to judge as a great improvement upon the Old or English Phonography, especially for reporting purposes. By very clear and full explanation, by ample illustration, and by other valuable and novel features —among which is a series of carefully prepared questions on the text—the 'Hand- Book' is fully suited to the wants of the schoolroom, and* EMINENTLY ADAPTED TO THE PURPOSES OF SELF-INSTRUCTION. *In this respect, Mr. Graham's book secures a valuable advantage for the large number of persons who, though desiring to avail themselves of the important benefits of the rapidly-spreading art of Pho- nography, have found the old text-books insufficient in many respects to convey an adequate knowledge of the desired art. We advise our readers who wish to learn Phonography to secure this work, which, while it does an honor to its author, becomes the most valuable assistant to the cause of Phonography.*

From the New York Day-Book.

"*The immense value of the system of phonetics is conceded by every one, and Graham's system of teaching this science, and the improvements he has introduced while preserving the principles of English Phonography, render his work to-day the most valuable extant. Graham's system is the only American system ever introduced. It is concise, full, and complete, and is an unmistakable improvement upon Pitman's introduction, which was made in 1837, and which, up to 1857, had undergone no less than nine modifications or changes.* [☞] *Graham's 'Hand-Book of Standard Phonography' may be strongly recommended for the use of schools, as the art either in the business world or the literary world is indispensable, and the education of youth would be incomplete without it. To those who would desire to take up the subject and teach themselves, this work will be found particularly serviceable. The work is admirably gotten up—the stenographic illustrations by Thorne—paper and typographical character unexceptionable.''*

From the Poughkeepsie Gazette.

"*This volume makes its appearance very opportunely as a standard work, when Phonography has again become unsettled in consequence of proposed improvements and alterations [by the Messrs. Pitman]. The 'Hand-Book' is a work of more character and completeness than any previous work on this subject, carrying the student progressively from the first elements of the language, as represented by Phonography, to the briefest reporting style. The books heretofore published have fallen far short of being complete expositors of reporting, from the fact that all reporters have resorted to expedients not recognized by the English Phonography, to insure success. The author's great experience as a practical reporter has suggested many valuable improvements, and enabled him to reduce these various expedients to settled principles.* [☞] *This system of American Phonography is capable of recording speech one third faster than the old or English Phonography, thus enabling many to become masters of this much envied art, who could not hope to become such without it.*

"*But Phonography is not for reporters only—it is for the people ; and without discussing its merits as an educational system, it may be used to great advantage in all mercantile and professional pursuits where it is desirable to economize time.''*

From the Home Journal.

"*The want of a complete illustrated work on the subject of Phonography has long been felt by the great body of reporters in every branch of their business. This work will supply the requirement.''*

From the New York Sunday Courier.

"*It has every appearance of being a most comprehensive and excellent treatise on phonographic writing.''*

From the New York Leader.

"*The old and clumsy systems of stenography have been improved upon and crowded away, by the working of the phonetic alphabets, and to no man in America is the phonetic student more indebted than to Andrew J. Graham. As may be supposed, the 'Hand-Book' is a full and carefully prepared digest of the whole matter, valuable to all, as a means of research into the science, and indispensable to students of the art—to reporters who wish to be reliable, and writers who realize the advantages of rapid and condensed expression."*

From the Brother Jonathan.

" *It is the most elaborate work of the kind in the United States, or probably in the world. To persons who desire to perfect themselves in the art of writing down a speech, a debate, or the proceedings of a public meeting, this book will be invaluable. With the aid of this work, a person needs only the necessary practice to become a proficient phonographic writer. Besides the ample rudiments explaining everything necessary—writing exercises, etc.—there are thirty pages of engraved examples for practice. Nothing appears to be wanting to make this book* A COMPLETE INSTRUCTOR *in the art of writing short-hand."*

From the Christian Advocate and Journal.

PHONOGRAPHY—IMPROVEMENTS.

" *Some time since the inquiry was made in the* Advocate *with reference to the advantages of the best system and the best instruction-books in Phonography. In reply to these inquiries several communications appeared, speaking highly of the advantages, and recommending Pitman's system and books as being the best. Since that time, however, there has been a change, and an improvement of Pitman's system has been brought to our notice, in which some changes that had been recommended for trial have been tested and incorporated, together with some other changes resulting from the introduction of these improvements. This new system is styled ' Standard or American Phonography,' to distinguish it from the Old, Pitman, or English Phonography, and it seems to be well adapted to the progressive age in which we live ; and being founded on the same principles (more fully developed) as Pitman's system, it becomes a very easy matter for one who has studied the old to become acquainted with the new, while, at the same time, one who studies the new system can read the old as readily as the new, consequently no disadvantages result from studying the new system.*

" *The fact becomes self-evident to any phonographer who investigates the matter, that the American is decidedly preferable to the English system.* ❋ ❋ *We do not wish to be understood as finding fault with Mr. Pitman ; on the contrary, he is entitled to great credit for what he has done, and what he is still doing in the cause ; but we think that our American friend, Andrew J. Graham, of New York, has better succeeded in reducing it to a standard system.*

" *We wish, however, to speak of the instruction-book as being* THE BEST ADAPTED FOR SELF-INSTRUCTION, AS WELL AS FOR CLASSES, *of any ever issued. Mr. Graham styles his work ' The Hand-Book of Standard or American Phonography,'* AND TREATS THE SUBJECT IN SUCH A LUCID AND SCIENTIFIC MANNER THAT ANY PERSON POSSESSING ORDINARY INTELLIGENCE CAN NOT FAIL TO COMPREHEND THE PRINCIPLES UPON WHICH THIS BEAUTIFUL ART IS FOUNDED, AND TO ACKNOWLEDGE THAT IT IS ENTITLED TO TAKE HIGH RANK AMONG THE

ARTS AND SCIENCES. *In support of what I have said, I quote from the January number of the* Quarterly Review, *the editor of which is a practical phonographer. Speaking of the 'Hand-Book,' he says:* [*See the notice from the* Quarterly Review *on a preceding page.*] THIS COMMENDATION, COMING FROM SUCH HIGH AUTHORITY, IS ENTITLED TO, AND WILL HAVE, GREAT WEIGHT WITH ALL WHO READ IT. *It is unnecessary to add more, perhaps; but allow me to say, in conclusion, that I have been able to write with accelerated speed by adopting Mr. Graham's system, and can and do heartily recommend it to all my brother preachers and others as the best system of rapid writing extant, and recommend them to send to Mr. Graham, 348 Broadway, and to procure a copy of his work, which will furnish complete instruction in both the corresponding and reporting styles."*　　　　　　　　　　　　　　　W.

WILTON, *Jan.*, 1859.

From the Constellation, *edited by Park Benjamin, Esq.*

"*Mr. Andrew J. Graham has published a work of great ability, entitled 'The Hand-Book of Standard or American Phonography.'* ✿ ✿ *Mr. Graham claims for his system, that it is capable of representing with accuracy the sounds of the English language, and of the principal languages quoted by English writers and speakers; that it secures considerable speed of writing, with ample legibility, so as to answer all the purposes for which long-hand is employed; that it secures, for reporting purposes, ample speed of writing, without illegibility; and that order and simplicity are observed in every department. Mr. Graham also claims for his system a superiority to all others.* THESE CLAIMS SEEM TO US TO BE COMPLETELY SUBSTANTIATED BY THE BOOK, WHICH IS ADMIRABLY MADE UP, AND IS, NO DOUBT, BY FAR THE MOST COMPLETE GRAMMAR OF THE ART WHICH HAS EVER BEEN PUBLISHED. WE PREDICT, THAT THE DAY IS NOT FAR DISTANT WHEN PHONOGRAPHY, AS WELL AS SIMPLE CHIROGRAPHY, WILL BE TAUGHT IN OUR COMMON SCHOOLS, AND THIS BOOK WILL HASTEN THAT DAY."

From Life Illustrated.

"WORTHY OF ALL PRAISE."

OPINIONS OF REPORTERS AND TEACHERS.

From Mr. Chas. B. Collar, Phonographic Reporter: for several years one of the Official Reporters in Congress; and Reporter of the Constitutional Conventions of Massachusetts, Virginia, Ohio, and Iowa, and now a Law Reporter in New York.

"'*The Hand-Book of Standard Phonography,' in my opinion, is by far the completest work on Phonetic Short-Hand, ever published. The system it presents I regard as* A GREAT IMPROVEMENT *upon the Old or English Phonography.*

The phonographic public have now A THREE-FOLD INSURANCE AGAINST THE PERPLEXING CHANGES TO WHICH THEY HAVE HITHERTO BEEN SUBJECTED; first, *in the 'Hand-Book' itself, which has been produced at great expense;* second, *in the system, whose completeness and standard elements render further change unnecessary;* third, *in the conservative character of its author. Mr. Graham's great experience as a practical reporter, and his ability as an author, should assure the public that his work possesses eminent advantages over any phonographic text-book heretofore published."*

From Mr. A. J. Marsh, Reporter for the New York Evening Post ; formerly Reporter for the Boston Atlas, and Congressional Reporter for the National Intelligencer.

"I have examined carefully and thoroughly Mr. Graham's 'Hand-Book of Standard Phonography,' and find in it EVERYTHING TO COMMEND, AND NOTHING TO CONDEMN. *I think I hazard nothing in the prediction,* THAT ULTIMATELY EVERY GOOD REPORTER IN THE UNITED STATES WILL WRITE THE SYSTEM AS IT IS TAUGHT IN THE 'HAND-BOOK.' *Mr. Graham has departed from the Pitman system only where some positive advantage was to be gained, and this fact especially commends Standard Phonography to those who have already become phonographers. What I most highly value in the system of the 'Hand-Book' is its skillful avoidance of the lifting of the pen or pencil, which has always been a great tax upon the time of the short-hand writer. Next, perhaps, to this in importance are the rules for forming contractions, and the valuable list of word-signs and contractions. I shall adopt Standard Phonography in its entirety; and I firmly believe that no further improvement can be made in Steno-Phonography without an injury of legibility."*

From Mr. Felix G. Fontaine, for several years one of the Official Reporters of the United States Senate, the Official Reporter of several State Conventions, and at present a Law Reporter in New York.

"A word in regard to your new 'Hand-Book of Phonography.' I have given this work a most careful examination, have tested and adopted, without exception, all the improvements suggested, and do not hesitate to pronounce it the most valuable and perfect treatise on short-hand that has come under my observation. To the learner it must prove a useful acquisition in simplifying the process by which he is to arrive at a complete knowledge of the art; and to the reporter, if I may speak from my own experience, it furnishes, in the shape of your novel and beautiful contractions and phraseograms, the most important auxiliaries to rapid, legible, and perfect writing. Indeed, it was only recently that I heard a friend say that he was enabled to report nearly a third faster with your improvements than without them, a result which, I doubt not, will be the experience of every short-hand writer. With my best wishes for your success, and with hearty co-operation, I am truly yours, F. G. FONTAINE."*

From Mr. Wm. Anderson, Reporter of the New York Herald.

"*Mr. Graham's 'Hand-Book of Standard Phonography' is, in my opinion, the most elaborate, thorough, and able exposition of phonetic short-hand that has ever been issued, and I think I have perused every work that has emanated from the phonographic press.*"

From Mr. T. J Ellinwood, an experienced Phonographic Reporter and Teacher, New York.

"*After a thorough examination of Mr. Graham's 'Hand-Book of Standard Phonography,' I have no hesitation in pronouncing it the most complete exposition of phonetic short-hand that has ever been presented to the world. It reflects great credit upon its indefatigable author. I am convinced, from the use I have already made of his improvements in Phonography, that they, in no small degree, enhance the value of the art. The 'Compendium,' which constitutes one of the five parts of which the book is composed, is of itself worth the price of the whole. The advantages arising from its superior arrangement can not be over-estimated either by the teacher or the learner. I predict for this excellent work a very extensive circulation, and believe it is destined, in a short time, to be adopted in this country as the standard on the subject of which it treats.*"

From Mr. Finlay Anderson, Phonographic Reporter for the N. Y. Daily News.

"*By Mr. Graham's excellent work, 'The Hand-Book of Standard Phonography,' the pupil is easily conducted from the elements of speech, through the corresponding style, to the briefest kind of phonographic writing. The sys-*

by securing much greater speed than the Pitman Phonography, and by other features, it arrives at results which Mr. Pitman has laboriously but unsuccessfully endeavored to effect."

From Mr. Henry B. Brown, Reporter, and Teacher of Phonography in the Wesleyan University, Middletown, Conn.

"*I can not speak of the 'Hand-Book' in too high terms of commendation. * * It is far beyond any other work which has been published.*"

From a Review in the Liberator, by J. M. W. Yerrington, Esq., an accomplished Phonographic Reporter of Boston, Mass.

"*The author of this work is a widely-known and very skillful phonographic reporter and teacher, who has embodied in it the fruits of a careful and thorough investigation of the principles on which Phonotypy and Phonography are based, and of many years' experience as a reporter. We regard it as* BY FAR THE MOST COMPLETE AND COMPREHENSIVE WORK ON THESE SUBJECTS THAT HAS YET BEEN PUBLISHED. *The five parts into which it is divided are—*1. *An Introduction to Phonotypy and Phonography.* 2. *The Compendium of Standard Phonography.* 3. *Phonographic Reading Exercises.* 4. *Phonographic Writing Exercises.* 5. *The Phonographic Or-*

thographer ; an Expositor of Principles for the Ascertainment of the best Phonographic Outlines. The matter embraced in the several parts is presented in a clear and intelligible form, and with a careful adherence to scientific principles. The student of Phonography will find in them ALL THAT HE NEEDS, so far as any book can give it, to perfect himself in the art ; while to the advanced writer, and even to the experienced reporter, the information and suggestions with regard to the best methods of attaining speed and legibility of writing will be found to be of great service. 'There is nothing without labor,' and the art of reporting, like any other valuable art, is not learned in a day, or a month; but by the aid of this book, with time and patience—which the Eastern proverb says, ' turn the mulberry leaf into satin '—the student may hope to attain a degree of skill that will abundantly repay him for his efforts. TO ALL INTERESTED IN THE SUBJECT, WE HEARTILY RECOMMEND THIS VOLUME."

From Mr. Charles Segar, Phonographic Reporter for Messrs. Fowler & Wells, and formerly Teacher of Phonography at the Providence Conference Seminary.

"The 'Hand-Book of Standard Phonography' is, among phonographic works, whether English or American, without a rival. As a text-book for phonographic teachers or self-learners, and those who would become competent phonographic reporters, I can recommend it, without qualification or exception, as the best. As a standard work among phonographers, it must be, is, and will be. I regard Mr. Graham's improvements upon the Pitman system as of great value."

From Mr. Wm. H. Orr, Phonographic Reporter, and Publisher of Phonographic works for Canada.

"It is worth almost all the other phonographic books which have ever been published put together. The phonographic world must thank you heartily for such a splendid production. * * I prize it more than all the dusty old relics of phonography which I have collected together from the birth and infancy of the cause down to the present time."

From Mr. N. F. Ethell, Phonographic Reporter for Messrs. Fowler & Wells.

"I have examined nearly every work that has been published on the subject of Phonography, and can say, without hesitation, that Mr. Graham's 'Hand-Book of Standard Phonography' is the best and completest book yet presented to the American people. I can safely recommend it to all who wish to make themselves THOROUGH and RAPID short-hand writers. I am gradually adopting its principles, and find from their use a great acceleration in my speed of writing."

From Mr. Wilbur F. Whitney, Teacher of Phonography in the Wilbraham Seminary, Mass.

"The best book of the kind now published."

From Rev. Chas. M. Powell, Wilton, Conn.

"The 'Hand-Book of Standard Phonography' is the most scientific work on phonetic short-hand ever issued from the press. The changes made from the old system are decided improvements. For CLEARNESS OF ELUCIDATION, as well as for CONCISENESS AND SIMPLICITY, it is a work that I can heartily recommend to any and all who desire to understand the PRINCIPLES on which this art is founded."

From Chas. M. Plumb, Esq , Holly, N. Y.

"I think I know enough of the merits of the 'Hand-Book' to speak advisedly, and I do so when I say that it is not only IMMEASURABLY SUPERIOR to any and every other phonographic instruction-book, but so PERFECTLY SYSTEMATIC, SO DEFINITE IN DETAIL, as to be a perfect treasure, not only to the phonographer, but to every student—to the elocutionist and the literary amateur."

From Wm. T. Harris, Esq., St. Louis, Mo.

"I have carefully examined the 'Hand-Book of Standard Phonography,' and do not hesitate to say that Standard Phonography is as great an improvement upon the Pitman Phonography as that was upon the old stenographies. To the reporter it is indispensable. Phonographic reporting may now be said to have become a science. What was formerly anomalous. now gives place to general principles ; and the materials which previously were presented in a confused, chaotic way, are now reduced to the order of science."

From James A. Kirkpatrick, Esq , Professor of Civil Engineering, and Teacher of Phonography in the Central High School, Philadelphia.

"I have carefully examined your 'Hand-Book,' and have been so delighted with its clearness and completeness, that I have taken the necessary steps to have it introduced as the text-book in the Philadelphia High School. I am well pleased with the appearance of the book, paper, type, and everything else."

From Prof. G. F. Comfort, Fort Plain Seminary, Fort Plain, N. Y.

"I am about to organize a class in Phonography in the Seminary here, and have decided to introduce as the text-book your 'Hand-Book of Standard Phonography.' "

From Rev. Aaron Rittenhouse, Teacher of Phonography in the New York Conference Seminary, Charlottesville, N. Y.

"I am very much pleased with the 'Hand-Book.' It exceeds my highest expectations in very many respects. I did not think there could be so many DECIDED IMPROVEMENTS, nor that a work of its size could be sold at such a low price. I have introduced it into my classes here, and find it SUPERIOR AS A TEXT-BOOK. No one can know what phonography is until he has made himself acquainted with Standard Phonography."

OPINIONS OF THE PRESS, CONTINUED.

From the United States Journal, New York.

This manual of Phonography is most welcome. It is the whole science compressed in covers, so that he who reads may learn. In these *fast* days short-hand writing has become an actual necessity, and it *should* form a part of our common-school education as much as penmanship and grammar. The difficulties hitherto have been that no well-digested system of Phonography was available for schools, although enough of the science had long been in existence to enable rapid writers and intelligent men to become good reporters. But order has at length come from confusion; and here we have the desideratum, in a very fine volume, adapted to every ordinary emergency, and to the fullest development of the rapid and sure short-hand writer or reporter. Would that it had come ten years sooner, to have saved our own failure to become an expert in short-hand writing. Mr. Graham has evidently made Phonography a life-study, has digested, philosophized, simplified, until a Hand-Book contains rudiments, elements, and results as clearly set forth as geometrical formula. We commend it to those who desire an insight into the mysteries of writing as rapidly as speech itself can utter—to authors, editors, ministers, lawyers—all who would save themselves the drudgery of the tedious and debilitating process of ordinary composition.

From the National Standard, New Jersey.

A New Work on Phonography. — The Hand-Book of Standard or American Phonography.—We have examined the work with the above title, published by Andrew J. Graham, Phonetic Depot, New York, and pronounce it, unhesitatingly, to be the most elaborate and the most comprehensive work upon the subject that we have ever met with This new system is denominated "Standard or American Phonography," in order to distinguish it from the old Pitman or English Phonography, and is admirably adapted to our progressive age. The author has remedied many defects which existed in previous works, and, with the improvements, offers his present work as a standard, since it embodies everything requisite for the easy acquisition of a knowledge of Phonography. The subject is treated in such a manner that any one possessed of ordinary intelligence can master the art in a very short time, as the lessons are of an inductive nature, and intended to obviate the necessity of an oral teacher ; an important consideration to those who are situated where a preceptor can not be afforded or obtained. Mr. Graham has evidently written his book with the view of placing his knowledge of the subject — obtained by long and successful experience in the office of instructor — in the possession of every one who is disposed to exert himself in any way proportionate to the good he desires. The editor of the *Quarterly Review,* who is a practical phonographer, in a notice of Mr. Graham's work, in the January number of that magazine, says : " This treatise is the production of a gentleman who stands at the head of his profession as a phonographer, and has done much for the diffusion of that beautiful art. It furnishes, perhaps, the best aid extant for a full acquirement, by easy steps and lucid explanations, of the entire principles. Mr. Graham has furnished some modifications of Pitman's system, by which, we are informed by high professional authority, the contractions are rendered more effective, and the rapidity of the reporter's performance is greatly accelerated." Such commendation, from high authority, will do much to introduce the book to the public. While the art may be so easily and certainly acquired by those willing to apply themselves, we see no reason why Mr. Graham's work should not meet with a large demand, especially when it is considered what benefits a knowledge of Phonography confers upon the possessor. To those who desire the *best* work upon this highly useful art, we say, inclose $1 25 in a letter, and direct to "ANDREW J. GRAHAM, Phonetic Depot, New York," and you will receive a copy by return of mail.

From Hull's Journal of Health, New York.

A book on this subject [Phonography], *able, systematic, comprehensive, and clear, has long been a want,* which the author has fully met.

AMERICAN PHONOGRAPHY vs. ENGLISH PHONOGRAPHY.

Part of a communication from the author to Messrs. Fowler & Wells' Life Illustrated.

I. The Standard or American Phonography attains a very important function, a capability, which the English or Pitman Phonography could not produce—it enables the practiced writer of it to report *verbatim* the most rapid speakers. Or, to state this matter in a different light, if it be claimed untruly that the more rapid speakers could be reported absolutely *verbatim* by a very few of the best writers of the old system, without resorting to devices which would not be recognized as belonging to that system, then I say that Standard Phonography will place that ability within the reach of thousands who otherwise could not hope for it, and render the reporting of fast speakers a far less difficult and life-exhausting task. There is no use of attempting to conceal the fact that the Old Phonography was a reporting system for a very select few, for too many writers of it have been made painfully conscious of that fact by their failures after most persevering effort. In respect of speed, Standard Phonography exceeds the English Phonography more than that surpasses the best of the old systems of Stenography. And all this is capable of mathematical demonstration. It can be sufficiently demonstrated to any reporter by the Old Phonography by less than five minutes' examination of the Reporting Style of Standard Phonography.

II. Standard Phonography recognizes details less, and general principles more, than the English or Pitman Phonography. It is constructed fully in accordance with the fourth foundation principle of a standard system, namely, that "order and simplicity should be observed in every department." If you could afford the space for it, the demonstration of this proposition could be readily afforded by a comparison of the two systems in respect of their rules, etc. In regard to this second point, the advantage obtained by the American over the English Phonography is a very valuable one ; for, of course, the greater the order and simplicity of a system, the more easily is it impressed upon, and the more securely retained by, the mind, whose first law, intellectually at least, is Order. In Standard Phonography it will be found that even details arrange themselves into Orders, Groups, and Classes, and that Exceptions obey a Law.

III. Standard Phonography is capable of being applied with *convenience* to the representation of the principal foreign languages, the signs, for the foreign elements being chosen in accordance with certain general principles, which not only distinguish the native from the foreign sounds, but teach with precision the pronunciation of the foreign elements. In all these respects English Phonography is unlike, and inferior to, the American Phonography.

IV. The system of Phonography presented in the "Hand-Book" comes in the nick of time as a standard system—a system of harmony —a ground of repose from the numerous and perplexing changes of Pitman's system.

☞ *For Catalogue of Phonographic Books, etc., see close of the* "*Hand-Book.*"